ACCOLADES FOR

DARE DISTURB THE UNIVERSE

"The US entrepreneurial ecosystem has made a significant positive impact on our economy, society, and innovation, by creating jobs, wealth, and life-changing products and services. In his book, Chuck Newhall highlights the importance of patient, resilient, and long-term investors; strong, values-driven venture firms; and the starring role entrepreneurs play on the journey to success. The successes of venture-backed startups over the past fifty years—thanks in part to Chuck Newhall, his peers, and NEA—have helped make the US venture industry the envy of the world."

—BOBBY FRANKLIN, National Venture Capital Association

"Considering that we benefit from an economy made—and remade— by venture capital, we know little of its inner workings. Here, Chuck Newhall III, a pioneer of VC in the 20th century, offers a deeper historical perspective and an insightful take on the industry's challenges and triumphs over the past five decades."

—DR. ARTHUR DAEMMRICH, Smithsonian Museum

"I have had the privilege to serve on NEA's Board of Advisors for almost all the forty years they've been in existence. Chuck does a wonderful job of explaining the longer history of venture capital, including NEA's founding and what venture capitalists struggle to do in starting and building companies. His insights are revealing and informative."

—PHIL PAUL, Founder, Paul Capital

"Love the book . . . so rich, so authentic, so Chuck. It was hard to put down. Chuck has uniquely captured the great personalities while telling the deep-down story of our industry. It is a story that has never been told in this depth."

—JIM SWARTZ, Founder, Accel

"An amazing story of family ingenuity in the venture capital industry. Chuck Newhall writes a beautifully candid and compelling account that integrates personal triumph and tragedy into the history of New Enterprise Associates, and more."

—TOM NICHOLAS, William J. Abernathy Professor of Business Administration, Harvard Business School and author of *Venture Capital: An American History*

"*Dare Disturb the Universe* is a fascinating description of the venture capital industry with a particularly human perspective. While many investors think about data rooms, investment gains, and losses, deals per partner, pre—and post-money valuations, et cetera, the reality is that the venture and entrepreneurial ecosystem is all about people. Chuck Newhall, through the lens of NEA's forty-year-plus history, relates the very personal and emotional highs and lows that are involved in creating new products, new companies, and new industries. It is a real-life story that is rarely documented."

—BON FRENCH, Adams Street

"A compelling memoir revealing the heart and mind of a leading venture capitalist who shaped the industry. Chuck Newhall shares unflinching stories—both personal and professional—that shed light on how venture capitalists over the past half-century have contributed to America's ascendance as an entrepreneurial power."

—MARGUERITE GONG HANCOCK, Computer Museum

"In the venture capital business, one can easily become bipolar with every phone call. One call will be a president talking enthusiastically about the company's good fortune while the next call is from a CEO lamenting that they are out of cash and facing layoffs or worse. The highs and lows of our business are extreme, and unfortunately, the lows outnumber the highs. In dealing with early-stage companies struggling to cross the chasm of success, one deals with more failures than successes. This is particularly painful when the need to fire a founder becomes apparent. These are people that originally had our confidence, respect, and fondness but have become an impediment to the growth or even survival of the enterprise. These are very difficult conversations explaining to the founder that the company needs new leadership. Over my thirty-five years in venture, people have often told me how easy the business looks. You just invest in a company, you take them public, and everybody makes a lot of money. They say. The truth is that happens on occasion, but there are way more gut-wrenching challenges than victories. It is easy to celebrate magnificent wins in a portfolio, but successful venture capitalists know that the real satisfaction comes from doing the hard work and long hours helping struggling companies become successful. This part of our business is not visible from the outside looking in."

—FRANK ADAMS, Grotech

Dare Disturb the Universe
by Charles W. Newhall, III

© Copyright 2021 Charles W. Newhall, III

ISBN 978-1-64663-435-4

Published by

 köehlerbooks™

3705 Shore Drive
Virginia Beach, VA 23455
800-435-4811
www.koehlerbooks.com

DARE DISTURB THE UNIVERSE

A MEMOIR OF VENTURE CAPITAL

Charles W. Newhall, III

VIRGINIA BEACH
CAPE CHARLES

From "The Love Song of J. Alfred Prufrock" by T. S. Eliot

In the room the women come and go

Talking of Michelangelo.

. . .

And indeed there will be time

To wonder, "Do I dare?" and "Do I dare?"

Time to turn back and descend the stair,

With a bald spot in the middle of my hair—

(They will say: "How his hair is growing thin!")

My morning coat, my collar mounting firmly to the chin,

My necktie rich and modest, but asserted by a simple pin—

(They will say: "But how his arms and legs are thin!")

Do I dare

Disturb the universe?

DEDICATION AND A GIFT

"... my glory was I had such friends."

—William Butler Yeats

JIM SWARTZ, ACCEL'S FOUNDER, SAYS, "Venture capital is best practiced as a calling, not a job." It has been a calling for me. I have been fortunate enough to spend most of my life working and growing up in the world of venture capital.

When asked about my career, I always say that one of the most important decisions you make in your personal and professional life is who you choose as your partners. I have been very fortunate to have made good choices.

This book is dedicated to my New Enterprise Associates co-founders Dick Kramlich and Frank Bonsal. Our voyage was a lot of fun. I could not have had better partners. It is also dedicated to Mary Ambrose, my assistant, who kept my life from spinning out of control for twenty years.

This book is my gift to venture capitalists, to entrepreneurs who are thinking of asking venture capitalists to finance their companies, to students of finance, to politicians who must learn how important venture capital is before they destroy it, and to any general reader who wants to know how our great american economy was created.

Some will say that my part of the book is ancient history, since my narrative stops in 2012. It no longer has relevance. They are wrong. There is much to be learned from studying history. It keeps the current generation from making the same mistake prior generations have made.

"If you do not know history, then you do not know anything.
You are a leaf that does not know it is part of a tree."

—Michael Chrichton

TABLE OF CONTENTS

Foreword xiii

CHAPTER I: UUNET 1

CHAPTER II: Is Venture Capital Important? 10

CHAPTER III: My Role Models: Laurance Rockefeller &
General George Doriot 20

CHAPTER IV: NEA's First Fundraising 34

CHAPTER V: NEA Culture 44

CHAPTER VI: HealthSouth 63

CHAPTER VII: Friends And Mentors 86

CHAPTER VIII: Amy 112

CHAPTER IX: They Broke The Mold 125

CHAPTER X: Dick Kramlich 133

CHAPTER XI: Triumph 146

CHAPTER XII: Biotech Adventures 194

CHAPTER XIII: The Bubble And Saving NEA's
Healthcare Practice 221

CHAPTER XIV: Saving Capitalism 236

CHAPTER XV: Scott Sandell, Forrest Baskett,
And Exploratory Drilling 249

CHAPTER XVI: Creativity 262

CHAPTER XVII: Ducks On A Pond 272

CHAPTER XVIII: Lower Costs, Better Outcomes 293

CHAPTER XIX: A Farewell To Arms 304

CHAPTER XX: The Apple Does Not Fall Far
From The Tree 315

FOREWORD

MANY BOOKS HAVE BEEN WRITTEN about the venture capital industry. Everything from academic treatises to profiles of individual venture capitalists. But no one to my knowledge has captured what really goes on inside the venture firms, how the individuals think and function on a day-to-day basis, and how people and events play off each other in unpredictable ways. If there is one book to read about how the industry really works, this is it.

Chuck Newhall has seen it all. Ups and downs of business, positive and negative dynamics of partner relationships, multigenerational transitions, personal tragedy, business tragedy, and enough successes to lead a satisfying life. His is a very personal account of a life lived fully in the rapidly changing fast lanes of entrepreneurship. It is a no punches pulled full-on account of Chuck, his personal and business challenges and the complex characters that he encountered along the way. Rich in historical detail, painful in some of its language, the accounts are always forward-looking and in the best interests of all.

I have known Chuck from his early days in the venture business and he has been a good friend and personal confidant through the years. We rarely interacted directly on projects but shared a long history covering many of the same experiences and personalities. I envy his ability to make these stories and people that I know so well come to life with astonishing memory and attention to detail that I know to be accurate.

Or at least largely accurate. Most accounts of history are written well after the fact by authors who rely on biased or nuanced second and sometimes third-hand accounts of events. Few are contemporaneous and written in the first person.

Anyone who knows Chuck knows that he is a refined and compulsive personality. His gardens, his collections of objects and books, and his wide-ranging interests reflect his brilliance. In this masterpiece of recall, he turns his observational skills and collector talents to documenting deeply and curating skillfully the story of his life with legions of entrepreneurs and venture capitalists.

Many areas of business are misunderstood by the public. The practice of venture capital, with its potential for life-changing products and the creation of massive wealth, is a prime example. The press focuses on highly visible successes and spectacular failures; in the process, the industry comes across as a giant gambling casino, which in fact is quite far from the truth. In his writing, Chuck does great service to the daily long hours working under continuous uncertainty, and the long years of twists and turns that go into every venture project, all the time keeping a keen eye on the personalities and personal frailties that shape the course of history. You will meet Chuck and his partners up close and personal, and you will learn as much about them as you want and probably more, definitely more than any autobiographical account ever would reveal. The unvarnished observation of a friend is infinitely more penetrating than any of us are willing to divulge. Chuck Newhall has made a major contribution to the world of venture capital with his continued leadership over the years. He brings a singular breadth of life experiences and knowledge to bridge the early days of venturing of Laurence Rockefeller, J.H. Whitney, and General Georges Doriot through to the flowering of the industry in the '70s and '80s, on to the internet age and the subsequent bubble and up to and including the excesses of the moment. I know of no other person who has had this span of connections. And there are very few who have such an astute ability to observe events and people. Chuck's career, and those of his partners, span the full breadth of the industry, from the early days of financing manufacturing companies to the computer era, the internet and modern communication era, the social media explosion, and the healthcare service and biotech worlds. There are few others who have seen and been inside the technical developments in all these sectors.

As someone who always put others ahead of himself, Chuck devoted hours and hours to collecting information from a wide range of his many friends and relationships. He has personally funded the largest collection of oral histories from noted venture capitalists through the National Venture Capital Association and Harvard Business School. These along with the continuing oral history project at the Computer History Museum, also funded by him, are the most definitive collection of venture histories that exist.

Beyond a historical trove, however, you will find this book to be a fun and engaging read as you are transported inside the everyday workings of those individuals who are full-on engaged with building the next big things that will change the world. There is no Amazon here, no Facebook, no Google, no Apple, no Twitter, none of what the press and Washington think is "tech." This book is about the thousands of companies that venture capitalists fund day by day and that really are the backbone of the tech industry.

We and all future readers owe Chuck and his colleagues a huge debt of gratitude for capturing this slice of the industry that has been and continues to be so impactful to the health of the American and the world economies. May we all strive to be as impactful, resourceful, and generous to others as Chuck Newhall has been to us.

By Jim Swartz
May 2021

I.

UUNET

"A leader is one who knows the way,
goes the way, and shows the way."

—John C. Maxwell

WHEN THE SUN CAME OUT, the wind was blowing hard as Peter Barris made his way to the service. Clouds of fallen snow scuttled across the roads around the hotel like ghostly claws. Many cars that had been parked the night before were snowbound, jamming the lot, but somehow, everyone found a place to park. We approached the hotel somberly. It seemed to tower above the streets like a fortress over the battleground of my friend's life. This was John's last triumph—his parade's end. We entered the warm foyer, shaking off snowflakes.

Randi Sidgmore, John's wife and now widow, stood in the hotel's ballroom, remembering the Latin phrase, "Sic gloria transit mundi," or "The glories of the earth are fleeting." All triumphs fade. You may be a big deal now, but tomorrow, no one knows your name. Still, some names stay with us, and John's will be remembered for a long time.

John Sidgmore's dream had been to make money, yes, but he also wanted to change the world and make it better. The birth of the internet set the stage for this, and even in the short span of UUNET's existence, John's work and the internet he helped create did indeed transform the world. In this new world, where the internet made communications ubiquitous and nearly instantaneous, dictators could no longer keep their populations blind to ideas and events around the world. The Hitlers and Stalins of the future would find it harder to enslave their countries. Nothing would be the same. This greater connectivity is not without a cost—fake news and cyberbullying are scourges of our time—but the benefits are inarguable.

So as Randi thought about it, John had indeed given his life for something greater than himself, and she was proud, too, since she had been an equal partner in his life's work. They had shared the dream.

My first encounter with the internet was in the early 1990s, with my partners, Dick Kramlich and Frank Bonsal. It was at an annual meeting for our venture capital firm, New Enterprise Associates (NEA). Stewart Alsop, also a venture capitalist, as well as a computer guru and a reporter, gave a presentation about the potential of the internet. Even at the time, his exciting talk reminded us anew of one of the great privileges of being a venture capitalist: it pulls you into the future.

Alsop stood on the stage, with a giant screen behind him. On his laptop computer, he took the 400 of us in the room on a voyage around the world, visiting scientific and informational websites. It was riveting. Still, what stood out to me wasn't what we were seeing but rather the potential of a World Wide Web. As Stewart clicked through the personal website of a Swedish professor that served as his autobiography, I felt like I was wandering through the man's house, looking at his most precious possessions. We met his wife, their daughters, and their dog and cat. It captured me because it contained enough information to inspire a novel, and for some reason, that is when I knew I was looking at a revolution. At that time, most people considered the internet to be an academic curiosity, not a new frontier or a serious disruption in the way we live and tell stories and do business. Though I realized its importance that day, it was my partner Peter Barris, along with two extraordinary entrepreneurs and the many unsung heroes on their teams, who were truly the internet pioneers.

Peter joined NEA as a general partner in 1992. Prior to this, he had worked under Jack Welch for nine years at GE Information Systems, which was, in some ways, a model for what UUNET would become. Decisive and bold, with a strong operating background, he always followed what Welch taught him: "Make a hard call and face reality today, not tomorrow."

Before his NEA days, Peter met one of the founders of Accel, another venture capital firm, and they had several meetings. The topic was whether Peter would be the best choice to be CEO of a company called UUNET that Accel had sourced in Washington. Peter found out more about the company from a board member and adviser to UUNET who was close to NEA. He learned it had about $3 million in revenue, but only half of that was from the internet. The company was unprofitable, and most of its business was with the government, although due to Peter's GE Information Systems background, he immediately understood UUNET's broader possibilities. While GE Information Systems had a proprietary global network that delivered value-added services to large corporate customers, UUNET could provide these services inexpensively over the internet.

Menlo Ventures was also interested in investing, so NEA, Accel, and Menlo all decided to invest together in 1993. Before the deal was done, however, Rick Adams, UUNET's founder, came to Peter and said he wanted NEA as his sole investor. He argued it would be less complicated than dealing with three venture groups.

Peter declined. Although Peter understood Rick's point, he knew the company would be stronger with the diverse expertise and connections that the three firms brought to bear. He encouraged Rick to see it this way, adding, "We came to this dance together, and we will finish it together."

Unlike UUNET's competitors, Rick and Peter chose to pursue the business market, which was much larger than the consumer market and didn't require the large upfront losses that entering the consumer market would entail. Peter insisted Rick bring in an experienced business manager to run UUNET, but the decision to give the business market priority was made before the new CEO was hired. Rick agreed to participate in hiring professional management. He had no aspirations to become the next Bill Gates. Soon, Rick, too came to see that UUNET's promise was so great that a new "operating" CEO truly was needed.

Even before they found a CEO, the first person Peter and Rick hired was the VP of operations, Joe Scaurzini, who had held the same title at GE Information Systems. Joe was older than most UUNET employees, but he was also a child at heart, and he related to younger people easily. He was also one of the most experienced people in data networks, having run the biggest one in the world. Rick liked Joe, a man from a different generation, and respected his competence.

Their next hire was Peter's customer support person, Dave Boast. Peter had worked with him at GE Info Systems and knew that he could do the job.

At this time in the CEO search, Rick and the board asked Peter to become CEO of the company, but he declined because he had just signed up as a general partner in NEA's sixth fund. Instead, Peter thought of John Sidgmore, another GE Information Services alumnus. John had risen to the rank of COO for GE Information Systems, so when Peter introduced John to UUNET, he too had the background to see the tremendous potential of the company. In 1994, he joined it.

UUNET's initial plan was to acquire several small, regional internet service providers (ISPs), which were typically owned by universities. UUNET initially acquired ISPs at MIT, Stanford, and NYU. Many of Peter's NEA partners were skeptical about UUNET because, in their minds, there were no barriers to entry. It seemed anyone could do what UUNET was planning to do. However, internet resources were scarce in the early '90s, and few people understood how to operate ISPs, and even fewer understood their potential. If the company could acquire ISPs, then build mass, then win regional dominance, it would soon establish a large competitive barrier. Like any service company, UUNET was a land grab—buy the best properties and end up with something close to a monopoly.

But the internet was no longer just a curiosity. Its potential was being realized by the public and touted by the media before John arrived. The cost of regional ISPs shot up, which meant additional acquisitions were not going to be the path forward for UUNET.

Fortunately, Peter's experience at GE gave him an idea of how to solve the problem. UUNET's customers used the networks during business hours; at night, the pipes were empty. There was no marginal cost to use the network before and after business hours. Therefore, all that was needed was to add consumer customers that could use the network during off hours.

America Online had consumer customers. Peter knew Steve Case, the CEO at America Online, and introduced him to John. If perfect matches existed, this was one. The idea was that America Online would make a major investment in UUNET and Steve Case would go on the board. America Online's investment would fund the build-out of UUNET's network, and its consumers could use that network before and after business hours.

Before the deal was finalized, however, Steve Case bought ANS, one of UUNET's competitors, a company John had also tried to buy. Unsurprisingly, ANS would not share its information with UUNET, threatening the deal. Looking for other potential partners, Peter and John asked themselves, "Who hates AOL the most?" The answer was simple: Microsoft. They decided to create an auction by letting Microsoft know they were in serious negotiations with AOL. Microsoft responded instantly, allowing John to negotiate a fantastic deal.

Microsoft invested $16.4 million in UUNET, buying 15 percent, which the company used to build out its network. Dave Boast, John, and Joe Scaurzini were the reason why Microsoft invested. They had total confidence in this UUNET management team. Microsoft funded the build-out of a dial-up network and provided the customers to use it, laying out a win-win situation for both companies. In the meantime, PSI and other consumer ISPs were raising debt from outside investors.

As UUNET grew, they leased AT&T lines just as GE had. Some board members felt it was risky, fearing that AT&T would willfully put them out of business, but it never did, just as it had never put GE Information Systems out of business. During this time, Peter and John were on the phone every day discussing the company's business and long-term strategy. The closer they became, the more Peter realized that John was an incredible business leader.

At their first meeting, when they were both working at GE, John was sitting behind a desk, chain-smoking and drinking coffee by the gallon. Peter remembered John's phone ringing nonstop, and every few minutes, people would stop in to talk. He learned John was a man in constant motion: he'd pace the floor while talking on one of his several telephones, tethered by a long cord to his desk, and he only slept three hours per night. Twenty-two years later, when he joined UUNET, John moderated his coffee intake a bit, but he was still on a different level of busy, complete with three cellphones and a BlackBerry. As UUNET succeeded, he came in contact with all the titans of the technology world.

Although he was small in stature, John was big in personality, big in presence, big in thinking. Soon, UUNET turned him into one of the rock stars of the internet. He was always moving, moving, moving. Surprisingly, he never let his ego get the best of him, as it does for many successful entrepreneurs. He was a regular guy, deemed "approachable" by just about everyone. While riding in an elevator with an employee, he would ask them about their lives and what they did. He only had to meet someone once, and he never forgot their name. He cared about people, harnessing an uncanny ability to make everybody feel special.

John wasn't the type to stay in one place, or in his office. He was usually popping in and out of his employee's offices or meeting them in the halls. John viewed his role as more of a helper and supporter than a manager, which meant that for him, it was a personal responsibility to help people become successful at their work. If an employee was no longer compatible with the company's direction, he didn't make them feel tossed aside but guided departing employees to new positions where they could be successful. As such, former employees were some of his best references. John's employees responded to him with a fierce loyalty that is certainly scarce today. He was the rare leader who could routinely get his employees to do the things they believed impossible. At his all-hands meetings, employees were known to wear "I love John Sidgmore" T-shirts.

There was nothing ordinary or predictable about John. His office was decorated with Jim Hendrix posters, guitars autographed by the band U2, and lava lamps. He could play an air guitar with the best of them. He would send out his first emails of the day at 3:00 or 4:00 a.m., while the rest of the world slept. His negotiating skills were legendary. He had a reputation for getting what he wanted, but he also never did a deal where both sides did not win. John poured himself into the job to make the company justify its price. And his enthusiasm was contagious: if he was having fun, so was everyone else.

UUNET was a band of pioneers, exploring untouched country, making miracles as they went. The thirty-five-person company he joined in 1994 grew into a multibillion-dollar enterprise with thousands of employees. In January 1994, the company's monthly revenue was $340,000, but by August 1999, UUNET's monthly billing was up a thousandfold, to $303 million. John also acquired compatible companies, and he felt responsible for them, too.

One of the unique things venture capitalists must do is develop a vast network of relationships. NEA, over its history, has financed more than 1,000 companies. Add a venture capitalist's direct relationship with the CEOs of their portfolio companies to the ones they form with university scientists, with companies being acquired or sold by their portfolio companies, and with countless other venture capitalists, investors, and entrepreneurial executives, and you have a vast contact file.

Leveraging these relationships after UUNET was a success, NEA's managing partner Dick Kramlich invested in Juniper, a communications infrastructure company that made high-speed routers. Those routers made possible the creation of very high-speed networks. After Peter introduced UUNET to Juniper, UUNET put Juniper on the map by becoming their largest customer. Mike O'Dell, UUNET's CTO, who later became an NEA partner, decided to buy Juniper Equipment for UUNET. NEA made 95 times what it invested in UUNET; it made 1,000 times its Juniper investment. When John died, Juniper's CEO simply said, "We owe our success to John Sidgmore and UUNET."

In August 1996, Metropolitan Fiber Systems (MFS) bought UUNET for $2 billion, a significant step up over market price, and a few months later, MFS was itself bought by the communications conglomerate WorldCom for $12.4 billion. At the time, UUNET was the world's largest internet access provider, with 6,617 employees and 70,000 business customers in 114 countries. John could have become the next CEO of WorldCom if he had wanted to, but he didn't. WorldCom was too big. His true love was being an entrepreneur, so instead, he became CEO of Electronic Commerce Industries (ECI). Others questioned why John went to a startup rather than becoming CEO of a Fortune 500 company, but his passion was working with a small group to build something of lasting value.

Several years later, John was standing in a Fresh Fields parking lot next to Randi when he got the call—a plea to come back and save WorldCom. Its board had asked Bernie Ebbers, WorldCom's legendary CEO, to step down while the company was being investigated by the FBI for overstating its earnings. The board believed John was the only one who could save the company.

WorldCom had 20 million customers, $30 billion in revenue, and 60,000 employees. It handled 70 million phone calls every weekend and provided services in 100 countries on six continents.

The US government, including the Social Security Administration, the Federal Aviation Administration, the Defense Department, and the US Postal System depended on WorldCom to function. Given the magnitude of WorldCom's responsibilities and his sense that he could help, John decided he would commit to saving WorldCom. "There could be no harm in that," he reassured Randi.

Randi disagreed. She thought it would kill him.

Time would prove her right.

John had to put the spotlight on the accounting fraud and was forced to take the company into bankruptcy in 2002. He found himself testifying in front of congressional committees whose members were more concerned with showing themselves to advantage in front of the cameras than in learning the truth from WorldCom's new CEO, who had never participated in the fraud, who because of his integrity, competence, and love from workers had been hired to clean the company up after it. In 2002, the Sarbanes-Oxley Act, also called the "Public Company Accounting Reform and Investor Protection Act," became law. It was in the best interests of senators and congressmen to go for blood.

John was a conveniently wounded animal to them. His honor, which was all-important to him, was shredded on national TV. People who knew John understood the price he was paying for his service to WorldCom, and if anything, his trials endeared him more than ever to the Washington, D.C., technology community. They saw him as a man of honor, trying to do the right thing.

For John, the hardest part wasn't the congressional hearings or the bankruptcy. WorldCom employees blamed him for what happened. He had remained on the board of the company, with the title of vice-chairman, when he was managing ECI. Several years later, the WorldCom board discovered Ebbers' fraud. John had had no idea of its magnitude.

John received death threats. One morning, when he went out to get the paper, there was a package at the end of the drive. It was an inoperative bomb. The FBI arrived and cordoned off his house. A man acting out of love for the company's employees, and love is not too strong a word, was vilified by them. Peter is unsure when it started, but around this time, John started drinking too much, often at night. The job killed him because alcohol destroyed his immune system.

While taking independent study as an undergraduate at Penn, I spent half a year studying Joseph Conrad's tragedy *Lord Jim*. Lord Jim was a man who put his honor above all considerations. Like Lord Jim in this respect, John felt he had a moral responsibility to UUNET employees and the companies he acquired. When we built NEA, we wanted partners with honor like this, just as Peter demonstrated when he kept Accel and Menlo Ventures in the UUNET investment. The key to NEA's success is treating entrepreneurs, limited partners, all employees, partners, and general partners in an honorable manner. For some people, honor is the most important thing in life. Conrad called these men "one of us." John was "one of us" and a model for all of us.

Peter's eulogy for John's lasted fifteen minutes. No one moved. The hotel ballroom was silent as everyone listened intently. He concluded his eulogy with this:

"John Sidgmore won't easily be forgotten. He touched countless numbers of people in a really significant way. A man with a big heart who always sought to help others, who gave freely of his riches to people and causes. We loved him for being who he was: a thoughtful, compassionate man of the highest integrity who always sought to do the right thing, regardless of the consequences. Everything he did, he did with passion. Some say his passion killed him. We know better. His passion kept him alive. John, you truly made a difference in this world. Forgive me for paraphrasing a Sinatra song—I know John preferred Dylan, but the message seems appropriate: 'You had a life that was full. You traveled each and every highway. And more, much more than that, you did it your way.' Wherever you are right now, John, I know it's a good place. I have no doubt you have negotiated a great package for yourself. You're the 'real deal,' my friend. I will miss you terribly. It was a privilege knowing you."

Everyone filed out silently. When they exited the building, the sun was shining, and the light was reflected in the snow.

II.

IS VENTURE CAPITAL IMPORTANT?

"Three things cannot be long hidden:
the sun, the moon, and the truth."

—Buddha

THE STORY OF UUNET IS an example of what venture capitalists can do for a company. Though much has been written about entrepreneurs who change the world, good venture capitalists, who charge into the fray and shield the entrepreneurs while wars are being fought all around them, haven't been given their due. I had the opportunity to watch great VCs in battle, including Laurance Rockefeller, General Georges Doriot, and my father, Charles Newhall, Jr. I learned from their successes and failures. It seems like only other venture capitalists understand what VCs do and the important role venture capital plays in the American economy. Venture capital is indeed a type of private equity, and a small portion of the private equity universe at that. Most people, especially and problematically politicians, dump all private equity into one bag. But venture capital is significantly different from other forms of private equity in the work it does for our economy and to propel innovation in technology, medicine, and other sciences.

Venture capital is a much different class of private equity than hedge funds, which make money trading stocks, sometimes "hedging" by taking a short position. Leveraged buyout funds buy companies using debt, then restructure them by selling off non-strategic assets and unprofitable businesses increasing buy-out firms have used financial engineering when making investments. They use more debt to buy a company and then recapitalize it with a public offering from which the proceeds are used to retire debt. This increases potential equity returns but also can increase risk. Instead, VCs create ten-year partnerships with entrepreneurs to build pioneering new businesses that change the world. The role of the VC is not only to provide startup funds but to act as a strategic advisor to the entrepreneur, working together to form a winning strategy, just as Peter Barris and the other VCs partnered with Rick Adams and, later, John Sidgmore at UUNET. Good VCs help recruit skilled management and directors, plus they introduce the company to important customers, investors, and service providers, such as accountants, lawyers, and banks. VCs mentor founders and CEOs, helping with their leadership challenges while also providing governance through the board of directors.

Today, the institutional venture capital business is a significant business managed by a small number of firms. It is tiny compared to other financial asset categories, including stocks, bonds, mutual funds, leveraged buyout funds, and hedge funds. It properly exists alongside angel funding, in which an individual, usually a former entrepreneur, provides very early startup capital in exchange for convertible debt or equity ownership.

Institutional venture capital is responsible for only 15.5 percent of private equity funding in 2018, but it is the glue of the American economy. Over the past century, venture capital financing has helped to create the vast majority of the companies that lead growth on the New York, American, and NASDAQ exchanges. Forty-three percent of all public US companies founded between 1979 and 2014 were backed by venture capital. Our role as VCs is to find out what will be, not what is or what has been, because when we see the future, we can make it happen. Venture capital financing has created innovative companies that have immense economic and sociological effects. The camera, the computer, biotechnology, the internet, and high-speed data communications are only a few of those innovations. The venture capital industry has grown significantly since 1950, when the number of firms was estimated to be around fifty. In 2005, the number was 1,009. However, that number fell to 798 in 2016, according to the National Venture Capital Association.

Year	$ Invested in Venture Capital	# of Firms
1950	100M	50 (est.)
1960	250M	150 (est.)
1970	.4B	230
1980	.7B	350
1990	2.9B	383
2000	105B	866
2010	23.5B	853
2018	130.9B	1,047

Through research, and with conversations with WWII era venture capitalists, the early numbers are my estimates. 1960 to 1980 numbers appeared in old newspapers, magazines, and other sources. Recent numbers were provided by the NVCA.

While at Harvard Business School, from 1969 to 1971, I became bored with a statistics course, "Analysis of Business Decisions Under Uncertainty," which taught statistical analysis to evaluate risk. I doubted whether these techniques would be useful in venture capital, my chosen career and life's mission. I spent all my free time at the HBS library, delving into the history and practice of venture capital, to find out what metrics were useful in venture capital risk-taking.

In my second year, I wrote a thesis titled "Financing Change: The Role of the Venture Capitalist in the American Economy." I described how the venture capital industry drove American innovation and how it is was practiced. With my father's help, I interviewed fifteen of the best East Coast post-World War II venture capitalists and spent thousands of hours further researching what they said. Over the years, I have been an avid amateur historian studying my industry.

Still, I'm sure many professional historians and venture capitalists will disagree with my conclusions. For instance, many people in the industry think VC started in 1970, while I would argue that it is one of the world's oldest professions. Few people understand the true significance of the venture industry. The NVCA studies show that venture capital has created 17 percent of the American economy, but in my estimation, venture capital is responsible for close to 50–75 percent. (This is without academic justification because to find out whether my number is correct, we would have to sift through countless forgotten corporate histories to see how the initial financing was obtained.) A recent Stanford study by Ilya Strebulaev and Will Gornall shows the industry is much more important than even the NVCA data shows. They have written a book about these findings.

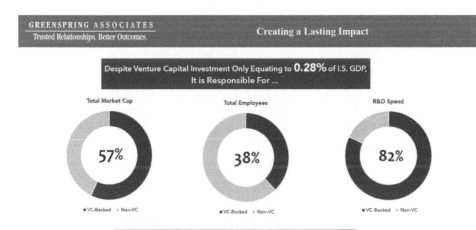

GREENSPRING ASSOCIATES
Trusted Relationships. Better Outcomes.

Creating a Lasting Impact

Despite Venture Capital Investment Only Equating to **0.28%** of I.S. GDP, It is Responsible For ...

Total Market Cap   Total Employees   R&D Spend

57%   38%   82%

■ VC-Backed ■ Non-VC   ■ VC-Backed ■ Non-VC   ■ VC-Backed ■ Non-VC

... of Public U.S. Companies Founded Since 1979

Source: Stanford University. The Economic Impact of Venture Capital: Evidence from Public Companies   34

Several organizations are pursuing the history of venture capital today, and over the past 20 years, along with the Bancroft Library, the National Venture Capital Association, and Harvard Business School, I've helped fund the oral interviews of seventy venture capitalists who, combined, have thousands of years of experience in the business. Until recently, the history of the industry has been primarily oral, and when Laurance Rockefeller, Benno Schmidt, General Doriot and General Draper died, their stories were lost. I hope the histories we've recorded and others that are being written will provide the source material for future study.

The world of private equity is fashionable today, attracting a lot of attention from the media, and it can be divided into three parts: leveraged buyout firms, hedge funds, and venture capital firms. Leveraged buyout firms and hedge funds are important financial asset classes.

My experience with the leveraged buyout business goes back to World War II. My father's boss in the Air Force then was Colonel Charles Dyson. At a very early age, Charlie was a senior manager at Price Waterhouse, and many considered him a genius. He was anointed one of the whiz kids in WWII, working out of the Pentagon. There were hundreds of them, and their job was to reform the American economy. They transformed watch factories into manufacturers of bombsights. They turned Caterpillar and John Deere into manufacturers of tanks. They created a scientific research community that drove scientific knowledge forward five centuries in just four years. Working under Charlie, my father's job was to supervise the development, production, and allocation of fighter aircraft. He was the rocket man.

When the war was over, Charlie tried to recruit my father to be his partner in a business that would come to be called leveraged buyouts, but my father was more interested in creating the future than in turning around old, established companies. Charlie went on to create the Dyson Corporation, one of the first leverage buyout companies, which later became the Dyson-Kissner-Moran Corporation. In the beginning, he had no money, so to acquire a company, Charlie borrowed millions from the First National Bank of Boston, his signature serving as his collateral, and repaid the loan three weeks later. Using debt, Charlie would acquire an established business with undervalued assets that had no relevance to the company's ongoing business (e.g., real estate or buildings). He would then sell them. He would later focus on turning a moribund business heading for extinction into a prosperous one. In the process, he might have to fire hundreds of people who made inherently unprofitable products. As these companies grew, he would hire new employees to work on the profitable product lines.

Charlie was tall and lean, and he wore a gray fedora with a black overcoat. His elegant hands were encased in gray suede gloves. He was the epitome of a New York financier, but he did not have three-martini lunches. There are still Charlie Dysons out there, restructuring stagnate businesses and making them successful; however, increasingly, the leveraged buyout business has relied on financial engineering that entails acquiring massive amounts of debt, buying a company, taking it private, getting rid of excess employees and unprofitable lines of business, then taking the company public to reduce debt. The average holding period now is usually three to five years. These buyouts can make good returns for their investors, but they do not shape the economy of the future.

The leveraged buyout business was institutionalized in the late 1970s and '80s, when firms like Kohlberg Kravis Roberts & Company, Golder Thoma Cressey, and Forstmann Little & Co raised billions of dollars from institutional investors. Today, fueled by cheap credit, the leveraged buyout boom, which had been building since 2004, has exploded. Private equity deal volume doubled in a few years. Leveraged buyouts accounted for almost 20 percent of the $3.5 trillion in global mergers and acquisitions, according to Thomson Financial. Until 2007, the buying binge continued.

The hedge fund business is widely believed to have started in 1949 with Alfred Winslow Jones, Ph.D. Before that, Dr. Jones had been a diplomat, a reporter for *Fortune,* and an academic. His novel investment approach was based upon hedging his long-term stock positions by selling short the stock to protect against market risk. He used leverage to enhance the returns. In 1952, he transformed his general partnership into a limited partnership, introducing a 20-percent-of-profit incentive fee for the general partners. Jones' results were excellent, but the hedge fund industry as a whole limped along until the early 1990s, when the spectacular returns of George Soros' Quantum Fund and Julian Robertson's Tiger Fund were published. New hedging tools like derivatives were added to portfolios, the industry exploded, and by 1999, there were more than 4,000 hedge funds in existence.

In the history of venture capital, we should remember this: it takes one cent to do basic research, but it takes 99 cents to turn that basic research into a company. Basic research comes with little cost or bloodshed. It's with the 99 cents—the creating of a company—that blood is spilled.

Historically, there are two types of participants in venture capital: syndicates of investors and angel investors. Angel investors are wealthy and usually entrepreneurs. Every $1 an angel or venture capitalist invests in starting a company is usually followed by $8 more in ensuing financings before the company goes public.

HISTORIC DEVELOPMENT OF VENTURE CAPITAL

(with the exception of the Phoenician Trading Voyages and the Whaling syndicates, I created this chart)

2000 BC	Phoenician Trading Voyages
1500 AD	Exploration Venture Capital Christopher Columbus Marco Polo
1800	Salem and Baltimore merchant banks funding letters of marque and China trade, English merchant banks funding railroads Nantucket angels funding whaling voyages
1880	Andrew Mellon—Gulf Oil, Carborundum, Gulf Oil, General Reinsurance, Alcoa

1902	Lucius Ordway—3M Sherman Fairchild—IBM Rochester Angels—Eastman Kodak
1911	Bessemer Securities
1930	Payson & Trask
1938	Laurance Rockefeller—Eastern Airlines, McDonnell Douglas, Thiokol
1938	Warburg Pincus JH Whitney
1946	G. Doriot—American Research and Development Corporation California Firms

Venture capital is a much older business than hedge funds or leveraged buyouts. It is one of the world's oldest professions. Phoenician syndicates funded their explorers and merchant traders to make risky voyages all over the ancient world, seeking exceptional profits. The merchants that put up the capital got 80 percent of the profits. The sailors and captains of the ships received 20 percent, according to Colin Blaydon, Ph.D., of Dartmouth. Dr. Tom Nicholas of Harvard describes the whaling ventures that used similar compensation structures in his pioneering book *Venture Capital: An American History*.

According to PitchBook, VC firms invested $132 billion, or 15.5 percent of the $717 billion raised by US private equity firms in 2018. Venture capital, the oldest form of private equity, is the business of funding early-stage businesses with the potential to be highly profitable because they offer something new, even paradigm-changing, in the fields of technology, healthcare, or consumer services and products. One can say that Ferdinand and Isabella were venture capitalists when they backed Christopher Columbus to discover America, or say as much about the Venetian merchants who backed Marco Polo's exploration of the Orient. In America, during the late 1790s, thirty or forty merchant investment banks in Baltimore and Salem were started to fund the clipper ships, then trading with China, or to fund pirate ships with letters of marque to raid, rob, and capture British ships. Representatives for these investors sailed with the clipper ships, much like venture capitalists attending board meetings today. What's more, the terms of the syndicates financing the ships were strikingly similar to today's legal documents drafted by Silicon Valley lawyers.

The merchant banks in eighteenth—and nineteenth-century England organized similar syndicates to finance change. In 1830, Hambros Bank raised four million pounds for Count Camillo Benso di Cavour, the finance minister of Sardinia. Bonds, eventually converted into stock, financed railroads and other new industries. Cavour became finance minister for Victor Emanuel, working with the Hambros Bank to use similar English financial syndicates to build a national railway system for Italy. This very profitable business would unify Italy's politically divided city-states into the single country we know as Italy. Similar British merchant bank syndicates funded such diverse American ventures as railroads and the fur trade. The same convertible preferred structure of investment is the standard of the venture industry today.

Let me make a biological analogy. The human body consists of cells. But the body originated from the cells dividing and multiplying furiously to create a large mass. In some ways, cells are like companies. Our national economies are largely made up of the interactions of large numbers of these bodies. The venture industry combines capital and extraordinary individual human talent that leads to the creation and growth of an enterprise, the proliferation of cells.

Institutional venture capital in the United States started in the late nineteenth century. Unfortunately, much of the early modern history of the venture capital business is not widely known. In my opinion, Andrew Mellon was the father of the institutional venture capital business at the turn of the nineteenth century. As a banker in Pittsburgh, he inherited and then expanded a small bank, but the Mellon family empire as it exists today was built by investing in startups. Mellon's holdings in Mellon National Bank were dwarfed by his later venture successes.

For example, in 1894, Arthur Vining Davis, Captain Alfred E. Hunt, and George H. Clapp approached Mellon. They proposed a commercially feasible product called aluminum, which was to be made from an electrolytic process invented by Charles Martin Hall. Mellon was so fascinated he loaned the company $4,000 and purchased $25,000 of its stock. He helped the company in its early years, and ultimately, he ended up with the majority of the ownership in the Aluminum Company of America, which became known as Alcoa. In 1890, Mellon decided to finance W.L. Mellon, his nephew, who wanted to enter the oil business. Mellon invested first $10,000 and later another $100,000 in Gulf Oil. Mellon always looked for men of "competence and character," he said, and the rules that govern VCs today are the same ones that governed Mellon's strategy.

That strategy, as described by the journalist John K. Barnes in the early twentieth-century magazine *World's Work:* "Find a man who can run a business and needs capital to start or expand. Furnish the capital and take shares in the business, leaving the other man to run it, except when it is in trouble, then replace the manager. When the business has grown sufficiently to pay back the money, take the money and find another man running a business in need of money and give it to him on the same basis."

III

MY ROLE MODELS: LAURANCE ROCKEFELLER AND GENERAL DORIOT

"Venture capital is best practiced as a calling, not a job."

—Jim Swartz

BEFORE THE ONSET OF WORLD War II, a new kind of venture capital appeared in the United States. With full-time, professional management, family venture capital firms were organized to finance new startup companies. The descendants of the founders of some of the great American industrial corporations sought to continue the tradition of their forefathers. Laurance Rockefeller, for instance, the child of wealth but also a man of vision, helped to start professional venture capital in the United States. Because he didn't talk much about his role in business or his many successes, many people tend to overlook Laurance Rockefeller's contributions to the nascent venture capital industry.

Laurance was a man who could have gone through life without working. As a Princeton freshman, Laurance was asked why his allowance was the same as most of his classmates. He reportedly joked, "What do you think I am, a Vanderbilt?" Blessed and cursed by the wealth and expectations he was born into, Laurence believed that it was his obligation to change the world. In 1935, from behind a door with a simple sign that read, "5600 Rockefeller Center," Laurance started a new enterprise, Laurance Rockefeller Associates. It was a loose association of principals (Rockefeller family members and their associates), but it was neither a partnership nor a corporation.

In 1938, Laurance backed Captain Eddie Rickenbacker, the World War I fighter ace famous for having the most German kills, when he bought Colonial Airlines from General Motors. His vision was to create an airline that would provide low-cost air transport around the world. Eddie's company, Eastern Air Lines, was nicknamed "Rickenbacker's Body Haulers," and it made both him and Laurance pioneers of the commercial aviation industry, along with Howard Hughes and Juan Trippe.

The next year, as a capital partner in Schroeder-Rockefeller, Laurance backed an inventor with a passion for lens technology who started a company that went on to supply virtually all the sunglasses worn by fighter pilots in World War II. At the end of the war, the inventor wanted to develop a new type of camera. Laurance believed that the inventor knew nothing about consumer products like cameras, so he eventually sold his 78 percent interest in the company for a pittance. He had second thoughts about the man he invested in and so failed to profit personally from the inventor's camera lens company. The inventor's name was Dr. Land, and the company was Polaroid.

And yet, Laurance's backing of Land is still a great example of venture capital dollars moving technology forward. Without them, Land might not have been in a position to take the next step.

Laurance also backed John McDonnell, who started McDonnell Aircraft Corporation (later McDonnell Douglas) in St. Louis in 1939, to develop the single-engine jet fighter plane. Laurance also invested in Cessna, founded in 1946, which created the market for consumer aviation. That same year, Laurance founded Reaction Motors, which became the rocket division of Thiokol Propulsion and led mankind to the stars. Piasecki Helicopter, also begun that year, pioneered tandem rotors for helicopters and was another Rockefeller portfolio company. Piasecki became Vertol Aircraft in 1956. Later, it was sold to Boeing.

In other words, when we look at what Laurance Rockefeller did between 1938 and 1950, we can see a classic pattern that recurs in venture capital. Laurance played a role in the development of commercial aviation that was probably of greater significance than all of Howard Hughes' contributions. He identified a fundamental trend and backed multiple companies associated with it, each one creating pieces of the future. The companies were often related to each other, and they were steppingstones along the path of advancing a technology, in this case, aviation. Over time, it has become clear they were also steppingstones in turning the world into a global village. In 1880, traveling around the world required rail, ship, and motor car transport and took eighty days. It could take weeks to move from place to place before World War II. Yet twenty years later, commercial air travel had transformed American lives. It was one of Laurance's major contributions to the world. His investments ultimately made it possible to cross the United States in five hours, to fly from New York to Paris in three-and-a-half hours by Concord, and to fly around the world in twenty-five hours.

The independent publicly financed venture capital firm came into existence in 1946, with General Doriot's American Research and Development Corporation. The objective of this firm was to create companies and, by doing so, create long-term returns on investment for its shareholders. Following Doriot's tradition, the firms Draper, Gaither & Anderson; McMicking & Company; and Davis & Rock were organized as a private partnership in California between 1940 and 1960. I was very fortunate because, early in my career, I had the privilege of knowing the World War II whiz kid generation of VCs. Each of them influenced me greatly.

During the war, my father was a whiz kid, too. At the Pentagon, Charlie Dyson and Robert McNamara managed this group of young businessmen who transitioned America's economy from peacetime to wartime production. When many American men left for the islands of the South Pacific or the deserts of Africa, whiz kids helped women enter new previously inaccessible sectors of the workforce, becoming riveters, streetcar conductors, tank mechanics, and munitions factory workers. It would have been thrilling to see these Pentagon desk commandos at work as they drove world industry to a level of innovation not to be equaled again in American history, including advances in atomic power, radar, aviation, radio, lasers, antibiotics, and countless others—all achieved in five years.

Laurance hired my father to help him create what is now called the aerospace industry, the industry that put a man on the moon.

Father was ideally qualified for the job. He had been well trained to become a master of the universe. He had graduated from Shattuck-St. Mary's School, in Minnesota, at age 16 and began attending Carleton College. At age 17, he transferred to MIT, where he earned a degree in electrical engineering. After MIT, Father received a Master of Business Administration degree from Northwestern in Chicago.

He went to work for Britton I. Budd. Budd was managing the restructuring of the Insull empire after its bankruptcy. British-born Samuel Insull was an entrepreneur who had built a holding company by acquiring public utilities and transportation companies. He created Chicago's transportation and electrical infrastructure during the 1920s and was a major philanthropist, but he financed his company with debt. When the Great Depression arrived, his company's revenues collapsed, and it could not pay interest on the debt. Budd was appointed by the courts to fix the problem, and Father was one of his lieutenants. Budd sought out Father because Father held patents in electrical generation systems in addition to his MBA.

In 1938, it was obvious the world was going to war, so Father joined the Army Air Corps and was commissioned as a captain, rising in rank over the course of the war to colonel, under the command of General Charles Dyson. One of Dyson's roles in managing the whiz kids was to focus some of them on developing and producing better fighter planes.

My father was captivated by Laurance Rockefeller, so he did not complain when, in the spring of 1946, he received a call from him at 2:00 a.m. Laurance had received an early morning call himself from Robert Patterson, the secretary of war, asking for his help. A struggling company in Morristown, New Jersey, with strategic value to the US, would go bankrupt the next day unless Laurance found a solution. President Truman had said that, without this company, the future of the US was in jeopardy. The company hoped to build rockets, and Laurance asked my father to figure it out.

Father picked up a $350,000 check from Laurance at 4:00 a.m., which was a lot of money in those days, then drove to a little office outside of Morristown, where the scientist Wernher von Braun and several other Germans sat in one corner and New Jersey bankers sat in another. Father paid off a loan, and Reaction Motors was born, the company that would build the engines that powered the rockets that would one day carry men into space. This was the dream of von

Braun and the other members of the V2 rocket design team that had fled from Hitler's Germany to Sweden, and then, after the war, to the United States to escape further exploitation by Hitler.

Von Braun was a troubled man, tormented by the knowledge of the suffering his V-2 rockets had inflicted on England. In the wrong hands, a great scientist's work had become an instrument of death. Ultimately, his "apology gift" to the Allies was pointing the way to the stars. His Reaction Motors would ultimately merge with Thiokol, becoming the basis of much of the rocket technology behind NASA. Von Braun wound up in Huntsville, Alabama, and his legacy was the US Space and Rocket Center.

One cold February evening, Laurance and his wife, Mary, came to dinner at my parents' home in Baltimore. Mother and Father were extremely excited and eager to make the best possible impression. If you could imagine what the Pope would go through for a visit from Jesus Christ, you can imagine our family the week before this visit. My mother spent days on the meal and prepared for what the army calls a "government inspection." Pillows were puffed, the floor was vacuumed four times a day, and all the tiny crevices of the house were wiped clean. Nothing remained unpolished except my small, live alligator, a present to me from my parents. Unfortunately, the night before the Rockefellers were due to arrive, the alligator escaped! The alligator was only twelve inches long, but still, my mother had to lecture me on dangerous pets.

She envisioned Mr. Rockefeller arriving and being dragged by a thirty-foot croc into a pool of quicksand that had suddenly materialized on our living room rug. Our house on Malvern Avenue looked the best it ever would on that evening in February. (The alligator was never seen again.)

During the cocktail hour, my mother brought me into the living room, silencing all conversation. For the first time, I saw the great man. From the tales I'd heard, I expected to see Achilles, glorious in full armor. Instead, Laurance was tall, slender, and wore an immaculate, charcoal-gray suit. His hands were graceful. I remember admiring his fine features, his dark eyes, and his aura of quiet self-possession. By not saying a great deal, he could say everything, listening more than he spoke.

My parents dressed me in a black suit that fit like a burlap bag with a Countess Maria tie of my father's. The tie was a colorful display of Zeus' lightning bolts, five inches wide. (My chest was only twenty inches wide.) My hair was greased. I looked like a waiter at Al Capone's birthday party. From the photograph of that evening, more than fifty years ago, I see a child rigged out as a cross between a grease monkey and the maître d' of a third-rate Italian restaurant.

Despite my appearance, Laurance politely asked me to sit beside him. Since he made everyone he spoke with the center of his attention, he helped an insecure boy feel at ease.

"How do you like school?" he asked, and I started enthusiastically babbling about an upcoming speech I was giving at my school, Gilman School, about Hannibal crossing the Alps on his elephants, the Punic Wars, and the defeat of Varus at Cannae.

"You sound like a war lover," he said.

"What do you do, sir?" I asked.

"I work with a small group of men like your father. We create companies with the power to change the world."

"What do you mean?"

I sensed he was disappointed with the question. He asked me what I thought was happening when my father and I watched the Vanguard rockets launch and the memories of that day are still clear to me. I remember the fire and the noise. The rocket released the guide wires, moving slowly upward, then it sprang up to the sky incredibly fast. As a child, I imagined I was a passenger on that rocket, riding it to the stars. Laurance's questions helped me understand what my father truly did: he helped lead us to the moon.

Ten years later, Laurance joined my father for a day of golf at Burning Tree in Bethesda, Maryland. The news was not good. Flight Refueling, the company my father then ran, was going out of business. General Curtis LaMay said, "All future wars would be fought by strategic bombers. Ground troops would not be needed." Flight refueling was sold to Aeronca, a manufacturer of small private aircraft. However, the company's headquarters property, next to the airport, made Laurance four times his investment, not that making money was the only point.

The other bad news was that Father's expertise was in the aerospace industry, and venture capitalists no longer did aerospace deals. Laurance was now funding computers, peripheral devices, software, and semiconductors. This was the future, a future in which Father would have no place. Both Father and Laurance believed that wars would always be won or lost when soldiers faced each other on the ground. They mourned the loss of flight refueling because our soldiers would no longer have the close air support they would need to win such wars.

Laurance carried Father financially after that. He hired him for another seven years to consult for his last aerospace companies. He did what he could do to give Father work, but a retainer like that could not continue indefinitely. From the age of 55, father lived by his wits—a job here, a job there—all while putting a child through college and supporting a family as if nothing happened. An accountant by nature, he became a master at controlling costs. I have looked at his ledgers and wondered at a 20-cent entry for toothpaste. What must have gone on in the mind of a man who helped America win World War II, who helped create the path to the moon, and for whom positively impacting the future now had come to mean carefully controlling our family's toothpaste usage? He was no longer a master of the universe. It must have taken considerable courage to accept his fate. I know it hurt him.

His attitude toward life changed after that. All his life he had dressed well, but from that point on, he never changed his style of dress again. His remaining life was caught in a time warp of the mid-1950s. He did not blame Laurance; he understood economics. He had failed to retrain himself for the future, which meant he was at fault. It was like trying to stop the sunrise. Father, the former whiz kid and wunderkind who believed in the future, could no longer see himself in that future.

I do not think of my father as a failure. He recovered as best he could after he left Camelot. He also gave me an excellent education at Penn and Harvard, he let me travel and see the world, and he let me make some investments in his best companies that gave me enough money to finance my career.

Father never complained, although what he loved most, his work, was now an unpleasant, thankless task. His situation also served as a warning: if you ever cease to evolve as a person, if you do not continue to re-educate yourself, you may face an unpleasant end—obsolescence. Careers, like living things, have a life cycle: birth, adolescence, maturity, old age, and senility. This is also true of corporations.

Many of us are led down the path by fate. Father followed that path with courage. His peers admired him. His friends always gave Father his best business opportunities and visited him constantly; however, his problem was that his self-confidence had dwindled. He had lost the will to dare.

I will never forget when my mother awakened me one morning in the mid-1960s. She said that Father had driven to Washington to put Laurance on a plane the previous night, but afterward, on his way home, he had gotten in an accident. Somewhat tipsy and sleepy, he had driven over a hill's rise and collided with an empty car stalled thirty feet ahead. He was in critical condition, having lost a quarter of his skull.

The doctors implanted a steel plate to replace the piece of skull bone, but he was never the same. Most importantly, his mother, who was his pillar of strength, died around the same time amid what he considered the ruins of his life.

I still think that night and dream of my father with his skull open, which mingles with my memories of a similar brutal injury I saw inflicted on a soldier in my platoon during Vietnam. Father received his eventual death sentence that night: traumatic brain injury combined with a genetic predisposition to Parkinson's. My grandfather had also had the disease, slipping slowly and painfully into death. Traumatic brain injuries dramatically increase the chance of Parkinson's. In time, the combination of genetics and the car accident would overwhelm my father.

All his working life, Father had a cherished image of what his retirement would look like: he would live stress-free and play golf. After my grandmother and my Aunt Clara died, he had inherited enough money to retire. But shortly after their deaths, a week before he moved with my mother to Florida, he was diagnosed with Parkinson's. The last eighteen years of his life were spent in steady decline, enduring the loss of mental and physical capabilities. At the end of his life, sick with Parkinson's, he kept a pistol beside his bed. I took it away, saying that his suicide would destroy his grandchildren. He nodded in acceptance, but I noticed a tear run down his cheek.

My father's tragic accident and his ignominious exile from Laurance's Camelot foreshadowed other lessons of the VC's life. Small, entrepreneurial businesses are personal. They are life and death experiences, just like combat, so anyone seeking a normal life and job security need not apply. Venture capital is Darwinian, often with a businesslike veneer covering the potent mixture of genius, passion, and greed boiling below the surface. It is a life of great dreams, continual crisis, disasters, and life-changing victories. If you fall in love with it, it becomes an addiction: you cannot live without a technicolor ride through space on a rocket ship of your own creation. This is another lesson I carry with me: learn to enjoy overcoming stress, because it is a part of a venture capitalist's life that cannot be avoided.

One of my father's greatest gifts to me was the seed of that dream, which arrived in the form of the pioneering venture capitalist I mentioned earlier, General George Doriot. I remember the first time my father introduced me to him. He had an impeccable voice. Father said he practiced his French accent every day in front of a mirror. He was a great man and a showman. It was an honor to be in his presence. Both Doriot and Laurance Rockefeller changed my life for the better, though I hardly knew them. In a crazy way, my father chose those instructors for me and passed on their lessons. He knew he was no poet, but when he met poets, he did recognize them.

It was one of those October mornings only to be found in Boston. The sun was bright, caressing my face. Even though I was wearing a blue Brooks Brothers suit with a vest, the wind blew fiercely, and I was cold. The shrapnel in my arm ached, reminding me that only six months before I had been a warrior in Vietnam killing communists. It was 1969, and Father and I walked across the Boston Commons, surrounded by a neoclassical iron railing. Boston's streets were narrow and twisted, in keeping with their seventeenth-century origins. For me, Boston was the most beautiful city and the only one where I felt totally at home. That day, on the anniversary of Paul Revere's long ride, I felt that I, too, marched to Lexington Green in April 1775 with a musket in my hand as my ancestor, Joel Newhall had done when he fired the "shot heard around the world." I followed in the footsteps of those Minutemen. For me, this was half pilgrimage, half homecoming.

Father said we were going on to the American Research and Development Corporation (ARD), which a 1967 *Fortune* article called a "dream factory." He knew I wanted a job at ARD and was trying to help as the general was an old friend of his. ARD was at the peak of its power, with offices occupying the top floors of the Hancock building, a skyscraper on the edge of downtown Boston. Founded in 1946, Doriot's venture capital firm opened its doors the same year my father entered the business, and until that time, venture capital had been merely the province of wealthy families and angel investors. Now, ARD, open to public investors, had started hundreds of companies, and Doriot had dedicated himself to changing the field forever. A hypomanic missionary, Doriot preached his religion from every pulpit he could find. Childless, he treated ARD companies as the closest thing he had to children.

At ARD, we met Jim Morgan, Dan Holland, and John Shane, the young men who served as warrior monks to Doriot's abbot of the monastery. Since I had always believed that a person's office reflected their character, I immediately noticed ARD's quarters were sparse and utilitarian—no period furniture, no oriental rugs, no old hunting paintings, nothing to distract from the mission. The furniture appeared to be Army surplus. The desks were painted gray with rubber tops the color of pea soup and dented aluminum trim. Everywhere there were neat piles of business plans and, on the occasional tables, piles of product literature from ARD's portfolio companies. With no window curtains to hinder it, sunlight streamed into the office. It was the ideal environment for these monks to toil under their austere and demanding leader. The phones never stopped ringing.

We were greeted by Dorothy Rowe, ARD's major duomo and the general's right hand, who made certain that this tidy little world kept humming along smoothly. Most days, General Doriot walked from home across the Boston Commons to ARD's spartan offices, dressed in a dark, tailored suit with a vest, white shirt, cufflinks, and matching tie. He wore wire-rimmed glasses, and his mustache was a thin line above his lips, trimmed like David Niven's. Though he looked like he might be going to a luncheon at the Ritz Hotel in the Place Vendome, he usually had a roast beef sandwich at his desk.

Born in France and a naturalized US citizen, the general wore a Distinguished Service Medal on his lapel. During the war, General Doriot's task was to prepare soldiers effectively for war in all climates while limiting waste. The Army had a series of regulations that made no sense, such as that old equipment had to be used before new equipment could be designed.

As a result, the Army was using tents designed for Normandy in World War I. When they sent them to the Philippines in the 1940s, they rotted in the jungle climate in two weeks. The accelerator pedal in World War I tanks was designed for someone with a size-five shoe. The average foot size by World War II was nine and a half. Doriot, as a quartermaster general, rectified these errors and sought out smart innovations. For one thing, he replaced combat boots' leather soles with rubber grooved soles.

American forces fought bravely on the ground, and our warrior generals proved themselves equal if not superior to Germany and Japan's aristocratic officer castes, but America's edge lay in its war production and innovation system, the greatest the world had ever known. To put it in perspective, there was more innovation in weapons technology in five years of World War II than in one thousand years in the ancient world, during the height of the Greek and Roman civilizations. The US outproduced the rest of the world, thereby supplying our allies, who lacked the production capacity. Most importantly, we became the modern world's center of invention, which was and is our enduring competitive advantage as a nation.

We started World War II with leftovers. Our planes could hardly beat a horse in a race; our tanks were sitting ducks for advanced German weaponry; our Navy was ill-equipped to face the Imperial Japanese Navy. Yet, by the end of the war, we were the undisputed masters of technology. Our planes, ships, and tanks were the best in the world. Our research labs had created nuclear technology and weapons and had developed early rocket science that would later propel man into space. All this change occurred in six short years.

All his accomplishments and contributions to the war and the world after the war were in my head when I met with Doriot that day in 1969. His words at that meeting electrified me. I wrote them down in my journal that night. This is how I recalled them.

He looked at me across his desk, and said, "So you want to be a venture capitalist."

I tried to answer.

Doriot drummed his pencil on the desk. "How many young men ask to join ARD? Many want to find a place at this table, but there are few seats."

The General offers, "During World War II, our country created a new world of technology. We moved five hundred years in six. That technology is still being created in corporate research labs, in university labs, but unless we transform ideas into commercial reality, it will be meaningless. So, we search for the exceptional man or woman, the entrepreneur. We become a partner in creating a dream. It is not a dream of just making money or creating capital gains—it's a dream of creating a company, a real business that changes our world. If we do this successfully, over time, capital gains will follow. The venture capitalist is not the hero. The hero is the entrepreneur who builds the business. We are a mentor, a coach, and we help in every way we can, using our knowledge and connections to facilitate the building of great companies. Not many entrepreneurs can run the gamut of company formation—from the startup with five employees to the giant multinational corporation with 100,000 employees. In these cases, we must be the instrument of change, attracting the management that can manage the large enterprise. But the hero is the entrepreneur. We, the venture investors, are a footnote in history.

"How do you know who is an entrepreneur? It takes time. You meet his family, you visit his home, and you try every way to get inside his head. The technology entrepreneur must be thoroughly grounded in the science of his area of innovation.

"The real entrepreneur is totally obsessed with his mission. He must believe that nothing can stop him—all risks he will overcome. If you finance him, you become part of his vision. Until a company is successful, you will not be able to sell your investment at a profit, so your destiny is inseparably tied to the company that is being created. The original business plan is nothing but an idea: dodge left, dodge right, find success. The entrepreneur must succeed even if the world falls apart around him. The only thing that counts is success.

"You go on sales calls with the entrepreneur, have dinner with him, you understand how he solves problems. Take for granted that the entrepreneur is hardworking. Judge him by the people who he attracts to his company, for he must not be afraid to hire people better than himself. The entrepreneur, a driven man, is usually motivated by money. He wants access to the intoxicants of life: art, houses, sports, gardens. But money is only one tiny element of the equation. The true entrepreneur must be in love with his product. It sounds odd to love a microwave radio. What I mean is that the entrepreneur must lose a piece of himself to that which he creates. Is this not what the painter or the poet does? The company is a part of its creator. The act of creation becomes its own intoxicating reward, and to not create unleashes dark moods which often lead to depression. It's the same for Henry Ford. He returns from a vacation and inspects his manufacturing line. He finds that some overzealous vice president, in his absence, has painted one of his beautiful black cars a dark blue. He grabs a sledgehammer and maniacally destroys the car in front of him in an hour of frantic violence—it is as if someone has violated his soul. Can you imagine that painting a car blue could be a violation of the soul to any other man than Ford? But to understand why Ford has no choice but to grab that hammer is to understand the creative passion of an entrepreneur.

"Unfortunately, in the business, your life will be spent dealing with serious problems, often crises, and sometimes situations of life and death. Because you find yourself sharing a vision, you will naturally be drawn to save it at all costs. Two bad deals may absorb you, and you may spend only a little time with the company that ends up making your investors one half-billion dollars. Entrepreneurs never admit defeat, nor do good venture capitalists. *Nil desperandum.* You must never lose the courage to dream on a grand scale. You must hold on to that dream at any price, any sacrifice. The most important quality besides honesty is optimism. Many of your dreams will die, but there will always be a dream that becomes tomorrow."

The general was just getting going when Dorothy Rowe interrupted, saying that a new company had arrived to make a presentation. He had to leave.

I'd almost missed my moment. I blurted out, "General, I am willing to work for nothing; can I have a summer job?"

Frowning, he shook his head. "Didn't I say that an entrepreneur must have a sound technical grounding? This also applies to venture capitalists."

His message was not subtle. English majors with MBAs need not apply. He nodded to my father and thanked him for the introduction to Reaction Motors and Airborne Instruments. He looked at me and said, "If you have any questions, call Jim Morgan. He can help you." With that, he was gone.

The next time I saw the general was in the spring of 1970 at the ARD annual meeting at a large convention hall. Doriot was at the podium with shareholders sitting in the center of the room in rows of metal seats, while booths of the portfolio companies lined the walls.

It was almost like a *Star Trek* convention. I visited each company and discussed its vision for the future. Doriot manned the podium with his velvet voice and a French accent. A formal man, he acknowledged friends with a firm handshake and a tilt of the head that was a slight bow. His eyes sparkled as he began his sermon on entrepreneurship.

The room was silent, except for the great man's voice. It seemed as though he was speaking to each one of us personally. And when I looked up, he was looking at me.

I remembered that the general kept a three-by-five-inch card on every person he met, carefully making note of that person's history, taste in wine, and any other relevant facts. Before making someone's acquaintance again, he checked his notes and could resume a two-year-old conversation almost as if it had not been interrupted. Maybe I was on one of his 3x5 cards.

My account of the general would not be complete without mentioning one last thing. Like all students, my first wife Marsi and I wanted to escape the heat of Boston during the summer, so we often would drive two hours to Manchester by the Sea where we visited our friends, Linzee Coolidge and Dick Hall.

After we left our friends, we would drive to the southern end. Doriot's summer home was a small cottage on a large piece of property there, separated from the road by a low stone wall. It looked like a Norman cottage. A quiet seemed to permeate the earth. Flower stems bent in the ocean breeze. When I saw the general and his wife, Emma, tending the garden together, their arms moved in rhythm. The only sound was the rush of the sea, the wind, and the waves crashing on rocks below.

I peered over the whitewashed stone into the general's private world, recognizing the stark contrast between his workday, a chaotic battleground, and his garden—a secret place of total peace and relaxation, a creation of his imagination, where he found relief from his frantic reality. In truth, the garden was the anchor of the general's sanity. May God give me a chance to create such an island where my dreams may be free from the intrusion of unpleasant certainties. To use Psalm 23's description, a garden is the "still waters." Following the general's example, I made note of this on my own three-by-five-inch card.

IV.

NEA'S FIRST FUNDRAISING

"First, think. Second, dream. Third, believe. And finally, dare."

—Walt Disney

IN THE SPRING OF 1977, it was frightening for me to think of leaving a secure job at T. Rowe Price. There were only four venture firms in the mid-Atlantic: Bro Venture in Baltimore, Maryland; Greater Washington Investors and Allied Capital, both in Washington, D.C.; and Data Science Ventures in Princeton, New Jersey. It was time to break into venture capital, I thought, but I also could not build a firm on my own.

Before NEA took shape, my friend John Nehra was a young analyst at Alex Brown, covering medical device companies. We often worked together. We analyzed small companies, then I bought them for T. Rowe Price through Alex Brown. John received the commissions. He had another client, Howie Wolfe, who managed the estate of three heiresses of the John Deere fortune, so John suggested that the three of us spend some time together at an upcoming medical conference in Montreal, the Society of Artificial Organs.

In the spring of 1976, John, Howie, and I discussed the opportunity in the venture business over dinner. I explained my frustration: we had an investment team, a plan, and a partnership agreement drafted for T. Rowe Price, but then they had lost interest in starting a T. Rowe Price venture capital business due to the energy crisis. Howie said, "Pull it together and I could have an interest."

Immediately, I called Loring Catlin, a Payson Trask partner to see if he would join my new venture partnership. He had already agreed to join a T. Rowe Price-sponsored partnership. He told me that his life was in New York, that starting a firm from scratch was far more challenging than starting a firm with T. Rowe Price's support, and that he doubted if I knew what this would mean to me and my family. Though he was happy to have a challenging job, he said building a company can destroy all that is important to you, your wife, and your family. He declined my offer.

However, Frank Bonsal, Marsi's second cousin, occurred to me as another option. Frank was one of the younger senior partners at Alex Brown, a Baltimore investment bank that traditionally underwrote Maryland tax-free bonds. He had led them into the volatile business of high technology underwriting. He also invested Alex Brown's partners' capital in a few venture deals. I had known him for many years and appreciated his athleticism. He had won the great steeplechase race, the Maryland Hunt Cup in 1957, so he was an Olympic-quality athlete in Baltimore's favorite sport. Frank was also funny, while I was an all-too-serious young man. Frequently, I served as the butt of his jokes.

Meanwhile, Kirk Miller, the chairman of T. Rowe Price, had invested some of the firm's free capital in a private North Carolina company called Terminal Communications, Inc. (TCI) and he asked me to help with the project. TCI's CEO, Carl Southard, was the president of IBM's peripheral equipment division, which manufactured printers. He believed he saw an opportunity for a new generation of printers. The TCI board invited me to dinner at a steak restaurant close to the Raleigh-Durham airport. Although Carl Southard was quite overweight and breathed with difficulty, he enjoyed a steak.

I was distracted. It's very exciting to be sitting with an entrepreneur and a collection of venture capitalists. When Kirk called on me to analyze TCI's competition, it was my chance to shine, and I gave a serious fifteen-minute presentation. I called the printer a "Me too!" product. Competition from other companies with better products would kill it.

Frank leaned back in his chair, and said, "Kirk, that young fella is too wet behind the ears to know a computer from a printer!" Everyone laughed.

While I admit I lacked their knowledge of computers, my analysis was correct. Soon, TCI would be bankrupt.

Over the next several months, Frank and I started to work together visiting small companies. Frank was no longer popular because the small companies Alex Brown had underwritten were casualties of the energy crisis. Stocks had collapsed. Customers were unhappy. Many partners were also tired of Frank's acerbic humor.

Together, we visited Rolm Computer, in California, which manufactured a rugged computer for the army that could withstand use in the field. I was familiar with these computers, having used them in Vietnam. They were solid and easy to use, controlling airstrikes and artillery along with a host of other tasks that required computation. Frank was excited because Rolm used its technology to enter the PBX business, an automated phone-switching system for small-business offices. At the time, computer and communications science were merging. There was a block of Rolm stock for sale, strangely enough, from the notorious Saudi arms dealer, Adnan Khashoggi. He had evidently invested in the startup but needed cash.

We learned shortly after our meeting that the VC firm Greylock bought Khashoggi's stock. Rolm would later go on to be purchased by IBM for more than $1 billion, which spurred Frank to complain that he was an ambassador without a portfolio. Frank was there in the early days of Intel, but at Alex Brown, he could not act quickly. Decision-making did not happen in a small group, instead, for each deal, he had to round up a group of Alex Brown investors.

I suggested a solution: he and I could form our own partnership. In the spring of 1977, we began to plan, and we made several trips to New York to visit with Howie Wolfe and his Landmark partners. We also visited with three T. Rowe leaders Cub Harvey, Jr., then manager of their New Horizons Fund, Cornelius Neil Bond, manager of the Growth Stock Fund, and Don Bowman, the CEO. I had sent them a proposal outlining my plan for a new venture firm. T. Rowe decided that it could not start its own venture firm, but it could invest in NEA.

Though Cub and Don both agreed that this was the time to enter the venture business, T. Rowe Price had too much going on.

In addition, many believed that it was not right for the people who managed one of the firm's product lines to have a direct economic benefit from that single product. Instead, the theory went, individual compensation should be based on the firm's performance across the board. Also, a system that allowed three people to have profit interests in their product could create jealousy. Discord of that kind could tear a firm apart.

Don, Cub, and Neil were right about how standard compensation works for investment managers, but managers of venture funds have to share in the capital gains. The business, at that time, simply did not control enough capital to justify large fees, so compensation in the form of sharing capital gains provided incentive and reward in light of the long lead times and the myriad difficulties of creating great companies. The three men encouraged us to proceed and said they would try to get T. Rowe Price in our fund. They even agreed to give us an office and secretarial support when I left my T. Rowe job.

Towards the end of our meeting, Cub took me aside and offered quietly, "I'll support you, but you need to find a real venture capitalist as a partner. Why don't you give Dick Kramlich a call? I bet he must be tired of playing Arthur Rock's Bob Cratchit."

There was no need for him to say it. Dick was already the California venture capitalist I respected most. We had worked on numerous public companies together, but for the moment, I knew he was trying to sort out the financial impact of leaving Arthur Rock. Arthur could be draconian even when he was in good humor, and God help you if you approached him on the wrong day—he could be vindictive.

Nevertheless, Dick, Frank, and I talked and met often. Dick often helped us in every way he could, always holding out the possibility that he might join us. At about this time, I wrote a prospectus for our proposed firm, outlining its values and strategies, and thirty years later, the values described in that document still governed the firm that came to be.

In the meantime, Frank and I knew we needed a third partner with substantial venture capital experience. At this point, Howie Wolfe and the Deere Family had committed to backing us for $4.5 million and Don and Cub had overridden substantial internal objections at T. Rowe Price, resulting in a $1 million commitment. Today that might seem small, but at that time, all the firm's profits were being used to buy out retiring employees. They were investing 17 percent of the firm's net worth in our fledgling fund.

Both Frank and I knew Jim Morgan, one of the ARD partners. Jim could see the writing on the wall. He knew his firm was not going to survive. Yet he desperately loved the venture business. We courted him, spending weekends with him and giving him and his wife tours of Baltimore. Jim flirted with us, but he loved his home on Marblehead, outside Boston, so on the day we printed the prospectus, he told us he would not join us. I wondered if it might pique the general that an English major like me was trying to poach one of his own.

The one great thing Jim did was to introduce us to Dick Testa, ARD's legal counsel and the best venture capital lawyer in the business. In an amazing stroke of good fortune, Dick said he was willing to represent us at no cost until we raised our funds. If we did not succeed, he would eat the cost.

As it turned out, General Doriot held no grudges, whispering something to Dick about supporting the two liberal arts fools. Very kindly, Dick also delivered a letter to me from the general. It read, "Best wishes, Chuck. I admire your determination. I welcome you to the band of brothers who seek to build companies that change our destinies. By the way, I am giving to you the name 'New Enterprise Associates.' It is the first name I selected for American Research and Development Corporation. In retrospect, it is a better name for what we do. Take it if you want and bon chance." That letter astounds me to this day. We had the general's blessing, despite our backgrounds.

Frank and I stalled in our fundraising. After all, who wants to back a thirty-something-year-old analyst and a middle-aged investment banker? Still, Tom Roberts, the CEO of the Dekalb Corporation, and his advisor John Mabie committed $500,000. When I was an analyst at T. Rowe Price, I had invested in Dekalb, and Tom and I became friends. It was a strong vote of confidence, but it was not propelling us toward the $20 million goal. We were still determined, but when we received a call from Dick Kramlich confirming he was coming on board, it was one of the happiest days of my life. I felt that NEA was real because Dick was joining us. Dick joined NEA in December 1977.

T. Rowe Price truly helped us. Cub, Don, and Neil put their shoulders behind our fundraising effort by introducing us to Hughes Aircraft, Hewlett Packard, Merck, and Phillips Petroleum. The group at Phillips became enormously interested. They alone could fund the partnership because oil prices were high, profits were at record levels, and they knew that couldn't last forever. They wanted an insight into the entrepreneurial world, but the group we were meeting with needed the CEO's approval first. The Phillips CEO rejected the investment.

Dick negotiated an agreement with Arthur Rock, allowing him to join our firm, but he had to give 50 percent of his time to Arthur for two and a half years. He was paid by Arthur for his services. (Frank had a similar deal with Alex Brown, where he continued as a broker earning commissions on stock sales.) It had already occurred to me that perhaps Dick believed he had joined a bunch of overly optimistic losers when he was approached by Tom Perkins and Eugene Kleiner, two of San Francisco's famed venture capitalists, who asked him to become the third partner in their new fund.

They told Dick he should join them, friends with known qualities, not this Chuck Newhall, a young analyst with no technology background, an amateur, and Frank Bonsal, an investment banker pretending to be a venture capitalist.

The truth behind the comparison was not lost on Dick. However, Dick was no Arthur Rock. Dick had always believed his word was his bond, and he had given us his word. He told us that when Kleiner and Perkins asked him why he wouldn't join up with them, he responded, "I believe we share the same values, and besides, I just like them."

Kleiner Perkins became a legend, of course, and while NEA continues to compete to this day, Kleiner Perkins and NEA could not be more different firms. There is something to be said for staying with people who share your values.

What is still astounding to me is how three people with as little in common as Frank and Dick and me could make such a precarious partnership work. Frank was an aristocratic East Coast investment banker with a wicked sense of humor. Dick was the West Coast venture capitalist, and then there was me who Dick often called "the poet" or "preacher man." Ordinarily, a partnership with people like us wouldn't get off the ground, much less thrive for forty years together. How do we explain NEA's success? I think it's because we had shared goals, complementary skills (i.e. board member, bird dog, analyst), and we were committed to our partnership and each other. We enjoyed each other's differences and joked about them often.

We also made a point of focusing on succession and on making sure the careers of our younger partners were successful. For me, NEA would become Camelot.

Forgoing a salary for nearly a year and a half, I set out to raise funds. I invested $350,000 of my capital, mostly from venture investments made at Harvard in Computer Vision and Combustion Power, one of my father's companies. To start NEA, I felt I was building a bridge, perhaps to nowhere.

The commitment was not limited to the three of us in the partnership. Our families were committed to this adventure as well. Marsi was pregnant with our second son, Adair Brantley, at this time, and when her water broke, she had to drive herself to the hospital because I was in a business meeting. Dick, Frank, and I traveled almost seven days a week trying to interest people to invest in our dream. NEA would not exist without Marsi's support because her commitment equaled mine. I will never be able to repay her for the trust she placed in us. She was a child of privilege who still bet everything on my wild idea. She backed everything I did, and she gave me the courage to continue when I thought I was defeated.

Frank and I tried to leave no stone unturned. We discussed our planned partnership with many local wealthy families, and despite spending one-third of our fundraising time in Baltimore, we could not find an investor at home besides T. Rowe Price. Many of our committed investors so far were individuals who knew me well: Bob Krieble, co-founder of Loctite; Bill Robinson, chairman and CEO of the John H. Harland Company; Tom Roberts, Jr., who headed DeKalb; Tim Timken, who ran Timken Company through a T. Rowe Price introduction; and Harry Vernon and John Oakland of 3M, through Don Bowman's introduction. We were significantly helped by 3M consultants Ed Glassmeyer and Stewart Greenfield, who later founded OAK, another leading venture fund, which became one of NEA's best allies. In addition, Frank had a relationship with Ezra Zilkha, a director of the massive Insurance Company of North America (INA). John Riddell, INA's manager of private equity for INA, invested for his firm and became our largest non-founding investor, as well as an invaluable counselor. What's more, Frank's friend was Peter Morse, who'd married Martha Ford. Peter got the Ford Family to commit to NEA.

Dick knew Hal Bigler, who led Connecticut General's venture investment team, because his brother worked for Hal. Hal and his assistant Hanse Halligan took a chance on us and they both joined NEA's board. Dick's good friends Jim and Barbara Goodbody brought in investment from the Ball Family. Dick also brought in the Mugar Family, who owned the Starr Market chain in Boston, and the Fred Meyer Charitable Trust from Seattle. We closed NEA's first fund in June 1978, and the first thing we did was pay our lawyer, Dick Testa. His confidence in us was finally proven when he received that eighteen-months-overdue receivable. We'd been raising money since March of 1977 when we made our first official call on Howie Wolfe. While Dick says that the firm started when we closed NEA's Fund 1 in June of 1978, I say it was 1977, when I invested $350,000 to pay for the firm's expenses.

In the offering document I wrote when we started NEA, I described the kinds of companies in which we were looking to invest. Those same criteria are very close to the ones the firm uses today. While analyzing potential investments, NEA's general partners were to emphasize the following criteria, although we did not expect any one company to fulfill all of them. The following is from our first prospectus:

Management: Because people are the most important factor in the success of any business, the general partners believe that it is possible to judge an entrepreneur's abilities by the caliber of people they attract, appreciation for finance, willingness to delegate, integrity, ability to make difficult decisions, and their strategic orientation towards the chosen market. An entrepreneur's record of prior accomplishment and the thoroughness of their business plan are often excellent indicators of potential.

Fertility of Field: The sales of a portfolio company should have the potential of increasing in excess of 20 percent to 100 percent annually, depending on their size. It's important that a substantial portion of this growth comes from increasing primary demand rather than gains in market share. Primary demand exists where a product, process, or service will be more frequently used by current customers, will benefit from varied usage by current customers, or will attract new types of users, or new uses will be developed for a basic material.

Distinctive Competence: Although this factor denotes companies in terms of patents, trademarks, and manufacturing know-how, it actually refers to a company's ability to defend itself against price competition combined with a plan to capitalize upon a unique opportunity. Barriers to entry can be an important part of a distinctive competence.

Real Value of Product: The entrepreneur must identify how a product, process, or service satisfies a real need for a customer. In this sense, the word "need" is not limited to the economic benefits derived from cost savings.

Market Leadership: This is reflected in a company's success in capturing or its realistic plan to capture a dominant market position within its defined area.

Market Size and Concentration of Effort: The ideal market for the small company is one that is initially too small to attract the dedicated efforts of a large company yet has the potential for substantial expansion based upon marketing or technological vision. This is the disruption factor.

Return on Capital: While new enterprises seldom have the ability to self-finance, it is important they have the potential to achieve above-average returns on capital employed, usually greater than 20 percent (or much higher).

Recurring Revenues: Recurring revenues from a company's sales cushions the impact of adversities that a company will inevitably encounter in its formative years.

Freedom from Government Interference: Companies operating in fields free from substantial government regulation or direct interference are preferred.

Conservative Accounting: This permits a more reasoned investment analysis while avoiding unanticipated and undesired developments. Portfolio Diversification: An attempt will be made to reduce both the risk and volatility of the Partnership's investments by diversification.

Portfolio diversification will be characterized both by the number of companies and the variety of industries in which investments are made.

Willingness to Accept Counsel: Because of the general partners' experience with small businesses, they believe they can make a useful contribution to portfolio companies, whether as directors or on a more informal basis. Since stockholder control positions in portfolio companies will not be intentionally sought, a willingness to accept business counsel from the general partners is important.

NEA's differentiating quality lay in our willingness to invest in many industries outside the typical California partnership's focus (semiconductors and computers). I wrote a ten-page document at T. Rowe Price, outlining my small company investing strategy that became NEA's bible. We chose to focus on medical devices, molecular biology, healthcare services, material and chemical science, semiconductor applications, alternative energy and energy services, food and agriculture innovation, the communications industry, analytical instruments, computer services companies, specialty retailing, and defense electronics. Dick, Frank, and I were generalists with experience in all these fields. From the very start, we were asset allocators, adjusting our asset allocation to the industries we considered most interesting. After completing our first fund, we were on to the next. Our starting salaries were $50,000 per year. Frank and Dick both took major cuts in compensation. For me, $50,000 was a substantial increase over what I had been paid at T. Rowe Price.

V.

NEA CULTURE

"No man can become rich without himself enriching others."

—Andrew Carnegie

A GARDEN, LIKE A CORPORATION'S culture, can take years to cultivate, and just as hail shreds even the best-nurtured petals, a culture can be destroyed in a dizzyingly short period. But hail is inevitable. You have to prepare for hail and adapt to new circumstances. A culture cannot remain constant. It must evolve and change over time, adapting to a changing world.

From the moment we started it, NEA's culture was in flux because everything around it was in flux. The mission we gave ourselves was to structure each investment and provide governance to new businesses. We had to know when to bend and when to stand firm. We prepared for success, which meant enforcing transparency, ethical partnerships, and avoiding conflicts of interest.

NEA wanted to start companies that would change the world. We wanted to build a firm that would last a century. This was much harder when establishing a series of fund partnerships with finite lifespans versus creating a corporation that could last indefinitely. We told our investors we wanted to build a leading VC firm in the US. We wanted to dominate venture capital in the same way that JP Morgan came to dominate investment banking around 1900. Our limited partners listened to us and invested, although they must have thought we were slightly unhinged.

They were not too far off the mark. Essentially, NEA was an organ grinder with two monkeys. Dick Kramlich the experienced venture capitalist, was the organ grinder, and Frank Bonsal and I were very definitely the monkeys. Frank, the investment banker, was still shell-shocked from watching his clients' small company portfolios collapse after the energy crisis. I was an analyst for T. Rowe Price and a portfolio manager of a tiny part of the New Horizons Fund dedicated to investing in venture-backed companies. So, yes, I was a monkey.

Soon after we founded NEA, I attended the Western Venture Capitalist Conference, feeling proud to be a general partner (GP) in a firm that I was sure would become one of the industry leaders. To me, it was a forgone conclusion that NEA would be great. When I arrived, however, I was stunned to see that I was registered as a junior analyst. This must have been Dick's or Frank's joke. For years after that, however, I embraced my junior analyst role and wore my junior analyst hat when I presented at NEA annual meetings. My grandmother always told me to dream big and change the world. NEA was dreaming big.

The most important aspect of NEA's culture was that everyone involved had to win: limited partners, entrepreneurs, general partners, and anyone else involved with the partnership. We believed if any one constituency did not win in the long term, it would lead to the failure of the partnership. In this light, we created a compensation system then unique in the industry. In my mind, the road to hell is paved with bad incentive systems.

We founded the NEA partnership upon ethics. Incentive systems must be designed to promote ethical behavior. In our case, the interest of our entrepreneurs and limited partners was in capital gains. The fees we general partners received did not pay salaries; they were loans that had to be repaid with interest. Our only compensation was a share of the profits after all capital and loans had been repaid. This usually took eight to ten years. The world would be a better place if all investment managers had to earn superior returns before they were paid their fees. This incentive structure is common practice now for many of our competitors, but not all.

There was an old story in the investment world about JP Morgan. Mr. Morgan took a young associate to the New York Yacht Club. He gave the young man a tour of the dock. "This is my partner Bill's yacht.

This is my partner Tom's yacht. This is my partner George's yacht," Morgan said. The young man interrupted, "Where are the customers' yachts?" NEA's structure made sure its customers had yachts.

Three things adversely degrade returns for partnerships that return less than five times invested capital: 60 percent of the degradation is attributable to fees and 30 percent is degraded by not recovering fees before you start sharing gains. Carried interest was responsible for only ten percent of the return degradation. This was true for the 30 percent carry firms, the 25 percent ones, and the 20 percent ones. Imagine that Partnership A has 30 percent carry, does not recover fees, and has a 3 percent annual fee. This is an extreme structure one partnership did have in the 1980s. I use it to illustrate that fees impact return degradation far more than carried interest. The partnership has a ten-year life, so thirty cents of each dollar of the partnership's contributed capital goes to fees. Because the partnership starts sharing gains when 70 percent of the capital is recovered, another ten cents per dollar of the contributed capital disappears. Therefore, in Partnership A, only sixty cents per invested dollar goes to investments.

Now let's take Partnership B (aka NEA), which took a 1 percent fee with full recovery of fees. Full recovery of fees, in this instance, meant you did not share in gains until 110 percent of the capital was returned. Most partnerships in the early-stage VC environment did not return capital for at least eight to ten years. If the carried interest was not paid until late in the fund's life, the discounted present value was very small. Ninety cents on the dollar went to investments. As noted today, most venture compensation structures are more competitive than in the early days of institutional VC. Investors have come to recognize fees and recovering capital matter much more than carried interest. Investing ninety cents of a dollar is always better than investing sixty.

The philosophy was we would respect our investors by putting more dollars to work for them, and we would respect and incentivize our younger partners by giving them more carried interest than most of their peers at other private equity firms. This philosophy helped our culture, collegiality, and mindset. Young partners had three times the dollars working in carried interest than they would have made at other partnerships, but their salaries were in the middle range. Salaries for administrative assistants were at the top, and in addition, each year they received $10,000 after taxes starting in the 1980s, which was invested in our "Ven program." The "Ven program" would invest in the first deals the partnership invested in each year. Between NEA's 401K program and the "Ven program," an NEA administrative assistant who started working in the 1980s and who left the money in the "Ven program" pool would have walked away with several million dollars after a thirty-year plus career in addition to their salary over a thirty-year career. In those thirty years, the "Ven program" would certainly have invested in one of those startup companies that returned 250 to 1,000 times the investment.

Gradually, our dreams at NEA became reality. We became industry leaders, and we did indeed invest in companies that changed lives. We helped create and commercialize balloon angioplasty, therapeutic lymphokines, human gene therapy, and Medicare and Medicaid case management. To this day, NEA continues to finance innovation in exciting fields like epigenetics and nuclear fusion. Epigenetics is the field of study devoted to harnessing our relatively new understanding that genetics aren't entirely fixed at birth. Because many genes can be turned on and off or simply dimmed, many genetically influenced diseases potentially can be modified or prevented. Nuclear fusion has even greater disruptive power with the potential to end a global energy crisis by producing low-cost, totally clean energy.

On the technology side of NEA, we helped to create the company carrying 70 percent of all early Internet traffic. We identified, invested in, and mentored the companies that built the ethernet, high-speed data communications, software as a service, and the cloud. We pursued these dreams and we are still pursuing them.

If we could follow all the NEA-funded companies as independent or public companies or even as acquisitions that grow after they are acquired, I believe their revenues today would exceed two trillion dollars. While considerable growth comes post-acquisition or after the IPO, we were the ones who started the boulders rolling down the snowy mountainside, creating avalanches.

Ethics drove NEA. Our incentive systems were designed to promote ethical behavior, and the only interest of our entrepreneurs, our limited partners, and our general partners was capital gains. As mentioned before, our only compensation, besides mid-range salaries and merit bonuses, was a share of the profits after all capital and loans had been repaid. The fees we received had to be repaid with interest. For some, the concept that an investment manager had to make money for his clients before getting paid was disturbing. As a result, our approach worked as a natural employment filter.

We modeled NEA around the ideal that partners should do whatever it takes to make the firm successful, even if it was not in their self-interest. Initially, full general partners were all equal partners. Eventually, the managing partner was given a slight premium. I have observed in my career that senior partners at investment firms find it all too easy to create statistical analyses showing themselves to be the best investors in the firm. They then argue they deserve most of the compensation. This was and is not a winning strategy. For one thing, their analyses were often flawed. Eventually, the unfairness becomes evident, internal competition exploded, and the firm would start to decline.

Today, NEA gives bonuses on top of this "flat and equal" structure if general partners start producing unicorns. In other words, we reward gigantic outcomes. Also, in 2005, we established a management company—intended to reward lifetime, not short-term, performance. It received some small fees and 16 percent of the carried interest. Earlier, NEA had given the partner who sat on the portfolio company's board all the performance credit. In truth, this was flawed. Originating a company or providing it extraordinary assistance (e.g., customer contacts, recruiting key managers, finding acquisitions) deserves credit too. NEA also gave full credit for performance to all the partners on a board, which, in effect, was double-counting when two full general partners sat on the board. The gains should have been split in half in that case. The same was true for losses: the wrong incentive systems can undermine a firm's success.

Forest Baskett, a general partner at NEA, spoke about our corporate culture during an interview in 2018 with the Computer History Museum's Len Shustek:

"NEA is a partnership culture. That sounds a little odd. Venture capital firms are partnerships in a technical sense. NEA has a partnership culture in more of a spiritual sense, so that everyone has the opportunity to have a voice, and everyone is expected to participate and contribute, and everyone is listened to.

"It is very collegial in that respect, and it is really nice to be a part of and to contribute, know that your ideas are being heard, are being listened to, and to feel like you occasionally made a difference in terms of whether the firm did something or not."

NEA was transparent. When we started NEA, most venture capital firms only communicated with their investors via a Christmas card, whereas NEA sent out complete annual reports. When we started, every quarter, our investors received a report that showed how our companies did versus their budget. NEA focused on the entrepreneur's success in good times and bad because we built loyal relationships with entrepreneurs. As a result, we were proud to say that 70 percent of our deal flow came from people we had worked with before, including repeat entrepreneurs. I have included letters from entrepreneurs attesting to the contributions of NEA partners at the end of this book.

NEA's livelihood depended on whether we built companies with firm foundations and not on investment fads or stock promotions. As of 2012, more than ninety of NEA's companies had achieved billion-dollar or multibillion-dollar market caps. We were very conscious of avoiding conflicts of interest with our entrepreneurs. As Forest Baskett said also in his interview with Shustek, "We try not to invest in companies that are clear competitors to our existing investments. But this is a guideline. What a company starts out doing is not always where it ends up. So companies do become competitors that are in our portfolio. When that happens, we try to be sure that when we have discussions about those companies, that the person that's on the board of Company A is not part of the discussions about Company B, and vice versa."

NEA's culture had rules. When a CEO left a portfolio company or a partner left NEA, we tried to help them find new positions. Six of our departed partners became successful CEOs. Barbara Dreyer is a great example. In 1984, Barbara first came to me looking for a job, and while she lacked fancy credentials, she was street smart, driven to do something of substance, and a hard worker. I could tell she had the potential to be a great leader. Perhaps more importantly, she put her mission and her comrades-in-arms above self-interest. Being an old soldier, I identified with an unselfish leader who could persuade her team to follow her and achieve the impossible. Getting people to do the impossible is the definition of leadership.

In addition to these virtues, she had a toughness of soul which enabled her to survive. It would be naïve to think of life as a one-way elevator to the top or that it had some magic button that led to success. We knew life was not that way. It was our ability to face adversity that determined our success in this mad world. Barbara was a true warrior, which is the highest compliment I can give to anyone. Over her life, she overcame many personal trials and has always returned from defeat with style, grace, kindness, great courage, and the respect of her peers. She was my example of a leader. If we could learn to approach each obstacle as an opportunity to learn, as Barbara did, then perhaps we will be able to equal her accomplishments as a partner, parent, and entrepreneur.

Barbara started at NEA as CFO. She, along with Nancy Dorman, another NEA leader, helped to build our back-office excellence. After some time, she decided she wanted to be an investing partner. In that role, Barbara made a number of disastrous investments in support of a general partner who was in favor of investing in financial service companies. Though we had to let her go, I followed her career and helped her find a job as CFO of one of our defense companies, Communications Systems Technology, Inc. There, she was vital in the company's turnaround. Later, the CEO wanted to take the proceeds from the sale of the defense division and invest it in a commercial conferencing system competitive with WebEx. Barbara disagreed, resigned, and started her own lifestyle company making commercial videos. As it turns out, the CEO's idea was a total failure. I became the first customer of Barbara's video company, but she had even greater goals.

In the mid-1990s, Barbara founded Connections Academy, an online education company for young children. Backed by the founders of Sylvan Learning, she replicated much of what she saw in NEA's culture and cultivated a group of dedicated employees who would follow her to hell and back. She built this very profitable company with $500 million in revenue, then sold it for a larger sum. In recognition of this extraordinary result, the board and the company's financial backers belatedly increased the option pool. They wanted to give Barbara 70 percent of the pool and the employees 30 percent. She refused and gave 70 percent to her employees. Right after the sale, we developed and began giving ethics lectures to business schools together. Unfortunately, eighteen months later, she died of cancer. I tell her story to entrepreneurs or anyone who will listen.

One element of NEA's culture came via a suggestion of Jody Bond, who was NEA partner Neil Bond's wife. She said, "Your business is very stressful for the partners, but it is also stressful for their spouses." To build a sense of shared purpose among partners and their spouses, she suggested, it would be good to spend three days a year in a nice spot where the couples could all get to know each other personally. "Keep business to a minimum," she said. "We are spread out over the country and should get to know each other. The spouses could learn what the others are feeling and learn a different unrelated third party perspective on how NEA is performing." We did it and I think in the early years this helped enormously to build comradery and joint purpose in the firm. As the number of general partners increased, the practice was terminated, which I still think was a mistake.

The NEA founders brought a culture of sharing our best deals. Frank Bonsal directed or passed along to younger partners somewhere between twenty to thirty of deals he sourced, including Advertising. com, Amplica, Soft Switch, and Progress Software. He received no credit on his performance evaluation for this selfless action.

I originated twenty companies and directed them to younger partners, including Tripod, Pharmion, Geltex, Myogen, Xcel Pharmaceuticals, Comp Health, and Amerigroup. These companies helped turn our younger partners into general partners.

Dick functioned as the partnership's turnaround artist. If a partner gave up working on a company or left NEA, abandoning their "garbage" investments, Dick took them over and tried to rescue them. Therefore, if the company failed, Dick took on other peoples' losses on his investment record. Remarkably, when Dick took over Visual Edge in the early 1980s, he managed to save the company after many years of crisis. That is why, within the partnership, Dick became known as *nil desperandum* or "never say die."

Sometime in or around 1987, Dick assumed responsibility within NEA for a portfolio company called Forethought, founded in 1983 by Rob Campbell and Taylor Pohlman. A young associate had made the investment, then left NEA. Dick naturally took over nurturing it.

Both Rob and Taylor came from Apple. Although Taylor had a solid management background, Rob had been, before Apple, a car salesman from Denver. Forethought's first product was a mini-grade database designed for a large tech company, but when that company changed its mind, the rationale for starting Forethought disappeared. When Taylor decided he could no longer stand the risk of being part of the company and resigned, Rob hired Bob Gaskin, who had studied computer science, linguistics, and English at Berkeley, to help him develop a proprietary electronic presentation product for Apple's Macintosh. But he needed NEA to provide the capital.

Since NEA had voted to turn down the next round for Forethought, Dick funded the company himself, saying, "If the investment is a loss, then I'll absorb it, but if it's a winner, the partnership has the right to buy me out at cost." The company needed $60,000-$70,000 per month for the next ten months. That was real money for Dick— the only topic at the monthly board meetings was how to survive until the next month. Bob Gaskin would call potential customers to find out what features they wanted, and within a few days, the presentation product would have the new feature. Rob thought that when the FileMaker product was introduced, it would generate around $5 million in revenue.

He was significantly off the mark. In 1987, Microsoft bought Forethought and FileMaker, now called PowerPoint, for $14 million. Instead of losing its investment, NEA made three times on it. Dick again offered to sell his stock back to NEA at cost, but I refused his offer (with the permission of the investment committee) because he deserved to keep the profits on the bold and generous investment he had made. With great risk, he saved PowerPoint's and NEA's bacon. Extraordinary efforts should be rewarded. Dick said that venture investing is "broken-field running." It was true, and Forethought was an example of this.

NEA had a history of mentoring young partners. This sounds self-evident, but it's not. Many venture firms have trouble letting new talent rise.We gave each associate a book that outlined exactly what was expected over a five-to-ten-year period to become a principal, then a partner, then a general partner, then a management company owner. Every year, we reviewed our younger partners' progress over the year.

As Forest Baskett explained in that interview with Len Shustek for the Computer History Museum: "We do keep long-term track investment records. There's a saying in the industry, 'It's a very slow way to get rich.' Because the typical deal takes eight years or longer to achieve liquidity. It's a long time before you get to the point where people can look at your record and say, 'You're a good investor,' or 'You're not a good investor.' But that is one of the things that we try to be able to do. Getting to be a general partner is a very slow process because being a general partner is like having tenure at a university, it's something that you don't go into lightly. Generally, the people who get there do have very good track records."

Many NEA general partners started as associates and worked their way up the ladder. In the early 1980s, I drafted "The NEA Career Path," a memo for young employees joining the firm without significant work experience. I divided the career path into six levels: 1) research associate 2) senior research associate 3) investing principal 4) partner 5) general partner 6) management committee.

The management committee that runs the firm was a group of four or five senior partners with twenty years or more years of tenure at NEA who had excellent investment records. The research associate (who generally had two to three years of experience) was tasked with learning the NEA way and assisting GPs and the partners. There were eight goals that the associate had to accomplish. The senior research associate (who had an additional two to three years) had three goals to achieve. The investing principal (with another roughly two years of experience) had four goals, one of which was to build an investment track record. A partner had to help raise money and improve his investment track record. A general partner had seven goals, including investor relations and an active role in fundraising. To become a general partner, one had to be a key driver of the firm's investment results. There were twenty-one goals that the GP had to accomplish, including reaching a dollar goal for dollars distributed. There were seven goals management committee members had to accomplish, including building a national reputation. The career path memo was re-written or updated every four to six years. I have only shared a few details because the memo is considered proprietary information by the firm.

Depending on at what stage you started, and of course, whether you were successful, it could take five to ten years to become a general partner at NEA. The path to GP was not the same length for the med team as the tech team. Promising technology team members were often promoted faster than med team members because their companies reached liquidity much faster. Tech partners could generate great records in five years. It would be unheard of for a Med partner to make GP in five years. For most Med partners, it took close to ten years to become a GP.

Because of the requirements to invest in each new partnership, it took me ten years to reach cash flow breakeven. For some, it took longer, which was one reason we made loans from the partnership to junior partners, so they could invest in each partnership. Needless to say, the partners who joined NEA with successful entrepreneurial or investing careers already under their belts tended to have totally different career paths. Many of them had successful careers as entrepreneurial CEOs, were qualified, and became GPs right away.

NEA had several core values we repeated all the time. We aimed to achieve superior investment returns for our limited partners. We partnered with entrepreneurs to build transformational companies with exceptional growth potential. We grew an enduring institution with shared values, goals, and rewards. We ensured junior partners and associates knew the firm's strategy, could articulate it as well as any GP, and continually focused on long-term goals.

This meant significant responsibility for our junior partners, who were regularly expected to present at annual meetings and board meetings and had to be able to speak about the firm's strategy, fund performance data, personnel, and other matters. Conversely, many other VC firms hamstrung their junior partners and associates by discouraging them from having significant contact with limited partners. They feared that a junior partner might not represent the firm well or might spin out and take LPs with him or her. Usually, we met about twenty times a year for all firm or team dinners. The general partners introduced new people at these dinners and recognized the accomplishments of junior partners in their toasts. The newest partners were expected to give witty toasts that also demonstrated their in-depth knowledge of NEA.

We even made spouses of new partners give impromptu speeches. Frank started this practice of "singing for your supper," modeled after early Baltimore debutante parties, where the debutante's dance partner sang her praises in a humorous toast.

NEA fostered a team system, where teams voted on all major decisions. It was the opposite of a star system, where a few people or even a single person made decisions and kept their rationale close to the vest. The challenge in a team system was to get a group of talented people with big egos to work together.

Everyone at NEA was held accountable for overall fund performance. Associates and partners filled out annual reviews in which each partner or associate evaluated his or her own progress towards goals. The two GPs who worked most closely with each associate or partner evaluated them and compared the evaluations to the self-evaluations. We also evaluated partners on long-term performance (their previous five to ten years). Mistakes were tolerated. We knew that certain sectors would be hot or cold. We did not confuse wisdom with a bull market, and we did make big asset allocation changes with every fund to ensure we were investing in the most rapidly growing industries of the future, not the past.

The med team lagged the tech team's performance for years, but the partnership never gave up on investing in medical companies. Eventually, this perseverance paid off in a big way.

NEA also worked hard to foster strong relationships with other VC firms. Each partner had their own list of preferred co-investors. Forrest Baskett describes this in the Computer History Museum interview:

"We like to co-invest. I think our ideal investment would be a co-investment with another well-established, experienced venture firm. We like to co-invest on a fifty-fifty basis. The idea is that there's no lead dog, and both investors are equally committed and equally expected to do the work that's needed to help the company succeed. We do, many times, become the only investor. That happens when the company either doesn't need much money initially or is already highly valued for whatever reason, and the only way to get a decent ownership percentage is to be the only investor. The ownership percentage is something that counts a lot for us. Our most critical resource is the time of the partners, the time that we spend working with companies and trying to make them successful. For that time to be valuable, we need to think that there's going to be a decent return for our investors. To have a decent return, the company has to become big and successful; and secondly, you have to have a notable ownership stake. These are the two parameters that push us either to partner with someone else or to go it alone."

At NEA, some behaviors were not tolerated: dishonesty, lying with statistics, manipulating the scientific data, or taking credit for what others did. Exaggerating investment results showed a partner did not share the firm's core values. When we found intolerable behavior, which occurred in even the most ethical of firms, we did not accept it and terminated the employee.

NEA was a flat, non-hierarchical organization—albeit one with a managing partner. When Dick, Frank, and I began eyeing retirement, the question of how to reward us and other long-term partners for what we had built and our ongoing contributions became a major issue. It was the younger partners who proposed creating the management company as a solution. It gave us an ongoing interest in investment returns and provided some of the long-term incentives of a corporation for future leaders.

NEA sought more efficient governance: a real board of directors with real powers. The Bigler budget is a perfect example. When the small company stocks collapsed in the early '80s, Hal Bigler, one of our board members, asked us to reduce our expenses. We did, thinking, "What is good for the goose is good for the gander." When we invested, we went on the boards of our companies to give them governance and provide strategic advice. Our board provided 70–80 percent of our capital when we began a new partnership, which immensely contributed to the firm's success. This degree of oversight was almost unique in the industry and still is today.

Everyone needs some form of governance. Children need parents, enlisted soldiers need officers, and companies need directors. The Constitution of the United States is essentially a blueprint for a governance vehicle, elaborating a system of checks and balances. Since absolute power corrupts absolutely, all human institutions should demand continuous accountability. Yet, most venture partnerships do not have governance. Governance bodies should understand the details related to compensation, expenses, and personnel issues. This group is also responsible for challenging management's strategic plans in response to an ever-changing reality.

We initially called NEA's board the "investment committee,"

but eventually the name was changed to the "board of advisors." I simply refer to it as "the board." At first, the investment committee approved our investments. That lasted about eight months because it was unwieldy. The board approved our salaries and the budget for the firm. Our annual meetings lasted two days, though we met with the board four other times throughout the year.

The special contributions from specific board members, such as John Riddell, helped to guide NEA. In the beginning, while raising money for NEA, we found ourselves desperate. Our only investors included the Deere Family, T. Rowe Price, and the Roberts Family. My partner Frank Bonsal knew Ezra Zilka, a director with influence at the Insurance Company of North America (INA), and while Ezra declined the investment personally, he did introduce us to John Riddell, one of INA's senior investment officers.

It was a cool winter day when we met in his downtown Philadelphia office, a brown mahogany room full of reproduction colonial furniture. He invited us to the Union League club for lunch, where I remember adding to the snapper soup a good dose of manzanilla sherry.

We began our conversation about the dream of NEA. If ever there was a man who would never invest in NEA, it was Riddell. Dressed in a dark grey suit, he was the epitome of the "Prudent Man Rule," a law that if a fiduciary made a risky investment and lost money, he could be prosecuted. It has since been overturned.

We headed back to Riddell's office, where the sunlight beamed through the blinds. John's desk sat in front of the windows, and we had to squint to look at him. He said, "I like you guys. I like what you want to do. This is a very unusual investment for INA, but if you check out, INA will invest $3.5 million." Charles (Chief) Burton, John's associate, did the due diligence. Burton would go on to found Philadelphia Ventures, and would be a great ally to NEA until his premature death. (You never know when you start a new relationship how it will turn out long-term. Make an effort to ensure all relationships work out well.)

I was floored that we had another big, prestigious investor. After almost a year of fearing we wouldn't be able to raise our first fund, I now knew for sure that we could do it. A year of fears and doubts flew right out of John's bright window. John Riddell became the chairman of NEA's investment committee.

In early 1978, we visited the merchant bank Kleinwort Benson in England, hosted by two partners, Harry Conroy and Bobby Nicole, both of whom were urbane English gentlemen. He invited us to a luncheon in the elegant drawing room adjacent to Kleinwort Benson's dining room. It was equal to a grand country house, filled with art, silver, and eighteenth-century furniture. Drinks were served in the early afternoon, and while most of the Kleinwort partners had gin and tonics, Frank and I favored the dry manzanilla sherry. The servers and chefs were young and attractive who had studied at the Cordon Bleu School in Paris.

I will never forget that lunch. To start, we had a flavorful fish soup with a great French white burgundy, Puligny Montrachet. The fish course was sole menuière, followed by English roast beef, cooked and carved to perfection by a stunning French chef. It was accompanied by claret, a 1961 Château Lynch-Bages. (I was taking notes!) The questions flew fast and furious because our hosts knew their audience.

In vino veritas, they say.

We answered questions about everything, our childhoods, our wives, what activities we liked, crooks we had known, how well we knew British history. They asked about our best investments and our outlook for venture capital. They felt that many had abandoned it, Then they asked us if we really thought there was a place for women in business. (We did.) We were baited to make fools of ourselves.

The cheese and fruit followed with a great port, a 1963 Quinta do Noval. Next was a Grand Marnier soufflé with an acceptable sauterne, a 1967 Château Suiderant. Feeling as comfortable as we did in our own homes, we adjourned from lunch to the drawing room for brandy and cigars.

Later, Merck approached to see if we would start a separate life science fund with Merck as the only investor. It was clear the corporation might want to invest for strategic scientific purposes rather than for purely economic gain. Who would make an investment on a healthcare company, NEA, or the dedicated life science fund? Bobby Nicole said no. The potential conflicts we could envision multiplied to the point that we knew we had to decline. Bobby defined a cornerstone principle of our partnership: avoid conflicts of interest.

In 1987, Tom Judge, who managed AT&T's pension fund became an NEA investment committee member. He joined a general partner dinner and gave us a lesson in tough love.

For years, NEA had followed a strategy of setting up affiliated funds around the country. Our hypothesis was that to work closely with a company, we (or an NEA-aligned surrogate) needed to live close to it. As such, we saw affiliated funds as a way of not missing opportunities in more remote locations where we didn't have a presence because our offices were in California and Baltimore. We also established affiliated funds based not on region, but on promising specialized industries, like defense electronics, to increase our deal flow.

To our horror, Tom began an NEA board meeting by saying that NEA had too many partners, too many investments in too many industries, too many partnerships, too many limited partners, and too many distractions. It was a difficult, heated discussion because NEA had invested six years of effort in establishing that network. Eventually, though, we admitted Tom was right. The affiliated funds partners received significantly more in distributions from their interest in NEA than NEA received from its interest in their funds. The program was not a financial success and was a major distraction when we helped the affiliates raise money.

We took the advice and set about winding down the affiliate program, which took a decade to accomplish, and we honed our focus investing in the two sectors where we had achieved the best results: healthcare and technology. We abandoned specialty retailing and financial services, to name just a few areas. Two of the affiliated funds continued as independent entities, and we closed our books on the last affiliated partnership in 2005. Tom, by raising the issue was invaluable. Refining our mission helped generate the success of NEA Fund V, along with the future fund partnerships.

Later in the partnership's life, Tom would make another great contribution. We were trying to figure out the proper size for NEA 10. I was concerned we were squandering opportunities by not heavily investing in the later rounds of our best companies. Tom said that if we did this, we would expand from early-stage investing into what he called "venture growth equity" and we would need much larger fund sizes. We jointly decided that NEA 10 should be a two-billion-dollar fund. Tom and other investors related to AT&T (Legent and the Baby Bells), invested hundreds of millions of dollars into our new fund.

Thanks to an introduction by T. Rowe Price, 3M was an investor in NEA funds I through VIII. Over the years, we got to know several members of the 3M venture team, and their philosophy was simple: make small investments in a variety of venture partnerships. They were motivated in large part by the desire for knowledge and access, as opposed to acquisition targets.

It's only a slight exaggeration to say that 3M became a key customer of virtually all NEA companies of that era. Forty NEA companies entered into joint ventures with 3M for marketing or R&D. Of all the corporate investors that became NEA limited partners, I think 3M got the most out of its relationship with the fund partnerships, profiting from NEA returns like other LPs, but also making the most of the new technology and great management teams they were exposed to. 3M would have a trade show at their corporate headquarters where many of the Venture companies had display booths. Hundreds of employees visited the show. Of course, NEA also benefitted immeasurably from having this strong, consistent, and well-known investor. Its firepower and active interest made NEA an attractive investor to startup founders.

The mastermind behind 3M's strategy was George Hegg. He managed 3M's memory division and strategic planning services. He also came to assume a sort of father confessor role at NEA. He introduced us to 3M's CEO and joined the boards of several of NEA's portfolio companies. Throughout the good and bad times, George was our enthusiastic coach, and it was his enthusiasm that helped us get through the dark days of the mid-1980s, when investment returns declined after the bull market of a few years earlier. He said, "What you are doing is important. The world will eventually appreciate what you have done." The entire investment committee gave us support during this time, but George was especially vocal. He always kept us grounded in times of excess and built us up when times were bad.

At some point, George learned that I had spent four years in Minnesota and enjoyed northern lake fishing. I have vivid memories of taking a group of twenty Shattuck (my military high school) students ice fishing for smelt in Duluth. Fifteen of us caught enough fish to feed the whole school (400 people) on that outing. I dreamed of going Muskie and pike fishing on the Canadian lakes. Since 3M had an old, wooden yacht to entertain business friends, George decided to act on this fantasy and invited me, Dick, and our wives to join him on a Canadian fishing trip.

For a few days, we fished and ate fresh fish and fries on tiny islands while discussing venture capital. For most of the trip, the sky was incredibly blue, and white clouds floated by like God's confections. The nights were cold. The days were sultry. Together, we flew north on a small plane with pontoons and landed on a seldom-fished lake, where golden sunsets bleed into the water.

As dusk faded each night, the darkness would swallow our moored boat. I'll never forget George standing on the boat's deck with his mass of white hair silhouetted against the sunset. A few years later, he died of cancer, and I lost a great friend. Soon after his death, 3M terminated its venture program, and NEA lost one of its best corporate friends. Somehow, I feel that George is forever shouting at me, "Dare disturb the universe."

Perhaps the biggest contribution to NEA came from Bondurant "Bon" French of Adams Street. It was 2001 when the internet bubble burst, and we soon realized that we had over-distributed NEA Fund VIII, due to the pushy greed of one partner who made statistically impressive but inaccurate analyses of NEA's distribution policy. The partnership elected to start distributions of Fund VIII to the general partners before the capital was recovered. Dick and I strenuously objected, but the partnership elected to move forward with the expectations of a significant return. NEA forecasted Fund IX to return eight times the original invested capital, but we "conservatively" based our distributions on a more cautious return of four times invested capital.

You know how this story ended. In the end, the fund returned only 2.7 times capital. It was a good result, and one with a high internal rate of return (IRR), but by distributing early and too much, the general partners who had received a share now owed the limited partners millions of dollars. To solve the problem, we pledged some of NEA Fund X's carry, plus a portion of the firm's fees, to satisfy our limited partners that our debt would be repaid. Unfortunately, this left us with insufficient fees to cover the partnership's expenses.

Keep in mind that NEA's fees were much lower than those of other firms in the industry, and our LPs knew it. So although we had over-distributed, and at a time LP governance groups in our industry were forcing GPs to reduce the size of their funds and lower their fees, Bon French led the board to raise our fees to help cover our clawback liability. He was supported in this by the rest of the board. His foresight, the board's flexibility, and our LPs' forbearance all kept us from having to reduce our staff at exactly the wrong moment in internet investing history. We learned a valuable lesson. Never distribute until fees are recovered.

Other board members like Ray Held and Jonathan Roth from Abbott Capital and Phil Paul of Hillman Ventures made similarly important contributions to NEA. NEA is a book written by many authors.

A final characteristic of NEA's culture is management succession. If you want to be a 100-year partnership, you must have management succession. Current NEA generations are always training the next generation. Dick was the first generation of managing partner. He passed it to Peter, who was recruited by Art Marks, but Dick and I mentored him. The third generation is Scott Sandell, who Dick recruited and mentored. Scott has identified Mohamad Makhzoumi (Mo) and Tony Florence as the fourth generation of managing partners. I am proud to say I recruited and mentored Mo.

VI.

HEALTHSOUTH

*"Success consists of going from failure to failure
without loss of enthusiasm."*

—Winston Churchill

OF THE SIXTY COMPANIES I helped launch, HealthSouth is
one with a special place in my heart, despite how it ended. It is
simultaneously one of the best and worst examples of what venture
capital and an entrepreneur can do together. The company positively
affected millions of lives. The sheer number of patients treated at
HealthSouth facilities is in the millions. Being a part of that was one
of the most satisfying and exhilarating experiences of my life. But the
founding CEO, Richard Scrushy, fraudulently overstated earnings.
That ruined lives and careers and almost forced the company into
bankruptcy. I still wish I could return to the years when we were first
creating HealthSouth.

In 1983, when the country was pulling out of a recession, the
American healthcare system was in crisis. Congress had changed
the Medicare and Social Security programs to slow the growth
of national healthcare spending. The government controlled
reimbursement for medical procedures, irrespective of what
that cost the provider. For an industry accustomed to cost-based
reimbursement no matter how inefficient the delivery of care, it was
a rude shock. One way for hospitals to reduce costs was to reduce

the time patients spent on expensive hospital stays. As you might imagine, hospital visits became shorter. As one example, the average time spent in psychiatric hospitals dropped from thirty days to two, which practically eliminated that business.

Richard began his career as a physical therapist before becoming a senior officer of Lifemark Hospitals, a multibillion-dollar company based in Houston. At Lifemark, he realized rehabilitation care could be moved out of hospitals and into outpatient facilities, significantly reducing costs. Although Richard proposed starting an outpatient rehab chain to his superiors at Lifemark, they did not pursue it. Shortly after, in the fall of 1983, the company merged with American Medical International.

Richard decided to pursue the rehab chain himself, and along with four other veteran Lifemark executives, he created a business plan and sought out venture capital. It was unusual in the venture industry to find a complete startup team whose members had already had many years of experience building a large and successful business together. The five founders called their company Amcare, and each invested $50,000 to capitalize the company. This meant they had skin in the game, which venture investors always consider to be a good sign.

With one million dollars in seed capital from Citicorp in New York, Amcare was launched. The founders located it in Birmingham, Alabama, a well-known healthcare center that was also close to Richard's hometown of Selma, Alabama.

When Amcare opened its first comprehensive rehab facility in Little Rock, Arkansas, in the spring of 1984, the facility had serious trouble making money. It finished its first year with an $800,000 loss. The company opened a second facility in December of 1984 and obtained a second round of financing mainly from the venture firms New Enterprise Associates, Smith Barney, and William Blair. The founders were out of money and needed that second round, but the model seemed like it could be profitable in three years, with almost unlimited growth potential.

Richard drew a cartoon at a staff meeting early on that came to represent the company's culture. The picture showed several stick figures pulling a wagon together. Some stood watching, some pulled from the front, some pushed from behind, others pushed from the sides, and some were riding in the wagon, talking to each other. The message was simple: moving the wagon forward requires teamwork. Everybody had a responsibility to push it forward. That cartoon was given a prominent spot in every HealthSouth rehab facility.

Everyone knew that Richard was the leader of the team, the one pulling the wagon from the front. When he spoke, it was like listening to a machine gun. Richard talked as fast as he lived his life, at a sprint. He knew every financial and clinical detail of his company's operations and had the passion of an evangelical preacher. He renamed the company HealthSouth. It became his life. He picked the company's colors, designed the facilities, and developed standard rehab practices. He traveled constantly, always immaculately dressed in dark suits and Hermes ties. The senior managers tried to emulate Richard, so Hermes ties and dark suits became the company's uniform. Most of HealthSouth's executives were homegrown, and Richard made sure they looked professional as they represented the company. By September of 1986, the company had opened ten facilities and raised $15 million in an initial public offering managed by Robertson Stephens, a San Francisco-based underwriter.

HealthSouth was booming, and Richard Scrushy along with it. A cult of hero worship was developing around him at this time. He redesigned and renovated a mansion in Birmingham. He created and played in a country-western band called Dallas County Line. He surrounded himself with fast boats, fast cars, famous athletes, beautiful actresses, and other celebrities.

To be sure, being around a brilliant entrepreneur with a compelling vision was exhilarating. Richard was a captivating person. He lived his life in turbulent, brilliant Technicolor, totally consumed by his vision. When he looked you in the eye, you understood his vision so deeply that it became yours. He spread his vision to others, and the company soon managed 10 percent of the freestanding outpatient rehab centers in the country. HealthSouth ended 1986 with $20 million in revenue. Richard added George Strong to the board because he had helped to fund and start five New York Stock Exchange-listed healthcare service companies.

Board meetings were held frequently, and twice a year, the HealthSouth board met with facility managers to strategize for three full days. Richard hosted an awards banquet to recognize employees with outstanding performances. These ceremonies had the excitement of modern-day revival meetings: flashing laser lights, multimedia performances, large flower arrangements, and over-the-top colorful decorations. Richard's band often played. At the end of his musical performances, workers rushed to the stage to touch the man himself.

It seemed that everything Richard did was magic. He was awarded a gold record for the Dallas County Line song, "Honk If You Want to Honky Tonk." On one of his first fishing trips, a marlin tournament, he won a million dollars for catching the largest marlin. But the magic was always no accident. Richard supervised preparation for that fishing contest himself, organizing his crew, paying close attention to the details. He bought a boat specially built to be the fastest in the field. He drew the flight plan for a spotter plane he paid to fly ahead of the fishing boat looking for marlin. He brought this win-at-all-costs attitude to everything he did. Foolishly, the board drank Richard's Kool-Aid, but my wife Amy did not.

While Richard was not a refined man, he longed to be refined. He started buying art and sculpture and hosted a variety of cultural events. For the most part, his eye for beauty was unproven, but standing on the loggia of his house overlooking Birmingham, ablaze like Los Angeles at night, was spellbinding.

HealthSouth started buying up rehab hospitals aggressively. Business doubled, and by 1989, HealthSouth had $300 million in sales and was listed on the New York Stock Exchange. Richard began every meeting with a speech about honesty in billing and in dealing with regulatory agencies. Our patients' medical experience had to be pristine, he said, and government billing conservative and accurate. There would be zero tolerance for any employee caught cheating or violating the company's code of ethics. After all, HealthSouth was to be the future of healthcare, and, Richard said, he was determined to set the highest moral standard within the industry.

The company also opened sports medicine orthopedic clinics, offering rehab programs for workers injured on the job. With proper rehab therapy initiated within days after an accident, more injured workers could return to the workplace quickly, saving their employers vast sums in disability payments. Pointing to these savings, Richard started marketing to insurance companies, so they would select HealthSouth as a preferred provider.

HealthSouth eventually acquired a fleet of aircraft so executives could make daily visits to facilities in fifty states. But the rapid growth was straining the organization. There were crisis meetings regularly for acquisitions or financings. While overcoming the challenges together, the board of directors created close bonds and trust; however, the challenges continued.

The company overcame each crisis, beat its competition, and produced regular and predictable earnings growth. It attained one of the best growth records in the country and became a Wall Street darling.

HealthSouth's principal competitor in the rehab business was Rocky Ortenzio's Continental Medical Systems. Both companies needed to raise debt or equity to fund the land-grab acquisition and development strategies that made each company the largest or second-largest provider in every geographic area. Continental decided to do a convertible debt financing. Its stock declined, and it found it could not raise an additional equity financing or borrow more debt.

HealthSouth faced much the same challenge. The investment bankers, the CFO, and several directors wanted to raise convertible debt because it entailed less dilution. Sage Givens, who led Smith Barney's investment in HealthSouth, and I thought convertible debt would remove the company's financial flexibility, so we argued for an equity raise. Sage and I ended up winning the vote by a majority of one, allowing the company to later raise more equity and debt.

As HealthSouth expanded rapidly, it left cash-starved Continental behind. Our stock declined as well, eliminating the equity option, but we could raise more debt. From that point on, HealthSouth did not have effective national competition in the rehab market.

Since most board members had been patients at one of the company's facilities at one time or another, we knew employees at all levels of it. The company had a hierarchy—it certainly wasn't flat—but it was a warm company culture where people on all levels knew and respected each other. As the largest rehab provider in America, HealthSouth became not just a regional but a national brand name, well-respected and trustworthy. I've sat on the boards of sixty companies and I have never experienced the intense camaraderie I felt with the other HealthSouth directors and employees in the company's glory years.

Richard involved HealthSouth in all sorts of charities. In 1995, he organized the "Go For It! Roadshow," highlighting famous sports medicine doctors, cutting-edge new medical procedures, and the inspiring life stories of famous athletes. Bo Jackson, Roger Clemens, Lex Luger, Michael Jordan, and Kristi Yamaguchi toured the country visiting underprivileged, inner-city kids. The athletes stressed the value of fitness and honesty and spoke to the students about avoiding drugs and alcohol.

Richard did do some very peculiar things. At HealthSouth board dinners, before board meetings, the Scrushy family's table was on a raised dais, as if it were a medieval banquet. The board and HealthSouth employees would sit below the family, "below the salt," as it were. I also found it alarming that my wife Amy did not find Richard trustworthy. Richard certainly had an irrational hatred of his competitors, calling them "crooks" and suggesting that we paint their faces on the company toilet bowls. Everything about Washington, D.C. made Richard paranoid, because the government could destroy a sector of the healthcare market in an instant.

Highlighting that point, in 1995, the company fell under the shadow of the proposed Clinton healthcare reform package, which would have tightened government controls over the healthcare system. HealthSouth's stock dove from $27 per share to $12. Everyone at the company was depressed, although it posted excellent results even as the stock price declined. The healthcare legislation died after vociferous opposition from Republicans and the insurance industry. Democrats did not unite behind the plan. Amid reform upheaval, Richard completed the massive acquisition of National Medical Enterprise's rehab division.

Although Richard believed that HealthSouth's future could lie in new business areas, such as diagnostic imaging and outpatient surgery, he did not want to frighten Wall Street by appearing to be a medical conglomerate. He envisioned turning the company into the outpatient equivalent of a medical-surgical hospital, dramatically lowering costs and improving patients' results. To do this, Richard, HealthSouth, and its venture capital investors started a series of specialized healthcare companies. If the companies succeeded and proved strategically compatible with HealthSouth's core business, HealthSouth would be in an excellent position to buy them. The VCs would, in effect, look after these companies, and if HealthSouth did acquire one, they would recuse themselves from all board of directors' votes. Acquisitions had to be approved by the company's outside counsel. In this way, in four years, the company strategically diversified its business.

During the board's strategy discussions, we debated the merits of new products, marketing strategy, brand creation, and every potential acquisition. Usually, management proposed a strategic direction or initiative, then the board constructively altered it. When we did decide to acquire a business, there was little debate except over price and financing strategy because we had already discussed the strategic value at prior planning meetings. Essentially, the companies we acquired were in the same business, broadening HealthSouth's national footprint.

In 1995, after acquiring two venture-backed companies, Diagnostic Health and Surgical Health, HealthSouth had the other businesses it needed to complete its national outpatient strategy. Surgical Care Affiliates (SCA), the leading provider of outpatient surgery, was the underbidder for Surgical Health. It had been built from scratch by Joel Gordon, the legendary Nashville entrepreneur. Richard convinced Joel of the validity of his vision for a full-service national outpatient company, and Joel sold SCA to HealthSouth and joined the board, holding on to all his stock.

HealthSouth now had acquired and united the two most important outpatient surgery pioneers. Richard continued his consolidation strategy, buying rehab outpatient centers from Caremark International and Advantage Healthcare. By February of 1996, the company had $2.5 billion in revenues, 32,000 employees, and $221 million in net income. It soon would have facilities in every state.

In a departure from common practice, HealthSouth requested that its audit firm, Ernst & Young, conduct the normal financial audit but also conduct a physical audit of all the HealthSouth facilities they visited each year. The audit included lengthy checklists that covered facility cleanliness, operating procedures, and employee attitudes. The company also started a university to train outpatient facility managers. All the university programs focused on training hospital administrators. Richard used a McDonald's-esque template for standardizing the education necessary to work in HealthSouth's outpatient facilities.

HealthSouth moved into a new $50 million headquarters in 1996, a Taj Mahal of a building that adjoined Richard's home. It was 130,000 square feet with a conference center, a university center, and adjacent buildings on seventy-four acres. It was a symbol of the company HealthSouth was becoming. When I walked on the company's campus, I stopped by a glass room that modeled the room where the company was founded, complete with mannequins of the founders.

The capstone upon which HealthSouth was built was Richard Scrushy's personality. Everything was either named for him or another founder. There were stainless-steel statues to reflect the company's priorities, rehabilitation therapy, surgery, diagnostic imaging, and pulling the wagon. There was also a monument to a poor boy from Selma who did something with his life. He projected the carefully crafted image that seemed to demonstrate what determination and willpower could do for those born into poverty. His country music band even had a song about him called, "Now That I Am a Rich Man Living on the Hill."

Richard was demanding when it came to his compensation, and he threatened the board when he talked about what he thought was entitled to. He occasionally got angry at the compensation committee, pounding his fist on the table. He thought he was owed everything because he worked harder than anyone else and because he had built the best healthcare company in the United States. One moment, Richard was like a charismatic preacher, generous and earnest. The next moment, he was a tyrant. Still, for twenty years, he did deliver on his promises, although sometimes those around him paid a price. To ensure HealthSouth was in line with comparable companies and complied with the rules of Institutional Shareholder Services, the compensation committee hired outside compensation consultants. Sometimes they would reject some of Richard's demands, but they would also compromise.

Richard's emotions grew out of control in the late 1990s, and he used seemingly any opportunity to take his anger out on others. He once physically threw a comedian off the stage for using crude language at one of the company's awards banquets. When he wanted to fire a senior manager, he would do it at a meeting, working himself into a tirade and, without fail, claiming the employee had committed some great moral failure. They were unfaithful to their spouses, they took inappropriate gifts, or they just wouldn't pull the wagon. The employee's humiliation in front of the full board, of course, made staff members feel horrible and board members uncomfortable. But the chastised employee was never really fired. They always resurfaced in other (less important) positions in the company.

As a master of intimidation, Richard used similar tactics with the board. If they denied him something he wanted, he yelled at them. If they gave in, he'd welcome them back to the family. For some reason, I was never placed on those difficult committees dealing with compensation and audits. I was able to remain his greatest supporter because I got the fun jobs, like helping to shape the firm's strategy. I didn't see Richard the way Sage Givens, George Strong, Jack Chamberlain (an experienced director), and Joel Gordon saw him, and they had tough jobs on the compensation, audit, and compliance committees.

At our annual awards banquet, Richard recognized the fifty best facility managers. He knew the sales of each facility, its inventory turn, its operating margins, its personnel problems. He was a financial genius who knew every number in the company, and he could run rings around any investment banker ever born. When we made an acquisition, he could model its impact on HealthSouth's earnings and debt structure extemporaneously.

Like a character plucked from a Greek tragedy, Richard was a man favored by the gods, with a talent admired by the gods, but his human flaws would bring him down, along with his family and all those around him. Increasingly, Richard believed that the government was persecuting him.

One of Richard's passions was the board of directors' dining room. He would plan the menus, paying attention to every detail to create the perfect meal. There was a strategy behind every one of his decisions. He told us we were the best board in the country and knew our company inside out. We believed him.

In a piece published in *Fortune*, Richard said, "Coke is what, 100 years old? It has $20 billion in sales and a $130 billion market cap. We've been around for only ten years. Our brand name is just beginning to get known, and we have $2.5 billion in sales and over $5 billion market cap. I think we'll get to where Coke is quicker than they did." Everyone tied to the company—employees, shareholders, and directors—lived in Richard Schrushy's dreamy spin. He created the yellow brick road that we traveled through the Land of Oz. Richard promised that in ten to fifteen years, HealthSouth would have $25 billion in annual revenue. "It is in your hands," he told his employees and board. "Y'all knock it out of the park."

Back in the real world, the Balanced Budget Act of 1997 passed. To balance this budget, Medicare and Medicaid reimbursements for inpatient and outpatient hospital services were greatly reduced. Reimbursement rates for providers were also reduced. The Act and these managed-care cutbacks put many healthcare services companies in financial jeopardy, but because HealthSouth's cost structure was lower than other providers, we still made money. The company bought Horizon CMS Specialty and Rehab and sold its long-term care business to Integrated Health Services (another NEA company). Even the dot-com bubble did not seem to affect HealthSouth. All the young internet geniuses were claiming "brick and mortar" businesses were dinosaurs and that in the future, all business would be conducted over the internet. They were right, but it took twenty years to happen.

In 2000, however, HealthSouth began to encounter problems. While the company met its forecast, it had to write off hundreds of millions of dollars in "extraordinary items," which are losses deemed unusual or infrequent. Examples included when the government changed its reimbursement on a service, when we discovered a problem with an acquisition, when the patient mix ratio changed, any of a hundred other things. We were on plan, it seemed, except for these many circumstances beyond our control.

The stock slipped, but that had happened before. HealthSouth responded by announcing a $1 billion capital-spending plan to upgrade its technology, a needed initiative that helped to shore up the stock. The company improved its website and launched a Web-based exercise clothing business. Physicians who practiced in HealthSouth facilities got web pages and patients were able to access their own records. via the internet. Patients received home therapy instructions and even purchased medical supplies remotely.

Perhaps HealthSouth's most ambitious project was the digital hospital. Its goal was to change the practice of medicine. The dream was that above patient hospital beds, there would be screens with detailed medical records and digital images of x-rays and MRI images, and patients and medical staff would be able to communicate via secure wireless technology. The dream was that technology would lower healthcare costs, greatly reduce human error, and improve patient care. A digital hospital like this could treat more patients and generate the higher margins necessary to justify its large capital cost.

There would be robotic systems to rehabilitate people recovering from strokes, spinal cord injuries, and other mobility-reducing diseases. Many of America's leading technology companies were interested in the concept, and they entered into a partnership with HealthSouth to design the facility. At this time, the company also started its own TV station, allowing patients to watch the "Go for It!" Roadshow while receiving therapy in HealthSouth facilities. I introduced Richard to NEA portfolio companies like Healtheon and WebMD so he could increase his internet savvy.

One of the problems of being a revolutionary is that it is necessary to go against conventional wisdom. Richard's next battle was against Continental Medical System, HealthSouth's major competitor in the rehab market. He won that battle. The second war was against Rick Scott, CEO of Columbia Healthcare. HealthSouth wanted to make the hospital system obsolete; and to Richard, Rick was the poster child for hospitals.

Over twenty years together, I had watched Richard fight a government that did not understand the industry it was attempting to manage. But it seemed to me that Richard took his animosity to the next level. To him, President Clinton was the personification of evil. He felt Clinton had eviscerated the US intelligence system and had consciously unleashed the FBI on American healthcare providers to find evidence of criminal activity. In hindsight, we should have known Richard had to hide his crimes from the FBI. He used his bluster to hide the fraud. But in the late 1990s, I thought his emotions were just pitched at a different intensity than other people's. According to Richard, Clinton was angry with healthcare providers for rejecting his reform proposal, so it was payback time. Richard thought FBI agents were being taken away from chasing crooks, murderers, and terrorists to make them into bounty hunters. It was a reasonable position, perhaps, until you learned later what we all now know about the magnitude of the Medicare fraud that HealthSouth had regularly and systematically perpetrated.

Still, as the government began to look for malfeasance, most of the board thought, *We are the pioneers. We are the good guys.* When the agency that governed healthcare reimbursement attacked us for overbilling and the stock collapsed, we remained calm, thinking, *We have seen this storm before. We will prove ourselves innocent and survive. We are the company that dared disturb the universe.*

During this healthcare perfect storm, with the technology bubble bursting and the ensuing collapse of the technology sector of the stock market, the most important life raft for me was believing I had played a small role in building one of America's most important companies. We board members flew on a HealthSouth jet to Birmingham, after which a company helicopter met us to take us to the company's sprawling campus, where we passed over what was to be America's first digital hospital. Like all HealthSouth structures, it was beautiful, built with gleaming glass and chrome, surrounded by gardens. It seemed like the future was here and that it was good.

But starting in 2001, the atmosphere on the board of HealthSouth started to change. The company experienced another raft of extraordinary write-offs. Hordes of outside experts were brought in for independent audits, and they explained to us how external events had conspired against us but that the outlook for the future was good. Richard railed against the unjust nature of the government, hitting the table again and again. Our stock, which had been as high as $39 per share in the late 1990s, collapsed. It recovered to $17 a share before drifting down to the single digits. But the company was approaching $6 billion in revenue and had $1 billion in EBITDA (earnings before interest, taxes, depreciation, and amortization). It was still possible to think, *This has happened many, many times before. We always recover.*

All of us on the board were affected economically by the share price collapsing. At NEA, we had made about five times on our investment, distributing the stock in the mid-1980s. But I had also invested personally and significantly, and I had never sold a share of that stock except to pay taxes on exercised options. The value of my holdings had fallen now to less than $1 million from $10 million in the late 1990s. Other HealthSouth directors also owned stock and suffered losses accordingly. Most of our stock ownership was due to options.

Joel had not lived through a stock recovery after a serious decline like this one at HealthSouth, and he became increasingly critical of Richard and the company's management. Jack Chamberlain joined him, both aggressively questioning the one-time charges to earnings. The irony was that only Richard had sold stock and generated over several hundred million dollars of liquidity. His sales of millions of dollars in stock had coincided with market highs. As the stock slipped to $5 per share, several shareholder lawsuits were filed. To mollify criticism, Richard added two new directors to the board. Bob May and John Hansen were supposed to be white knights, although they had no healthcare experience. If Joel and Jack were critical, Bob and John were openly hostile. I supported Richard in his skirmishes with these four directors because I did not yet understand that I, the employees, the stockholders, and the rest of the board had been betrayed.

I called Richard at this time and demanded, "You swear that the company has $1 billion of EBITDA. Our stock price is therefore absurdly undervalued. Will you support an NEA bid to buy the company? We expect HealthSouth's management to invest alongside us, and we will invite our venture friends and limited partners to join."

Richard swore to me that the numbers were accurate, saying, "In all the years you have known me, I have never lied to you. You know that." He insisted that I recuse myself from any decisions that HealthSouth's board made regarding NEA, but he agreed to send a plane to pick up an NEA group to begin due diligence.

NEA's Peter Barris and NEA venture partner George Stamas agreed to lead a team of healthcare partners to begin the company analysis. Such an analysis would, of course, include a forensic audit, which was always part of such a management buyout. We did not mention the audit to Richard. Peter, George, and others flew to Birmingham. They were impressed by what they saw on the ground, and they began their due diligence. Then, on March 19, 2003, we received a frantic call from HealthSouth's CFO that the FBI had raided the company and confiscated all records.

Company management was being accused of overstating earnings significantly. I could not believe what was happening. It was inconceivable to me. Life suddenly became surreal. Yes, at NEA we were rebuilding our healthcare team and producing good investment results. But all that went by the wayside. The other directors and I were caught in a national scandal mentioned in the newspapers every day.

It was hard to get a grip on what was real and true. For twenty years, I had devoted a lot of myself to helping build this company. At least NEA had exited its position more than a decade ago, but now, under my watch as a director, a terrible fraud seemingly had been committed. The people I had trusted for twenty years had betrayed me.

How could it happen? Worse, Richard was actually trying to cheat me again, by lying to me and letting me put at risk my own firm—the thing I had built from scratch—while we pursued the buyout of a company with billions of dollars in debt and overstated earnings. Did he believe me to be a loyal fool? My whole world was tossed upside-down and shaken by the crisis of HealthSouth.

A few days after the raid, I flew to Birmingham for a board meeting. The atmosphere, of course, had completely changed. Bob May and John Hansen were convinced the veteran board members should resign immediately because HealthSouth needed fresh faces to restore confidence in the company. But as the long-term board members, we were convinced we knew what was best for HealthSouth, and we also felt we were truly accountable for fixing the mess. All of us on the board were at risk as the lawsuits against HealthSouth multiplied, but we were allowed to stay. The company and our directors' insurance stood between the board and the lawsuits, but all bets would be off in the event of bankruptcy, which would cancel our insurance.

Our first official act was to relieve Richard as President and CEO. The buck stopped at his desk, which means that he was either the mastermind of this great tragedy or grossly negligent. He left the room whispering, "Chuck, I am not a crook." It is a line I have heard before from a president's lips. When someone has to say this, it is because they are covering something up.

A week before the FBI raid, we added Betsy Atkins, a former executive at an NEA company, to the board. Betsy and I were given the task of finding a restructuring firm and a forensic accountant. We knew we had $3 billion in debt, but we did not know the company's real earnings power. Was it sufficient to service the debt? We were a bleeding, wounded whale chased by sharks and orcas, blind to what lay ahead. Betsy resigned her board seat after nineteen days.

When the government claimed damages for fraudulent billing, the insurance companies denied us our coverage, and shareholders were suing. Most of our long-term bondholders had sold their bonds, which were bought by vulture debt investors. The vulture hedge funds bought the cheap bonds and used the power of the debt in liquidation to suck money from the company.

We had problems with our shareholders as well. The long-term investors sold their stock, replaced by a group of bottom-fishing speculators. To complicate matters, a law firm specializing in suing companies whose stock dives sued us. When there is fraud, they have a field day, claiming to be protecting innocent shareholders, but those promises rang hollow. They did not care about the long-term potential of the equity or shareholders; they wanted cash, no matter what the fate of the company might be. In the end, the rewards went to speculators who bought penny stock rather than those that truly lost most of their money.

The HealthSouth board did not know whether the company was profitable enough to carry its debt, and we had no idea what our liabilities were. We knew that the cash balances were deliberately misstated, and the $500 million on the books was closer to $5. We did not know who participated in the fraud. Were any honest employees still working in the finance department?

Joel Gordon became chairman, and he volunteered to move from Nashville to Birmingham. Here you had a 70-year-old man, who should have been living on Golden Pond, but instead, he chose to step into the gates of fire. It was the worst crisis of his life. For the next two years, he had to work twenty-four hours a day, seven days a week, away from his wife and family. Only proven leadership could give our employees, shareholders, and bondholders enough confidence to believe that we could survive. Everyone on the board spent at least a third of their time on HealthSouth.

Bob May stepped in as CEO after a while to help Joel with the huge task. He and John Hansen restructured the firm's compliance department and led a committee to analyze our financial standing. Everyone on the board was involved in what should have been the job of management in a normal situation.

Betsy reminded me that I knew the healthcare businesses. "Who do you know who has turned around a healthcare company? That person should be able to tell you all you need to know." The solution to my problems was self-evident to me. Mac Crawford, one of the best turnaround experts in the healthcare industry, was our man.

It was a simple call. Mac began the conversation by telling me that he knew I was honest and scrupulous and that my self-interest was secondary to whatever company I was helping. So how the hell did I land myself in such a terrible situation?

Well, it was hard to argue with the truth of that statement. I needed his help. "You are the best restructuring guy I know. Can you save HealthSouth?"

Almost Yoda-like, Mac replied, "That is a big favor you ask of me."

"Yes, it is, Mac."

He acknowledged that while he might be able to do it, as CEO of Caremark (another turnaround), he was out of the restructuring business and into the company-building business. Who could blame him? It was a lot more fun to build a company than save a crooked one.

He did offer several pieces of good advice. When he was working to save Magellan (another turnaround), he had worked with Guy Sansone from a firm called Alvarez Marsall. Mac said that Guy's boss, Brian Marsall, was even better than Guy. He told me that Price Waterhouse Coopers and Trusted Information Systems were the best forensic accountants. A little overwhelmed, I thanked him and reminded myself that I owed him a nice bottle of wine.

Within five days, we submitted our report and recommended Alvarez Marsall, Trusted Information Systems, and PWC. The board would interview them and make their choice. Two decisions combined to save HealthSouth. One was to make Joel the chairman, and the other was to bring on Brian Marsall as chief restructuring officer with Guy Sansone as his aide-de-camp. Later, I learned that J.P. Morgan, one of our debtors, told Joel and Bob that they would have called their loan if we had not hired Brian Marsall.

What happened next was my worst nightmare. The media discovered the fraud in Enron and WorldCom. HSRC was the next crooked company. Due to this negative coverage of the fraud, we lost our honor. We did not lose our honor, but losing it in our own minds was almost as bad.

When there is a crisis of this magnitude, bad news sends out ripples everywhere. An SEC investigation immediately painted all management, the board, and the employees as a band of crooks. Our attorneys forbade us to talk to any members of the press. At the same time, our competitors, disgruntled employees, and perhaps some board members and senior managers (with their own private agendas) leaked information to the press that was often inaccurate and almost certainly taken out of context.

Dissatisfied shareholders, their lawyers, and hedge funds circulated rumors to enhance their financial self-interest. With all this bad press, the bond rating agencies lowered the rating of our bonds. That scared our banks. They started to call in their loans. Our suppliers and vendors were requiring cash payments, which further complicated our cash problems. We created a special account, away from the company, to pay creditors who made the most noise since a few of them could force us into bankruptcy.

We were forced to liquidate all nonessential assets at prices below market in a frantic rush to raise cash. We terminated all marketing expenses and new product development costs, then began a study to determine which of our large facilities we could sell to raise more cash. We had to pay off the claims of our debtors, our shareholders, and the government. Physicians, who had been loyal supporters of the company, became disillusioned due to misinformation. They threatened to take their business elsewhere. Every time I turned my head, I discovered five more fires that had to be extinguished instantly. The SEC and Congress conducted investigations where Teddy Kennedy ranted about the evils of American capitalism in front of a TV camera.

The lawyers proliferated geometrically. Skadden Arps served as Corporate counsel, Bruce Vanyo and Wilson Sonsini served as special litigation, Willke, Farr & Gallagher represented the audit committee, Weil & Gotshal covered financial restructuring, and Akin Gump became the director's counsel. These were only a few of the lawyers that became involved. Lawyers were essential, but ultimately, they cost the company $500 million (another huge cash drain).

Board members met with separate legal counsel. It was impossible to keep them acting with a common purpose, for each member was advised on what was in their interest, not the company's.

With HSRC under criminal investigation, everything we did was scrutinized. We operated on a totally transparent basis, so we established a series of special committees. They met very frequently and reported to the board where we voted on actions to be taken.

The character of the board inevitably changed in a crisis because all the directors faced different levels of risk. Meetings were tense.

Tempers often flared, and as HealthSouth's disgraced directors, we could not show our faces in public.

The bright light at HSRC was Brian Marsall. Brian had turned around a number of healthcare companies or had shepherded them through bankruptcy. Within a week after he arrived, he told us the company was not in financial jeopardy. We had $600 million in real EBITDA, we could liquidate assets, resolve our problems with the bondholders, and settle shareholder suits. It might take five years to stabilize operations and begin to grow again. While many people were responsible for saving HealthSouth, the combination of Gordon and Marsall deserved the most credit.

The congressional investigations were a nightmare for those of us who had to testify and those of us who watched the process on television. The HealthSouth board was crucified. Our integrity, competence, intelligence, and diligence were all maligned by politicians who never allowed us to answer their questions. As I watched the proceedings, my blood pressure increased, and a hot, unhealthy flush covered my face.

Our greatest stress was grinding through the legal examinations. First, we gave depositions to the FBI and Alice Martin, the US Attorney in Birmingham. She was intelligent and remarkably respectful of the board. We gave depositions to the FBI. Before each deposition, our counsel briefed us for hours and we had to review all appropriate documents. Whenever one testified in front of a court or a congressional committee, one had to be thoroughly prepared. This process took thousands and thousands of hours, and throughout this time, we could not read articles about the trials of HealthSouth officers who had pleaded guilty.

We could not read about Richard Schrushy's shenanigans. We could not speak to the press without risking prosecution. The feeling of being defenseless against constant attack was the most enraging experience.

While the board took action to save the company, I felt like I had stepped on a land mine. To me, the world was flipping over. One moment, I had helped finance the best healthcare company in the world; the next, I was accused of crimes in the *Wall Street Journal*. My greatest accomplishment as a venture capitalist had become a nuclear wasteland.

A hundred more lawsuits followed, and some board members had to testify before Congress: a televised inquisition. The politicians showed the public how they were hard on corporate crooks, but they did not seek the truth.

None of the directors were charged with any crimes. At the trial, I testified as a director, looked Richard in the face, and told the court how he controlled everything that happened in the company.

Joel Gordon, a board member and creator of the surgery center business, saved the company. HealthSouth employees were devastated by the drop in the company's stock. Lives were lost to suicide. Lives were ruined. My "$10 million" in stock virtually had no value. The company gave up its dream of changing the American healthcare system and withered back to a chain of rehab hospitals.

Like Al Capone, Richard was found not guilty of the major crimes, but later, in a separate case, he got seven years for bribing the governor of Alabama. By December of 2004, it was evident that HSRC would make it. We had not hired a CEO yet, but there were several final candidates. Rightly, Hansen and May pressed for the old board members to resign. I volunteer to be the first (although it could conceivably put me at risk).

The other, old board members set their resignation dates.

It was freezing when I flew back from Birmingham to Baltimore. Guy Sansone, Brian's partner, shook my hand when I left the plane and patted me on the back, saying, "You have done the right thing. The directors have saved the company, and we all know HealthSouth deserves saving."

It was too cold as I walked to the car. I heard nothing. There was no traffic, no sounds of conversation in the airport hallways. Grief overwhelmed me. What did an experience like this do to people who go through it? To those closest to the blast, it had been catastrophic. Joel Gordon was devastated financially. He had to live in Birmingham, away from home. He worried about his safety. He had reason to.

Several weeks later, Joel sent me a plaque honoring my twenty years of service and contribution. That made me feel that I succeeded in keeping the respect of the other old directors, the people I valued the most.

Sage Givens, the second woman in venture capital who had started her own firm (the first being Annette Campbell White), suffered the

most. She was an unrecognized hero of the HealthSouth fiasco. I called
her the venture capital "Maid of Orleans—Jean d'Arc." There were ten
to twenty female venture capitalists in the industry of the '80s and '90s
who had great track records and had real power. Sage was one of the
best. She had accomplished great things but was ultimately brought
down. She kept her courage, but her world collapsed around her. She
had a traumatic divorce from her husband of twenty years and was
awarded full custody of their children. While this was going on in her
personal life, she had to testify in Schrushy's trial in front of Congress,
which she later described:

"In a rather bold and unprecedented move, Richard and his
lawyers subpoenaed me to be a witness for the defense at his trial.
They assumed correctly, given the low education level of the jury,
that they would assume if I were called on to testify for Richard, that
I was supporting Richard. The prosecution asked me meaningful
questions and my responses implicated Richard. But the lawyers for
Richard called on me just to read pages and pages of board minutes
that were meaningless but looked like it was proof that Richard was
innocent. Richard and his lawyers nodded dramatically as I read each
sentence that had no bearing on any of the charges, but the jury took
that cue to mean that I was testifying in Richard's support.

"The worst moment of the day for me came after I testified, and
someone 'official'-looking approached me and asked me to step into
the courtroom (I had been sequestered in the witness chambers). I
went to the courtroom and they motioned for me to come to the front
of the room, whereupon one of Richard's attorneys physically picked
me up and twirled me around as if to enthusiastically congratulate
me on great testimony on Richard's behalf. My attorneys, who had
accompanied me into the courtroom, were taken off guard (as was
I) and had to wrestle me away from Richard's attorney and exit the
courtroom quickly as the jury looked on. In retrospect, it was just
part of the circus that the rest of the trial was, but it was breathtaking
in its audacity."

Sage's law firm, Cooley Goddard, added a term to her partnership
agreement for a new fund she was raising during the HealthSouth crisis,
forcing termination of her new venture partnership if an investment
was not made for six months after the partnership was started. Neither
Sage nor her investors wanted this term. She had managed two very

successful parnerships. Her record would have been even better if Amerigroup, one of her startup companies, was held. But the bubble had occurred, and her large institutional investors were told by their investment committees that no new venture capital commitments could be made at that time. She could not raise another fund. She described the experience:

"We were close to the goal of our $200 million for our third fund and had already had a couple of closings. What we didn't know was that while my lawyer from Cooley Godward was vacationing in Tahiti, he had left the fund documents to be finalized by a couple of new associates. This was the internet boom time, when law firms were incredibly busy and sloppy. Unbeknown to Acacia [Sage's fund] or any of its LPs, one of the associates inserted a brand-new term which required that there be a new investment prior to six months of the fund's first close presumably. [This was to preclude the cash sitting idly for too long.] This term was not requested by Acacia or its LPs, and it was never discussed with us. When we made the fund's first investment six months and a couple of weeks after the first closing, we were informed that due to not meeting the new term, the fund would automatically be dissolved. We would have to raise Fund III all over again. This was coincident with the internet bubble bursting, and many of the LPs were overextended and chose not to recommit at their original levels, despite the past performance of the Acacia funds. We chose not to go forward with a smaller fund because the economics didn't make sense and my time was beginning to be monopolized by the HealthSouth situation."

Sage threatened suit and won a large settlement from the law firm out of court, but it was of little satisfaction. She, a woman and a member of the compensation committee, had to bear the brunt of testifying in front of Ted Kennedy and the Governmental Inquisition, along with Joel Gordon and George Strong. This was all going on while she spent 25 percent of her time saving HealthSouth. Eventually, she started an internet company called Gambol Life and was back building an entrepreneurial business. Sage is unsinkable.

Jack Chamberlin, a man of the highest integrity, was publicly disgraced. In our subsequent interactions, it appeared that being under such enormous stress had changed his personality. My good friend, George Strong, had accidents following the scandal, then went through several difficult surgeries. About five years after resigning from the board, he died. As for me, I was a victim of the great train robbery, the pillaging of a great company for the personal gain and greed of the few. Like the feeling following a loss in war, stress exacerbated my chronic illnesses. I increased the potency of my medicines, and their side effects depressed me. I drank heavily. It was hard and embarrassing, but what was most painful was that there would always be an empty place in my heart.

During the trial, I put my BlackBerry beside the bed every night. When I could not sleep, I nervously checked its messages, hoping for some tangible good news. Even at 4:30 AM, I was worried. I was a venture capitalist, and my life was war. I had thought the companies I had started would change the world and make it a better place to live. How could I have been so wrong? HSRC for years was more important to me than my family: yes, I would have given my life to save it. It was a matter of honor.

The HealthSouth crisis was one of the greatest traumas of my life. It sent me back in time to Vietnam. During the HealthSouth trial, I was taken back to my valley of the shadow of death, to Vietnam's A Shau valley, to the rain and blood. Again, I had to face the horrors of war.

It was my duty. I had to call the airlines, make a reservation to fly to Birmingham, where our company was located, and save it. I woke my wife, sleeping beside me, by accidentally hitting her while flailing in a nightmare. My children were in their beds, dreaming of victories on the basketball courts. They knew nothing of what I faced. I kept it from them.

Joel Gordon, Bob May, George Strong, and Jack Chamberlin hired Jay Grinney as CEO. He had a great hospital background. HSRC stock had a five-for-one reverse split. Now the stock was $58, but if you adjusted it for the split, it was around $11.50.

That was double its low of $5, but a long way from $39, its all-time high price. We saved the company: in 2016, it had $3.66 billion in revenue and $246 million in net income. But it may take twenty or more years to go back to the stock price of $39. The dream of saving the American healthcare system was lost.

Jay deserves credit for stabilizing the company, though I believe the old board, under great adversity, really saved it. Although no one will sing my praises, playing a small role in that rescue was one of the greatest accomplishments of my life. I also got to watch two great men, Joel and Brian, do the right thing against "fearful odds."

VII

FRIENDS AND MENTORS

"As iron sharpens iron, so one man sharpens another."

—Proverbs 27:17

MOST VENTURE CAPITAL DRAMAS FOCUS on famous entrepreneurs and the all-knowing venture capital partners who finance their companies. Yes, those people are important, but those dramas do not tell the whole truth. They don't explore what's going on under the hood or what turns the engines of venture capital firms. The unsung heroes of the venture business are undervalued and dismissed as actors with minor parts, but while they may have few lines in the play, they have their own great stories to tell.

Mentors help you become what you could not be on your own. Credit is often claimed by a single individual, but in reality, it is most often shared by several. Success cannot exist in a vacuum. To some extent, you make your own luck, but when you do find someone who shares your values and wants to be supportive, befriend them, learn from them, and help them in return. Often, friends in competing venture capital firms have as much to teach you about living life as they do about business. Mentors can show you how to build your destiny.

To share the entire story, to fully detail the machine that is NEA, I must acknowledge my mentors, including Lewis H. Sarett, John Lockhart, C. Vincent Prothro, Frank Zenie, Bill Robinson, Paul

Wythes, James Swartz, Jim Blair, Tony Evnin, Dick Testa, Anthony Montagu, but I have to start with John Ridell.

From the Insurance Company of North America (INA), John Ridell was one of the lead investors in NEA I. He only lived for a few years after he invested, and he never knew how well NEA turned out, but he was an important contributor to NEA's success. He was an initial member of NEA's investment committee.

In the early days of NEA, I was emptying the wastebaskets and taking personal responsibility for every administrative detail. After one of our meetings, John took me aside and gave me advice that went something like this: "You are a general partner, and general partners should focus on investing. Find someone else to do administration, limited partner support/relationships, and marketing." He went on to add that most venture partnerships he knew were poorly administered and kept their limited partners in the dark. If NEA wanted to differentiate itself, the partnership would need to excel in those too-often neglected tasks.

As a result of that advice, I hired Nancy Dorman as administrative partner, giving her a piece of carried interest as large as some general partners. Nancy had worked previously for Walter Mondale, organizing and sometimes directing his hectic life. My thought was that if she could keep politicians on track, she could certainly manage to keep NEA on the right path too.

Nancy immediately took charge, and within a very short time built the best administrative marketing and limited partner relationship effort in the industry. She brought on Lou Van Dyke, a General Electric alumnus, as CFO. At the point she came in, the primary communication between venture partnerships and their limited partners was a Christmas card. Under Nancy's directive, NEA published annual reports, quarterly reports, held a series of meetings with its limited partners, and stayed in touch with them all year. She organized our marketing and fundraising, so they look little of the general partners' time. Our investment committee was treated as a real board of directors and was consulted on major hiring and firing decisions and all strategic moves that the partnership made.

Nancy Dorman was largely responsible for the successful operation of this program, which she accomplished by working fourteen hours a day, seven days a week. Without her, NEA would have not been as successful as it was.

But without John Ridell's advice, I doubt that this hire would have been made. To this day, NEA general partners spend 95 percent of their time on investments.

🌲🌲🌲

An English gentleman titled the Honorable Anthony Montagu was Dick's good friend. When Lord Montagu died, his first son inherited 500,000,000£, according to the British laws of primogeniture, along with all the family property between London and Bournemouth. His second son, however, inherited just a pat on the back, a fine pair of Purdey shotguns, and an introduction into the family's trade—one considered embarrassing for an English Lord.

In the end, Anthony got the better deal. At an early age, he became managing partner of the merchant banking house of Samuel Montagu. Historically, merchant banks have financed countries, princes, railroads, and wars. Samuel Montagu's specialty was bullion trading. Since his family banks had survived hundreds of years, financing change around the world, Anthony was not just a patrician; he was, essentially, a lord of risk capital.

Anthony managed the firm and then sold it as the banking business began to consolidate in England. He went on to do something very unusual for a son of the aristocracy, even a second one. He started a technology-focused venture capital firm. In a general way, it was a logical career trajectory for him; he was carrying on the tradition of financing change. But at that time, the only question English investors asked when presented with an investment opportunity was, "How much does it yield?" Nonetheless, Anthony raised his money from farsighted families like the Bembergs, earning the position of England's greatest entrepreneur venture capitalist. He also had the guts to back a crazy English playwright on his first musical, a rock opera called *Jesus Christ Superstar*. The playwright, Andrew Lloyd Webber, became a good friend, and their country houses ended up next to each other.

Perhaps the best story about Anthony was how he became an investor in Apple. Introduced by Peter Crisp of Venrock and my NEA partner, Dick Kramlich, Anthony met Steve Wozniak and Steve Jobs, visiting the company shortly after it started shipping the Macintosh personal computer. In thirty minutes, he decided this was a world-altering company, and he wanted to invest. Anthony wouldn't leave the building until he manipulated his way into buying 4 percent of Apple's stock for $400,000. Primogeniture isn't such a bad thing when it leads you to Apple.

He began collecting contemporary British art, which was fitting since his grandmother was one of England's greatest collectors. While you might hear of the "goût Rothschild," you don't hear of "goût Montagu." In my opinion, Montagu's taste was superior to Rothschild's. His collection soon became one of the greatest of modern and contemporary British art in England, including the artists Lucian Freud, Francis Bacon, and Graham Sutherland.

As a business mentor, Anthony was the most cultured, elegant man I had ever met, and very much the proper English gentleman . . . except for the facts that he drove a Cadillac down London's narrowest streets, used an American electric carving knife to cut his lamb, and loved Las Vegas. Anthony and his wife, Deirdre, invited Marsi and me to their country home in the Cotswolds after Andrew Lloyd Webber and Anthony had purchased the estate together. Andrew had the country seat, while Anthony converted the stables into one of the most beautiful living environments I'd ever seen.

During that visit, my first to the English countryside, he took to calling Marsi "Washington" because it was an English tradition to call a married woman by the name of her most illustrious ancestor. It's amusing because my children, Ashton and Adair, have daughters that are therefore entitled to this august title. As the grandson of a schoolteacher, I was always a plebeian aspiring to become a "new man" of Rome. No matter how wealthy or famous in battle, the Romans could only hope that their sons could become true Roman patricians if they were first anointed "new men." I hoped to do this in Baltimore.

Great sweeps of lawn and ancient trees drew the eye to Watership Down, which was only a mile away. This property, and its rabbits, are the subject of the novel of the same name by Richard Adams. Anthony had an incredible walled garden that saved the heat and sheltered his roses. The faded, rose-white brick was the perfect background for the border garden, which surrounded a lawn of grass clipped close like a putting green.

Everything about the house was comfortable, down to the hot-water bottles warming up the beds at night. The sisal rugs and the fabrics were delights of color. Luxury was everywhere, but it was a home, nonetheless. Surrounded by great English furniture, I wanted to curl up on a sofa beside a fire to read a good book. Anthony was a collector of Regency antiques through Mallett Antiques, and he pointed Marsi and me into a direction that changed our life: Regency-era furniture.

More than anything, Anthony was a great teacher, and beneath that urbane exterior was a strong will. He saw much more than I did when NEA financed Integrated Health Services (IHS), a company with the vision of using a nursing home to do what was formerly done only in a hospital setting, calling it "sub-acute care." The premise was that many hospital patients did not need hospital care. Their recoveries were impeded by being awoken hourly and exposure to mutated, drug-resistant bacteria found in hospitals. Integrated created a better, safer option.

Anthony referred to Bob Elkins, CEO of Integrated, as "That Most Tricky Gentleman." Bob behaved like the typical hypomanic entrepreneur, showing both an appetite for wealth and a desire to reform the healthcare system. He proved sub-acute care produces dramatically better outcomes while significantly reducing costs. Still, he failed to meet his budgets. The managed-care companies demanded proof that all his claims about costs and outcomes were valid. Then, after NEA did a second and third round of financing, IHS took on too much debt. Anthony essentially had me living at Integrated. I updated him on our progress daily. When Maryland National Bank, Integrated's biggest lender, came under the scrutiny of federal regulators, those regulators found questionable loans. The Integrated loan was called, but the company did not have the cash to pay it back.

Anthony was apoplectic. The company was rescued by Ben Lorello, an investment banker, who raised public equity capital and retired the debt.

Anthony made three-and-a-half times on this investment, and though he taught me to behave like an English gentleman, he also taught me to be ruthless in the pursuit of excellence. Without his prodding, I do not believe that IHS would have been as successful an investment as it was. Without him, I would have been ill-equipped to handle the challenges.

Lewis H. Sarett came into my life when T. Rowe Price introduced NEA to Merck, the great pharmaceutical company. As the former head of R&D for Merck, Lew synthesized Cortisone, won the National Medal of Science, and was convinced that Merck should invest in our partnership. The head of corporate development, Kirk Maslin, supported Lew's view that Merck should have a window on outside technology, especially biotechnology.

Lew adopted me, and we went shooting together in Maryland, Mexico, and South America. We talked about Mexican silver, the science of genetics, and the habits of doves. He was a gentle person with incredible insights into everything. He loved fresh Chincoteague oysters but maligned them as "organic filters." The times I spent in his company were some of the highlights of my life.

Maslin and Lew entertained us grandly in the wine cellar of the exclusive New York restaurant, Le Cirque. They introduced us to Barry Weinberg, Chuck Hartman, and the boisterous sculptor/venture capitalist Walter Channing. Soon, Channing Weinberg became of one our best, healthcare co-investors. Lew became an invaluable advisor, assisting us as a director on the boards of many NEA portfolio companies. His advice and help were particularly crucial regarding Advanced Cardiovascular Systems (ACS), the company responsible for creating balloon angioplasty. This procedure is performed inside the body in a few hours, which is certainly preferable to open-heart surgery where the chest is split open like a lobster's on a dinner plate. Dick Kramlich had invested in ACS a year or two after NEA was funded.

As an aside, Dick was involved with John Simpson, who developed the Simpson catheter marketed by ACS and used to perform balloon angioplasty. The company had personal significance for Dick because his wife had just died of a heart condition. He was determined to find ways to alleviate heart problems, and because of his passion, NEA would continue to advance cardiology for thirty years. When ACS started, there were about 450,000 coronary bypass procedures in the United States. By 2005, there were about one-and-a-half million balloon angioplasties in the US.

For ACS research, Howie Wolfe and I called a hundred doctors. Half insisted it was a great opportunity to lower costs and improve results, while the other half condemned it as a nonstarter. They thought the patient's arteries would clog after the procedure and that it would never be commercially significant. Lew told me that doctors always disagree passionately, so I should just go with my instincts. We invested, and soon, ACS captured the market. Lilly, the global pharmaceutical company, bought ACS, increasing the value of its stock significantly. The transaction alone was worth nearly $1 billion.

The first time Lew Sarrett pitched the proposed investment in NEA to Merck, to Roy Vagelos, Merck's CEO, and Phil Roy, the CFO, I sent a letter to Phil, totaling our commitments to the fund. I added the total incorrectly.

Phil asked Lew, "How can we invest in a boy who can't add?"

He believed investing in NEA would be betting on the wrong horse. To him, a window to outside technology would just be a distraction to Merck. Besides, what could an English major (me), an economics major (Frank), and a history major (Dick) know about life science investing? Merck turned down the chance to join NEA's first fund. But Lew and Kirk were persistent; they convinced Merck to invest by NEA's second fund.

Lew also taught me how to do due diligence on groundbreaking companies that could change the future. Most people look at life through the rearview mirror, thinking, "The past predicts the future, right?" But that's not right. History has many lessons to teach us, but to see the future, you cannot be governed by the past. When I researched the future of the telecom industry, everyone believed AT&T's dominance would last forever. They were wrong. At this stage in my career, whenever I try hard to glimpse the future in my mind, I think of Lew.

Lew retired from his thirty-eight-year career at Merck in 1982 and moved to Idaho. He attended services for my wife Marsi after she committed suicide, but our paths did not cross again. Though he died twenty years ago, his lessons live on in me and in those I mentored.

✦✦✦

Dick Kramlich started his career working for John Lockhart, the COO of the Kroger Company. John had been Dick's mentor, and he also became mine. John grew up in the logging town of Mellen, Wisconsin. The nature of the work there had brought many different ethnic groups to the town over time, giving it a unique flavor. John's father was a doctor and, as a result, a key figure in the community. The Lockhart family immigrated to the United States from Scotland, fleeing the cleansing of the clans which followed the great battle of Culloden in 1746.

John left Mellen to go to college at Northwestern in 1927, at the age of 16. He was a backwoods boy, one who could pick up a hat off the ground while riding at a gallop or vault across a horse's back to mount. He was used to hard riding and the company of lumberjacks. His college years were spent in Chicago in the midst of the Great Depression and Prohibition. After college, he earned an MBA, then passed the CPA exam in 1934. From there, he went on to get a law degree.

In 1940, John was hired by Trans-World Airlines (TWA) to be the Assistant treasurer for a $5,000-a-year salary. The brainchild of Howard Hughes, TWA hoped to compete with Pan American Airways' monopoly on international airline service. Jack Frye, TWA's CEO, was 36 years old, six years older than John, and a cowboy pilot. He flew recklessly and lived extravagantly, but he probably did more to advance airline safety than any other man of his time. He had a simple mission: build the world's best, largest, safest, and fastest air transportation system.

Like Howard Hughes, Frye was an obsessed visionary. When Pearl Harbor occurred, he proved his mettle. He helped transform TWA into the nucleus of the Air Transport Command. Several senior officers of TWA left to become Air Force generals. At this time, John became TWA's treasurer and a full participant in the management of the company.

During the war, the military took over one-third of the nation's commercial fleet. With a shortage of commercial aircraft, TWA increased its aircraft utilization to nine hours per day for the military, versus only an hour and a half before the war. There were no vacations during the war years, though John did get to see Hughes in Hollywood, starlets and all.

Toward the end of the war, TWA focused its efforts on winning support to become an international carrier. TWA bought TACA (Transport Aero Centro Americanos) to expand their international operations and sent John to run it as CEO. The airline pilots were ex-military misfits from all over the world, many of whom had spent the last five years fighting one another. The fleet was likewise a hodgepodge of international aircraft. John managed to keep the ill-fated company alive until it could be sold to the competition.

Hughes was an incredible boss, but no rules applied to his behavior. He once flew a new experimental aircraft from Los Angeles to Las Vegas and tested the plane by stalling it. He was an engineering genius, had an eidetic memory, and was extremely generous. No details escaped his attention. He was also incredibly secretive. John had to go through three locked doors to find Hughes in obscure Los Angeles warehouses. Hughes worked from midnight until dawn and never read any document (no matter how complex) over one page in length.

When John was negotiating to purchase aircraft from Glenn L. Martin, Howard crashed the experimental H-1 racing plane and wound up pulling himself out of the burning wreckage. In 1946, John left Howard Hughes and TWA to take a job as COO of Kroger, the grocery store chain. He was hired by Joe Hall, who was then in a life-or-death struggle for control of Kroger with Charley Robertson. Later, John hired Dick Kramlich. They stayed close, and through Dick, I met John.

John taught me an important lesson about being a venture capitalist. He said that business plans are nothing more than a picture of a company at a moment in time—a single frame in a long movie. If you believe they are cast in stone, you will lose many good investments. If you try to manage a company by its initial business plan, you are effectively putting it in a straitjacket. You will fail.

In business, John always wore a dark suit that set off his silver hair and mustache. He was an invaluable educator who seemed to innately understand complex situations. He taught me the art of gaining a CEO's trust and how to work constructively with charismatic personalities. John was a tough taskmaster, and together, we had to fire several CEOs. Many young venture capitalists develop hostile relationships with their CEO almost immediately, forgetting their roles as board members and turning into micromanagers. John kept me from falling into this trap. I also recognized we shared some things: even though for years he dealt with political infighting at the companies he worked for, he could be too trusting. I have the same issue.

One of the greatest benefits of being a venture capitalist is getting to know entrepreneurs. Of those I got to know, C. Vincent Prothro, in addition to starting companies, became my partner for several years as a venture capitalist. Vin was truly one of Texas' greatest entrepreneurs. He was medium height at two inches shy of six feet, but he had the lankiness of a long-distance runner, and he filled the room with his stage presence. Vin was also the black sheep of his family. Instead of pursuing ranching or oil, he chose to make his career in the semiconductor industry. After earning several technical degrees, he went to work for Texas Instruments (T.I.) but defected in the 1960s with a group of other TI employees to help L.J. Sevin start Mostek Corp., a semiconductor company. Vin understood that he was not meant to play a supporting role, so he left Mostek. Vin added immense operating and technical credibility to any project he became involved with, but his influence on me extended beyond work.

Vin and his wife Karen once invited us to stay with them at their house in Santa Fe. It was straight out of a movie. The approach to their home was a ten-mile-long dirt road, through cactus and sagebrush. The house had a beautiful desert garden, illuminated by candles in terracotta pots with geometric, cut-out patterns on their sides. Karen introduced me to an array of Native American Indian artistry, Pueblo pottery, and her wunderkabinett (a kind of small treasure house). She was a yellow rose of Texas and opened up for us a kaleidoscopic glimpse into another world. The four of us sat on the back porch, drinking margaritas and watching the sunset over the Sangre de Cristo Mountains—pink, purple, green, and yellow—with violent shades of color towering over the dusty, desert horizon. Below, a herd of buffalos hunkered down for the night, while the lights of Los Alamos flickered in the distance and the coyotes began to sing.

In 1984, Vin started Dallas Semiconductor, which developed application-specific semiconductors. Ultimately, he helped it grow to $1 billion in sales. Today, Vin's semiconductors open our car doors when we press buttons on our keys. Later, after several years managing a venture fund, he returned to his entrepreneurial roots, installing himself as CEO of Dallas Semiconductor.

Watching Vin's skillful approach to communication was a great lesson for me. As a venture capitalist, Vin gave effective lectures on the nature of the business. One of his slideshows began with a picture of a woman in a sultry pose, with bright red lipstick and a cigarette dangling out of her mouth. It is a classic image at the time. Vin said the first question a venture capitalist must ask is, "Are you really in love with the company in which you have invested? For only if you have a feeling as strong as love will you have the passion to help create the company." Later came a slide he titled the "Management Resignation Box," showing losses increasing while sales lagged and the cash ran out. The slide meant that the time had come for management to resign. Vin showed this slide to every entrepreneur, clearly explaining that their future would be in jeopardy if they continually failed to meet budget.

When Dallas Semiconductor made its first profit, Vin sent every shareholder a Payday candy bar. He was the master of using simple images to quickly convey complex messages.

In 1988, I was sitting on a porch with Vin at the Rolling Rock Club in Ligonier, Pennsylvania, and he lamented that his parents had not traveled but were now too old to experience the world. Vin and Karen always traveled. He talked of visiting Venice in the winter, a medieval city filled with cold mists, of trattorias filled with Venetians drinking wine and telling stories by firelight. Vin's philosophy was simple: spend money you do not have, make time when it is unavailable, but make the effort to travel. You never know when the opportunity will be lost forever.

About eight years later, Vin was attending a Dallas Semiconductor board meeting when he died instantly from a stroke. Years after that, when my son Ashton raised his first fund, Karen, his wife, and her children were among his first investors, and they have invested in almost every fund Ashton has started since.

Vin taught me so many things: how to use the management resignation box, how to communicate complex ideas with a single word or image, and how to appreciate Southwest Native American art. Even after his death, he continues to add so much to my life. Vin also taught me how to take a bite out of the reality sandwich (also known as recognizing when you are in serious trouble), but his most important lesson is embedded in a brass plaque that I must walk over to enter my office garden: "Carpe Diem." Try to enjoy the moment because you don't know when the bullet will take you out.

Bill Robinson was the CEO of the John Harland Company, one of T. Rowe Price's investments I made before we formed NEA. When we started NEA, the John Harland Company became one of our initial investors. Bill was something of a business legend, having led Harland from a small regional presence into the second-largest check printing company in the world. Harland had grown by 20 percent each year for twenty-five years, and Bill served as a constant reality check for me. At times, when the California technology markets were frothy, my partner, Dick Kramlich, became euphoric and our investment rate would accelerate. During those times, Bill was sure to sit us down and talk to us about how long-term growth rates were what determined a company's real valuation. Often, the rapid growth rates experienced in a technology company's first introduction of a product are impossible to maintain, so valuations will come down precipitously as growth slows.

We learned this lesson all too well. We invested NEA's third fund too rapidly in technology companies at high valuations, and the results were disappointing. We also made investments in fields far outside of our core competency. We let new partners commit capital too quickly, before they had shown themselves to be proven investors, in industries we did not really understand such as specialty retailing and financial services. NEA III became a difficult partnership that produced mediocre results. We never should have believed that our portfolio companies' outrageous multiples were sustainable. NEA I had returns of 37.5 percent, and NEA II was 14 percent. Bill was too gracious to remind us that he saw it coming, but like Vin, he too was the master of the reality sandwich.

When we closed NEA I, we took down the total fund of $16.1 million. It took us five years to invest most of it, and we continued investing the rest over 5–8 years. Had we taken the money down as needed, as we did in all the other partnerships, I believe the annual return would have been over 80 percent. To add insult to injury, we kept the uninvested money in bonds. The largest loss in the fund was a $500k–$1m loss in our bond portfolio.

An avid hunter, Bill often invited me on hunting trips. On one memorable occasion, the John Harland Company took me and a group of senior bank executives to Cali, Columbia, for a dove shoot. Because the bank executives were major lenders to the company and Columbian government, we were given a military escort that included a .50 caliber machine gun mounted on a Jeep and a platoon of soldiers. (Could there be a better hostage for a Columbian drug lord than a senior US bank executive?) The soldiers fanned out and established a defensive perimeter around the freshly harvested fields where our shoot took place.

Despite our overall returns being satisfactory, Bill's successor terminated Harland's venture capital investment program.

After Bill retired, he continued to invite me to shoot with him. In 1991, Bill invited me to his home, and we shot wild quail. There was nothing like it. We rode horses through pine forests while the dogs ran in front of us. It was winter in Georgia—sunny, but chilly. The underbrush was burned annually to provide an ideal environment for nesting quail. Suddenly, a dog would go on point, prompting us to dismount, grab our guns, and approach behind the dog. Then, there would be an explosion of birds' flapping wings. The covey would rise, darting away in every direction. The line of guns in a quail shoot must maintain order so no one accidentally kills someone else. Everyone must be careful not to shoot low birds or birds behind the line. Hunters are tempted to covey shoot, of course, banging away at the whole group rather than focusing on one bird. It's an exhilarating experience in the pine forest, amid the woodland scents, as sunlight filtered through the canopy of tall pine trees. Watching the dogs work while mounted on a tall horse is a lot like watching ballet. After the day's shooting, we'd have a wonderful dinner of roast quail, complemented by claret, and we relived the events of the day.

I never was able to thank Bill for his advice or the introduction to his wonderful hunting lifestyle. My last contact with him was in 2002. He sent me a note along with a copy of a news article about Richard Schrushy's compensation as the CEO of HealthSouth. The note was two short words: "Watch Out." Unfortunately, Bill was correct, as usual. Often, the best friend is the one who gives you the worst news. I failed to recognize his wisdom, crumpling the notes and throwing them into the trash basket.

When Bill died, I had a board meeting and could not attend his funeral. He would have done the same thing. He would have said, "When you cannot change the outcome of an event, ignore it, and focus on what you can change."

I met Paul Wythes, co-founder of the Sutter Hill venture capital firm, through Cub Harvey, the CEO of T. Rowe Price. Over the next twenty years, Paul became a close friend and mentor to me, helping me to grasp the nature of the venture capital business. When Paul joined the board of T. Rowe Price's New Horizons Fund in the late '80s, he began making regular stops to my house in Baltimore to visit. During one of the most memorable of those visits, Amy, Paul, and I sat in the den, eating Chinese takeout food while watching the shock-and-awe bombing that initiated Operation Desert Storm.

Paul was born in 1933 in Camden, New Jersey. He grew up in nearby Haddonfield, surrounded by the history of the Revolutionary War and the Underground Railroad. His father was a teacher, and like most educators, the Wythes lived a modest lifestyle. His darned socks were handed down from his brothers. He mowed lawns and had a paper route to add to the family income. His father pushed Paul to get an Ivy League education, and Paul worked through every term at Princeton to pay for it. Paul majored in mechanical engineering, signed up for Naval ROTC, and after graduation, he joined the Naval Supply Corps. Paul was eager to see more of the West after his time in the Navy, so it seemed appropriate that he chose to attend Stanford Business School.

Until Congress passed the Small Business Investment Company (SBIC) program with the Small Business Investment Act of 1958, most venture capital was practiced by family groups such as the Rockefellers, the Whitneys, and the Phippses. The SBIC program enabled a venture team to put up some equity, then leverage it with funds borrowed with a Small Business Administration guarantee. Paul's friend from Stanford Business School, Greg Peterson, started a real estate company with Frank Lodato called Sutter Hill Company. Greg and Frank were brothers-in-law, and they set up an SBIC in 1962. In 1964, they hired Paul to run it.

It was a risk for Paul to leave his secure job at Beckman Instruments to join a real estate business that had an SBIC venture arm as a side gig. In those days, no one knew what a venture capitalist was. Paul drove around in an old car, cold calling on technology companies. In California, there were only three other firms in the venture business: Davis and Rock, Bryan & Edwards, and Draper, Gaither & Anderson. The Sutter Hill Company's SBIC eventually became Sutter Hill Ventures. Paul was joined there in 1965 by his co-founder, Bill Draper, who previously had worked at his father's firm, Draper, Gaither & Anderson. Today, Sutter Hill is one of the oldest and best California venture capital firms in operation.

In 1972, Paul played a significant role in founding the National Venture Capital Association. Ned Heizer, who founded and managed the largest venture partnership, the Heizer Corporation, was the driving force behind that association's start. Ned tried to conduct venture capital on a corporate scale with divisions: investing partners, lawyers, work-out specialists, and so on. For years, Ned was a constructive force in the industry, but his complex business structure never produced the kind of investment results that attract ongoing capital. The NVCA was one of Ned's and Paul's significant accomplishments and gave the venture industry and entrepreneurs who raise private equity a small voice in Washington.

One of the major accomplishments of the NVCA in the early '80s was convincing the US Department of Labor to exempt pension plans' investment in venture capital firms from the "Prudent Man Rule." Up to that time, a pension plan could not invest in venture capital because if one investment in the plan turned out to be imprudent (i.e., lost all its money), the plan beneficiaries could sue the pension plan for a breach of fiduciary duty.

Of course, the rule was totally inappropriate for venture capital, where portfolio performance must be evaluated on the results of a whole fund, not the performance of a single investment. The Employee Retirement Income Security Act (ERISA) ruling, encouraged by the Department of Labor, totally altered the venture industry by opening the floodgate to pension fund investment and creating the institutional venture business. Paul accomplished his goal when ERISA became law.

Paul used to say to me that he would often lie awake at night, wondering what would happen, plagued by the problems and scandals that sometimes occurred. Paul once got a call saying that a CEO was missing, and no one could find him. Another of his CEOs started a firestorm by having a relationship with a co-worker. From Paul's responses, I learned to stay calm on the outside even if you're churning on the inside. I knew these types of things could happen in my companies, too, and you had to handle them. That's the predictably complicated nature of venture capital.

Throughout the 1960s and well into the 1980s, the venture industry remained collegial. In the mid-1980s, investment banks entered the business, claiming to be one-stop shops for entrepreneurs. They would say "we provide all your capital from startup to the initial public offering; you don't need a venture capitalist." Some venture capitalists started believing that they could fund a company by themselves without forming a syndicate. During the 1990s, Sutter Hill stayed with its historic investment strategy. They passed on deals that were too high-priced, preferring to invest $2.5 million to $5 million, hoping the investment would return $50–$100 million. Between 1970 and 2005, Sutter Hill's internal rate of return was 36 percent. Although Paul, who retired in 1999 and died in 2012, underplayed his role in building Sutter Hill, he considered it one of his lasting legacies.

In an oral history I funded, Paul said what motivated him. "It is the idea of building a team that works well together over time, keeping the place going, doing well, and lasting for a very long time. Sutter Hill is viewed today as a good firm, not one that imploded or one that doesn't deal fairly. We work hard and have a good reputation. That means a lot to me. When entrepreneurs visit us here, we want them to remember the people, not the furniture. We feel the same way about our portfolio companies. We want entrepreneurs to be the heroes and the stars, not the venture capitalists behind them. Some other venture firms become the big name behind their companies; we are not that type of firm. We try to make the companies the success story. A partner who may have contributed a great deal to the success of a company may never go on the board, and except for a few people around here, no one knows the integral part that individual played. Everyone knows Sutter Hill invested in a company, but they don't know who the partner is who actually made the investment. The business is not one person; it's a team. What's discussed in the partners' meeting in terms of deciding whether to invest is a team effort. 'Did you check this?' or 'What do you think about that?'"

The lessons I learned from Paul helped me to craft NEA's culture.

🌲🌲🌲

When we raised NEA's first fund, Frank Bonsal took me to meet his old friend, Arthur Patterson, a tall, lean, and elegant man who looked like he stepped out of *GQ*. He worked at Citicorp with his good friend, someone who would later have a vast impact on my life, Jim Swartz. If ever there was an odd couple, it would be Arthur and Jim. One is the silver spoon, the other a tin spoon.

Let's start with the tin spoon. Jim looked like a linebacker on a football team, which, at one time, he had been. He grew up outside Pittsburgh, earning money by pumping gas and working on road crews. His father was a firefighter while his mother managed a hospital-based pathology lab. He grew up in a very healthy family, but without a lot of financial resources.

One day, a scout for Harvard University, a former Army officer, Colonel Gallup, showed up at Jim's school and asked if they had any promising scholar-athletes. Gallup visited local schools to find outstanding athletes also qualified to withstand the rigors of Harvard's academics. At the time, Jim was being courted by numerous football powers, and he had been encouraged to attend the Air Force Academy. Colonel Gallup gave Jim the money to visit Harvard, and after that, Jim was sold.

Jim majored in engineering and applied physics at Harvard, and he experienced it as a jock, not a patrician, joining the Harvard equivalent of Animal House. After Harvard, he received a full scholarship from Carnegie Mellon and earned a Master of Science in industrial administration. After graduating, he worked as a consultant, which was just a stepping stone in his career trajectory, a training session to solve business problems.

At that time, the New York venture community was dominated by old-line firms such as Venrock, Newcourt Private Equity, Payson

& Trask, and J.H. Whitney & Company. Jim lived in Princeton and came to know Mort Collins and Jim Bergman, who had just founded a Princeton-based firm called Data Science Ventures. Those were the days. There were no references to venture capital in the library or anywhere else for that matter.

Mort had a Ph.D. in engineering and took Jim under his wing by introducing him to Wall Street bankers interested in technology. One of these bankers was Hardie Shepard of Payson & Trask. Hardie's son-in-law, Jim Stevens, was the number two person at Laird, a research boutique investment banking firm that did both leveraged buyouts and venture investments. Thanks to Stevens, Jim got a toehold in the world of venture capital and joined Laird in 1972. Laird's principal source of income was providing high-quality research to investment firms, but when regulation reduced brokerage rates, that economic model no longer worked. Still, despite its financial difficulties, the firm was a force in the venture capital and leveraged buyout business in the 1960s and 1970s.

With Laird in trouble, Jim Swartz left to join Arthur Patterson at Citicorp Venture Capital (CVC) from 1974 to 1978. Arthur and Jim played football together at Harvard and became close friends at CVC, cementing a long-lasting relationship that continues to the present day and that defined both of their futures. Jim and Arthur made direct venture investments at CVC, while Arthur also ran a small public portfolio. Citicorp, however, never gave Jim and Arthur a profits interest, which they both wanted, so in 1978, Jim left Citicorp to join Fred Adler in establishing a small venture fund, Adler & Company. Shortly thereafter, he recruited his trusted friend Arthur to join them.

Jim met Fred when they sat on the Board of Acuity Systems, an ophthalmic testing equipment manufacturer. Fred was one of the legendary founders of Data General, the minicomputer company, and also managed a New York law firm that specialized in litigation. He bought shares personally at one cent per share, then invested from his fund at significantly higher prices. He offered Jim and Arthur the same deal, but they knew they could not do this and still adequately represent the interests of their limited partners. Despite this morally questionable behavior, Fred had some great qualities: he conducted effective board meetings, had a great sense of humor, and could laugh at himself. There is no question he was the sun, and all other mortals revolved around him like planets. He was a genius, capable of making instant decisions in multiple, unrelated areas. The funniest meeting I ever had was a board meeting in a hospital. Fred had his leg in a cast, suspended from the ceiling. He had broken it while playing tennis or with a pretty twenty-year-old model.

Arthur and Jim learned a tremendous amount from Fred Adler, both what to do and what not to do as VCs. In Jim's opinion, Fred had an exceptional mind to match his complex character. As a businessman, he was brilliant. Still, he could be highly manipulative and angry; he definitely had a dark side. It was this difference in character that eventually led to a split, but the three men made many good investments when they were together. During their stay with Fred, Jim and Arthur funded pioneering companies in healthcare, networking, and software, including Med21 (the first outpatient surgery centers), Ungermann-Bass (a pioneer in local area networking), Daisy Systems (the first computer-aided engineering company), and MicroPro (the first word-processing company).

I asked Jim about what motivated him in business and life. He once said in an interview, "I find myself in almost every situation wanting to be competitive and wanting to be the best. I love learning for itself, but to be honest, my primary motive is to succeed. I have always been driven by peer group acceptance, not acceptance like you find in a large corporation, but the acceptance you get when you excel in a small group of highly talented professionals, a venture partnership.

"I don't mind doing things differently: most of my investment success has been in things that go against the crowd. I never go with the crowd. I like people, but at my core, I'm really a loner. I'm very comfortable in my own skin. I have a strong sense of self-confidence, not overbearing (I hope), and I get along with almost any type of person. I've always cared about everybody. I have always had a desire to create my own environment. If I retired and just went and sat on the porch, I'd go crazy."

In 1983, Arthur and Jim form Accel, closing a $68 million fund the year after. Accel's core strategy, to borrow a phrase from the oil field, was to do developmental drilling rather than "wildcatting." Developmental drilling entails drilling a well near an established field (a philosophy established by Laurance Rockefeller in the 1940s and

1950s), whereas wildcatting is drilling for oil in entirely unproven areas. In venture-capital terms, exploratory drilling means finding cutting-edge technology like high-speed data communications, networking, and conferencing, then funding successive generations of companies in those fields. It was through conversations with Jim that I learned to appreciate exploratory drilling. It would become a central tenet of NEA that I also used in my healthcare service investing.

One of Arthur's favorite phrases was "Chance favors the prepared mind." About this, Jim said, "It's a brilliant encapsulation that has come to define Accel. We work hard to know a lot about certain businesses. When we see the right opportunity, we can react quickly. I sometimes think successful venture capitalists have special glasses on top of their heads. They, like someone who works in the mines, can turn on a light and see in the dark. Venture capitalists see into the future. They also have exceptional situational awareness. Venture capitalists, the good ones, walk into just about any kind of meeting and in about five minutes figure out who's doing what to whom and exactly what the issues are. It is not that we predict the exact future, instead, we predict a trajectory.

"Some of us can do this consistently, but we all get it wrong sometimes. It is a gift, a form of pattern recognition. But if you do it long enough, it becomes self-reinforcing. Sometimes you see something and say, 'this is stupid.' The big misses are where you get hung up on something irrelevant, the entrepreneur is too difficult and you don't move on it as quickly as you should, or you believe it is too high-priced. When I work with a company, I hope to make a difference in a way that doesn't interfere with what's going on within the company or with the management team. I try to find out what isn't getting done and make a difference there."

From 1985 to 1987, Jim served as President of the National Venture Capital Association, after first joining the NVCA board in 1979. It was a great, personal honor. Together with Chris Brody, the NVCA director, they helped liberalize the ERISA Labor Laws, which culminated in the passage of a 1986 law defining Venture Capital Operating Companies (VCOC). For the first time, fiduciaries of the nation's pension funds had a way to deploy pension funds in the venture capital business. As we now know, this unleashed a huge pool of capital for venture investing and provided the foundation for the modern venture capital industry.

With the formation of Accel's sixth fund in 1998, Jim Breyer, who had joined the firm in 1987 directly out of Harvard Business School, took over as managing partner. It was during the internet boom, but the firm was heading into a perfect storm. It was about to get hard for investors.

Accel had a long string of good luck starting telecom and software companies such as Teleos, UUNet, Portal, Real Networks, Veritas, and Remedy. The funds' internal rate of return (IRR) then was off the charts. Within eight months during early 2000, however, the entire market collapsed upon itself, and once-promising companies had no market for their innovative products. Like most venture firms, Accel overinvested their 1999 fund.

The late '90s were difficult for Jim. He was a firm believer that either you lead, you follow, or you get out of the way, which is one of the most important pieces of advice given to me. As Jim said in an interview I funded, "The bubble is very rough and raw. You might call it a civilized firefight. You have ideas coming at you every which way, and what do you do to survive; who do you grab onto; who do you avoid? In my lifetime, it has happened three times: 1966–1970, 1981–1983, and 1997–2000. It takes fifteen or twenty years for everybody to forget; a new generation comes along and thinks they know it all. During the bubble, I become depressed because there are plenty of good people around me whose respect I've lost. They are worshipping another god. I no longer enjoy going to work because I no longer have the principal respect that I was used to my entire career."

In the mid-2000s, Jim Breyer stepped down from the role of sole Managing Partner, and the firm reverted to its former flat structure, in which all partners were equal. Jim, like Jim Swartz before him, released the wheel of the ship to other partners and reverted to being a member of the crew. Perhaps the greatest challenge for a venture firm is management succession. Accel has handled four of them. Continuous, active involvement on the part of the founders helped Accel stay on course through the successions, adapting to changes in management.

When Jim Swartz addressed the graduating class of his business school, he explained a venture capitalist's purpose: "Venture capital has always been about helping a person or a project succeed. It is about adding judgment, perspective, and a selfless desire to see the company succeed. Venture capital is best practiced as a calling, not a job. It was never about maximizing wealth . . . Venture capital must be practiced with absolute integrity and ethics."

When Jim Swartz stepped back from actively managing Accel, he and his wife Susan started to apply a venture-capital approach to charitable projects. They sought out projects where their gifts alone could make a difference. A good example of their charity is what they did for the US ski team. Ski team members must postpone their college education for years while they train. Jim and Susan were involved with the team and underwrote the tuition of each member so they could complete college once they finished their skiing careers. Jim and Susan taught me that to live life fully, you must excel and give back to society in other ways than your business.

🌲🌲🌲

NEA would not be what it is without our mentors. Especially Dick Testa and his able younger partner, Dan Finkleman. Dick founded Testa, Hurwitz & Thibeault in Boston, which rapidly became the most important law firm representing venture capitalists on the East Coast. Dick was General Doriot's lawyer and was referred to us by Jim Morgan. When we hired Dick for our first fund, he promised two things: one, if we didn't raise the money, we wouldn't have to pay him unless we succeeded, and two, he would never give us a purchase agreement over thirty pages nor one not written in understandable English. Dick kept his promises.

Dick was as much a business partner as our lawyer. Both he and Dan attended our meetings, and when tensions were high, they always calmed us down. After thirty years, our partnership prospectus and agreement remained virtually unchanged. We consulted with them when we had to fire a senior partner, and we sought their counsel on every other major issue. Dick was always composed, and he always gave the best advice. When he died, Dan remained as our corporate counsel and advisor.

🌲🌲🌲

Frank Zenie is an entrepreneur. I first met Frank when he was CEO of Waters Associates, a public company which I invested in while at T. Rowe Price. Waters created the market for high pressure liquid chromatography (an important analytical instrument used in research.) It was the only stock that out-appreciated Intel for several years after its public offering. He went on to found Zymark, the company that created the market for laboratory Robotics with his chief scientific officer, Burleigh Hutchins, and his Chief Marketing Officer Jim Little. Frank was a business philosopher and certainly one of my most important mentors. I called upon him for advice throughout my career. His business advice is described in the book StreetSmart Entrepreneuring.

I recently asked him what advice he would give today's entrepreneurs, here is his response:

ENTREPRENEURIAL TRUTHS

Preface—my opinion.
Venture Capital is a dying art practiced by only a few today. It has been replaced by early-stage Private Equity. These young professionals call themselves VCs. They think you can know the right path to success by managing the numbers. There is much more to creating a company than managing it's numbers. I don't think you, Dick and Frank or Jack Dulaney believed that.

Always remember:
Starting a company is easy, building a successful business is hard. Sixty plus years ago, Peter Drucker explained that the purpose of a business was to create customers. I believed it then and I believe it now.

My company once had a German Professor as a chemistry consultant. I never understood the chemistry, but he gave us an important insight:

Your customers aren't always right, but they are always your customers.

1. **When faced with choices, always ask; "How does each choice add value to your customers.**

We often refer to markets; but markets don't actually exist, only customers. Marketing professional define customer groupings as markets, entrepreneurial innovators simply disrupt these artificial definitions by defining new ways to fill unmet customer needs. When entrepreneurs continue delivering high customer value, they earn the profit and resources to reward their leaders, employees and investors. Customers enable reward. No matter how large the numbers, never aim for a small share of a large market. Define a new niche and dominate it. Your customers then truly need you and want you to succeed. Your customers will actually point you toward future opportunities.

2. Building a successful business—Vision, Culture, Impact and Execution

Entrepreneurs are leaders, not managers. Leadership begins with Vision and Culture. Vision is not a strategy; it's an image of a place where other leaders, employees and investors want to join and help you get there. Vision energizes an organization. Culture is the shared values that builds trust and teamwork. Culture is the enemy of politics. Ensure accountability and then delegate. Expect passionate execution driven by Vision and Culture.

The successful entrepreneurial CEO is the Chief Vision, Culture, Customer and Accountability officer. He/she can delegate most of the rest.

3. If you're lucky, you will find three to five High-Impact players. They will propel your business. Enable, energize and reward them, they're invaluable.

Think impact not management. There is no right organization. Get the best people you can find, ensure that they share your vision and culture and then play to their strengths. Don't try to fix people. If they can't deliver impact, move on.

Two essential impact people:

Technology Architect—Creates innovative products and services that uniquely address unmet customer needs and disrupts existing markets Rainmaker—Identifies important and influential customer targets and converts them to customers and advocates

Your key impact people are smart and somewhat arrogant; and, therefore, high maintenance—but they're worth it.

Remember, no customer has ever used your truly innovative product or service before. Version 1 only reflects your perception of customer needs and preferences. Correct the technical flaws and get on the field of play quickly. Connect with early customers. encourage criticism, don't defend your product and learn how to make it more valuable. After two iterations, Version 3 should be pretty good.

4. Entrepreneurial Leadership; don't forget.

Use compensation to energize impact. The employment marketplace dictates cash compensation. Use equity-based compensation to attract, incentivize and reward impact. High impact > high reward!

Set and encourage ambitious goals. Over achievers aim high. Think Olympics; the best athletes go for the Gold, but only one wins it. Yet we celebrate the Silver and Bronze as winners. I doubt they would not have achieved Silver and Bronze had they not aimed for Gold. Aim high.

Learn how to manage Urgency, Patience and Focus Act boldly, then fix your flaws—Ready> Fire > Aim, > Fire > Aim . . . Your customers want you to succeed and will love your caring and attention. Urgently execute really important initiatives and Patiently learn from your customers and enhance the value of your products and services based on real-world results. Discover your bandwidth constraints and Focus your valuable time and resources on truly important initiatives and problems.

5. **Understand and respect competition. Your job isn't to crush the competition, it's to serve your customers better.**

Compete for business, but focus on customers. Your job isn't to crush the competition, just push them aside when they get in your way. Don't be intimidated by big company competition; yes, they have lots of resources, but these are often blocked by bureaucracy or committed to defending existing products.

My mentors helped to shape my success in business and my appreciation of life, and my debts to them can never be repaid. Other VCs from competitive firms turned out to be some of my best teachers. The limited partners on our board also guided me, but most importantly, many of my NEA partners mentored me. The wonderful thing about mentors is that the relationships last, and now some of my mentors also mentor my children.

VIII

AMY

"My most brilliant achievement was my
ability to persuade my wife to marry me."

—Winston Churchill

ONE CANNOT ADEQUATELY MEASURE A spouse's significant contribution to a venture capitalist's career. Marsi, my first wife, was my most ardent believer who gave me the courage to invest everything we had into NEA. My obsession with my business probably contributed to her death. Amy, my second wife and partner in life for decades now, has been the fuel that propelled our rocket to its destination.

After Marsi's suicide, my psychiatrist insisted that I not move my family to the West Coast, which is what I wanted. That would only further disrupt my boys' lives. "Ashton and Adair must keep their schools, their friends, and remain in familiar surroundings," he said.

Finding a partner, a wife, willing to accept these constraints was understandably challenging. When Amy came into our family, she saved my life and the boys' future. She is beautiful, intelligent, professionally accomplished, and best of all, Amy knows how to make a family work. On the advice of our psychiatrist, she was willing to forgo having her own children and devoted herself to Ashton and Adair, formally adopting them.

By the time I met Amy, I had already created a mental list of all the things I hoped my next wife would have: extreme intelligence, perhaps an M.D. or Ph.D. in the sciences with a focus on CNS disorders so we could both pursue funding cures for PTSD and bipolar disease. I hoped she would have equal knowledge of literature, so we could be mental travelers together (not an easy task because I usually read one to two books a week). She would be lean, athletic, a published writer, have significant business experience, an understanding of medicine, history, and art. She had to understand and respect the military if she wants to understand me, a warrior. Finally, she had to be a passionate lover.

I wanted a soul mate with all these things—someone who could be my companion in love and adventures of the mind—a person that never existed, and who, if she had, would probably have fought with me as much as she complemented me. What Amy lacked in formal education, she more than made up for in innate intelligence and common sense, a characteristic my "ideal woman" would probably have lacked.

I did not date women after Marsi died. Instead, I went searching for a wife, giving myself one year to find her. I knew my life depended upon pursuing the dream of creating world-changing companies. I also knew I could not raise the boys by myself. I had to find a partner. When I invited a woman for dinner, I'd refer back to my soulmate checklist, but I would also watch to see if the boys put their heads on her shoulder.

When I met Amy, I threw away that crazy list because I discovered that those things didn't matter. What matters most is family. Amy has a Ph.D. in family, and I am so lucky she loves me, despite all the baggage I carry.

Amy is and always has been a practical, tough survivor who has made her own way in the world. While Marsi and her prep school classmates may have had several of the traits on my list, they had the misfortune to be raised in the 1960s and 1970s. They were raised by WWII generation parents who wanted them to be wives, mothers, and socialites. They went to boarding schools and colleges where those values collided with feminism. The class reunions of women's schools like Garrison Forest, St. Timothy's, and the Northeastern prep schools in the early 2000s were attended by unhappy women that had lived through divorces, infidelity, careers that were not satisfying, and children who never got their acts together. Marsi was a poster child for that generation.

I never appreciated it at the time, but Amy gave up an awful lot to jump in and swim through a tsunami. She was a 32-year-old single woman with a good job and an active social life. She gave it up to marry a man suffering from PTSD and sometimes violent nightmares. She gave it up to marry a man who was obsessed with his job and often traveled six days a week, who was also obsessed with collecting, gardening, reading, and travel, and hardly had a minute to spare for her, a man who knew nothing about children or being a father. She gave it up for sometimes having to play nursemaid (A legacy of my time in Vietnam was a back that had been ground up as if in a Cuisinart. Disk alignment, the discs between the vertebrae, and the fascia were a mess. This led to long confinements in bed, accompanied by my caustic temperament). She gave it up to live with a man whose heart is in the early nineteenth century, whose mind is in the twenty-third century, who has very fixed ideas about how things should be done, and who is not above interfering with how she would run the house. She gave it up to take full-time responsibility for a four-year-old and seven-year-old boy, both of whom faced enormous challenges and required 24-hour-a-day attention. As an added benefit, she could not have her own children because of those needs. In retrospect, I think she did not get a very good deal.

At 5 years old, Amy lost her father, then shortly thereafter, her grandfather—the most important men in her life. Rather than pursue college, she chose to start work and earn a living with her first job typing exams at the University of Maryland, Baltimore County. She left UMBC to work for Jeff Miller, who helped inspire Baltimore's rebirth, and she played an important role in downtown Baltimore's revitalization. She educated herself, pursued charity work, and worked her way up through the First National Bank to become the vice president of corporate events. Respected in the local business community, Amy didn't have the prep schoolgirl's problem of being caught between the expectations of two generations.

"One thing is for sure: I will not make the same mistakes I made before," I said to myself when I married Amy. "I will stay very close to Amy, travel less, and try to be the perfect husband, granting her every wish." Despite this promise to my new wife, my guilt over Marsi's death drove me to become obsessive about my work and my hobbies. I mistakenly felt I could make my wife happy by giving her everything she wanted in material terms, but not my time and my soul.

Life before Amy had been Hell. After Marsi's death, I employed a series of housekeepers, and it was disastrous. The silver lining was that to survive this experience, the boys learned how to look after each other. Our first housekeeper, Jessica, was a disheveled, self-proclaimed born-again Christian. It infuriated me that she fed the children nothing but McDonald's hamburgers (at $420 a week . . . 20 percent were consumed by the boys and 80 percent by Jessica). What I already knew was a big problem became even bigger when Ashton walked in on this housekeeper in bed with her (married) minister.

That weekend, we drove to Long Island with Jessica and spent the weekend sailing with the boys' aunt and uncle. On the New Jersey Turnpike, Adair needed to use the bathroom, but the heavy traffic kept us from pulling over. Jessica encouraged him to pee in an empty milkshake cup. Traffic started to move forward briskly, just as she tossed the urine forward out of the window. The urine was blown back into the car. She was drenched and her mood for the rest of the weekend was likewise unpleasant. Three days later, she informed me that she had found a new job, unsurprisingly as her minister's assistant, and she left our house forever.

Our next housekeeper, from Trinidad, was even worse. In hindsight, it's truly frightening how reckless and irresponsible she was. Occasionally, when the neighbors dropped by the house in my absence, they found this housekeeper entertaining her gentlemen friends in a locked bedroom. This was terrible, but not nearly as disastrous as when the same neighbors found Adair, still a toddler, wandering on a country road one mile away from our house during rush hour. A week later, Ashton showed me the latest game he had created with Adair: they stole kitchen knives, stood on my bed, and threw them on the floor and through the carpet. A week later, the housekeeper vanished, stealing as much as she could carry with her.

What went on in my absence, I will never know, but there was an unexpected, albeit fortunate, result. Both Ashton and Adair have an uncanny ability to detect when the other is in danger. Fortunately, at this point, Amy was moving in with us, and we lucked out beyond our wildest dreams when she hired Lorna Williams, a Jamaican woman, to be our new housekeeper. Lorna said she could only stay for two years. She stayed for thirty-five. She became a valued and loved member of our family, and I looked forward to dinner most days with Amy, Lorna, and the boys. The boys called Lorna their mother. I don't know how that term of endearment will go over in modern times, but it was a pure expression of love and gratitude. It will be the saddest day indeed when I do something wrong and realize I will never again hear Lorna putting me in my place, "Oh, Mr. Newhall, you are very bad."

I don't get to hear it as often anymore. We have the honor of supporting Lorna in her senior years at a nursing home, but we visit and get together for holidays, both at our home and the boys' homes.

Perhaps the greatest discovery for me after Marsi's death was learning about the importance of child development. In addition to dealing with the vagaries of housekeepers in the B.A. era—that is, Before Amy—there was also the problem of the boys' rooms. They were a mess. It was torture for an old soldier. My young cadets were slobs at ages three and six. I instituted a nightly inspection before bed. My sons stood at attention at the ends of their beds, and each night, they failed and were admonished. My father had always insisted that I get all A's, and I never failed an inspection. Why weren't my boys the same?

I was referred to a child development expert. When she showed up at my home, I explained my problems and she took each boy to his room, and about forty minutes later, she returned for me. First, she showed me the boys' closets. There was a steel closet rail about five feet from the floor—a good height. She pointed out that neither boy could reach the rail. Hooks were far better than hangers suspended far above their heads. Then, we went into the bedrooms. They both had diminutive, antique desks, and she asked me to open one of the drawers. I opened it: it took some wiggling, but it wasn't difficult. She noted that the motor skills of my six-year-old were not sufficient to open the drawers. Both boys need plastic bins on rollers to store their possessions. Antique chairs look wonderful, but the boys needed plastic ones with wheels if I wanted them to move the chairs to their desks.

She handed me a book on child development and opened my eyes to parenting. It's amazing how so many of us have children and yet are totally unfamiliar with child development, let alone the host of psychological issues confronting our children. The story of my anger and frustration at the children's failure to clean their rooms is amusing now, but the danger in my reaction was that it could be damaging to their self-esteem. When you are overtired or have had a couple of drinks, you should not hold an inspection when you know the result will be a failure. Praise is a much better motivator than fear.

All these experiences and worry about my children caused me to lose more than 30 percent of my body weight before I married Amy. It was a time of survival. I started to hear loud sparks of electricity crackling in my ears. Travel for work was unrelenting, so my partners often accompanied me on business trips to ensure that I arrived at my destination and successfully found my way back home, as much as to help with the work. I was back in Vietnam, back in the valley of the shadow of death in so many ways. Then, on June 4, 1983, I married Amy.

Amy immediately immersed herself in Ashton's and Adair's care and development. We learned from the boys' psychiatrist that both Ashton and Adair had severe learning disabilities and PTSD from their mother's death. He recommended further testing at the University of Maryland under the direction of Dr. Regina Cicci, winner of the famous Orton Award.

For two Saturdays, we took both boys to the University of Maryland to undergo Dr. Cicci's testing. She concluded that the boys suffered from learning disabilities, which, coupled with their mother's suicide and ensuing PTSD, put them both at severe risk. If left unchecked, they could suffer a crippling loss of self-esteem. The doctor gave us volumes of reading so that we could learn what the expectations were for us as parents. Then, she told us the bad news: statistics showed that our sons had a 95 percent chance of ending up in jail by the time they were 21 years old. There had simply been too much trauma.

The doctor helped us form a strategy, encouraging us to spot any difficulty in class and immediately hire a tutor in the subject, including speech and language therapists. Our boys saw letters backward and pronounced words incorrectly. We played to their strengths. That meant getting them both involved in athletics, hobbies, or sports where they could achieve more than their peers. We were instructed to attend all these events and make sure the boys received proper recognition for their victories. These victories would offset any failures in class.

When I look back, I realize that my soulmate checklist was one of the stupidest things I have thought up. If I ever met a woman like that, the last thing on earth she would have wanted to do was to love a man like me. She would have wanted to cure a disease and be awarded the Nobel Prize, write the great American novel, or start a company of her own. At best, I would have been an amusing distraction. Women are much more practical than romantic men like Lord Byron. For Byron, love overcomes everything. In real life, this is not true.

When I wrote my first book, *Fearful Odds,* I used my diaries and Marsi's diaries, short stories, love letters to me, and others as my source materials. When *Fearful Odds* was published, I gathered my family around a fire pit and burned Marsi's papers. It was a formal ceremony that ended in my silent prayer.

When I proposed to Amy in December of 1982, it was around a roaring fire surrounded by Amy's mother and my boys. Ashton delivered the emerald and diamond engagement ring to Amy, in a glass of champagne, as her mother watched. A few hours before the proposal, I had a private ceremony burning that list. That time there was no silent prayer, just a sigh of relief.

In *Fearful Odds,* I wrote about how coping and defense mechanisms helped me to deal with PTSD. It was Amy who introduced me to my most important coping mechanism—being involved with raising my children. As described in *Fearful Odds,* my parents let my grandmother and the Army raise me. I was clueless about my children until Amy brought them into my life.

She required me to be helpful with their homework. Ashton's science project was to prove a universal truth about motivation. Someone suggested that mice responded to colors. We built two mazes. The mouse in the pink maze would find its food faster than the mouse in the black maze. Our mice were named Frodo (pink) and Bilbo (black). Halfway through the experiment, I called the science teacher and told him about our experiment. He told me that mice were colorblind. Time to change our plans.

We decided to reward whichever mouse got through the maze first with extra food. Frodo was the fastest, so he got the extra food. Unfortunately, Bilbo died on Sunday morning, the day before the experiment's conclusion was due. I left at 5 AM on Sunday to find a new Bilbo. Believe it or not, I found one by 10. The great race was run. Frodo trounced the new Bilbo and we conclusively showed that mice rewarded with food ran faster than mice without a reward. Now, this was all foolishness, but who can be sad when such a comedy of errors was going on? The boys became for me a source of happiness and endless amusement, keeping PTSD far away.

Dinner became a sacrosanct hour. We would discuss each day as a family with a positive attitude. Instead of denying the children sweets, we purposefully left them around the house, then praised the children when they exercised self-discipline. Remarkably enough, neither boy developed any interest in sweets.

For me, perhaps the most important lesson was how to establish limits to keep two very impulsive boys safe. We sternly forbade any behavior that posed any danger, which was exceptionally challenging since both boys were intelligent and impetuous. Whenever a ball flew into the street, they pursued it, acting like they were invulnerable to cars rushing past. On one such occasion, I had to tackle Adair to prevent a car from running him over. It was our job to sit them down and explain how good they were when they finished their homework and completed their chores, but it was also our job to help them recognize that chasing a ball into the street without first looking is an impulse that must be checked. I appealed to their emotions in these situations, asking, "How sad would your brother feel if you killed yourself doing such a thing?" In short, the setting of boundaries is most effective when accompanied by a self-esteem boost. Intimate parental involvement with every aspect of childhood came to seem necessary to me to ensure that victory is respected while putting failures into perspective.

The hardest thing for me to overcome, as my parenting approach evolved with Amy's help, was my own childhood, which was radically different from that of my children. In marrying Amy, I got a new, extended family who welcomed me and the boys, but it was a family with ways and interests that were completely foreign to me. Amy's family was like a Norman Rockwell painting seen through a wide-angle lens. They assembled en masse every Christmas, Easter, Labor Day, Fourth of July, President's Day, plus a number of other holidays I didn't know about. Instead of family dinners, they had family luncheons. The strangest thing for me was that no alcohol was served, and few, if any, non-family members attended.

When I wasn't in school, I grew up in an outwardly focused family with exciting guests, whereas Amy's family was in a secure, family cocoon. When they got together, they used a private language they had developed over sixty years of commonly shared life experiences. I didn't know why Aunt Betty was called "The Crab," and I didn't understand the joke that Aunt Sally played on Uncle Jim twelve years ago, nor did I remember the name of Dotty Ann's fourth-grade teacher. I wandered amid picnic tables spread with food, all sugar-laden (which I did not eat), feeling ill at ease, and trying too hard to please. The conversations did not center around art, science, business, or the host of other topics which had been my very life until that time. I would talk about the weather because I did not know the latest Orioles' baseball scores.

The wonderful thing about Amy's extended family was that it focused on children. I had never seen so many children. There must have been thirty or more of them, and they swam together in the pool, played basketball or baseball, and made family gatherings warm and fuzzy mayhem. Ashton and Adair joined in, spending most of their time with Amy's sister's children, whom they saw often, leaving a trail of mayhem behind.

I moved into my parents' home with Marsi in the early 1970s. I had explored every inch of the property and knew every secret hiding place in the house. One thing that always fascinates me about a house is the baseboards—where the wall meets the floor. You can tell a lot about the quality of a house from the baseboards. How high are they? What is the thickness of the wood? Are they seamlessly joined? Can you see the nails or holes? In some ways, baseboards are a metaphor for the quality of the house, and that was the problem with my house with Marsi. For close to twenty-five years, 3210 Caves Road was my home. This home, my parents', was a 1950s tract house, quickly and carelessly built using shoddy, inexpensive materials. The baseboards were 3 ½" high, ½" thick, and made of cheap, white pine. Worst of all, there were noticeable gaps along seams, where the boards should have been flush. We tried to fix the house up by installing a new kitchen and adding a substantial wing, but in the end, we did little more than putting lipstick on a pig.

Amy and I moved into a new house before Thanksgiving in 1983. It would have been a mistake to continue living in my childhood home and the one that I once shared with Marsi. I purchased Brightside, which belonged to the Lalleys, my parents' friends. It wasn't far away (just a few blocks down the road), but I felt as though I was living in a foreign land. I will say, however, that it was comforting to know that Brightside's baseboards were of an infinitely higher quality.

Before I married Amy, my idea of playing with Ashton was having him crawl towards a stone enemy bunker I had built while I fired live rounds over his head. We went to the ravine on the side of the old house to play war games. I showed him the devastation of the firepower of an Uzi at close range and then celebrated a warrior's rage. We threw dud grenades together as we crawled toward the bunker. We cleaned and field-stripped weapons together—for in those moments, I was in the A Shau again, fighting for my life, teaching my child to survive. That felt necessary.

Amy taught me to go galumphing with my children—*galumphing* being a word from Lewis Carroll's nonsense poem, "The Hunting of the Snark." The woods behind our new house became a magic land where, instead of war games, I tried to convey the beauty of the giraffe while we searched for the snark and avoided the boojum. I bought a bow to show the boys how to shoot, all the while telling stories of Robin Hood. Together, we read *The Hobbit* and *The Lord of the Rings.* We watched old movies like *Treasure Island.* I unleashed my imagination to compensate for the literature they were not reading in school, and while I tried hard, it was tough—very tough—because Amy rightfully insisted the boys become involved in athletics. Consistently, she was the essence of intuitive reasoning. Athletics saved the boys' self-confidence.

In Vietnam, I slept with my M-16. After Marsi died, but before I met Amy, I slept with an Uzi off safety. It was the one thing that would make me feel safe when I was trying to fall asleep. Amy required every gun to be locked away in the closet. Weapons, once my solace, were rightfully denied me. I changed as a result. So did the boys.

One of the most important pastimes in the boys' lives occurred during spring and summer. The boys played little league at the Green Spring Valley Hunt Club. The teams were called the Foxes, the Hounds, and the Horses, and they battled it out for three months every year. Parents were asked to coach or serve as umpires. I could field strip an M-14 in twenty seconds, but I didn't know enough about baseball to be an effective coach. I ended up as an umpire, behind the plate with a black face mask, chest protector, and knee guards.

I will never forget the last day of one of the club's World Series, the Hounds versus the Foxes. Ashton and Adair had shone all season as the stars of the Hounds. Adair was on third base with two outs. At the bottom of the ninth, the Foxes were ahead by one run. The batter hit the ball, a hot-skipping grounder to the shortstop. Adair ran for home. I was sweating, and my glasses were filthy. Adair slid, running into the catcher and me amid a cloud of orange dust. I thought, *Is he safe or out? I can't see!*

The other parents looked at me. They were always so biased towards their children, and I shouted, "You're out!" All hell broke loose. I had ruined my sons' lives, but I had shown them how to be impartial.

I did not understand baseball or sports in general. Athletics, for me at their age, meant learning to kill. My world was incomprehensible to most people I knew. I longed for the certain world of my youth at Shattuck where good was good and evil was evil. It was a world where I was a part of a larger family: the US Army. It was a world where I could bear a sword in mortal combat and know that life belonged only to the victor. I taught my boys how to call things as you saw them, for to not do so was dishonorable. It was what warriors learned.

As a parent whose children were not attending a school surrounded by gray, gothic stone towers, learning about the value systems of the Greeks and the Romans, I could only wish them well and give them an education in how to be gentlemen, not bigoted. The boys' teachers at St Paul preached that "It is easier for a camel to go through an eye of the needle than for a rich man to enter the kingdom of Heaven." This statement references an extremely small gate in Jerusalem, known as the eye of the needle, through which no camel could pass. The school ethos told my children that their parents were rich people who would be denied the kingdom of Heaven. Fortunately, Ashton and Adair learned that these self-serving, self-appointed moralists did not speak the truth, and were trying to force their values and beliefs on my children.

It was difficult to see the children I loved having such a banal educational experience. I realized that the key to life was not what you learn in school. As my godfather Freddy Rowe used to say, "An education is just a key to the world's libraries. You are what you read during your life." So it was my job to help the boys find the key, which they could earn through sacrifice and hard work. They could enjoy their epiphanies when they made the world of literature their own. So be it. Later in life, I was to be rewarded beyond expectations when the boys recognized their education, at least in high school, was lacking. They discovered they must read and work seriously to know that the world had a history—that history was reflected in art, and the key to the future was always resident in the past if you knew where to look.

I did not blame the boys' school. It was no better or worse than most preparatory schools of our time; however, in the pursuit of political correctness, they failed to effectively teach reading, writing, and arithmetic. In their pursuit of political correctness, they actually taught bigotry, for they allowed no other "truth" but their own. There were a few exceptions, like the boys' favorite English teacher, who fueled their imaginations. Otherwise, for the most part, their high school encouraged pursuing grades rather than an education. We became involved in the school community, encouraging the school to change, but there was just too much organizational inertia against us. Amy became a trustee on the board of St. Paul's, and while she monitored the boys' progress, it became a full-time job for her. I cried for the lost cadences of Shakespeare which were such an important part of my childhood.

Whatever happened, the boys were not normal children. They were different from the other children I encountered because they worked together so closely. Tragic events can create strength, or they can be crippling; the challenge is to turn tragedy into the growth of the spirit. In Ashton and Adair's case, this strength first manifested itself in a bond of mutual trust. At no time in their lives has either boy hit the other in anger. When they did get angry, it was because one or the other is endangering himself by doing something foolish. They faced their enemies together back to back, swords outstretched, their minds acting as one. Each one had a unique personality and interests, but they shared an exceptional relationship that helped them face what was ahead. They, too, had had to overcome fearful odds at a young age. The school bubble-wrapped them, but Amy and I did not. We wanted them to be hard men, which is what my grandmother would have wanted. For example, they couldn't ride, so we sent them to camps where they had to ride forty miles a day. We let them overcome adversity by themselves.

At this time, my parents were living in Florida. We visited them for a week over the spring vacation, however, as my father's Parkinson's disease advanced, our contact with my parents decreased. If they did call, it was usually a request to help them visit Johns Hopkins. As my father slipped into the advanced stages of Parkinson's and senile dementia, the family that I knew as a child only existed in my memories, memories that Amy of course did not share. Nor had she even heard me speak about them, since we had only been married a year. For a person who lived in the past, who could remember how cold it was on the day he was confirmed, who was there, and the conversation afterward, it was torture having the past recede. I lived continuously suspended between two lives, between the present and the past, never sure which one, if either, was the true reality.

My sons, both of whom have ADHD and PTSD, are successful VCs with lives that mirror mine. We all work together at Ashton's firm. I see them weekly, talk to them daily, live close to them. Amy has given me the gift of sharing their lives, something that surely would have never happened if I had been left on my own. She also sees that our houses are always filled with beautiful flowers. You cannot be unhappy if you are surrounded by flowers.

Ashton and Adair now have wonderful wives and children that are part of our life. Like General Doriot, they have gardens to give them solace in the never-ending battle that is venture capital. Without Amy, I would have failed the boys and failed to help NEA accomplish its great mission. I describe Amy's role in saving me and my children because she is an important reason NEA is the partnership it is today. I believe that many of my NEA partners would say the same thing about their wives or husbands. The contributions that spouses make to their mates' careers are often the difference between triumph and failure.

IX.

THEY BROKE THE MOLD

"If you want to succeed, you should strike out on new paths rather than travel the worn paths of accepted success."

—John D. Rockefeller

THERE WILL NEVER BE ANOTHER Frank Bonsal. The mold is broken. Being around him was like being in the middle of a tornado. Frank could do six things simultaneously. At work, when he called an English limited partner, he would use a southern drawl that would make his ancestors proud. On the other line, he might have a Boston CEO waiting, and Frank could switch to the Boston entrepreneur using a Brahmin Bostonian accent while he put the other partner on hold. He kept one hundred Rolodexes behind his desk, and he was always thumbing through them to see who he would call next. He read research reports while looking at pictures of horses in equestrian magazines. To add to his list of talents, he was also an Olympic quality steeplechase rider. Frank taught me many things, but most importantly, he showed me how to develop a sense of humor and laugh at my own foibles.

Once, on a flight to Boston for a board meeting, I asked the passengers on the plane how many of them knew Frank Bonsal. Half of them raised their hands. In the early years of NEA, whenever he traveled to a city to raise money or see a company, he'd be sure to go to a phone booth, rip out some of the yellow pages, and search for interesting companies. If he found one, he called the company's CEO and made an appointment. He walked into the company and introduced himself to the CEO. Frank always shook hands confidently, saying, "Hello, boss man. I'm the money man." CEOs loved him. I think he probably knew a little about every entrepreneurial company in the United States.

Frank made an art out of political incorrectness, but he never offended people, and he always made them laugh. He taught me how to pull off being politically incorrect. We are anachronisms, but even today, no one seems offended by our humor. In fact, they seem to like it. We both delighted in the things that made people different. Our jokes always shine a light on someone's talents or qualities. We only tease those for whom we have sincere affection. Most of all, we like to make fun of our own follies and laugh at ourselves.

Frank is a contradiction in that he is messy and yet very organized. His office at NEA usually had five tons of paper in it, and in some instances, the piles stood five feet high. There were always countless investment analysts reports on companies, business magazines, and newspapers—God knows what else. Once, the men who shared his office at Alex Brown threw everything out while he was gone. Frank's heart nearly stopped upon his return. Another time, a reporter who was interviewing Frank was impressed by the disheveled papers in his office and challenged him to identify the content of ten papers randomly pulled out of the stacks. Frank identified every piece. His memory was incredible.

Several companies a day came to visit Frank, and he often asked me to join him. If he got bored, he would excuse himself, leaving me to finish the hour-long meeting with a company we would never invest in, while he ran off to make calls. Eventually, I realized what was going on and pretended to be on a board call whenever he came to my office to pull me into a meeting.

Frank always had a great sense of humor. He raced in the Maryland Hunt Cup, one of America's most difficult point-to-point races. He once lost to a rider from Pennsylvania. That night, he invited the riders from Maryland and the surrounding areas, Virginia, Pennsylvania, Delaware, and Washington, D.C., to a white-tie dinner, and he greeted his guests while lying in a coffin with his face painted white. This unsinkable sense of humor was important to NEA's operation. Whenever we had a crisis,

Frank could always make us laugh, easing the stress of uncertainty. With his unruffled attitude, he effectively relieved the tension so we could make good decisions. One of Frank's greatest contributions to all of us at NEA was that he made business fun. It was an invaluable gift.

Successful partnerships demand fortitude and loyalty. Frank was always there for me in a crisis.

I was a board member of Bethesda Research Laboratories when the CEO, Steve Turner, nearly spent the company into bankruptcy. After the board fired him, they tasked Fred Adler, a new white-knight investor, with saving the company. My job was to get the banks not to force BRL into bankruptcy, which they could easily do if they wanted to. Frank was well known to the bank presidents who loaned the company money. He attended every meeting with me, ensuring that the banks did not foreclose. Gradually, we closed or sold the unprofitable divisions, the banks were paid, and BRL became Life Technologies, which was successful and eventually merged with a larger biotech company.

I will never forget coming back from BRL in a blizzard, driving a Volkswagen station wagon with wipers that did not work. Frank and I took turns driving while the other leaned out of the window to brush the snow off the windshield. It was a miserable two-hour drive home with frostbite gnawing at our fingers.

Perhaps the most endearing characteristic of both Frank and Dick is their loyalty. It is the glue of our relationship. The three of us might argue with passion, but whenever one of us is in trouble, the other two are there to protect him.

When my first wife, Marsi, took her life on March 13, 1982, it was spring vacation, and most of my Baltimore friends were out of town at the time and did not return to attend the funeral. By mid-morning the day following Marsi's death, both Dick and Frank arrived in Baltimore, leaving their families to be with me. Without their support, I would not have made it through my darkest hour.Once, very early in my career, I helped Kirk Miller, the Vice Chairman of T. Rowe Price, with a venture investment. We were both attending a board meeting in Raleigh, North Carolina, and all the investors were there.

Kirk asked me, "What do you think of the company?"

I said, "I think it's hard for a company that copies IBM Terminals to make a long-term go of it," This was an obvious attempt to impress my boss and the other venture capitalists in the room.

Frank blurted out, "Kirk, shut that kid up because he knows nothing." Soon after that board meeting, though, Terminal Communications went bankrupt. Afterward, I started working closely with Frank because we both loved entrepreneurial companies.

Frank's hypomania and hyperactivity worked to balance his depression, a disease that has plagued his family. When Frank was in his manic phase, such as when he greeted everyone coming to his party in a coffin, everyone loved him. But when he was in a depressive stage, he became quite pessimistic. He was still funny, but his sense of humor was gloomy and self-deprecating.

During the energy crisis in the 1970s, we tried to get Bob Levi, a prominent Baltimore investor, to invest in NEA. In 1975, Newsweek published an article titled, "Are Equities Dead?" and Frank's investments in small companies declined precipitously. Frank was markedly depressed when we went into the meeting.

Bob Levi wondered aloud, "What will happen to the price of oil in ten years?"

"It will be twenty times higher," Frank said dolefully.

"What will the American economy look like in ten years?" he asked.

"We will probably be in a bad recession," Frank answered.

Bob asked one last question, "Frank, if you are so pessimistic, why are you getting into the venture capital business?"

And as we left the building, Frank started laughing at himself. "I guess I made a mess of that sales call," he offered, prompting a hard laugh from me. Many investors were equally pessimistic in those dark days. What kept Frank functioning, when all around him seemed lost, was his unfailing belief in entrepreneurs and their capacity for innovation.

Frank's greatest contributions may have been in helping, and truly in some cases creating, the investment careers of many young partners. After NEA invested the first few funds, we gradually expanded the partnership in both the total number of partners and the total assets under management. In the early 1980s, NEA brought in Art Marks, a Harvard Business School classmate of mine who was also friends with Peter Barris, to help us make software investments.

Frank and I made quite a few investments in the software business, including Soft-Switch, Sage Software, and Data Language Corporation, which would later become Progress Software. Frank was the point person and board member on all those investments, while I was the co-sponsor. But Frank and I and the other NEA partners recognized that he and I didn't know a lot about the software business, so Art took over Frank's three board seats. We had made those investments three years before Art joined the partnership, and they worked out very well. Art got the credit for them, but so should have Frank. He had made them. In this way, Frank helped spread the success around NEA by encouraging younger partners. He always directed his best deals to them, and throughout his long career, he probably "gave away" twenty to thirty profitable projects to other partners at NEA, which helped them build the foundations of their careers.

Before leaving the partnership, Frank steered us toward global investing, believing that global venture capital would outperform our US results. Eventually, Dick Kramlich and Scott Sandell led us into China, and Mark Perry led NEA's investments in India. Perhaps they were influenced by Frank's tales of Bill Draper, one of the founders of Sutter Hill. A lot of venture money was being committed to global investing at this time, in the mid-2000s, particularly in China. Ultimately, NEA made a substantial commitment in both China and India. Frank's involvement was really through Bill Draper, who pioneered investing in India, and then Lip-Pu Tan at Walden Venture Capital in China.

Frank didn't just plant a flag in new countries; he also led NEA to invest in new sectors. We had the massive companies, the Intels, the Apples, the Microsofts, which were replaced by the Googles and Facebooks and Twitters. The universe changed. New York City had once been an entrepreneurial wasteland. No one spent time there. The internet changed everything, and New York became a hotbed for internet consumer venture deals. Frank discovered what was happening in New York before everyone else did. He was always everywhere things were happening, constantly chasing innovation.

Frank's most important deal was Vertex, an investment that highlighted his networking abilities. He visited Agouron Pharmaceuticals in San Diego because he was interested in their plans for rational drug design. Much of drug design involves creating medicines from molecules with specific physical shapes and charges that let them bond more effectively with their targets. Rational drug design could predict success and shorten development times. The

CEO of Agouron mentioned during their conversation on this topic a startup that was backed by Kevin Kinsella at Avalon Ventures. Since Kevin and Frank were friends, Frank went to visit Kevin and asked him about how he was investing in rational drug design.

"I can't tell you," Kevin said.

Frank tried another way. "Well, who are you doing it with?" "There's a guy out of a major pharmaceutical company." "Which company?"

"Merck," he replied. "I can't tell you anymore."

Merck was one of NEA's limited partners and we worked with Kirk Maslin there. Frank continued to pursue the mystery deal by calling Kirk. Frank asked Kirk, "I need to know who at Merck is the champion of rational drug design. I need to know his name and I need to know his home number." Kirk told him about Dr. Josh Boger.

Frank, of course, called the doctor, and said, "Dr. Boger, you don't know me, but I am a venture investor, and I understand you're leaving Merck to form a new company focused on rational drug design. I think NEA would like to consider participating."

Boger said, "That's very nice of you. I can tell you I'm working with Greylock and J.H. Whitney."

Frank asked, "Who is working with you at J.H. Whitney?"

"Benno Schmidt."

"Well, I happen to know Benno."

Frank then called Benno and said, "I understand you got a hot deal."

"Oh, I always have a hot deal. You mean Vertex? That is very interesting."

Frank jumped at this. "I want to be in your deal, Benno."

"Well, I'd love to have you come in our deal, but I think it's already fully subscribed," Benno said.

"Well, fine! Get me in the deal," Frank insisted.

Benno said, "Well, Delphi is looking at it now—if they don't pony up in a day or two, I'll call you back."

Benno did indeed call back, and Frank responded by getting a $1 million commitment from Dick and me. Soon, the unrelenting Frank Bonsal joined the board along with Benno at J.H. Whitney. Josh Boger was the CEO, of course, and Vertex was a tremendous success. Frank knew that rational drug design was an interesting scientific advancement because it allowed pharmaceutical companies to shorten the time for drug discovery, therefore reducing development costs significantly. Today, a share of Vertex is worth fifty times our original investment.

NEA always tries to maintain good relations with our competitors because they also become our partners when we invest together, plus they provide us with some of our best deal flow when they bring us their companies. Frank built loyalty with other firms and he has had an enormous effect on the venture capital industry by helping to start firms. One of these was Novak Biddle. Perhaps the best way to understand Frank's impact is through the account of Roger Novak, who said in an interview, "I left Grotech in '93 and was investing on my own account."

In '95, Frank Bonsal, who had founded NEA, called to ask me to lunch. You know that when Frank calls, there's always an ulterior motive. So he said to me, "You know what's happening in Northern Virginia?"

I said, "Yeah . . . "

"If you go back into the business and do an early-stage fund, I'll give you some of my money."

"Will you be my other general partner?"

He said, "No, I don't want to work that hard."

"Whom would you suggest?"

"Jack Biddle."

"I turned Jack Biddle down in '91 for financing, and every time I see him, he tells me I'm the stupidest person he'd ever met because he returned 20 to 1. There's no way I could ever be a partner with someone who thinks I'm that dumb."

But Frank talked about how Jack had put a company together and thought we'd make good partners. So Jack and I did get together and raised our first fund, Novak Biddle Venture Partners. We did very well with that first fund; out of 14 investments, only one did not work. I think we were at the right place and the right time with the right strategy. Frank had great ideas, and he spread the opportunities around.

What is NEA's secret ingredient? We did a lot of things over forty years to enhance our advantages over our competitors. I think what made NEA successful was that from the very beginning, Frank, Dick, and I were loyal to each other, trusted each other, and had a shared sense of mission. I have no doubt that Frank and Dick would do anything for me, just as I would do anything for them. We fought with each other, but we never lost respect for each other's opinions. The shared vision was key. Dick and I wanted to build a partnership that would last a century and that would benefit and change the world. Frank trusted us enough to go along with this madness. We were a band of brothers. Such brotherhoods, functioning as a single, core business team, do not last forever as organizations grow. It is right that things change: what makes small teams successful is not what makes large organizations successful. But these stories occurred during a time when we could run with wings on our feet.

X.

DICK KRAMLICH

"Nil Desperandum" ("Never Say Die")

—Horace

THE ONE THING I WILL always remember about Dick Kramlich is his wonderful smile. My face is stuck in a perpetual frown. I probably haven't smiled more than twelve times in the past thirty years. No matter how dire the future seems, Dick is always smiling. He has, in one hundred bad circumstances, helped me banish pessimism and seize opportunities.

If I ever remarked on this (sometimes offensive) trait, Dick would say, "People think I am a wild-eyed optimist, but I'm not. I just look like one."

There can be no doubt that Dick drove NEA's investment results, with the uncanny ability to see the future and identify exceptional entrepreneurs, some of whom had the most unlikely backgrounds, Dick has led the investments in ten companies that have gone from meager startups to companies valued at over a billion dollars: 3Com, Ascend, Silicon Graphics, Dallas Semiconductor, Immunex, Macromedia, Healthcon Corp., Juniper Networks and Financial Engines and X00M. He also served as the President of NVCA, and in 2001, NVCA honored him with their Lifetime Achievement Award.

I don't know who will die first: Dick, Frank, or me. Although I am the youngest, I think it will almost certainly be me. If it is, and I go to Heaven, I will rush to the bar and save two seats, so I can watch Dick smile and listen to Frank's stories of the deals he missed for the rest of eternity.

Dick was born on April 27, 1935, in Green Bay, Wisconsin. He came from a long line of wheat farmers, but his grandfather, Samuel Edward Kramlich, and the Skaggs brothers co-founded a company that ultimately changed its name to Safeway. They built a chain of 4,000 grocery stores that supplied the western US, completely changing the methods of food distribution. Dick's grandfather moved to Denver and sold his Safeway stock to Charles Merrill of Merrill Lynch, who took the company public in the 1920s. Dick's father graduated from the University of Denver in 1933, then founded Krambo Food Stores in Wisconsin because the state was relatively unaffected by the Depression. He built Krambo into the largest independent food chain in the state. In 1955, he sold Krambo to Kroger, then spent the next two years transitioning it to its new owner, reporting to the chairman. Before Dick's father sold the business, he called Dick and Dick's brother, Doug, to ask them if they wanted the business. Dick declined, saying that he "wanted to do his own thing."

Dick's mother was an incredible woman. She was an aerospace engineer and fiscally conservative, which is to say that she saved while Dick's father spent. One evening in California, Dick invited me to one of his regular family dinners and his mother sat at the head of the table, calling on every member of the family to make a report like a division manager, running the family like a corporation. I followed her example in running my own family. Everyone knows what the others are doing, plus we make many decisions as a group to hold joint accountability.

Although Dick was accepted to Yale, he went to Northwestern because he wanted a perspective that was not from the East Coast. He knew he was going to go to Harvard Business School, but before Harvard, he joined the Air Force. He worked for the Strategic Air Command in the SAC Headquarters carved out of Cheyenne Mountain in Colorado Springs. The day he reported for duty, Russia launched the Sputnik. The country went on red alert.

When Dick's father sold Krambo to Kroger, he met the executive vice president, John Lockhart, who worked closely with Howard Hughes. John was the founding CFO of TWA who helped pioneer

TWA's routes. When John joined Kroger, he helped reinvent the company. As Dick was graduating from Harvard Business School, John called Dick and invited him to visit him in Cincinnati.

Lockhart said that they were going to overhaul Kroger, bottom to top, which would be a huge challenge for such a large company because they had 80,000 employees and had not kept up with the times. John admitted that they had to automate and develop the best computer systems in the industry. He ended with a proposition: "I need a right-hand man, and if you join us, you will have enormous responsibility."

Dick accepted and was involved in everything at the company from accounting to law. In 1963, Kroger reached $2 billion in sales and was one of the first companies to have its own computer system. Dick was one of four people that could talk to Wall Street at the age of 26.

John was not surprised when Dick left to join Preston Moss & Company, a Boston family investment firm. He wanted to learn about venture capital. He had two friends in the business: Peter Crisp at Venrock and John Shane at American Research and Development (ARD). They were investing in small companies with big missions. It sounded fascinating.

Preston Moss was run by Jeremy Preston and Jim Moss. They had six other partners with an average age of sixty-eight. There were two types of Boston patriarchs, the kind that had a twinkle in his eye and the kind that didn't, and all the Preston Moss guys were the former. They were kind to Dick and taught him how to be a good investor.

Dick's job was to manage money and check out small companies. It was the age of Highway 128, Digital Equipment Corp., and General George Doriot's ARD, a venture capital firm that funded innovative tech companies. Dick thrived on stress. He believed that "without stress, you regress."

Eventually, Preston Moss merged with the Gardner office. George and Jack Gardner of the Gardner Museum family ran it. They were very good men, but venture capital was not the focus of the firm.

Dick read an article titled "The Money Men." Arthur Rock, from David & Rock, was listed as the number one money man in the late '60s. From 1961 to 1968, they turned $4 million into $80 million by helping to start Scientific Data Systems (which pioneered the mini-computer) and Teledyne, one of the first great conglomerates. In the article, Arthur mentioned that he needed a new partner, so Dick wrote a one-page letter, and within a few days, Arthur called him to set up a meeting in Boston. After that, for the next year, they spoke often and made a couple of investments together.

Dick had spent the last few years studying for, and passing, several certified financial analyst tests, though he canceled his final test to meet Arthur in New York, where Arthur asked him to be his partner. Dick found a replacement to take his place at Gardner, Preston & Moss and moved to San Francisco with his wife Lynne. At that time, Arthur was one of the most famous venture capitalists in the world, and he later appeared on the cover of *Time* Magazine. Arthur ran the show.

Dick helped Tom Perkins, one of the VCs mentored by General Doriot and co-founder of Kleiner Perkins, to raise money for his first fund in the mid-'70s in an unofficial capacity. By 1977, Dick and Arthur were burning out. It was a terrible time with double-digit inflation and high interest rates. In 1975, public offerings for venture-backed companies had dwindled to $16 million. Dick had become good friends with Cub Harvey of T. Rowe Price while collaborating on several investments, so I was elated when Cub introduced me to Dick, who already knew Frank Bonsal. Soon after, Frank and I approached Dick about being our third partner. We'd been courting Jim Morgan from ARD in Boston until he backed out at the last moment. While Frank and I had raised $6 million for our fund, we needed a proven venture capitalist as our third partner. Frank and I flew to California in December 1977, where we shook hands with Dick, our new partner.

Right after Christmas, though, Tom Perkins also asked Dick to be his third partner. Dick replied, "If you had asked me at Thanksgiving, I might have said yes, but I just committed to Frank and Chuck from Baltimore, and I never break my word."

Tom reminded him that Frank and I lacked real venture experience, plus we lived on the East Coast. "Dick, it will never fly," he said.

"You are probably right," said Dick, "but I have given my word."

In June of 1978, NEA closed on $16.5 million and began investment operations. Frank and I flew World Airways, the low-cost, no-frills airline to San Francisco, to see Dick and get started. When we arrived, we stayed at a boarding house in Pacific Heights called Hotel Drisco. It was a charming turn-of-the-century building. The white paint on the woodwork was peeling off. The walls were beige with a pinkish hue. The dining area was staffed by a group of gay waiters who moonlighted as stand-up comics. The surroundings were barebones, but the humor was irreplaceable.

Dick met us at the airport. On the drive from the airport to his house, Frank suggested we stop by and have a beer to celebrate the closing of our partnership. Dick knew of a new bar that had been completely renovated by a wealthy investor. When we entered, we saw the bar was hand-carved satinwood with matching toadstools for seats. It was spectacular and decorated with taste. Dick and I sat down at the booth and started telling humorous stories from our fundraising. Frank got the beers, then returned to the bar to talk to two striking girls perched on the toadstools.

About fifteen minutes passed, and Frank abruptly left the bar. His face was ghost white. He was shocked because he had just been wantonly groped. We paid our bills and left our beers unfinished. How were we going to run a venture capital firm when we did not even have the pattern recognition skills to find a gay bar?"

We went back to Dick's car, only to find his keys on the floor by the driver's seat, locked inside. Embarrassed, Dick had to call his wife Lynne to pick us up. Lynne was giggling when we opened the doors. In her pleasant Texas accent, she crowed, "Don't you boys know this bar is the hottest pick-up place in the whole city?" Then, throughout dinner, Lynne gleefully reminded us of our foolishness.

After our celebration, Frank and I visited the Western Electronic Manufacturers Association's meeting in Carmel to see West Coast companies. When I arrived, I realized that Dick or Frank registered me as a junior analyst, rather than a general partner, thus beginning a humorous dialogue that lasted for years.

During the period when we traveled around raising money, Dick, Frank, and I discussed our goals for the business. Dick usually led the discussion because he had the greatest VC experience. We decided we weren't just in the business of making money. It wasn't that money was bad, for it represented the freedom to express our values. We saw money as an important byproduct, but building real companies was the true mission. Excellence was the only standard we would accept. Also, we were not driving ourselves to defeat our competitors as much as we wanted to produce excellent results. That would make us the best. We were, in other words, in competition with ourselves.

As a venture capitalist, you always looked for the best and the worst in entrepreneurs since it was your job to guide the company towards success. As a VC, you were a change agent, and that could ruffle feathers. Analysis, therefore, had limited value. You continually exposed yourself to danger. You made mistakes and learned painful lessons, but this was how you developed intuition. How did a soldier survive a war? He sensed danger and responded appropriately. When the venture capitalist felt anxious, it was a warning. You lived your life on the edge. You were paid to lead, to check around the corner, to put yourself at risk, but if you were not at the corner, you could not hope to see around it. The business was not for all people.

For me, Dick was not only a partner; he was my mentor. I knew most of the players in the venture capital business and invested in some public companies (that should have never gone public), but I had no experience being on a company's board. Dick went on the board of Chomerics, one of our first investments, and so did I. It was the wildest ride of my life. When I finally stepped down from that board, I felt like I had earned a Ph.D. in being a venture capitalist board member.

Dick introduced NEA to Chomerics, a maker of conductive composites, glues, and seals capable of shielding electromagnetic interference and conducting electricity. Though the company had military customers, its CEO, Bob Jasse, wanted to enter the industrial and consumer markets. Its products went on to be used in everything from circuit boards in children's toys to the first commercial personal computer keyboard to iPhones.

Bob Jasse was a Messianic leader. In his youth, he was a juvenile delinquent, arrested for stealing from Filene's Basement in an inventive burglary. First, he had trapped squirrels in the Boston Commons. Then he had brought them into Filene's Basement in a suitcase and released them on top of the checkout counter. During the ensuing panic, Bob had packed his suitcase with merchandise. He had almost made it out the front door when a guard had apprehended him. He was taken before a judge who said, "You have a choice to make. Jail or Navy." Bob enlisted for four years, and the Navy transformed his life.

Jasse's mood swings were caused by his manic depression, and even when he was joking, his terrible temper was always just under the surface. He was a generous employer who funded endowments and gave special credit to the managers or scientists who made outstanding contributions to the company by naming buildings after them. But if you made him mad, he would become enraged. When we went on a walk through his manufacturing line, Bob spotted an employee incorrectly feeding an elastomeric sheet into an automated machine designed to minimize the loss of the valuable material. Bob screamed at him, brutally pushed him aside, then ran the sheet through the machine by himself. For twenty minutes, he watched the employee, correcting him incessantly as he fed the sheets himself. Bob's smile could make you smile, but when he turned angry, his face became reddish-black.

Around Dick, though, Bob could only be happy. Dick was Bob's antidepressant.

Dick had worked with the company since its inception, but Chomerics was on the East Coast, like me, and I had some familiarity with specialty chemical and materials businesses. We both went on the board, and Bob put me to work on company strategy. The company went public, and it enjoyed great success.

Every autumn, Chomerics had a pig roast. The great pig was soaked in marinade and spices, wrapped in heavy-duty aluminum, and lowered into the pit of hickory coals. It took four or five people to perform this choreographed action. Since the apples from Bob's famous orchard were harvested in September, they stood out, bright red, against the leaves yellowing with autumn's approach. The air was crisp, with no humidity. It was a beautiful thing to be alive and here at this place.

The whole company would arrive on the day the pig was unveiled. The employees seemed to worship Bob as he mesmerized them with stories of the company's recent successes, always personally thanking those who made the greatest positive contributions. As he clapped employees on the shoulder, you could see them light up with pride.

One of the perks being of being on Bob's board was that when he took great vacations, he took his friends along, although the only topic of conversation allowed was Chomerics. He was an avid hunter, so we went to the Orvis Shooting School together. We flew to Mexico to shoot doves and ducks by the Sea of Cortez. We drank tequila, told stories by the firelight, shot bats at dusk, and as night fell, we listened to the coyotes howling.

The following year, we went to the Yucatan and Columbia. My Vietnam rifle training with an M-16 came in handy with bird shooting. You move your weapon at the same speed as the target, swing through, shoot instinctively. Bob Jasse, along with Bill Robinson, the CEO of the John Harland Company, nurtured my love of bird shooting. It gave me the same excitement as a jungle firefight.

Dick played the nice guy on the board, but he supported me when I criticized Bob's often grandiose visions. Without someone else to check his impulses, Bob could have destroyed the success he worked so hard to create. I was thrown off the board—three times. I returned for a fourth, but when I was sent away again, it was the last time. Earnings growth stopped because the company overextended itself, and the stock price declined precipitously. Dick talked Bob into bringing a new CEO, Art Carr, and Art turned the company around. In the early '80s, the Grace Corporation acquired Chomerics at an all-time high value, after the company got its game back on track.

Marsi was not sympathetic when I was going through this cycle of being kicked off and welcomed back to the Chomerics board. She must have thought, *Who in their right mind would be a whipping post for a madman?* She resented that I would allow someone like Jasse to degrade me in such a way. I tolerated Jasse's treatment, however, because I knew that by speaking the hard truths, I had a direct impact on Chomeric's success. Today, when I use a phone or an iPad, I remember that what I did for the company helped make the touchscreen ubiquitous. Also, Chomerics taught me how to overcome adversity in a corporate setting. As I have mentioned before, Dick's motto was "Never say die," or "Nil desperandum," if you prefer the original Latin.

One day, Dick called us from San Francisco to tell us he'd found the next new thing. We immediately flew to California to visit a company called 3Com. 3Com was built on technology developed by the genius Bob Metcalfe at Xerox's Palo Alto Research Center. He had left Xerox with his patents to start it. It would eventually be everything we could have hoped it would be: the future of communications, creating the technology that allowed office computers to seamlessly communicate with each other in a network. It would be the grandfather of the internet.

However, when we first saw the company that day, we questioned Dick's sanity. Bob, the CEO, was a visionary innovator with incredible passion, but he was not built to be a CEO. His head of marketing and business partner seemed more interested in which debutante parties Frank or I attended growing up than in describing 3Com's business strategy. Still, as was customary within our partnership, when any partner believed in something, we allowed him to proceed. We are so glad we did.

The company was at the right spot at the right time. At first, we all wondered, *Who can help make it real?* Shortly after that, Dick thought of Bill Krause and recruited him to join as CEO. When 3Com started, Ethernet was not a protocol. There was baseband, broadband, and token ring. Over time, Ethernet became the standard, and eventually, billions of people all over the world would use it. Frank and I saw that we had underestimated 3Com as its sales started ramping up. Profitability was coming.

When Krause presented to us, we saw that the sales prospects were incredible. The market was immense. We were shareholders of a company that would change the world while eroding the Bell monopoly. The depreciable life of communications equipment would soon fall from forty to two years. Over the next decades, a host of technologies would follow the Ethernet rapidly, such as fax, mobile communications, and high-speed digital switching. With 3Com, we took the first step in making the world a global village. Another NEA company, UUNET, would later use this technology to help create the internet, and one day, San Francisco's famous Palisades Park would be renamed 3Com Park. In a significant way, Dick was responsible for 3Com's success.

Not all challenges to a venture capital firm are attributable to the business. Some are deeply personal. Dick called me in the spring of 1981 after he joined a 3Com board meeting via telephone. He was crying. About six months earlier, Dick's wife Lynne had gone into the hospital for a fairly routine heart-valve replacement, but during the procedure, Lynne went into a coma and never recovered. Dick had stayed by her side whenever he could get away. Now he was calling me from her bedside after he'd finished his 3Com board meeting. The doctors offered no hope, so I told him I thought after this vigil of many months, it was time to turn off the life support. Dick instructed the doctor to do so, and we listened together in silence as it was turned off. We were both crying as Dick watched over her.

At Lynne's funeral, which Marsi attended with me, Dick gave me his "Jonathan Livingston Seagull" tie that he wore to the funeral. One year later, I wore that same tie to Marsi's funeral after her suicide.

Both Dick and I buried ourselves in work to avoid the pain. Fortunately, Neil Bond, an investment committee member representing T. Rowe Price, resigned from T. Rowe and joined NEA as a general partner, moving to San Francisco. Neil helped Dick cope with a tidal wave of work while he was grieving for Lynne. Neil truly helped save NEA.

Late in 1981, Dick married Pam Buffet, a smart and elegant woman. She was an entrepreneur with a business designing and selling seed pearl jewelry. Dick and Pam put the Kramlich family back together. Before she died, Lynne had begun a pioneering collection of the "Society of Six," a group of California impressionist painters, and published a book about the artists with Su Wa Newton, the granddaughter of the Dragon Lady, the Last Empress of China.

Dick and Pam took Lynne's artistic mission one step further. They began what is now one of the most significant collections of video and media art, the Kramlich Collection, today housed in Napa. Collecting video art is a mutually shared passion, and fitting for them as a couple, since video art as a genre is truly at the intersection of technology and art. Pam and Dick have formed the New Art Trust to leave their collection to the San Francisco MOMA, the Tate Modern, and MOMA in New York.

Dick's two greatest investments were Juniper Networks and Ascend Communications. Ascend was a great case study because it had such a unique team, and Dick believed in them. Rob Ryan, the CEO, was a visionary, and he and the team were developing a modem-type product line for the cable television market. Two partners from Greylock, Roger Evans and David Strom, were also on the board. Tom McKinley, from ParTech Ventures, had introduced NEA to the project, and Dick thought it looked like a good idea, plus he liked that a proven manager, Mory Ejabat, was the head of operations.

NEA contributed to Ascend's second-round financing in 1991. Dick attended his first board meeting to learn that the product wasn't working, it wasn't selling, and there wasn't a market for it, but we still invested our money. Rob was a very smart, interesting guy, and Dick liked him a lot. Rob didn't look at people when he spoke to them; he looked sideways.

There had been some turnover within the company, so the VCs on the board rearranged the deck chairs, as it were. One day, Rob said to Dick, "You know, it looks like this original product is not really working. We've been working on another product, sort of a skunkworks-type thing . . . we're calling it the 'dynamic bandwidth allocation product.' It serves packet-based systems. We think it is a very, very strong product for the telecom infrastructure that's being encouraged by ARPANET." By ARPANET, Ryan meant the Advanced Research Projects Agency Network, which was the first wide-area packet-switching network incorporating distributed control.

Dick took all the analysis they had, threw it over his shoulder, and said, "That's what I love about startups!" In other words, it's impossible to predict what you'll end up with. Ascend moved forward to build a very good product, and in 1993, Dick decided to help them hire a strong CFO.

The board searched all over Silicon Valley. Dick found Bob Dahl, who had come from Rolm with excellent experience and a great reputation. Bob was conservative, putting everything transparently on the books, and he kept things on the straight and narrow. Mory Ejabat, the head of operations, had also been handling finances up until Bob's hire.

When Bob came in, Dick was interested to see what kind of write-offs we were going to have because we'd been operating on such an amateur level until that point. Surprisingly, there was not one change related to the finances. Dick said to himself, "Mory really knows finance." He had underestimated Mory.

Ascend was on the verge of going public, and Dick and the board needed to hire a new CEO. The company held a long board meeting via telephone. It was decided to ask Rob to take the position as chairman while elevating Mory to CEO. Dick drove this decision because he thought Mory was better suited for the job, and Rob was scheduled for back surgery immediately after the IPO. Ascend couldn't have its CEO out of commission for months right after going public, so it was left to Dick to break the news to Rob.

Dick went across the street to find Rob, who was in the middle of a discussion with the bankers, lawyers, and accountants. Dick said, "Rob, look, I have to be straightforward with you. The board has just had a meeting, and we've decided that as of now, you're going to be chairman. Mory will be our CEO. It doesn't mean we don't respect you or what you've done because we do. But you're going to have back surgery, and we don't think it's a good idea to have the CEO out of commission for as long as your recovery."

Rob looked at Dick and said, "Why is it, Dick, that on what should be one of the greatest days of my life, I feel as though I've just been kicked in the teeth?"

"You're absolutely right. You have been kicked in the teeth, but you'd better learn to handle it because it's going to happen."

Rob understood, saying, "I'm alright with it."

So Ascend made the changes and moved on. NEA held onto the stock for quite a while when the market was booming. NEA distributed it in 1997. Ultimately, the company was acquired by Lucent for $24 billion.

The story of Juniper is simple and not dramatic but stands as the single best investment in NEA's history. NEA VI fund invested $2.915 million in Juniper in August of 1995, near the startup stage, and distributed $1.534 billion in early 2000 for a return of 526 times the cost. Juniper's stock continued to appreciate after the distribution. Dick joined the board and helped to select the CEO while also engaging in strategy, company building, and governance. Juniper had the best software and networking capability in the communications industry.

Contemplating these successes again, I asked myself, "Why is NEA successful?" And I'm reminded of Dick saying that he believes Harvard Business School teaches "take the hill," which means "take it by yourself." NEA was the opposite. For a time, we were a band of brothers. Dick described it thus:

"A partnership is a great vehicle for accomplishment because you can listen to viewpoints of others. You're not limited by your personal boundaries. One of the purposes of a partner is to save another partner from himself. We really believe in that. That's why the original philosophy of NEA was shared goals, shared values, and shared rewards. That was the whole idea, but it is challenging to make anything last forever."

Dick's partner at NEA in creating the firm's telecom strategy was Peter Morris. Peter was the most remarkable partner in NEA's history. He made me look sane, and that was almost impossible to do. He spoke faster than an M-60 submachine gun, which, if I remember correctly, is 650 rounds per minute. You'd think he was spouting total drivel; except everything he said turned out to be true. After one annual meeting, when I was totally exhausted and could hardly stand or keep my eyes open, Peter cornered me and delivered a sermon that felt like it was longer than the New and Old Testaments combined. He told me how NEA's ownership of his companies could be worth $2 billion in the next twelve months. He predicted that four companies would be sold or go public. "You awake?" he asked. I mumbled in response.

Everything Peter said came to fruition. Dick and I nominated him to be a general partner, and we backed him despite the objections of another general partner who wanted to fire him. Peter often seemed to be calm, but underneath that stillness was a furious volcano, just waiting to erupt. He was a fierce competitor. If he had been in the Army, I would have called him a "berserker." That was what my men had nicknamed me.

One of Peter's most successful companies was Tele Atlas, which pioneered global positioning systems and is currently owned by TomTom. While the company's operations were headquartered in Moutstraat Gent, Belgium, it also had offices in New Hampshire and Massachusetts. Founded in 1984, by 2005 Tele Atlas was operating in thirty countries with 2,300 employees and revenue of $2.39 billion. I have no sense of direction (I get lost going to my bathroom), so every time I arrive at my intended destination, I kiss the ground and thank Peter Morris. He was among our best investors, a hell of a lot of fun to be with, and one of the few partners who laughed at my insanity.

Dick Kramlich's contribution to NEA, to my life, and to the careers of others has been underscored by his positivity. While his natural prowess and acumen drove his success in venture capital, it was his daring spirit that broke down the doors that others couldn't see. He saw—and still sees—around corners. Or perhaps, through them. As a venture capitalist, he showed his talent for spotting talent and his kindness, even in the bleak face of loss. I am who I am because of Dick and Frank and the business we built together.

XI

TRIUMPH

*"Success is a lousy teacher. It seduces smart people
into believing they can't lose."*

—Bill Gates

IT WAS THE IDES OF March 1996, fourteen years after my first
wife, Marsi, had shot herself in the woods behind our home. Thirty
years had passed since I had held Tiny Stanchfield's head in my arms
as his brains seeped from a bullet wound in the A Shau Valley in
Vietnam. I will always fear head wounds. Often, I feel like a sniper is
stalking me, preparing to kill me with a shot to the brain, because I
know what it is to be stalked by a sniper. Officers were always singled
out, and I thank God I was spared in Vietnam, although some bullets
whispered when they went by my head. The distance traveled from
Vietnam had been immense when I returned home and I was spat
upon by a bartender in the San Francisco Airport. That's what I was
thinking when I found out that I was to be honored by the Greater
Baltimore Technology Council. It was my triumph.

This award was the culmination of a journey launched in March of
1977, when we started raising money for NEA. At that time, I swore to
recreate a Baltimore at its apex, which was the period shortly after the
Revolutionary War, and the War of 1812. Baltimore then was a city on
a hill, a home for inventors, war heroes, entrepreneurs, art collectors,

artists, and authors. Baltimore was the city that repelled the British Army and Navy, captured a virtual monopoly in China trade, built the first American Railroad, created the American investment banking industry, and is home to many other innovations. That Baltimore, designed by Benjamin Latrobe to resemble Augustus Caesar's Rome, helped establish the United States in the form of the Roman Republic.

I co-founded the Mid-Atlantic Venture Capital Association, or MAVA, in 1985, with Frank Adams of Grotech. We were both determined to transform the Baltimore-Washington corridor into an entrepreneurial center, bringing the region's venture capital firms together. Between 1977 and 1990, the Mid-Atlantic had moved from capturing half a percent of the money invested in venture capital in the United States to getting 20 percent of it. Similar organizations played a significant role in starting the entrepreneurial ecosystems around Boston and San Francisco. In fourteen short years, the number of venture partnerships in the mid-Atlantic region had grown from four to one hundred and fifty.

The mid-Atlantic, when I stepped down from the Chairman's role at MAVA, had the fourth-largest concentration of venture capital in the United States, and the number of entrepreneurial companies in our region, stretching from Philadelphia to Northern Virginia, was second only to San Francisco. We had been successful beyond our wildest dreams. Our region indeed crossed several state boundaries, but measured in square miles, it was similar to the entrepreneurial corridors surrounding Boston and San Francisco. Elevating my city and this region is what I had hoped to do for the city that sheltered me. Baltimore was the only permanent home I had ever known, my only security as a young man, blown about like a leaf in an indifferent breeze.

By the 1990s, NEA alone had started thirty to forty companies in the mid-Atlantic and I was proud of them. They included Life Technologies (soon to be Invitron, that facilitated the biotechnology revolution), Integrated Health Service (creator of sub-acute care), UUNet (creator of the internet), and many others. These companies had billions of dollars in revenues and employed hundreds of thousands of people across the United States. In honoring me, the Greater Baltimore Technology Council chose to recognize my contribution to our region, my home, and my adopted ancestral land.

Amy and I walked up the stairs on a red carpet into the convention center where we felt like movie stars nominated for Academy Awards. Amy turned to me and whispered, "I don't like this. This is too good to last. It is a brief moment in time. Where do you think we will be five years from now? I doubt if we will be on a red carpet."

I, too, felt the chill of the ides of March and the haunting smell of the A Shau Valley. The whole evening was exciting, but to me, it was unreal, and I was ill at ease because I didn't enjoy being the center of attention. There were five hundred people at the award ceremony, including all my East Coast partners, along with most of NEA's CEOs in the region. Amy and I were seated with friends at the front table, close to the speaker's podium. We were on display.

Dick and Pam Kramlich had flown in from California. Frank was traveling and couldn't make it. Senator Barbara Mikulski was at our table, one of the country's leading Democrats, and although I am a Republican, I always voted for her. She was also one of the great supporters of Dr. Bernadine Healy, the new head of the National Institute of Health, and an acquaintance of Amy's. To me, Bernadine was a leader who had fought to allow NIH researchers to be able to work with private companies and develop proprietary products with strong patent positions under her CREDA program. Senator Mikulski helped make the Baltimore-Washington corridor a biotech hotbed.

This had led to a flurry of entrepreneurial activity north of NIH in Gaithersburg. First, Life Technologies commercialized the restrictive and modified enzymes to allow scientists to manipulate DNA. Human Genome Sciences used the science of genomics to develop compounds rapidly and, hopefully, shorten the pharmaceutical development cycle. MedImmune developed a pipeline of products that protected infants' immune systems during the first two years of life. Celara was sequencing the whole human genome, allowing pharmaceutical companies to unlock its secrets. Together, these companies combined represented $20-$30 billion of market value and were making a critical impact on medical science. In a limited way, by working with Genetic Therapy and Life Technologies, I had been a part of this revolution.

Bernadine Healey (director of the NIH) was trying to patent the human genome for the United States. She had discovered that 90 percent of NIH's research budget was spent on diseases afflicting men and was steering it to devote an equal amount of effort to women. Her passion for commercializing medical research promoted innovation, which drove the entire industry forward.

Also sitting at our table was Dr. Bill Brody, a California entrepreneur, who had recently been made president of Johns Hopkins University, a position in which he served for twelve years. He had worked with NEA for twenty years, and he would introduce me at the podium. One of his jobs was to change the university's attitude toward the commercialization of research. Guilford, Sol Snyder's small pharmaceutical company, was then the only commercialization of Hopkins science. Hopkins had only $100,000 of royalty income while Harvard and Stanford received hundreds of millions of dollars from royalties. This amount, however, was dwarfed by the gifts from entrepreneurs who were former students. Think of how much more research Hopkins could do with such funding and think of the impact of rapid commercialization would have on saving lives and the treatment of patients.

Bob and Shirlene Elkins were also at our table. Bob was the CEO/founder of Integrated Health, the provider of sub-acute hospital care in a nursing home setting whom I described earlier. NEA had helped start the company in 1984, and now it had $5 billion in revenues. During my time at NEA up to this point, I'd helped found four healthcare services companies that collectively had over $30 billion in revenue. I was a master of the healthcare services universe.

Like many VCs, I've tended to fall in love with my companies. When they prospered, I prospered. By prospering, I do not mean that the company went public and I made a fortune as a result of speculative excess; I mean that over a long duration of time, a company would develop good products, satisfy its customers, defeat its competitors, and generate exceptional returns for its shareholders. We built our companies to last. Unfortunately, when one of my companies failed, it was heartbreaking. I felt it intensely, as though I was a failure as well.

Amy and I left the Civic Center, after thanking all our friends who attended the awards ceremony on our behalf. Strangely, I felt no personal satisfaction that evening. As Dick always says, "The only thing that counts is the next time at bat." *After all these years, the next decade should be my best,* I thought, *unless they change the rules of the game.*

The night was chilly, just as I remembered on the A Shau Valley ridgeline. I thought, *Isn't it amazing that, in a few months, it will be the thirtieth anniversary of the A Shau.* I could still smell that valley after almost thirty years. It was the smell of blood, urine, and death, carried on the wind.

Beware the Ides of March.

**Three founders: Chuck, Dick, and Frank
(June 1978)**

Essentially, NEA is an organ grinder and his two monkeys. Dick Kramlich is the organ grinder, an experienced venture capitalist and the former partner of Arthur Rock. Frank Bonsal is a monkey, a shell-shocked investment banker who watched his clients' small company portfolios collapse after the energy crisis. I am a monkey, an analyst for T. Rowe Price and portfolio manager of a tiny part of the New Horizons Fund that is dedicated to investing in venture-backed companies.

Dick Kramlich on G. Hegg's 3M Fishing Trip (early 1990s)

Within our partnership, Dick is known as "nil desperandum" or "Never say die." Look at the typical Kramlich smile. There can be no doubt that Dick drove NEA's investment results, with his uncanny ability to see the future and identify exceptional entrepreneurs, some of whom had unlikely backgrounds.

Frank Bonsal (late 1980s)

There are forty Rolodexes on the bookcase behind him.
Frank contradicts himself in that he is messy and yet he knows where
everything is. His office usually had five tons of paper
in it, and in some instances, the piles stood five feet high.
When he visited a new company, he'd say to the entrepreneur,
"Hello, boss man. I am the money man."

Charles W. Newhall, Jr. at Reaction Motors (1949)

The Vanguard rocket (the first rocket in space manned by a monkey) and the engine of the Bell X-1 (the first piloted plane to break the sound barrier), are shown in the background.

**Meteor refueling on the run.
Flight Refueling Ltd., England (1950s)**

While I was stranded in the A Shau Valley during the Vietnam War in 1968, this in-flight refueling technology saved my life by keeping fighter planes in the air that gave fire support to ground troops. In the A Shau, we were out of artillery range. This example of the importance of technological innovation and its ability to change the world is one thing that convinced me to become a venture capitalist.

Reaction Motors rocket (1950s)

The scene depicts a Vanguard rocket launch, like the one I watched as a child. Laurance Rockefeller hired my father to help him create what is now the aerospace industry.

**Chuck Newhall (far right) with the Terminal
Communications Board of Directors (1974)**

It was my first venture deal at T. Rowe Price. Kirk Miller, the chairman
of T. Rowe Price at the time, asked me, "What do you think of the
company?" I replied, "I think it's hard for a company that copies IBM
terminals to make a long-term go of it," I replied, in an obvious attempt
to impress my boss and the other venture capitalists in the room.
My future NEA partner, Frank Bonsal, then an Alex Brown partner,
blurted out, "Kirk, shut that kid up because he knows nothing." Soon
after that board meeting, Terminal Communications went bankrupt.

**General Doriot, the Father of
Institutional Venture Capital (1960s)**

"So we search for the exceptional man or woman, the entrepreneur.
We become a partner in creating a dream. It is not a dream of just
making money or creating capital gains. It is a dream of creating a
company, a real business that changes our world."

Laurance Rockefeller (1970s)

"I worked with a small group of men like your father. We created companies that changed the world."

To meet Laurance Rockefeller, my parents dressed me in a black suit that fit like a burlap bag with a Countess Mara tie of my father's. The tie was a colorful display of Zeus' lightning bolts, five inches wide. (My chest was only twenty inches wide.) My hair was greased. I looked like a waiter at Al Capone's birthday party. In the photograph of that evening, more than fifty years ago, I see a child rigged out as a cross between a grease monkey and the maître d' of a third-rate Italian restaurant.

Dick Testa (1990)

Our lawyer, Dick, and his partner, Dan Finkelman, were instrumental in helping to create NEA. Dick, also General Doriot's lawyer, once delivered a letter to me from the general, which read, "Best wishes, Chuck. I admire your determination. I welcome you to the band of brothers who seek to build companies that change our destinies. By the way, I am giving you the name 'New Enterprise Associates.' It is the first name I selected for American Research and Development. In retrospect, it is a better name for what we do."

TESTA, HURWITZ & THIBEAULT, LLP OBITUARY FOR

Richard J. Testa
1939–2002

We mourn the untimely loss of Richard J. Testa, Chairman and Co-founder of Testa, Hurwitz & Thibeault. Dick Testa was a lawyer of few words and great vision, who altered and deeply affected the business and personal lives of many people in the private equity and high-technology industries.

In 1973, when Dick started this law firm, he stood at the beginning of the high-technology and venture capital revolution and never blinked. Dick's mentor was General Georges Doriot, widely credited with starting the venture capital industry through his founding of American Research and Development (ARD). Working with ARD, Dick provided creative legal guidance for the funding and launching of many private and public high-technology companies. Over the ensuing years, Dick worked with venture capitalists and entrepreneurs who laid the foundation for many of the venture-funded technology industries that have shaped the modern national economy.

Notwithstanding Dick's well-deserved status as a true pioneer in the venture capital and technology communities, he was fundamentally a quiet and self-effacing person. Dick made every effort to avoid the limelight. For Dick, the accolades were never about himself but instead were always about the client or other lawyers who put in the hard work and produced positive results for the clients. Nothing pleased him more than to receive embarrassingly glowing kudos from clients extolling the wonderful job others at the firm had done for them.

Nancy Dorman

At NEA, Nancy immediately took charge, and within a very short time, she built and managed the best administrative and limited partnership relationship team in the industry. Her contribution to NEA's success was invaluable.

Barbara Dreyer

Barbara started with NEA as CFO but left to pursue an entrepreneurial career. She took with her NEA values, which she said had deeply influenced her life. She epitomized the best of those values. When she sold that Connections Academy for $500M+, her board granted management a large option package. The board wanted her to take 75 percent of the options and give 25 percent to the management team. Instead, she gave 75 percent to her management team and kept 25 percent for herself.

Amy, Ashton, Adair, and Chuck with Ming & Pippin (1983)

Amy & Chuck just married. Our family being rebuilt. It was a process that took thirty years and, with grandchildren, continues to this day.

Ashton (1984)

My oldest son, Ashton, accepts and adopts Amy as his new mother.

My Toast at NEA's First Investment Committee Meeting—June 1978

One of the traditions at NEA is that we are all toastmasters. Every investing partner is expected to make clever and interesting toasts at partner planning meetings, annual meetings, and investment committee meetings. It is a rite of passage that all partners become good public speakers. Following is the toast I gave at the first investment committee meeting to our limited partners in June 1978:

Tonight, we the general partners, have had the opportunity to have had a few laughs and express our thanks to all of you who will be helping us start New Enterprise Associates. But now is the time to stop and consider that together we are about to embark on a very serious endeavor. It is a time when there is a critical shortage of risk capital in the US. The few men who have the dreams and convictions to build the companies that play so great a part in changing our lives today have great difficulty in finding capital to grow and expand.

Indeed, the system of free enterprise in this country is on trial.

In the past, these periods of trial have been times of opportunity for those with the foresight and conviction to risk capital. Gulf Oil, Alcoa, McDonnell Aircraft, Eastern Airlines, Polaroid, and Digital Equipment are all companies that have been financed by venture capitalists, spawned in times of adversity. Over the next decade, we will make NEA a leader in the difficult but rewarding field of venture capital. We will help to build real companies and, in doing so, handsomely reward our investors. We will create wealth and leave our impact on this country.

What we have undertaken is not easy. All of us know the risks and obstacles to be overcome. The long hours, the travel, the emotional strains of this business are rigorous and break men and women. Yet, this is a business that all of us love so much we could be content with nothing less. We say to you that we take seriously the trust you are placing in our hands. We look forward to working together. Let us all drink a toast to our joint future—the future of New Enterprise Associates.

NEA partners (1980s)

From left to right: John Glenn (a special part-time partner), Ray Bank, Tom McConnell, Dick Kramlich, Woody Rae, Frank Bonsal, Neil Bond, Howie Wolfe, Art Marks, Vin Prothro, Cub Harvey, and Chuck Newhall

Early 1990s

Peter Morris, right, one of NEA's best investors, discusses the future of global positioning systems (GPS) with Alain De Taeye, the CEO of Tele Atlas. Every time a GPS in my car gets me to my desired location, I thank Peter.

HealthSouth's Board of Directors (1991)

Clockwise from top left: Chuck Newhall; Dr. Allan Goldstein; Dr. Phillip Watkins; George Strong; former Ohio governor, Richard F. Celeste; Richard Scrushy, Sage Givens.

HealthSouth's Richard Scrushy drew this cartoon once at a staff meeting, and its iconography depicted the company's culture, with several stick-figure workers pulling a wagon together. Some stand in front, some push from behind, others stand to the side, and some are riding in the wagon. The message is simple: "Pulling the wagon requires teamwork. Everybody has a responsibility." The cartoon was replicated and had a prominent spot in every HealthSouth facility.

Ex-HealthSouth Chief Invokes a Higher Power As Fraud Trial Proceeds

Prosecutors Fear Scrushy's Preaching,
Daily TV Program Could Sway Jurors Dozens of Bench Conferences

By DAN MORSE

BIRMINGHAM, Alabama-As members of Point of Grace Ministries, a Pentecostal congregation, pulled into the church parking lot on a Sunday evening early this month, they drove past a blue-and white marquee blaring the featured attraction:

"Join us tonight at 6 p.m., for a good time in Jesus. Special guest Richard Scrushy."

An hour later, the founder and former chief executive of HealthSouth Corp., now on trial over a $2.7 billion (€2.11 billion), nearly seven-year-long ac counting fraud at his company, was at the pulpit. Jesus one day will separate the blessed from the cursed, he said, quoting Matthew, just as a shepherd separates his sheep from the goats. "We can choose to be a goat or we can choose to be a sheep. We can choose to walk with the devil," Mr. Scrushy said, stepping from one side of the pulpit to the. other. "Or we can choose to walk over here, with Him."

As a parade of witnesses has testified in US federal court here to Mr. Scrushy's knowledge of the HealthSouth fraud, he and his attorneyshave mounted a righteous re—*Richard Scrushy* joinder. They have pilloried government witnesses for their moral failings, while casting Mr. Scrushy as a target of overzealous prosecutors lost in their own complex accounting theories.

Meanwhile, Mr. Scrushy has been preaching regularly for months at fundamentalist churches and appearing daily in a Scripture-laced morning television show. Prosecutors privately contend it is all a bid for sympathy in this Bible Qelt city, or an effort to reach jurors indirectly through family or friends. Mr. Scrushy denies it is anything of the sort, as do his attorneys.

Joel C. Gordon (2003)

Joel had sold his company, Surgical Care Affiliates, to HealthSouth in 1995. He agreed to be the new interim chairman of HealthSouth in 2003. He was a good choice. He was the biggest individual shareholder and a legend within the healthcare business. Joel's leadership made possible HealthSouth's survival.

Jeff McWaters, CEO of Amerigroup Corporation (2004)

Jeff McWaters and Jeff Folick, the CEO of Bravo Health, are two of the finest, most dedicated leaders I have encountered in my career as a venture capitalist. Their companies encountered great difficulties, most often caused by government interference. In the end, they both triumphed, producing better healthcare outcomes at much lower costs, helping millions of patients over the years.

AMERIGROUP

CORPORATION

Charles W. Newhall, III New Enterprise Associates 1119 St. Paul Street Baltimore, MD 21202

Dear Chuck:

I know that we are in a business environment in which change is expected and generally positive, but it is hard to imagine AMERIGROUP without you on our Board of Directors. We are at a place today as a company that reflects tremendous accomplishments and is a testimony to our original Board's confidence and dedication -ten markets, more than $1.5 billion in revenue, 2,500 associates, eight acquisitions, and now a Fortune 1000 company. Most importantly, we are making a positive difference in the lives of more than 800,000 moms and kids, and the disabled. Today, AMERIGROUP is the leader in a field that did not exist a decade ago and proves every day that our challenges in reforming the health care system can be overcome. Can you believe, the little startup company you helped create had a major role in the President's Tax Bill by giving $20 billion back to the states.

In a time of uncertainty and strife, Harry Truman told Congress that "America was not built on fear. America was built on courage, on imagination and an unbeatable determination to do the job at hand." I believe Truman's words apply to AMERIGROUP as well. When we got started, most firms and venture capitalists were fealful of investing in health care, particularly in a company designed to do business exclusively with states and provide coverage for low-income families. Your courage in supporting our vision, your effort, to help us secure adequate funding and your involvement in building and managing this new company were largely the reason for our success.

In addition to your wisdom, experience and sense of humor, you brought a commitment to ethics and accountability to our Board. I believe that our dedication to being a company driven by mission, values and integrity is a reflection of you and will continue to distinguish us among our competitors.

Chuck, it's easy for me to thank you on behalf of our staff and members for your time, investment and service. But more importantly, 1 want to express my personal appreciation for your friendship, confidence and leadership. Without you, there wouldn't have been an AMERIGROUP. I hope that you are proud of a company that reflects your work and commitment! You will be missed!

Very truly yours,

Jeffrey L. McWaters
Chairman and CEO

AMERICAID
AMERi KIDS
AMERIFAM
AMERIPLUS
AMERIGROUP CORPORATION • 4425 CORPORATION LANE • VIRGINIA IIE AC H, VIRGIN IA 23462 • 757 490 6900 • WWW. AMERIGROUPCORP. COM

"These companies are more than successful investments for me. They are children of my heart."
Amerigroup's NYSE Listing (2001)

Commenting on his career as an entrepreneur, Jeff McWaters, the CEO of Amerigroup, said, "You work like crazy, partly because you believe in your product and your people and partly because you are too scared to do anything else. You improvise, take calculated risks, and create a result-driven culture of integrity, excellence and drive to improve every day . . . for true entrepreneurs and world-class operators, the dream never goes away."

From left to right: George Stamas, Peter Barris, Chuck Newhall, Dr. James Barrett, and John Sidgmore in my Baltimore office.

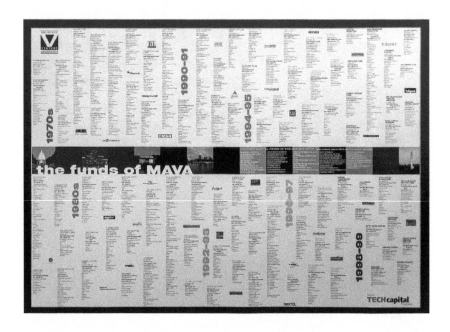

Timeline showing the funds of the Mid-Atlantic Venture Association's member firms and the companies they financed.

MAVA helped change the mid-Atlantic from an entrepreneurial desert into a significant player in the industry. At one point, the mid-Atlantic had more venture-backed companies than Boston, and its share of total venture capital dollars raised increased from half a percent of the total in 1970 to more than 20 percent in 1990.

Change Was Happening Quickly, Even Long, Long Ago

Recognition from Grant Thornton for those who contributed to the JOBS Act

Grant Thornton LLP extends its gratitude to a number of people who have helped focus attention on what is a systemic risk to the US economy—the lack of a properly functioning IPO and small-cap stock market.

In particular, we thank Duncan Niederauer, Chairman & CEO of NYSE Euronext, and Dixon Doll, founder of Doll Capital Management and recent former Chairman of the NVCA, for organizing the Blue Ribbon Panel to search for solutions to the "IPO Crisis"; Pascal Levensohn, founder of Levensohn Venture Partners, who has blogged about our report and the threat that the lack of an IPO market poses to US national interests (Pascal is on the Counsel of Foreign Relations and once worked for First Boston); David Coolidge, Vice Chairman of William Blair & Company, who called our attention to some additional items that we have included in this version of the report and that have served to reinforce our thesis that the loss of the IPO market in the United States is due largely to changes in market structure; Mike Halloran, former Deputy Chief of Staff and Counsel to SEC Chairman Christopher Cox and current partner at Kilpatrick Stockton, who believes that our recommendations for a new public market—one that would be parallel to the current stock market while retaining a very different economic model—not only make sense, but also should be politically viable. (Mike made a point that had escaped us completely: our recommendation for a new stock market model is one of the few changes the Obama Administration could make that would help the US economy without increasing the deficit. In fact, he believes that our market structure recommendations, if implemented, would help decrease the deficit over time).

Last, but not least, Grant Thornton recognizes Chuck Newhall, one of the founders of New Enterprise Associates (NEA) and a "Dean" of the venture capital business, for his passion and interest in helping to solve this crisis. NEA, back in the days of functional IPO markets, perennially topped the list of most active backers of venture capital IPOs.

Jim Swartz, Accel Founder (2015)

When Jim Swartz addressed the graduating class of his business school at Carnegie Mellon, he explained the venture capitalist's purpose:

"Venture capital has always been about helping a person or project succeed. It is about adding judgment, perspective, and a selfless desire to see the company succeed. Venture capital is best practiced as a calling, not a job. It was never about maximizing wealth . . . Venture capital must be practiced with absolute integrity and ethics."

Tableau listing on the NYSE. Forest Baskett and Scott Sandell, second and third from bottom right

Letter from KR Sridhar, the Founder of Bloom Energy, Thanking Scott Sandell for his contribution to the company

Bloomenergy

Dear Scott.

Recently, you and I had the rare privilege of standing shoulder-to-shoulder on the floor of the New York Stock Exchange as Bloom Energy celebrated its Initial Public Offering. As is evident from the photographs and video, it was a very joyous and proud moment for the two of us, a huge milestone that was possible, thanks to the amazing NEA-Bloom partnership!

The image from that event made me reflect on the incredible and unfailing support you as a Board Director and partner have provided to the company and me. That support from you and the other EA members were critical to our success, and to the significant contributions we are making to safeguard our planet for future generations.

Scott, you took a gamble on us when countless experts said, "Fuel cells would never be economical or robust." Well, they are robust and are saving money for our customers. The little company NEA backed fifteen years ago has built the most efficient power generation platform in the world. We have helped customers, AT&T, The Home Depot, Kaiser Permanente, Walmart, and others, reduce their CO_2 emissions by 3.5 billion pounds and counting. To put that in context, the company EA helped build has already eliminated as much CO_2 as would be sequestered by two million acres of forests.

It turns out, the timing of NEA's investment in Bloom was prescient. We are hitting our stride just as customers need us most: the grid is becoming more costly than ever to maintain; extreme weather events and outages are costing US business more than $150 billion per year, and the specter of cyberattacks on infrastructure is creating heightened demand for clean, resilient, on-site electric power.

Perhaps best of all, as Bloom plays its part in elevating the resilience of the global digital economy, we are also proud to be an engine of job creation in Silicon Valley and Delaware, including high-quality American manufacturing jobs. With your backing, we have demonstrated that America can lead the world in alternative energy.

So, in summary, you as a visionary venture capitalist took a bet on a futuristic electric infrastructure fifteen years ago. Today, that bet has created a platform that can offer clean, reliable, resilient, and affordable electricity. Today, that bet has created real manufacturing jobs and jump-started a new industry and established American leadership in clean energy. Thank you, Scott, NEA, and the venture industry, for making bets on entrepreneurs like me. Together, **we** can make the world a better place.

Warm regards,

KR Sridhar
Founder, Chairman and CEO
299 Orleans Drive, Sunnyvale, CA 94089 T 408 543 1500 F 408 543 1501 www.bloomenergy .com

Jim Blair, founder of Domain Associates

About how to build a culture that is friendly to entrepreneurs, Jim said, "In some firms, young partners are taught to put self-interest first. You can put things into a term sheet, and then if you don't sell the business for exactly what you wanted to sell it for, it can come out of the entrepreneur's hide rather than your hide. That is not consistent with Domain's culture. I'm not saying that those terms don't creep in, but we always ensure that management should retain incentives."

Tony Evnin, Venrock, 2017
Photograph by Ellen Jaffe

"The wonderful aspect of this business is working with very interesting, very smart, very dedicated people, both within your partnership and even more in the companies in which you're involved. It's just stimulating and exciting to work with people who are doing new things, who are thinking at the levels that you can't begin to think at, that are creating new products, new activities, and making a real difference. That is all great, but half the time, it's really difficult and unpleasant and not much fun. The other half is wonderful. Like any business or life, a lot of it is difficult and unpleasant. You have to raise money when no one wants to give it to you, you have to fire people, close things down. That's not fun. Or a project fails. That really hurts, so you live through that. But that's sort of life, isn't it? In the venture business, you have intellectual stimulation and learning. You don't sell the same story every day. You come in and there are new things to learn and always new people to meet. That is what excites me, and you can still make a little money doing this, and that's not all bad."

MONTAGU

NEWHALL

MONTAGUNEWHALLGLOBALPARTNERS IV, L. P.

Limited Partner Interests

CONFIDENTIAL

OFFERING MEMORANDUM

2000

Todd Ruppert,
T. Rowe Price (1998)

Todd was my son Ashton's mentor at T. Rowe Price. Ashton said Todd probably thought he was a bit brash when they first met. He remembers saying, "You don't know me yet, but I know you are going to hire me." Ashton said, "In the end, I think he appreciated my confidence. After the internship during my sophomore summer year, I was invited back to work more closely with the Institutional Sales Group and many of Todd's subordinates. After completing the program, I finished my senior year at Elon, and before I graduated, Todd hired me for the whopping sum of $27,500 per year."

My son, Ashton Newhall
(2003)

Ashton co-founded Greenspring Associates in 2000 with Rupert Montagu, Anthony's son.

The transcript of the speech I gave when I received the National Venture Capital Association's Lifetime Achievement Award in 2016.

I am wearing my decorations to honor Laurel Blevins and Ken Noldner. They took a bullet meant for me in Vietnam. Because of their sacrifice, I am alive today. I hope they are proud of me this evening.

Venture capital has been my family's lifelong passion. I would like to thank the officers and the members of the National Venture Capital Association for giving me the greatest honor of my life. I would like to thank my NEA Partners for making me look like a better venture capitalist than I am. I would like to thank venture capitalists in other firms who mentored me when we co-invested: Paul Wythes, Bill Edwards, Tony Evnin, Jim Blair, Jim Swartz, Sage Givens, and Jack Delaney. I would like to thank my NEA co-founders, Frank Bonsal and Dick Kramlich. Dick was my partner, but also my mentor in this business. I would like to thank my new partners at Greenspring Associates for giving me another war to win. Finally, I would like to thank my wife Amy, who has helped me to cope with PTSD, a forty-year war that continues to this day.

Our family has a long history in venture capital. My father entered the venture capital business in 1945 when he joined Laurance Rockefeller and Associates. He helped Laurance to create the aerospace industry. I co-founded NEA with Frank Bonsal and Dick Kramlich in 1977. My oldest son Ashton founded his venture capital firm Greenspring Associates in 2000 and recruited his partner Jim Lim away from Commonfund. My youngest son Adair was an entrepreneur and principal at Domain. He joined Greenspring last year. Now all three of us are working together in a business we love. If Ashton and Adair work until 2045, we will have 100 years in the venture business.

Today, the Drapers are the only four-generation family in the business, but look out, Bill and Tim, I have four granddaughters who will be coming up your tailpipe.

My father told me a story to illustrate what the job of a venture capitalist really is.

Let us go back to the spring of 1946. During World War II, Father was a whiz kid whose job was to manage the development, production, and allocation of fighter aircraft. Laurance Rockefeller hired him for his knowledge of rocketry. Laurance called Father at 3 AM. He had just received a call from the secretary of war. The secretary was calling Laurance at the request of the President of the United States. There was a small company in Morristown, New Jersey, Reaction Motors that will go bankrupt this morning. If this company goes bankrupt. the future of the United States will be in grave jeopardy. He asked Laurance to save Reaction Motors. So that morning, Father went to Morristown with a check for $300,000 to save a company founded by a group of escaped German scientists, Werner Von Braun, and the U2 Crew. Under Father, Reaction Motors built the engine that powered the Bell X1 that broke the sound barrier. The company then launched the Viking Rocket, the first trip in space. Thinkol acquired Reaction Motors to be its Rocketry Division. Thinkol went on to create the aerospace industry, put man on the moon, and one day will take us to Mars and beyond.

The point of this story is that the job of venture capital is to change the way the world is. The name Dick Kramlich gave me at NEA is "Preacher Man." If you give me a podium, I will give you a sermon. You have given me a podium, so look out, here comes the sermon.

How many of you know how important our industry is to our country? We have created the American economy. The merchant banks, institutional venture capitalists, funded whaling ships, privateers, and clipper ships, which had a monopoly on the China trade because of their speed with purchase agreements like we use today in the 1970s. Let us go back to 1880, to a bank in Pittsburgh, Pennsylvania. A banker named Andrew Mellon invested $250,000 in *seed capital to found four companies. He was an institutional venture capitalist who will create four companies: Gulf Oil, Alcoa Aluminum, General Reinsurance, and Carborundum. Sherman Fairchild and a group of angel investors in the 1920s recruited Tom Watson to create a company called International Business Machines that sold something called computers. About the same time, an angel investor named Lucius Ordway recruited William McKnight to run a startup called The Minnesota Mining and Manufacturing Company, which made its first product, called sandpaper. Eastman Kodak was seeded by an angel group in Rochester, N.Y., and created modern photography. Wal-Mart was seeded by an institutional venture capital firm within a small southern investment bank in the 1950s.*

Let's move on to Laurance Rockefeller. In 1935, he seeded Polaroid. He went on to seed Eastern Airlines, Rock Resorts, McDonnell Douglas, Iteck, and Thermo Electron. His firm changed its name to Venrock and funded the startup of Intel and Apple.

I believe that if you studied the history of the 500 most important companies in US history, that 80 percent will have received funding from institutional venture capitalists or angels. It has been my privilege to help fund, along with Pete Bancroft, the NVCA, and Harvard, the oral histories of venture capitalists about to die. The only histories of venture capital are oral. There is little written, and we need a written history of venture capital if we want to convince politicians of the importance of what we do.

For the most part, we know less about the history of venture capital than today's high-school students know about American history. Not knowing who Benno Schmidt, Georges Doriot, Joan Payson, and Laurance Rockefeller are is the intellectual equivalent of not knowing the importance of George Washington, Alexander Hamilton, and Thomas Jefferson to American history.

These oral histories have been conducted by Mauree Jane Perry, my partner Mark's wife, and Carole Kolker. They have enjoyed recording the histories of the men and women who have built companies that change the way the world is, but they feel the next generation of venture capital may be going in the wrong direction.

I am fortunate to have read the comments of Jim Swartz when he addressed the graduation of his business school. He explains what venture capitalists do. "Venture capital has always been about helping a person or a project succeed. It is about adding judgment, perspective, and a selfless desire to see the company succeed. Venture capital is best practiced as a calling, not a job. It was never about maximizing wealth." He goes on to add, "Venture capital must be practiced with absolute integrity and ethics."

All too often our new generation of venture capitalists says, "My goal in life is to make $1 billion today." I do not think this attitude works over the long term.

Let me repeat what my father told me: "Change the way the world is, cure cancer, or create super-intelligent androids. If you do this, do not worry. The economics will follow."

Thank you, again. Now, go out and change the way the world is!

Letter to Dick Kramlich

From Pradeep Sindhu, Founder of Juniper Networks, for his contribution to the company:

I first met Dick Kramlich in May 1996 at NEA's Sand Hill office when I was looking to raise the series B round for Juniper Networks a few months after successfully raising series A with Kleiner Perkins.

From the earliest meeting, I found Dick to be personable, as well as passionate. He was all about helping founders build great companies, and we connected immediately. Much of the discussion, as I recall, was about how and where he could help; Dick mentioned his numerous connections, his CEO network, and how he most enjoyed helping young entrepreneurs succeed. I believe at that meeting NEA had already decided they were going to invest in Juniper. My only ask was to have Dick sit on the board of the company—he graciously accepted.

In the subsequent years, Dick was there at virtually every board meeting and heavily involved in many important decisions for the company. One of the early decisions was the selection of the company's permanent CEO. (I had made it known to my board that I believed I did not have the experience needed to run Juniper and so we started a CEO search early on.) Dick was one of the board members instrumental in finally closing Scott Kriens, who went on to become Juniper's CEO and lead it to go public.

Without a doubt, Dick had a hand in helping build Juniper Networks. He was a mentor to me and an example of how to work with people with humility, grace, integrity, and most importantly, a sense of humor.

Pradeep Sindhu
Founding CEO, Juniper Networks

Letter from Kai Li, Founder of Data Domain, thanking Scott Sandell and Forest Baskett for their contributions to the company

35 Olden Street
Princeton, New Jersey 08544-2078
Phone: +1-609-2584637 Fax: +1-609-2581771

Kai Li

Paul M Wythes '55, P '86 and Marcia R. Wythes P '86 Professor

Dear Forest and Scott,

It is my great pleasure to write this letter, as NEA is celebrating its 40th anniversary, to express my sincere appreciation to both of you and the NEA organization for helping me and the rest of the Data Domain team from 2001 to 2009.

Since I am sending this letter to Chuck Newhall to help him with his book writing, I would like to provide a brief background about Data Domain, Inc. Data Domain pioneered disk-based "deduplication storage systems" for data center customers to build a local or a private cloud ecosystem for backups and archives, to replace the decades-old backup ecosystem with tape libraries and tapes. Data Domain started at the printer room of the old NEA office on October 12, 2001, went public (NASDAQ: DDUP) in 2007, and was acquired by EMC for $2.4B (more than two times of the market cap) in 2009. It created a new market segment called "deduplication storage for backups." Its product line exceeded over 60% of the market share of the market segment since 2005 with a gross margin of over 80%. The new market segment quickly displaced the tape libraries for backups. Since 2006, the revenue of this market segment exceeded that of tape libraries. New generation flash-memory based primary storage products such as Nimble Storage (NYSE: NMBL), Pure Storage (NYSE: PSTG), and XtremIO (acquitted by EMC) have successfully leveraged the deduplication technology Data Domain developed. For these reasons, the storage industry considers Data Domain as a rare disruptive example with game-changing disruptive technologies.

Over the years, quite a few entrepreneurs and students asked me about my startup experience. I shared quite a few small stories about the two of you with them. These stories also played the key roles for the founders of many startups such as Fusion-IO (NASDAQ: FIO), Tableau Software (NYSE: DATA), Nicira, etc) to take NEA early investments. These small stories are:

Finding dream co-founders

During my sabbatical from Princeton University in February 2001, I met Forest (whom I knew for 15 years at that time) and told him that I saw a startup opportunity in the storage market to replace the tape libraries in data centers for backups, but I did not have concrete ideas about what to do and had no co-founders yet. Forest encouraged me to pursue this opportunity. When I decided to do a startup in this area in the summer of 2001, you two invited and hosted me as an Entrepreneur-In-

Resident (EIR) at NEA to work on building a founding team and developing a business plan. Forest introduced me to Ben Zhu who was an EIR at USVP, looking for his next startup opportunity after 3DFX just acquired his previous startup GigaPixels. Ben immediately expressed his interest to work with me and introduced me to Brian Biles who was also an EIR at USVP. Over the following 8 years, the three of us prove to be a dream founding team.

Without Forest's help, we would not have this dream founding team. Although I met Ben when he was a graduate student at Stanford several years ago, Forest's "re-introduction" was important because I did not keep in touch with Ben.

EIR opportunity and building a good business plan

Being an EIR was a significant help for me. I was a first-time entrepreneur and did not know much about how to build a startup. By hanging out with other EIRs and partners at NEA, I learned many helpful lessons including building a good business plan. During that time, I received enormous help from Scott. I would stop by his office to chat without an appointment typically after 5pm and we did at least twice a week for several months. I would bounce new ideas with him. He would tell me some of the stories of his portfolio companies including successes and failures, and why they were successful, and why they failed. His insightful observations have stayed with me and some became my principles as an entrepreneur.

Both Forest and Scott spent a lot of time with the founding team to brainstorm our business plan. We had many meetings on the product roadmap, go-to-market strategy, and competitive analysis. Even after the company formally started in October 2001, continued such discussions for about 7 months. We implemented a prototype system for technical validation of our deduplication technology before designing our products and discussed our product and product roadmap with about 40 data center customers for customer validation. After the EMC acquisition, I looked at our business plan. We essentially followed it for 8 years.

Our business plan has passed the test of time and it is closely related to the help I received from the two of you and what I learned as an EIR at NEA.

Raising Fund and Finding a CE

The two of you gave me enormous help when we were looking for an experienced CEO and series-A funding. Year 2001 was arguably the worst time for raising funds by high-tech startups because the dot-com bubble had just busted and then the stock market had the worst crash in history due to the 9/11 terrorist attack. VCs were extremely conservative in terms of investing in startups. Although we seemed to be on an inside track as we were EIRs at NEA and USVP, it was very clear to us that we needed to have a good CEO and a great business plan to receive series-A funding at that time. We had a disruptive idea (deduplication storage), but we had no track record in building storage products. None of us had any CEO-level experience. We identified quite a few CEO candidates, but either we did not like them or NEA and USVP did not like them. A lot of time has passed without much success.

USVP finally introduced to us a former VP marketing of storage products of a large company who had the most convincing profile. Our understanding was that if we could work out with this individual as our CEO, we would be able to close series-A funding with NEA and USVP, which would be extremely important for us during the worst climate for fund-raising. We spent several weeks working together on a trial basis. We did learn new things from the CEO candidate, but we also felt differences on a few important issues.

A dramatic turn of events occurred in one late afternoon in the NEA's printer room. The CEO candidate came to meet me after a private meeting with the company's legal counsel about the formation of the company. The CEO candidate proposed to revamp the founder stock partition plan the three co-founders previously agreed, by giving the CEO candidate and me substantially more shares and reducing the shares of my two co-founders. The argument was that the CEO and I were the most important people for the company. This proposal would benefit me financially but would damage the integrity and trust among the founding team. If I disagreed with the proposal, it would be the end of working together with the CEO candidate and would receive no funding from USVP. Since the climate for fund-raising was very conservative, other VC firms would naturally ask the question why USVP was not interested in funding the company as two of the co-founders were EIRs there. This was a very significant decision for me.

Despite the risk of losing an opportunity for the company's series-A funding, I decided at the meeting that the trust among the founding team was much more important than my financial benefit and told the CEO candidate we had to part ways. I went upstairs and told the two of you that I just killed the working relationship with the CEO candidate and perhaps killed the funding opportunity for the startup. To my pleasant surprise, you not only took the news well, you fully support my judgment and decision. Scott told me that before that today, he was not so sure about the founding team. But now he had more confidence and he would like to provide us with a term sheet for NEA-only seed funding as the first tranche of series-A before midnight of that day. He would go together with me to visit other top firms to close series-A. Later I learned that this was typical Scott's style! A few days later, we went to Greylock together and convinced them to co-invest. Aneel Bhusri agreed to serve on the board and being our acting CEO. The rest was history.

Throughout the entire process of finding a CEO and closing funding, you reconfirmed that we shared the same values and culture. I also learned that you were on the entrepreneur side during a difficult time.

Developing disruptive products

In addition to Forest's dedication to helping the engineering team, Forest early on suggested to me to ask Scott to formally serve on the board and he would come to all board meetings without being a formal board member. As promised, Forest did attend all board meetings. As a result, we received help from two general partners of NEA. Such unselfish help was far beyond Forest's duty as a general partner and as a good friend.

Before ending this letter, let me say again, as the initial founder of Data Domain, that a lot of our success was due to the enormous help we received from the two of you. I deeply appreciate everything you have done for me and the entire Data Domain team.

Forest spent a lot of his time at many design review meetings with our engineering team and provided many helpful suggestions. We did such meetings bi-weekly for over a year, typically after 5 PM when Forest finished his daytime work at NEA. The early engineers all know that one of the key reasons for designing our successful product was due to these design review meetings.

Forest's feedback and ideas were instrumental during our design process.

I would also like to send my best wishes to the entire NEA organization.

Sincerely

Kai Li
Paul M. Wythes '55, P'86, and Marcia R. Wythes '86 Professor

**John Spitznagel, CEO of ESP Pharma
and my son, Adair's, first mentor (2005)**

Adair comments on his mentor, John Spitznagel: "John Spitznagel, ESP's famous CEO, bet one of my father's partners that I would wash out in six months. Beginning as a salesman, with no experience and little training, I was given the worst territory in the US. Within one year, I changed Washington, D.C., territory from the 57th to the 12th ranked territory in the US. I was competing with 60 other sales reps. After this, John Spitznagel adopted me and personally guided my career."

XII.

BIOTECH ADVENTURES

"Change means traveling in uncharted waters."

—John C. Maxwell

IN 1978, NEA INVESTED IN Bethesda Research Labs (BRL), a company that commercialized modifying restrictive enzymes. The enzymes, discovered by two great Hopkins physicians and Nobel Laureates, Daniel Nathans and Hamilton Smith, permitted the cleaving of strands of DNA. This technology allowed the manipulation of genes—the code of life.

Biotechnology was the gold rush of the late 1970s. Research spending by startup biotech companies and big pharmaceutical companies was exploding, and BRL was akin to the Levi Strauss Company, making a fortune selling jeans to the miners during the gold rush. While only one in one hundred prospectors found gold, Levi's sold jeans to all the miners. In the biotech goldrush, BRL was on the ground floor for the whole industry, making the tools needed to make the breakthroughs possible.

BRL's CEO was Steve Turner, a missionary who preached that biotechnology would change the world. We gobbled up his words almost before he spoke them. Steve was always busy doing twenty things simultaneously. He was a salesman who could sell iceboxes at the North Pole and a dream merchant, like all good biotech executives.

Steve had voting control of the company, which was problematic.

194

One of the first rules of venture capital is never to invest unless ownership is spread widely enough to prevent one voice from overruling all the others, but because of the magnitude of the opportunity at BRL, we decide to ignore that rule and buy 20 percent of the company for a million dollars. The company was raising money, and we felt we must participate. Soon, BRL made up 5 percent of our fund on a cost basis.

And Steve could not be held in check. He decided to enter the pharmaceutical business and hired twenty molecular biologists from one of the best California biotech companies, making BRL now a pharmaceutical and instrument and laboratory products company. The financing requirements were enormous. Without informing me, or the other board members, Steve committed the company to a $75 million building project, a new headquarters in Frederick, Maryland, in which he had an economic interest. Since BRL was, at the time, spread across five labs in Gaithersburg, Maryland, Steve argued that the sites had to be consolidated. Concurrently, Steve was divorcing his wife, Ann Turner, one of Farleigh Dickenson's daughters.

As a result, Farleigh, the son of the co-founder of the medical technology company, Becton Dickenson, would no longer be his financial backer. BRL was therefore facing bankruptcy, and we had to beg the Mercantile Bank to cover BRL's monthly payroll.

The bank agreed, trusting that NEA would be able to finance the company, so we began a frantic search for financing. Frank Bonsal and I visited Jim Blair, who managed Rothchild Inc.'s American biotech investments. With multiple doctorates, he was one of the leading investors in the burgeoning biotech business, and Jim understood BRL. He offered to help.

Jim said he would not help, however, if Fred Adler was in control. As a legendary founder of Data General Corporation, Fred ran both a venture firm as well as a law business as I have discussed before. He was a difficult genius at best and a litigator. Jim did not want Fred as a partner. Unfortunately, we were boxed in, since the brokerage firm that raised all BRL's money, F. Eberstadt & Co., represented the clients that now controlled BRL. Eberstadt wanted Fred, so Fred it was. Fred agreed to take on the turnaround, but he had a condition: Steve Turner had to sell him 10 percent of BRL at a penny a share, and then he would invest his partnership's money at one dollar per share. Steve agreed to the terms, and Fred immediately began the search for a new CEO.

Dick Kramlich was appalled, justifiably, and upset with me. NEA was being diluted, and our ten-times-the-investment gain was evaporating in front of his eyes. Many of our East Coast companies were disappointments. Several of them had to raise additional money at a much lower price than we initially paid. We all invested in BRL, Eberstadt, Adler, and NEA.

In the meantime, Fred Adler proved that he was a turnaround genius, hiring as the new CEO Jim Barrett, an enzymologist with a Ph.D. in biochemistry. Jim had run both research divisions and operating companies, including one of Smith Kline's largest operating divisions—its clinical labs. He was a quiet man who understood the science. His hair had turned prematurely white, making him look older than he was. He affectionately called me "young man." Many years later, I respectfully reminded him that we were the same age.

Fred Adler visited BRL only twice. Our board meetings were held at his law offices in New York, and when we entered an austere conference room there, his minions scattered. One of them would fetch Fred a gigantic mug filled with half milk, half coffee. He was divorced and dated young models and beautiful actresses. The reason I was aware of this is that he began board meetings with graphic descriptions of his sexual exploits. He once interrupted the board meeting for an hour while he negotiated the purchase of a multimillion-dollar condominium. Fred did have a good sense of humor about his excess, frequently laughing at himself. Our most memorable meeting with Fred during this time was in his hospital room, with his leg suspended from the ceiling by a pulley system because of some tennis injury, or perhaps because he could not keep up with his young actresses.

Fred did teach me a lot, including his recipe for turning around companies, which was as follows.

1. PRICING

Review all pricing of products. The following rules apply:

- a. Pricing should be four to five times labor and materials
    - i. For example, $1,000 labor and materials
    - ii. $2,500 cost with full manufacturing burden (150 percent)

iii. 50 percent GM; prices at $5,000 to generate 20 percent pretax margin
   b. Warranty: returned items should be at the customer's expense.
       i.   Partial down payment before shipment.
       ii. Customer product education at the customer's expense.

2. PAYABLES

Determine the magnitude of all payables. Identify critical vendors and develop a delayed payment plan. Keep a slush fund, that was not a company bank account, for small vendors, whose claims could force the company into bankruptcy. Usually, vendor payments can be 5–10 percent down, 1–2 percent a week. Insure shipments from critical suppliers. Meet personally with significant creditors.

3. RECEIVABLES

Develop an immediate plan to shorten receivables to 30–40 days. Push very hard. Offer a discount program to encourage collections. Monitor daily collections.

4. AREAS OF BUSINESS

Look at each major product segment. Check to see that there is a short, current business summary outlining the following:

   a. Sales expectations and assumptions
   b. Market Shares
   c. Competition
   d. Manufacturing cost, overhead, and margin assumptions.

This must be in writing for future evaluation. Key board members and any executive committee should possess it. If it is not written and signed by the person responsible, it is worthless. Determine which areas of the business are not central to the core technical strength or strategic thrust of the company: eliminate the less essential. Determine areas of business where it is possible to do a joint venture for research, marketing, and other activities.

Get people off payroll. Maintain core technical areas by keeping 2–3 critical developers and remove their support staff.

5. EXECUTIVE COMMITTEE

This is the critical mechanism for company control. Let management retain the title of chair of the board, but make sure you have the title of chair of the executive committee. The executive committee needs the power to act for the board under appropriate state law. Investors should have voting control of this body. President (COO) and chair should report to the executive committee. It is important not to have the COO report to the president if there has been mismanagement. When possible, put the founder's stock in a voting trust that must vote with the majority of the executive committee. Announce this mechanism in front of all shareholders (and rub management's nose in it for good measure).

6. PUBLIC RELATIONS

Take the initiative. Formulate a news release showing the financial stability of the company and announcing the formation of an executive committee. Name the new players. Put events at the company in a favorable light. Aim the release toward the financial rather than the trade press.

7. PERSONNEL CUTS

One cut is preferable to several; try to do it all at once. First, cut the service/support areas. Cut technicians and discontinued product areas but keep the core scientist pool and project teams intact. Reduce payroll to cash flow to break even immediately. Additional cuts can be made if necessary. Try to avoid constant attrition.

8. BANK

Keep the bank informed. Meet regularly with a senior loan officer. If necessary, keep funds outside the bank in escrow for advances to the company to pay bills as needed. Make sure creditors cannot attach funds.

9. PRESENCE

Be present at the company every day or have a representative there. Surprises may develop, so management may try to withhold information. If management is too shaken to make solid decisions, financial problems (such as the bank and payables management\) may be overlooked. If you are not there, the situation is, by definition, out of control.

10. NETWORK

Have contacts on several levels within the company that trust and confide in you. Use them to monitor internal politics and events, mainly to see if executive committee requests are being followed up.

11. SHAREHOLDERS

Immediately contact and inform major shareholders of the problem, plan, and status of implementation. Isolate and diffuse anyone who will try to stop the financing or cause trouble. The chair of the executive committee should dominate all shareholder meetings.

Remove management from shareholder contact.

12. THE CHIEF FINANCIAL OFFICER

The CFO must be a good comptroller and be held personally accountable for all numbers. He reports directly to the executive committee, not to management, daily. The CFO is informed of his reporting responsibility in front of management and shareholders. He is the critical source, although there should be several others in the finance department that feed information on the internal operations of the company to the executive committee.

13. PAYROLL TAXES

Must be current—this is one area in which control persons could face criminal liability.

14. DELEGATE

Develop a team of outside people who are present at the company every day on a rotating basis. One person should handle financial matters, one fundraising, one business planning, and so on. Keep them in constant contact. They must be trained to report efficiently to the chair of the executive committee. They should limit their reports to two minutes per conversation, so they must organize their thoughts beforehand.

In the end, Jim Barrett saved BRL. I was given the task of keeping the banks happy, meeting with our investors, and keeping them updated on progress. At great expense, we got out of BRL's $75 million liability for its Taj Mahal-like offices and paid off our lease, consolidating into the original BRL building. Eberstadt helped us analyze each business. Twenty molecular biologists were fired the day they arrived for work. We closed down the instrumentation business, while the laboratory supply business continued its rapid growth. We were cash-flow positive after six months. Jim had performed a miracle. I remember also that all this chaos occurred during a winter of profoundly heavy snow.

When BRL went public, Fred asked me to step off the board because he wanted only his people there. BRL bought a more substantial laboratory supply business from Dexter Chemical, and the company was renamed Life Technologies, which boasted growth above 20 percent per year. As of 2012, the company had a market capitalization of far over $20 billion. Dick was happy with this performance; perhaps the junior analyst really was a venture capitalist.

In 1984, Bob Johnston, a friend from Princeton, called me to recommend an investment in Sepracor, a research-based pharmaceutical company in Marlborough, Massachusetts. I knew that my friend, Tony Evnin of Venrock, had agreed to lead the financing of the company, which was subject to a lot of work on due diligence. Tim Barberich, Sepracor's CEO, had previously been an executive at Millipore Corporation, and Tony must have felt that my long-term knowledge of Millipore through T. Rowe Price would have rubbed off somehow. Sepracor aimed to combine separations technology with biological materials to mimic what was happening in a living cell. The potential was dazzling.

When there was biotech fairy dust in the air, Bob Johnston, an angel investor, started a group of companies that caught the public's attention. These companies showed great promise, but some of them failed to translate that enthusiasm into reality. In my view, Bob's only weakness was that he thought raising money at a high valuation for one of his companies was the only way to enter venture capital heaven. I thought building a successful company meant raising money at a reasonable valuation. During his career, he made outstanding contributions to the biotech industry, and I count him among my friends.

Tim Barberich was stocky. I like to describe him as Buddha crossed with a triathlete. When I met him, we reminisced about Millipore, Waters, and Zymark, companies I considered progenitors of the tradition that led to Sepracor. Tim was a fullback in college, skilled in changing directions, able to dodge right and left, which is essential in football, combat, and in starting companies. Tim's description of the founding of Sepracor is the best definition of broken field running I know:

"We are a company that has reinvented itself many times. I was working at Lederle Labs as a process chemist. I was drinking at a bar in Argentina when a good friend from Lederle joined me and said, 'We have to introduce our new product, a de-wormer, to a major cattle rancher.' We were in a small town in Argentina. Our customer, the owner of a prominent *estancia* [a Latin American cattle ranch], comes out with a famous giant bull festooned with ribbons. We inject the de-wormer, and the bull falls dead. The poor bull's death leads to the discovery that part of the drug worked but another part did not. Most pharmaceutical products at that time were racemic mixtures, the left and right hands of a molecule. Often, the left and right hands perform differently in the body. The moral of this story is simple: find the part that works.

"I never forgot this story. I worked at Millipore, a traditional biosciences company that specialized in membrane separations, for ten years. I thought, *Why not combine membranes with biologicals— selective separations mimicking the human cell?* Combine membranes with biologicals (enzymes and antibodies) to create a small filter. This led me to separate stereoisomers, like the shaking right and left hands, with each side being a different drug. What an idea for a company.

"You must remember that, at this time, genetics was emerging as a commercial technology. Everybody in the biotech business was looking for new proteins which could be given as drugs: Amgen, Genentech, and the wannabes. Between 1984 and 1988, Sepracor focused on biological and chiral separations (the left and right hands). We had a smörgåsbord of business potentials. Then, we came to an epiphany—to focus on single-isomer drugs, the left hand or the right hand. There were a lot of proven drugs that were racemic mixtures, combinations of both hands. But a pure product, left or right, could be vastly superior. We patented racemic mixtures that had $40 billion of potential sales. We could develop single isomeric products with better performance in the pharmaceutical industry to capture the market before others did. The remaining technology in the company was spun off to fund our interest in single isomers, so we reduced our staff from 400 to 101. In total, we spun out four companies, two of which became successful."

Sepracor would go on to raise $2.5 billion to fund its mission, the most money raised by any biotech company at that time. Their drug developers focused on the treatment of respiratory and central nervous system disorders. Sepracor then out-licensed products, including Clarinex, Allegra, Lunesta, and others, to other pharmaceutical companies.

I did not always have a peaceful relationship with Tim. He talked at length about his vision to make Sepracor a smaller, research-driven Big Pharma company with distribution directly to physicians' offices, plus the ability to do the R&D in-house to fill the pipeline with blockbusters. By the late 1980s, Tony Evnin and I were convinced that Tim needed a practical, buttoned-up number two to support him. We all had dinner together (I maintain this is the only one Tony ever paid for), overlooking the skating rink at Rockefeller Center in New York City, and I recommended a suitable candidate. Tim disagreed so violently that we almost got into a fistfight. Even though Tim outweighed me, I still think I could have broken more than his nose that day on Fifth Avenue.

Eventually, that candidate turned out to be a disaster. Tim, however, realized he needed someone, and he hired David Southwell to be the CFO and his number two. Tim never looked back. David was the perfect complement to Tim. The moral of this story is the important thing is getting the horse to drink; forget about forcing him to the water.

From the time I met Tim, our connection was not a rational one but an emotional one. Somehow, I knew it was my destiny to try to make him and his company a legend. And no matter what I did—whether it was raising money for crucial financing or just believing in its mission and shouting from the rafters that this company will make history—I knew that my contribution to the company's success was but a paper boat cast upon the stream. This was the way it should be. After all, "It's the entrepreneur that counts."

I think, at one point, sales of clinically pure pharmaceuticals topped $350 billion, Sepracor's sales accounting for a small portion of that. Sepracor's licensed products topped $2 billion, and the company's direct sales exceeded $2 billion.

In 1986, BRL's Jim Barrett introduced NEA to Genetic Therapy, started and funded by Wally Steinberg of HealthCare Investment Corporation (later Health Care Ventures), a health technology venture capital firm, to commercialize the science of Dr. French Anderson. French was one of the internationally known scientists working at the National Institute of Health (NIH). His core theory was that doctors would be able to use human gene therapy to both cure genetic diseases, such as sickle cell anemia and Tay-Sachs disease, and to make measurable contributions to the treatment of other conditions, such as cancer. Genetic Therapy would be the first company to cure genetic diseases. The company's breakthroughs would enable the bubble boy to leave the bubble. Their technology was based on using a retrovirus to carry genetic material to the cell, altering the cell's function. For example, if sickle cell anemia is caused by the absence of hemoglobin, then adding hemoglobin to the cell's structure would enable to cell to carry oxygen, just like a normal cell. This viral vector would also be used to carry toxins to cancer cells, killing the cancer and preventing its spread.

French was a great scientist, but he was also a skilled clinician. He had developed an approach that would enable his company to take gene therapy into the clinic rapidly. His work claimed the core patents on both ex vivo (outside the body) and in vivo (inside the body) genetic therapies. Several other companies pursued the same technology, but in the end, Genetic Therapy owned the intellectual property.

Meeting French was an incredible experience. You knew you were in the presence of a great scientist when he could quickly convey complex concepts in language easily understood by any layman. The newly formed CREDA policy at the NIH allowed the intellectual property from French's work to be transferred to a commercial enterprise. Without that policy, it would have taken another twenty years to introduce gene therapy to the clinic, delaying advances in treatment. One of my first tasks, once NEA decided to invest, was to convince French to take some ownership in the company. At that time, he was still burdened with the academic view that ownership would taint his scientific impartiality. I explained to him that the inventor must own stock to convince investors he is committed to the project through good times and bad, which finally persuaded him.

Jim Barrett was hired by Wally to be CEO of Genetic Therapy, and his first responsibility was to raise money to fund its clinical programs. Naturally, he contacted NEA, Abingworth, and a few other venture firms he knew well. Jim then introduced us to Wally Steinberg, the founder of HealthCare Investment. Jim had left Life Technologies because he became frustrated with Fred Adler's continual meddling with management decisions.

When I met Wally, I thought Jim jumped out of the frying pan and into the fire. Wally was an elemental force, focusing his passion on the future of human gene therapy. He claimed 20 percent of all pharmaceutical products would be based on human genome therapy by 2030. For the most part, Healthcare Ventures did not co-invest with other venture firms. They financed many of their companies themselves, not bringing in partners. They simply made a limited number of big bets on transforming technologies.

Wally's partner was Jim Cavanaugh, formerly the deputy assistant secretary of health, education, and welfare under Reagan, and before that, he was the COO of SmithKline Beckman. Whereas Wally was utterly exuberant, Jim was the consummate gentleman, occasionally smoothing some of Wally's rough edges. Each year, Wally hosted a "Future of Healthcare" seminar in Palm Beach. He invited some of the best scientific minds in the country, and they speculated about what might be the next paradigm shift in health science. Jim Barrett attended these meetings, as did most other Healthcare Ventures CEOs, perceiving them to be mind-bending experiences. Over time, I realized that Wally might be a Fred Adler but with a good heart. He could express his views with such fervor that you'd assume that he was intolerant of others' opinions, but when confronted with another view, he would discuss it openly and often change his mind.

Jim challenged Wally on science; I challenged him on financing strategy. Although Wally would finance a company himself when the world did not agree with his valuation metrics, I have never met an investment dollar I did not like. Jim, more often than not, sided with me, and together we led Wally through a number of painful financings.

Together, we tried to bring the science forward. One pivotal move for the company was raising public equity. When our offering was stalled, I called Ben Lorello at Smith Barney (Ben was HealthSouth's banker), who looked and behaved like Gordon Gekko in *Wall Street.* But unlike most investment bankers, I knew Ben cared about the companies he underwrote. He stayed with them through the good and bad times, and over the years, he turned many would-be disasters into victories. Ben took over the Genetic Therapy offering in 1991, and Wally experienced another painful financing.

Genetic Therapy continued to make progress in the clinic. The company received its ex vivo patent for human gene therapy.

One afternoon in 1995, I was stopped in my tracks to learn that Wally had died. An obstruction in his throat caused him to choke, and he died in his sleep. MedImmune, Human Genome Sciences, and Genetic Therapy all went on to prove the validity of Wally's grand visions. Jim Cavanaugh went on to lead HealthCare Ventures to become one of the best health care venture firms in the industry. He remains a good friend. With the loss of Wally, though, the world lost a great soul who really did care about his work.

Ironically, shortly after Wally's death, the great pharmaceutical giant Sandoz approached Genetic Therapy. They acquired it in 1992, at a valuation that would have pleased Wally. Although gene therapy ultimately has a hard time at the clinic, the fundamental value of French's vision was vindicated, and eventually, genetic therapy became an essential weapon in our arsenal against disease.

In 1992, Jim Barrett left the company to start Sensors for Medicine and Science (SMSI), where they hoped to develop a technology for measuring blood glucose levels continuously, without a finger stick. One everyday problem facing diabetic patients is they must draw their blood to measure their blood glucose levels accurately. If SMSI succeeded, it would transform diabetes treatment by increasing the efficiency of measurement as well as save lives. HealthCare Ventures, NEA, and Abingworth joined together to help fund the company.

French joined the board of Sensors, making invaluable contributions as chair of the scientific advisory board. He was brilliant, gentle, and in making many difficult ethical decisions, he always displayed the highest degree of honor. I respected his accomplishments.

In 2003, French was accused of sexually molesting a young woman whose mother ran French's lab and who had helped him with many research projects. French had a black belt in karate and said he had given the young lady martial arts lessons and mentored her academically. He claimed the girl was emotionally disturbed and that he and his wife, a famous surgeon, were merely trying to help her. The trial seemed to last forever. During the trial, the jury heard a tape recording of French saying incredibly damaging things.

The jury found him guilty, but neither Jim nor I were sure that French was capable of such an act. He had devoted his life to the service of others. Could my friend, this gentle scientist, have behaved in such a manner? The law said so, and the evidence was strong. Why does it seem that there is so often a dark side to creativity?

🌲🌲🌲

On December 22, 2005, NEA, OrbiMed, and Abingworth closed on a $45 million investment in Supernus Pharmaceuticals. Jack Khattar, CEO of the drug delivery division of Shire, a pharmaceutical company based in Maryland, had approached Jim Barrett to spin out the division and form Supernus. Jim had joined NEA as a general partner to beef up its biotech practice. For years, that division developed novel, specialty pharmaceutical products using drug delivery platforms, enabling existing drugs to have enhanced efficacy and better tolerability. With strong innovation and patents that protected these differentiated specialty pharmaceutical products, the products could have rapid and sustained revenue growth for years. We hoped for protection that would rival that of new chemical entities: their composition-of-matter patents could last ten years or more. Shire kept a minority stake in Supernus stock. The company's post-money valuation was $60 million.

The company had several drug development programs underway, in partnership with Shire and other companies, but such projects had little monetary value until the drugs were approved by the Food and Drug Administration. The company also developed its own products, selected based on their clinical differentiation and their marketability. These products were relatively inexpensive to develop and delivered drugs with enhanced efficacy. These Supernus products eventually came to be marketed under the names Trokendi XR and Oxtellar XR. Trokendi XR was used to treat epilepsy and migraines. Oxtellar XR was a second epilepsy product with a smaller market size.

If a company did not develop products with an eye towards efficient and effective commercialization, it could end up with a too-varied product line. For example, one that included, say, a cardiovascular treatment, an inflammatory disease treatment, and a central nervous system drug, all of which would require separate sales forces. It costs hundreds of millions to develop a research organization, but it costs even more to build a commercial company with multiple sales forces. Even if your company makes only central nervous system treatments, you must still develop treatments that only need a relatively small CNS sales force. You can market multiple products to mental health professionals with a two-hundred-person sales team, but a product sold to general practitioners will require a two-thousand-person sales force. From the very start, Jack Khattar focused the company on selecting products that were not as risky as new chemical entities and could also be marketed by a relatively small sales force.

The central nervous system market was not an obvious choice. It was large, and CNS diseases often had comorbidities, such as cancer, heart, and liver disease. As a result, these diseases were quite expensive to treat.

Making CNS drug development even less attractive was the fact that FDA approval of new CNS treatments was substantially less assured than it was for other diseases. If you spent $1.3 billion bringing a new drug for bipolar disease through a phase-three trial, the chance the drug would be approved was 4–6 percent. If you brought a cardiovascular drug through a phase-three trial, the chances of approval were 66 percent. If you got a CNS product to market, it was a goldmine that would not have much competition. Jack planned to build a company with more proprietary products, eventually, but he first wanted to develop a portfolio of specialty pharma products with significant revenues. Completing this plan would take fifteen to twenty-five years. He thought it was important to fend off acquisitions early on.

The problem was, how was Supernus going to finance this costly development? Although the company was entirely focused on research in the early years, it needed to transform itself into a commercial entity with in-house staff for regulatory affairs, formulation, production, marketing, and sales. The combined commercial development efforts would take more than $400 million to fund. Supernus had raised $45 million in its initial financing. It also had that pipeline of products it had developed for others, and as those treatments became FDA-approved, the royalty streams they produced would have significant value.

In 2007, Supernus sold its royalty stream for the medications Oracea and Sanctura XR to a group of investors for $75 million. A year later, it sold the royalty stream for Intuniv to Shire for $37 million. The company completed a series of non-dilutive financings that allowed it to survive the 2008 financial crisis until Supernus went public in May 2012. Just take a moment to consider that the company went from its Series A round in 2005 to an IPO in 2012 without any dilutive financing. In addition, during that period, it managed to complete development of two epilepsy products and submit its new drug applications to the FDA. Finally, it raised $90 million in a convertible offering in 2013, most of which was converted to equity by 2017. In six years, given the stock price in 2018, loyal investors in the IPO saw an eightfold to tenfold return.

In February 2013, Supernus launched Oxtellar XR, followed by Trokendi XR in August. The commercial infrastructure had been completed in 2012, before the launch of these products. The company needed to become cash-flow positive by the end of 2014, which is what they had promised investors in their convertible offering in 2013. At the same time, Supernus needed to put every dollar it could toward building out its commercial infrastructure and launching the two products. Supernus achieved profitability by the end of 2014 and executed the most successful launch of epilepsy drugs the industry had ever seen, outperforming some of the biggest players in central nervous system disorders. It did all this while transforming a research company into a commercial pharmaceutical company. The initial sales force was seventy-five people.

Supernus went on to advance new products through clinical trials: Molindone, an antipsychotic, for impulsive aggression; Viloxazine for ADHD; and Trileptal, which was the same drug as Oxteller XR, renamed for bipolar disorder. These products had longer patent lives than the company's initial product portfolio, plus they had greater revenue potential. Because the market knows the development risks in CNS products are high, the company's stock price did not significantly reflect its potential until the products were finally FDA-approved.

When asked what made Supernus successful, Jack replied, "Right products, right markets, multiple shots on goal, but more importantly, our values and our people." He was a meticulous manager and quick to give each Supernus employee credit for the company's success. "If we are driven by our values," he said, "then we can never go wrong. Success will always come."

He also said, "Caring about our patients and each other, being driven and committed to our vision of becoming a multibillion-dollar company, being innovative in everything we do, and finally doing all that with integrity, are the values that over the years allowed us to endure and overcome every challenge and achieve the success we have had so far."

Jack considered it a privilege to create a team that created such success. Jack and I met regularly to discuss strategy and operations throughout my time on the board. I feel my most important contribution to Supernus was encouraging Jack to build a great company and to commit to the long haul and not selling out. I also introduced him to two of the directors, Dr. Carolee Barlow and Fred Hudson, whom he put on his board, and Todd Horich, the director of marketing. I include Jack in my CEO Hall of Fame.

In some ways, we have similar backgrounds. I have PTSD from Vietnam, my first wife's suicide, and four other traumas. Jack was born in Lebanon in 1961, and he was only 14 years old when the Lebanese Civil War began. It was a ruthless war, full of dismemberment and other horrors. After graduating from the American University of Beirut, Jack left Lebanon in 1981, worked for two years in Greece and Dubai, then emigrated to the US in 1983 to get his MBA. Perhaps it was the trauma of our shared backgrounds that led us to try to make a great company for central nervous system disorders.

About three years ago, one of our investors, a director, and a large shareholder, tried to convince the board that they should sell the company at a slight premium on the company's $11 per share price. I persuaded the board to go for the long ball. The director resigned, and I became chairman of the board. Since then, the stock price has been as high as $61 per share, although recently, due to delayed new product introductions, it has declined.

Around 2007, I was asked to join the board of NeuroPace, a company that made an electrostimulation device to be implanted inside the skull. Like a pacemaker for the brain, it stopped epileptic seizures. The CEO, Frank Fischer, a proven leader of other successful medical device companies, led NeuroPace from inception on a decade-long quest for FDA approval of its device. It was in phase-three trials.

The FDA panel, which was led by a dentist, not a neurologist, refused to approve the device. NeuroPace's scientific advisory board, which developed the methodology for evaluating the device, engaged in a long and frustrating process of trying to educate the panel. It took three years and cost $75 million. Over this time, countless epilepsy patients were left to suffer painful seizures that NeuroPace's technology could have prevented. When the company contested the FDA's decision, the FDA convened a panel of neurologists, who immediately reversed the decision and approved the product. These days, it is maddeningly complicated to get device approvals. Not so long ago, more than sixty venture capital firms funded device startups. By 2010, that number was down to ten.

Medical device innovation is limping forward because the FDA has to balance safety with speed for new efficacious treatments. The industry's goal equates to saving lives above all, so when the pendulum swings too far to safety, innovation ceases.

Much of my biotech career was guided by two mentors, Tony Evnin of Venrock and Jim Blair, the founder of Domain Associates, both of whom specialized in biotech investing. At one time, there were "four wise men": Tony, Jim, Brook Byers, and Chuck Hartman of Channing Weinberg's (Chuck was a good friend as well, but he died about twenty years ago).

After graduating from Princeton in 1962 with a bachelor's degree in Chemistry, Tony went on to earn a Ph.D. in organic chemistry from the Massachusetts Institute of Technology. He became a researcher in Union Carbide's central laboratory in 1966, and soon after, he was promoted to group leader. In 1971, he joined Story Chemical, which was working to identify human pheromones. (Ultimately, this effort was unsuccessful, although it did produce products for perfumes.) The company was highly promoted but terribly managed, and the stock declined.

Tony was a business and a commercial development person. Although the company wanted him to move to its headquarters in Michigan, by that time, he knew his career did not lie with Story.

Instead, Tony went to work for Venrock, the Rockefeller venture firm. In 1974, Peter Crisp, a senior partner, had hired Tony for his background in the physical and life sciences. Peter also then hired Hank Smith for his electronics background. What great hires. Eventually, Hank Smith went on to invest in Apple for Venrock while Tony invested in Centocor, Genetics Institute, and IDEC Pharmaceuticals.

Tony described Peter as his most important mentor. He said, "Peter Crisp set a standard that required us to have extraordinary work ethic and a seriousness about what we were doing. You are working both as an investor, as a director, and as a partner with management. You have to do well, but if you do well, you do good, and this is especially true in biotech and is tremendously rewarding. It is a reflection of the goals of Laurance Rockefeller."

The business of genetic engineering really took off between 1974 and 1979, after the discovery that a piece of DNA from one gene could be spliced into another gene. Tony was one of the few VCs who understood both chemistry and the underlying biology. He was the proverbial one-eyed man in this nascent industry, king in the land of the blind. By 1980, Tony focused 85 percent of his efforts on biotech.

He became extraordinarily experienced, and he said about

biotech companies, "You have to ask a question about the business. How long, how expensive, and if you are successful, will the product clear the regulatory hurdles and make it to market? For example, if you want to develop a drug for what is a huge market, let's say the treatment of asthma or certain kinds of cardiovascular diseases, you want a drug that is going to be prescribed by family doctors, and you have to have an enormous sales force to deliver a product, something a small company cannot take on. That would be the kind of product you would have to partner with a Merck, with a Roche, with someone like that. A cancer drug or a specialty product for hemophilia is something a small company might be able to market."

Tony invested in Centocor, the company that Michael Wall founded in 1979. At the time Venrock invested, it was in trials testing Centoxin, its first therapeutic product, which looked to be a promising medication for heart failure. The company went public in 1983, and the stock burst through the ceiling, but in 1992, Centoxin failed to receive approval from the FDA after its phase-three trials. Its stock price collapsed, tumbling from sixty-five dollars to five dollars per share in one year. Michael Wall, who headed the board, fired the CEO and reduced the company's staff by two-thirds. Later, Centocor went on to develop ReoPro, a cardiovascular drug, and more importantly, Remicade, an anti-inflammatory biologic approved to treat rheumatoid arthritis and other rheumatic diseases. Johnson & Johnson acquired Centocor in 1999 for $4.9 billion in stock, or sixty-one dollars per share. By 2009, Remicade had $5 billion in annual sales.

About being on this roller-coaster ride, Tony said, "I'm emotionally involved. I get upset. I understand there are times when a company will fail. You just have to say, 'Well, it didn't work.' You try to salvage for your investors everything that you can. Then you pull up your socks and go on. The development of drugs is high-risk and high-uncertainty. You cannot take all the uncertainty out." As long as you have multiple shots on goal in biotech investing, you can grab victory from the jaws of defeat.

In 1980, Tony invested in Genetics Institute, along with Dan Gregory, co-founder of Greylock Partners, Benno Schmidt, co-founder of J.H. Whitney, and Bill Paley, from CBS. Paley left the board early, although Schmidt served as chair of the board until he retired in 2015, with Tony succeeding him in that role.

Two of Harvard's leading molecular biologists, Mark Ptashne and Tom Maniatis, founded the company. Harvard was not supportive of it; the creation of a for-profit company by academics was somewhat controversial at the time. The town of Cambridge was also resistant to the company because of concerns about having "dangerous organisms" present in their community. Genetics Institute developed hemophilia drugs, Factor VIII and Factor IX, in addition to erythropoietin, but they lost a US patent suit to Amgen.

After losing the patent suit, the stock price plummeted, and the board decided to sell part of the company. American Home bought a majority share of Genetic Institute's stock, with an option to buy the rest, while also allowing its management and the board to run the company. Tony had a significant role in interacting with American Home's management and negotiated the final sale of the company at full price. Genetics Institute was a big success. Today, its products generate billions of dollars in revenue.

About how he originated and vetted deals, Tony said, "Centocor and Genetics Institute found me. In other cases, we hear about developments and go out and call on the companies. It's fair to say that I have never been much of one to go walking down a university hall, find a researcher, and say, 'Gee, we should start a company.' There are people who do this or claim that they do this."

It is perhaps ironic, then, that Tony has subsequently become chair of the technology transfer committees of both Memorial Sloan Kettering Cancer Center and The Rockefeller University. "More typically, I respond to the entrepreneur who forms a company and somehow finds his way to us. If you fund several biotech companies, you develop a reputation for being knowledgeable, fair, and honest. You become part of a network, hearing about new companies as they are formed. Companies that you finance like Centocor give you leads to new companies being formed."

IDEC was another of Tony's best investments. Founded by Bill Rastetter, who later became a venture partner at Venrock, the company developed Rituxan, a cancer drug with $6 billion in sales in 2009. In 2003, IDEC merged with Biogen, creating a company valued then at $6.8 billion. Tony said, "The lesson is that all these companies all go down and have their crisis moments. If you can recover from them, you might go on to greatness, but you might not. Interestingly enough, in a company like that, if you hold all your stock, an enormous amount of the value creation might have occurred subsequent to the distribution from your partnership to your limited partners. So in the case of IDEC, Venrock realizes about three or four times multiple on its investment. If you then hold the stock for the next decade, you would get ten times that; you might get a thirty-fold greater return."

About cycles in venture capital, generally, Tony said, "When you have been this in the business as long as I have, you know it is very cyclical. The venture business started as a cottage industry. It was a business that was effectively the purview of a dozen firms, most of which were representatives of families of great wealth: the Whitneys, the Rothschilds, the Rockefellers, et cetera. It is now a professional and well-organized business. I have been a part of that transition.

"The cycles in the market have taught me a lot of things. One, once you think you've figured everything out, something bad happens. In the late '90s, everyone was a genius, and all companies were worth billions of dollars. Then the bubble bursts and you were devastated, everything was worth nothing. After that, there was sort of a nuclear winter where nothing happened. I never thought I was that smart during the bubble when things were going so well. To be honest, I also never had a clue that things were going to stop and turn down so abruptly. But what was obvious to me was that all ideas were not good ideas; not all twenty-six-year-olds who started web companies were going to be successful and build important things. The market got carried away, and it was impossible not to get involved. It was a good virus; whenever you got it, you had varying degrees of it. But I guess I was never convinced that I'd gotten ten times smarter all of a sudden. I did see people around me who made fortunes in two or three years and then lost them all in the next two or three years. They really believed that they had discovered the answer.

"I guess there was a good dose of humility that came along with that. I think one of the things I've always appreciated about Venrock is that it has never been a culture of arrogance, thinking we know the answers and we are the masters of the universe. If you went around Silicon Valley, some people might give you that impression. So if you can keep a little bit of humility, you are pleased when the times get extraordinarily good, and obviously, you're devastated when they crash and go bad. But if you avoid drinking too much of the Kool-

Aid, you can survive those things. I think the culture at Venrock has been helpful in that. We weren't necessarily the best when the times were good, but we were also not quite so devastated when the downturn came. The cycles in this business, the recognition that it's never easy, and if it is easy, watch out because the wave is about to crash. That is the essence of venture capital.

"The wonderful aspect of this business is working with very interesting, very smart, very dedicated people, both within your partnership and even more in the companies in which you're involved. It's just stimulating and exciting to work with people who are doing new things, who are thinking at the levels that you can't begin to think at, that are creating new products, new activities, and making a real difference. That is all great, but half the time, it's really difficult and unpleasant and not much fun. The other half is wonderful. Like any business or life, a lot of it is difficult and unpleasant. You have to raise money when no one wants to give it to you, you have to fire people, close things down. That's not fun. Or a project fails. That really hurts, so you live through that. But that's sort of life, isn't it? In the venture business, you have intellectual stimulation and learning. You don't sell the same story every day. You come in and there are new things to learn and always new people to meet. That is what excites me, and you can still make a little money doing this, and that's not all bad."

🌲🌲🌲

Jim Blair, of Domain Associates, was a valuable mentor for me and a close friend. We traveled together on vacations for twenty years. My son Adair worked at Domain for five years, and our two firms have had a productive relationship for thirty-plus years.

Born in Ottawa, Illinois in 1939, Jim was raised in Los Angeles. In eighth grade, he did something remarkable: he started his own company, raising and training parakeets, then sold the birds to Beverly Hills pet stores. Jim's mother helped him by cleaning the cages so that Jim could crawl in the aviary to train the birds. At fourteen, Jim was an entrepreneur.

Jim wanted to experience the East Coast and attended Princeton, eventually becoming one of the school's best football players. Even today, the marching band plays "Hail to the Chief" whenever Jim enters the stadium. One of his mentors was Franklin "Cappy" Cappon, a football coach who didn't believe in entitlement. "You just go out there and do your job," was his motto. With Cappy's insight, Jim was only impressed by others' actions, rather than where they went to school.

He graduated with a degree in engineering soon after Sputnik's launch, and his generation was the one that had to rise to meet the Soviet challenge. At RCA Astro Electronics, he helped design communication, weather, and spy satellites, while also earning a master's degree and a doctorate from the University of Pennsylvania.

At this time, funding for the space program was reduced due to the Vietnam War, and Jim, bored with writing proposals fated for rejection and dejected from laying off employees, took a new position with F.S. Smithers, a New York banking firm, where he could learn investment analysis. He focused on technology stocks. He ended up spending the next seventeen years in New York. Between switching careers, graduate school, and a family, Jim had a lot of balls in the air.

Describing what he learned at Smithers, Jim said, "I think one of the things that I've done reasonably well is have a good understanding that when you make an investment, you don't get wrapped up in the technology, but you ask, 'Is this something that is going to have broad appeal to the public marketplace?' I guess I would say, having started out with a lot of things that did well, I appreciated the value of stock picking as much as how to build a company."

Jim decided to start his own venture capital firm, Domain Associates, which commenced operations in 1985, in Princeton, New Jersey. He recruited Jesse Treu from GE Labs as a founding partner. Three years later, they added Brian Dovey, who was the president of Rorer Group, now a part of Sanofi, as a general partner. Jim wanted to find partners with both investing experience and operating backgrounds.

Jim Swartz of Accel offered some startup office space to Jim Blair, as well as some advice: "You will succeed. If you have any uncertainty, don't, because you've been successful in the environment, you're in. You will do better independently. You'll do better because you'll be making a lot of decisions more rapidly."

Jim Swartz's encouragement gave Jim Blair the courage to strike out on his own. It was a comfort to know people that had done it before. It gave him assurance when Jim said, "If you think you want to do this, don't have any uncertainty that you can't because you can."

Domain worked with people the firm's partners had worked with before, such as repeat entrepreneurs or teams they had backed in the past who had gone on to their next idea. If folks had done well in the past, Domain financed and supported them again. Usually, deals that came in over the transom rarely did well. Domain instead identified areas they were interested in and talked to teams they liked about starting companies around those areas. They'd say, "Have you thought about working on this idea or that idea?" Jim directed good teams towards things of importance to Domain. The businesses were often Domain's ideas, and Domain helped get them started.

Jim commented in an interview I funded around 2010, "I think our biggest challenge has been to manage the organizational change that has come with our growth as an asset manager over the past twenty-four years. When we started Domain in the 1980s, our philosophy was to bring in some industry expertise so we could help our entrepreneurs create new companies. The entrepreneurs, in those cases, were scientists that were not experienced in business. I would say that by the '90s, we started to see repeat entrepreneurs so the need for us to fill in on some of the business functions within their companies started to disappear. Those skill sets were not unimportant, but as we started to build our organization, we were able to do it by bringing in younger people that could support us in our due diligence, and hopefully become good life science VC investors, even though they had not spent long careers in the industry.

"We started to hire associates. In doing so, we built more of a hierarchy within Domain than we had in the beginning. In the beginning, it was four investment partners doing their thing with no support. In the '90s, we started to build that support team underneath us. That allowed the senior people to get more leverage on their activities. Now we have a very well-defined structure, where we have sorted a good mix of people from an age point of view, all the way from me down the line to our youngest analyst, who just turned twenty-six. I would say at the beginning of Domain, we had no need or requirement to develop the people within our team, but now that's a very big part of what we're trying to do to mentor, train, and sustain a good culture despite occasional organizational changes. I would say that's been both a challenge and a source of pride. It's a challenge in that it's not easy to maintain one's culture. We have to sit down and talk about it on a fairly regular basis as: Are we behaving culturally in the manner that we want to behave? Are we projecting, inside and outside the firm, the values that we think are important to us as a business organization? I would say that it has been a source of pride because our organization, from top to bottom, respects that culture, and individuals practice it in their day-to-day work.

"The other challenge is the government. Our congressional leaders have no appreciation for the capital formation process and what stimulates capital formation, and the capital flows in areas that they think are important. By way of example, they want to overhaul the healthcare system. There's no way they're going to have a favorable impact on that because the only thing that's going to change the economics of healthcare delivery is technology. And they've killed any interest on the part of the investment sector in putting money into innovative new technologies; they've killed it.

"They're trying to squeeze down patent life; trying to put systems in place that will in effect control the prices of innovative new products. They are putting bureaucracies in place that are ineffective. We're turning ourselves into a 'can't-do' economy, rather than a 'can-do' economy."

In the same interview, Jim explained what he thinks goes into building a culture that is friendly to entrepreneurs. "In some firms, young partners are taught to put self-interest first. You can put things into a term sheet, and then if you don't sell the business for exactly what you wanted to sell it for, it can come out of the entrepreneur's hide rather than your hide. That is not consistent with Domain's culture. I'm not saying that those terms don't creep in, but we always ensure that management should retain incentives. There are other things we do not tolerate. When an entrepreneur calls, does it take us five or six days to get back to them, or do we return his call right away? When we're sitting in board meetings, we do not look at cell phones. We listen to what is going on. When a company comes to present to us for the first time, we do not have twenty people getting up and down, running in and out of the room tending to other things. You are attentive. What is important in the long-term is how we are perceived by the entrepreneur. We're not perfect; we think these are our values. We try to ensure that those values are built into our culture."

"We also interact socially with our entrepreneurs. We take great pleasure in each other's company. I think you would find that it doesn't go on as much in other firms. I think one of the reasons they come back when they start another company is that we are focused on building great companies and the entrepreneurs are our partners. We do not jump over to investing in cleantech. We do not fund windmills or try to create new energy policy. The entrepreneurs we fund are not just pursuing funds. We tend to have good, steady dialogue and communication with them because the things that they're interested in are interesting to us. That may well create a whole other set of problems for us because the private equity investment community's attitude towards life sciences waxes and wanes with the times. We find in times like the present, people are concerned about the policies emanating from Washington and are less interested in deploying capital in our sector. We pay the price for that. We know it is because the investors' attitudes are: *We don't know what's going to come out of the current administration. We don't know what the FDA policies are going to be. We think this is a big, black hole. We're not sure what's going to happen.* So the investors express their lack of certainty in our convictions by basically not giving us as much money as they did. I understand that. But we think this is too big a sector of the economy to change radically any time soon, and that policies are going to have to evolve in such a way that innovation continues."

Jim stressed the necessity of an exit. "In the current environment, Domain adopts a strategy: 'Five Years to Liquidity.' We do not invest unless the firm can reach liquidity in three to seven years." Jim also believed that biotech investors were much more collegial than tech investors. They were a band of brothers. "The term 'band of brothers,' for the record, comes from the Shakespearean play, *Henry V.* He gives one of the most inspirational speeches I've ever heard. The essence of the speech is: 'We few, we happy few, we band of brothers.' They're going to go to war and half of them are going to die. It's a St. Crispin's thing. And so, we have a group now, within the venture community, which we call St. Crispin's Society. It was all created in the '90s when a lot of our high-tech fund brothers were doing very, very well. They were doing very well, and the life science people were having trouble justifying their role within these diversified firms. We kind of all hung together and supported each other. We refer to ourselves as a 'band of brothers.'"

Jim's board memberships today include aTyr Pharma, Axial Biotherapeutics, Clovis Oncology, Ocunexus Therapeutics, Gene Sciences Inc., ChromaCode, and IntegenX, Inc. Jim has more than forty years of experience with venture and emerging-growth companies, and he has been involved in the creation and successful development, at the board level, with over forty life science ventures, including Amgen, Aurora Biosystems, Amylin Pharmaceuticals, Applied Biosystems, Dura Pharmaceuticals, GeneOhm Sciences, Molecular Dynamics, NuVasive, Pharmion, and Volcano.

Currently, Jim serves on the board of directors of the Prostate Cancer Foundation and the Sanford Burnham Prebys Medical Discovery Institute. He is on the advisory boards of the Department of Molecular Biology at Princeton University, the USC Stevens Center for Innovation, and the Division of Chemistry and Chemical Engineering at the California Institute of Technology.

The mentorship, partnership, and friendship I received from Tony and Jim were the most important factor in making me a successful pharmaceutical investor.

XIII.

THE BUBBLE AND SAVING NEA'S HEALTHCARE PRACTICE

"[. . .] in all our quest of greatness, like wanton boys whose pastime is their care, we follow after bubbles blown in the air."

—John Webster, *The Duchess of Malfi*
Act 5, Scene 4, Lines 64–66

AS A VENTURE CAPITALIST, I have participated in several revolutions: the personal computer, biotechnology, high-speed digital communications, the SAS revolution, the cloud, and minimally invasive surgery. The Internet Revolution, however, dwarfed those innovations, not only in its importance but in the drama that went with it. If I followed this line of thought in the early '90s to its logical conclusion, I would have anticipated the economic tsunami that would soon engulf our country and our firm. In the old economy, we relied on conservative formulas to build value over time. In the new economy of the 1990s, the giant wave of internet investment broke under its own weight. The technology industry fell victim to its perceived success. While some of this was due to the market imploding, some of it was due to negligence and questionable ethics. The devastating results challenged some of our investing rules, remade others, and erased some altogether.

The '90s was a time of incredible growth for information technology venture investing. While the number of US venture capitalists climbed from 3,800 in 1990 to 8,000 in 2000, a quarter of new venture firms had only raised a single fund. They were naifs wandering into the slaughterhouse. It was a sign of trouble. It always is. Venture capital is an apprenticeship business, which means it takes most people ten years to master it.

Starting in 1990, when IT growth was at a robust 11 percent per year, spending on information technology grew until it came to represent 8 percent of the total US economy in the late '90s. Technology investment returns far exceeded any other industry's or asset class's returns. Historically, the venture industry had focused on building companies with proven business models, such as Intel, Apple, Cisco, Compaq, Silicon Graphics, Sun, Genentech, and Immunex. All were examples of the industry's success. Investment opportunities were thoroughly investigated, followed by staged financing linked to the achievement of milestones that progressively reduced risk.

Over time, such tech startups evolved into businesses with positive cash flow and rapid growth, producing unique products that captured new markets. Though it took five to ten years for venture capital to build value, the venture industry took pride in fueling radical change throughout the world. Today's economy was created by innovations financed by venture capitalists. Such funding was what the Scottish economist and philosopher Adam Smith called "the invisible hand" of capitalism, the unobservable market force that enables the supply and demand of goods to reach equilibrium in a free market. That is not to say periods of investment excess do not occur in a variety of industries, including biotechnology, computers, medical devices, software, and healthcare services, and specialty retailing, to name a few, but such bubbles always burst.

The commercialization of the internet, sparked by the Telecommunications Act of 1996, led many venture capitalists to believe that the old rules of building businesses no longer applied. Suddenly, I heard, "Who cares about cash flow?! The game is about eyeballs, dude!" in the buildings surrounding Sand Hill Road, the corridor running through Silicon Valley, outside of San Francisco, and the center of the venture capital universe. There had been a tremendous influx of capital into business, and as the 1990s progressed, many institutional investors came to believe that the twenty-year outlook for conventional public equity investing would not be as bright as it had been in the past—for many reasons. The Harvard and Yale endowments, the Ford Foundation, and numerous insurance companies had achieved attractive returns in the past by investing in venture capital, and gradually, other institutional investors such as the mammoth pension plans began to increase their allocations to venture funding, too. Between 1995 and 2000, at least $168 billion in new capital flowed into the industry.

In the late '90s, the initial public offering and merger & acquisition markets for venture-backed technology companies shattered expectations. As a result, liquidity came rapidly into venture portfolios, and distributions to investors exploded. Some thought it was a new norm, that the methodical approach to investing was outmoded. Competition for investment opportunities increased, which drastically shortened reaction times. Many partners responded by increasing their investment pace from one to two companies per year to six or seven. To succeed in the future, everyone thought, one need only copy what had been successful in the past. The early internet era truly was the age of comparables. Of course, NEA profited from the frenzy, too, and the internal rates of return on certain funds in this vintage ranged from 40–80 percent annually.

For the most part, NEA missed the consumer dot-com bubble. We prided ourselves in investing in real companies with proven models, so we were focused on the communications industry. While at T. Rowe Price in the 1970s, I spent a lot of time studying the communications industry and forecasting how it would evolve. Before Dick joined NEA, I sent my industry analysis (some forty pages thick) to him, hoping I could tempt him away from the computer and semiconductor companies he was focused on with Arthur Rock. Perhaps the best decision NEA made at the outset was to focus on the communications industry from the start of our partnership. Dick built NEA's reputation in communications, with significant assistance from Peter Morris, Peter Barris, and Frank Bonsal. As always, and as with Laurance Rockefeller, one company leads another; so it was with my partners. One of the best examples was Juniper Networks.

Although Mark Perry and Peter Morris did the original work to fund Juniper, the CEO, Scott Kriens, wanted Dick on the board. Our partnership's initial investment was $3 million, though the ultimate return in 1999, when it went public after $20 million in follow-on investments, was $1.5 billion. This success was due to Juniper's flawless execution of its business plan.

Juniper, Cisco, and other technology companies lived their lives on treadmills. They designed and mass-produced products that had marked advantages over their competition; still, the life cycle of these products, thanks to deregulation, could be one-and-a-half to three years, as opposed to the twenty to forty years that products lasted under the Bell monopoly. In the late 1990s, communication technology was the new gold rush. Thanks to Dick and Peter Morris, we were in the right place. It was not accidental.

During the Bubble, entrepreneurs reacted to the availability of capital by starting companies in unprecedented numbers. Competition among them was vicious. After Kleiner Perkins funded Netscape, the internet search engine, fifty new search engines popped up. Capital became a way to separate a startup from its competition, so it was not uncommon for a company to raise $100 million in its second round. Never had there been so much money made available so quickly. Venture capitalists acknowledged that it was a period of speculative excess even while it was going on and freely admitted that many business plans they were funding did not make sense. But if you withdrew from the market, choosing not to invest, you watched as your competitors made billions. To be successful, you had to balance belief and skepticism.

There was the new economy and the old economy. Believers in the new economy predicted the end of brick-and-mortar businesses, even supermarkets, and they started an online grocery delivery business named Webvan. When an old economy CEO pointed out that unless the company charged dramatically higher prices, Webvan could never make money, he was derided as an irrelevant fossil. Of course, eventually, Webvan did go bankrupt. The fossils turned out to be right.

Only twenty-year-old or thirty-something wannabes could understand the brave, new digitized world. Many of the gray-haired eminences of technology venture investing also came to believe this maxim and chose not to sell their hot tech stocks, for the future had no limit.

The bubble was more like a wave. It built strength throughout the late 1990s, only to crest on the shores of the year 2000. For someone like me, it was a time of trial. The values I'd come to believe in over a lifetime had been overturned in an instant. Age and experience, the things I have been brought up to respect since childhood, no longer mattered. They were equated with ignorance in the new, internet economy. Younger NEA partners had always joked, "How do you recognize an NEA founder?" Response: "He's the one who can't use a computer!" In the past, these jokes were well-intentioned, but during the Bubble, they were signs of disrespect from the young, who thought they had all the solutions to the puzzle of life. They believed they were entitled to a legacy that others had built for a quarter of a century. Our younger partners joked that to be a good investor, you had to be on the right side of gravity. I was on the wrong side, so, for me, going to the office each day became more painful.

Arrogance and greed were rampant, but during the Bubble, people treated wealth like it was a birthright. It did not matter when a company's vision had no merit and its business plan was built out of air. The reasoning was, if you started a company, you should earn billions. Entrepreneurs were not dedicated to their products, and they didn't care about them the same way Henry Ford cared about his black car. Neither did the dot-com entrepreneurs care about their founding partners and employees. After all, life was a gold rush, in which success necessitated climbing over the back of your fellow men to snatch whatever you could, as fast as you could and cheating your partners out of their ownership as subsequently shown in the movie *The Social Network*. It was a time of black clouds. The devil had set the rules.

What was this like for me? The Greeks say your soul is located in your stomach. I agree. It felt as if half a dozen people had punched my stomach, and I was in deep pain.

Not all dot-com entrepreneurs were elaborate hucksters. When the dust settled, many profitable and valuable companies that changed the world had been created: eBay, Amazon, and Google, to name a few.

But in 2000, the Bubble finally ruptured, although the future would bring new bubbles: shimmering, prismatic mirages that disappeared as soon as you started to track their trajectory. These bubbles are why venture capital is a bipolar business, with fantastic highs and devastating lows. I had loved a bipolar woman. I had grown accustomed to such extremes.

Nonetheless, my PTSD recurred during the internet bubble. I adapted, as I tend to in times of stress, but I was also haunted by Vietnam, by the valley of the shadow of death. That proximity to death pushed me, giving me motivation and vision—and it helped me save NEA's ninth and tenth funds, plus it simply kept me going into the office. I rebuilt the healthcare team after the dotcom bust with proven scientists, MDs, and senior healthcare managers. When they made investments, their visions became reality.

When the technology bubble burst, there was no Black Thursday to mark such a precipitous decline. Unlike the Great Crash of 1929, this economic depression was like water torture, as we were forced to watch one technology sector after another collapse. The dot-com sector was just the first to fail. The internet was a revolution, and in every revolution, there are fools and profiteers driven by greed and a savage lust for power. Only a few of the fools have good intentions.

After the dot-com guys went down like dominoes, Webvan went bankrupt, then the online marketing company Netcentives went bankrupt, and these companies were followed by a multitude of fake tech miracles. Most VCs think the bankruptcies were an inevitable form of justice, an invisible hand balancing the industry's unrepentant pride. Now it's easy to look back and laugh at the baby-faced entrepreneurs who wrote their business plans with fairy dust and not hard work. After the bubble burst, it would once again be refreshing to know young entrepreneurs who loved their product more than they loved acquiring a $400,000 Porsche just months after starting a company. False dreams create suffering for real people.

NEA made the vast majority of its technology investments in stable businesses in the data communications industry. The problem was that data communication was a cyclical growth business. During the 1990s, competition grew in the telecom business, as the giant monopoly fortress of the Bell System was torn down. Competitors to the traditional telephone carriers, such as ILECs and CLECs (the locally based carriers), entered the market. Everyone was after the best data communications equipment, switching systems, routers, and such. At the time, some thought data communications and the internet would grow 50–100 percent annually for eternity.

Of course, that was not the case. The local exchange carriers used too much debt, and when demand for telecom equipment suppliers failed, the ILECs and CLECs went out of business, alongside the equipment providers.

The great telecom companies, like Lucent Technologies and Nortel Telecom, also fell prey to greed. They used falsely inflated stock to buy companies that made nonfunctional products. They pursued extensive acquisition sprees using this stock to buy new technologies at insane prices. Companies that once took pride in being conservative were now playing a game of musical chairs, but when the band stopped playing, everyone would be without a seat.

A young partner at NEA invested in a startup company called Xros, and seven months later, in 2000, Nortel acquired it for stock valued at $3.5 billion. NEA made an $800 million short-term gain. The general partners could not sell before our limited partners, which meant we general partners had to sit on the stock until it would be a long-term gain. Ultimately, though, Xros' product didn't work during testing. Nortel, therefore, wrote off its $3.5 billion loss, and due to this and other investment losses Nortel incurred around this time, their stock dropped from sixty dollars per share to five-eighths of a dollar per share. Technology investing had had its comeuppance.

Lucent Technologies, born in 1996 when AT&T split into three companies, was part of this madness. It was a great institution, with all the fabled innovations of Bell Labs part of its corporate story. Lucent executives decided to reward themselves by building a $100 million golf course for themselves in Princeton, New Jersey. Lucent bought Ascend, a high-end data provider, an NEA portfolio company, for almost $20 billion. Although Ascend's product lines were sound, growth was slowing. The acquisition was unsuccessful. Lucent was making the acquisitions, so it could compete better with Cisco and Nortel. Lucent made a host of other purchases, and their write-offs escalated. Eventually, senior Lucent employees blew the whistle on their company because the CEO was overstating the company's prospects. In December 2000, the company announced that it had overstated revenues by $700 million. Its stock collapsed from a market cap of $258 billion to $15.6 billion. This was not too bad, believe it or not, given that between 2000 and 2002, the large telecoms lost almost $4 trillion in market value.

In the frenzy, telecom CEOs pushed their employees to produce unachievable results, so some of the managers cooked the books. As an industry, telecom had exhausted its capital for new technology, and a host of venture capital-funded startups offering the "next new thing" filed for bankruptcy. New venture capital-funded telecom startups had no customers to generate returns from the billions of dollars they raised to develop ever better products. The ILECs and CLECs, the locally based carriers, were gone, and Big Telecom wasn't buying. In this new economy, companies that at one time had a $1.5 billion valuation disappeared in eighteen months, and the telecom market devolved into chaos.

Software companies began to suffer. During the bubble, these companies hit valuations not justified by their business prospects. The growth of the companies did not falter; nevertheless, they imploded. The field of enterprise (or business) software, which for a time offered the best venture opportunities, had plateaued, and just as healthcare had its perfect storm, so did technology. Tech investors, formerly masters of the universe, realized they had been taken for fools. Many caught up in the mania did not or were not able to sell even a share before the music stopped. One day, you're worth $300 million; five hundred days later, you're worth $3 million.

In the spring of 2000, we were about to launch NEA X, and we held our annual meeting in Washington, D.C., while the cherry trees were blooming. The NEA investing staff drank cocktails at a historic house in the Georgetown neighborhood. Not everyone was enjoying themselves, especially the healthcare partners.

A divide had begun to emerge, with some partners (formerly on the healthcare team) claiming that healthcare investing did not provide satisfactory returns. They criticized proposed investments, suggesting that their former partners were suckers who didn't comprehend the new economy. This darkened the atmosphere at our partners' meetings, and they raised objections about every new healthcare investment, feeding the skepticism of other technology partners.

Dick later explained the situation this way: "A convert to a new religion is always on a jihad, and their old teammates are the unbelievers." Knowing this did not make it any easier to handle open attacks from the people you had mentored and whose careers you helped to build. This was a heart-wrenching experience because heated skepticism fueled my self-doubt and paranoia. The good news was that Mark Perry, a partner on the tech side, was also one of the partners like Dick who watched over NEA's med team during the worst of the Bubble, and he suggested the team bring in another senior medical partner.

Mark Perry was, to some extent, my alter ego on the tech side in the NEA general partner group. He was a Silicon Graphics alumnus, having served as vice-chair and executive vice president of that company, and he was a close friend of Dick's. He joined NEA as a general partner in 1996. Until that time, I had led NEA's fundraising efforts, which required organizing and maintaining close relations with the limited partners. I felt it was important that this function be delegated to someone else, so the partnership would not be too dependent on one person. Mark took that role over until Peter Barris, as managing partner, assumed the role in the early 2000s.

Mark and I viewed the NEA band of brother culture as our territory to protect. We were constantly working on ways to improve it, such as developing the "NEA Career Path." Of course, Mark's major focus was as an investor on the technology team, championing companies like Tivo, Broadcom, and Ariba. For me, though, the most important thing he did was to keep my head on my shoulders during NEA's debates about the future of healthcare. Mark and his wife Mauree Jane were always there for me when I needed encouragement.

Dick always said that he liked having partners as they keep you from making mistakes. Mark taught me that a good partner can get you through "the times that try men's souls" both personally and in business. After all, that is what being a true partner is all about.

Mark Perry recommended that NEA hire Dr. James Tananbaum, a friend he knew from the Bohemian Grove, to join NEA. It was a great idea. I'd known Jim since I brought him into Amerigroup, which was a very successful NEA investment, and later, he founded the NEA portfolio company GelTex Pharmaceuticals. An "enfant terrible," Jim had an MD and MBA from Harvard, a Ph.D. in molecular biology, and I wanted to hire him. To me, his decision to consider joining NEA was a compliment because he was electing to remain in the healthcare business and considered NEA as a base for his operations. He conceded that we were understaffed for the daunting task of investing $450 million in the new fund; still, he believed we had an extraordinary franchise and remarkable deal flow from our former entrepreneurs.

We discussed our first project together, Vitae. Years ago, NEA had backed Vertex, one of the companies that created rational drug design, and we found then that it took ten to fifteen years and $800 million to bring a drug to market. The last five to seven years of that span were the most expensive, when human clinical trials were underway. Although Vertex had introduced successful products, it had failed to realize the full potential of rational drug design, but its technology was a paradigm shift. The genomics revolution had created thousands of compounds that some said could extend the human lifespan by forty years. But how could you mine the mountain that contains the diamonds while sifting through millions of tons of worthless dirt? Rational drug design was the answer.

Vitae's management included pharmaceutical legend Gene Cordes, who has a deep voice like actor Ray Milland in *Love Story*. He had the experience we needed, given that he was an alumnus of Merck, a former vice president of research and development at Eastman pharmaceuticals, and a proven drug hunter. Gene's partner, Dr. Jack Baldwin, was a soft-spoken, drug-hunting genius. Formerly the chief scientific officer and a founder of Pharmacopeia, Jack helped Gene build an exceptional team of scientists. Jim Tannenbaum was responsible for conceiving the company's mission and attracting the team members.

The discussion we had about Jim at the partners' meeting where we were to decide whether to hire him was particularly volatile, with some of us firmly in favor and others violently opposed. We didn't get to a consensus, and the decision was delayed. All along, Jim had been transparent. He told me he was also talking to David Schnell and Alex Barkus, two former Kleiner Perkins partners who left that firm when it decided to stop making healthcare investments and focus only on technology investments. Together with Dr. Russell Hirsch, they co-founded Prospect Ventures, quickly raising $500 million from excellent investors. Jim called to tell me he was joining Prospect. I didn't blame him. But Jim's effect on me was exhilarating. His interest showed we did have a great franchise; all we had to do was rebuild the team.

Jim's focus was early-stage biotech investing. I had a successful biotech investing track record; but as you approach the age of 60, it's harder to invest in companies that may take fifteen years to commercialize products. Many of the leaders in biotech investing doubted the historic biotech model. Jim Blair, my good friend and Domain founder, and I crafted a new method for biopharma investing, asking "How do we cut the Gordian knot and generate investments that have shorter paths to liquidity?" The answer was right in front of us.

Big Pharma, through mergers and acquisitions, was too large to take an interest in some of its smaller pharmaceutical products. Most of the small, specialty biopharma companies had been acquired. Interestingly, a lot of Big Pharma's revenues came from products that had revenues of less than $100 million a year. It was obvious to us that small, neglected markets had the potential to grow significantly through promotion, marketing, and pricing. Over time, you could extend patent life by new formulation or drug delivery that would make them highly differentiated products.

Biotechnology, through the rational drug delivery concept, claimed to have the potential to shorten delivery times while increasing the probability of success in clinical trials. Early biotech companies wooed investors with sound and light shows, but they never came through on their promises. Despite the much-touted promise of biotechnology, it took just as long to develop new products, and the odds of clinical success remained about the same. By the year 2000, a company needed to have a product in phase-two or phase-three clinical trials to go public, or it had to have a multi-hundred-million-dollar deal with Big Pharma. Reality, not promises, ruled the drug pipeline. The state of the industry in 2000 was that small research-oriented companies developed products, while Big Pharma typically financed these new drugs through final trials and commercialization.

The old model for biotech investing no longer worked. In the past, an investor group might spend $10 to $20 million to assemble a team, develop several leads, and then do a massive biopharma deal with pre-clinical products. The next step would be to take the company public. The new model entailed venture syndicates investing $100 to $200 million just to get to the point where value is created, meaning phase-three trials or commercialization. It was difficult to attract public investors until those milestones were achieved. Occasionally Big Pharma would do a pre-clinical deal. This raised the stakes for biopharma investors because they had to invest substantial amounts in increasingly risky and uncertain outcomes.

Now, suppose we could do things differently. NEA and Domain had a stable of entrepreneurs that we had funded in the past: Mark Skaletsky (Biogen, Fenway Pharmaceuticals, GelTex), Pat Mahaffy (NeXstar Pharmaceuticals, Pharmion), and John Spitznagel (Roberts, ESP Pharma, and Esprit Pharma Inc.). A high percentage of our deal flow came from serial entrepreneurs like Jim Barrett, and those are the people we sought out to construct a biopharma company in three to five years instead of fifteen.

A proven entrepreneur like Jim approached his old friends in Big Pharma to buy a product that was too small to be relevant to a company with $30 billion in revenues. Biopharma would only sell its drugs to experienced teams because they did not want the residual liability of a mishandled product. The entrepreneur vastly accelerated a product's sales with a specialty sales force. Simultaneously, they found products in human clinical trials that created a pipeline of new products. Whenever Big Pharma companies merged, a significant percentage of research projects were abandoned. The companies combined their research pipelines, picking out the projects that were complementary to existing products. They closed down many research projects while out-licensing the rest. The serial entrepreneur could make a company overnight with revenues and a pipeline. Such a company could access public equity within two to five years of its founding, instead of ten.

The concept that Jim Blair and I arrived at became NEA's and Domain's healthcare strategy. Perhaps healthcare could now account for 40–50 percent of NEA X's invested capital and a greater percentage of its profit. We had only had 20 percent of NEA's carried interest (tech accounting for 80 percent), but we could invest half of the fund and pay back our technology partners for their distributions during the bubble. NEA's current healthcare team did not have the horsepower to do this. Traditionally, the NEA healthcare team had been made up of investors, but the new investment strategy required the expertise of M.D.s with extensive clinical experience, Ph.D.s in molecular biology, and pharmaceutical industry executives with extensive operating experience. Where would we find that kind of talent?

It was a typical morning for me in the early '90s. I woke up at 6:00

AM, exercised for an hour, took my pills, fed the animals, dressed, and drove to Gaithersburg, Maryland for the Sensors board meeting. Jim Barrett, the company's CEO, was trying to launch another miracle, a readout of blood glucose for diabetes. Sensor's tiny implant eliminated the need for finger sticks, which give diabetics accurate, continuous glucose readings. This was important because patient compliance in taking insulin improved patient wellbeing dramatically. Many diabetes patients failed to perform their finger sticks because it was too painful. This product would save lives.

Sitting across the table from me, Jim was an eloquent gentleman. We both recognized that Sensors was a two-step-forward-one-step-back company, by which I mean it made a dramatic scientific advance, but then discovered a critical problem, which delayed the product's commercialization. Jim exercised regularly and was in good shape; however, he had begun to develop heart problems, and he was considering slowing down.

Sensors rented a building that had once housed a Hillman Biotech company that went bankrupt. It's hard to live in the shadow of a vanquished dream. The place seemed to be haunted by the ghosts of what could have been, but the rent was low. I always sat next to the company's new CEO, Dr. Mark Schoenebaum, so that I would be across from Jim during meetings. Jim had moved, by his own choice, from CEO to chairman, and Mark was his chosen successor.

Jim was planning to step back and enjoy a well-earned retirement. He had already donated a significant portion of the money he had created over his lifetime to a charitable foundation his wife April managed. As I sat across the table, looking at Jim, I was reminded of the phrase, "to be in the company of gentle madmen." Jim was that gentle, hypomanic genius—marching to his own drummer, doing things that mattered. He did not like to promote himself and lived to deliver results.

It was frustrating dealing with Jim because he looked like a white-haired college professor missing his bow tie, and when you asked him what he had done, he would hardly respond. Yet, the three most important entrepreneurs in the history of the mid-Atlantic were Jim Kimsey, the founder of America Online, Bill McGowan, the founder of MCI, and Jim Barrett, the CEO of three companies—Life Technologies, Genetic Therapy, and Sensors. At that board meeting, I had a vision. Most of my visions related to the future; this one referred to the past. Jim Barrett knew the biopharma business. He knew the clinic where pharmaceutical battles are won and lost. He understood the science. And he had experience running a billion-dollar division of SmithKline. Here was one of the few men I trusted, sitting across from me on a sunny spring day. We needed him at NEA. Spring is such a confusing season for me, watching life reemerge after a winter of death.

I ask Jim to spend a few minutes in his office, saying, "Jim, I got a favor to ask of you."

"Well, I owe you, so go ahead."

"Let's change healthcare history together," I said. "You have created miracles in your thirty-year career. Let us suppose that, in the next ten years of your life, you can replicate what you have done to date tenfold. The venture business will allow you the time to take vacations and relax, but do not underestimate the challenge—it's life-and-death combat."

Jim just looked at me.

What the hell will he say to this bizarre request? I wondered.

Finally, he replied, "What will I do in retirement? I could watch shooting stars as an amateur astronomer, but that will be boring after a while."

"Why not become an NEA general partner?" I pushed.

Jim smiled and said, "I have to ask April, but she probably wants me out of the house."

Jim called six hours later, insisting, "I accept, but I am only signing up for three years."

After hiring Jim, we built a solid healthcare team at NEA, with partners who had the skills we were missing. The scientific partners we brought in were Dr. Josh Makower, Dr. Ali Behbahani, and Dr. Robert Garland. Our operating partners—people who worked for pharmaceutical firms—included Ed Mathers (from MedImmune) and Bob Croce (from Johnson & Johnson). Our investing partners were Jake Nunn, Paul Walker, and Mohamad Makhzoumi. The team was headed by Dave Mott (former CEO of MedImmune).

When we hired Jim Barrett, I had to convince my partners that he was not too old and had the energy for the business. When we hired Dave several years later, I had to convince them that he had not made so much money from the sale of MedImmune that he'd lost his drive for the business. Both Jim and Dave exceeded all expectations. Dave added to NEA's biopharma investing strategy in numerous ways. He invested in pre-clinical platforms of high interest to Big Pharma, which led to a family of products—Epigenetics is an example. These platforms were bought for multiples of invested capital. Healthcare was finally, at this time, back on a firm footing at NEA.

After I retired, there was yet another move by the West Coast technology partners to eliminate the healthcare practice and split the firm into separate healthcare and technology partnerships. Ultimately, the discussion was made moot by the incredible results generated by David Mott and his new team.

During the bubble, NEA had been spared severe losses, and while many technology companies failed due to overwhelming competition, many were driven to failure by greed. These companies published overstated earnings, then their write-offs contributed to a grab-what-you-can economy in which no one was held accountable. It's still a familiar problem today. For entrepreneurs like that, their passion was making money, not creating value in a useful product, so when they couldn't make money, they invented it. For me, money was not enough and not the purpose. It was an honor to build the best teams, innovate life-changing industries, and go to battle for what I believed in.

XIV.

SAVING CAPITALISM

"To dream the impossible dream
To fight the impossible foe
To bear with unbearable sorrow
To run where the brave dare not go
To right the unrightable wrong
To love pure and chaste from afar
To try when your arms are too weary
To reach the unreachable star
This is my quest
To follow that star
No matter how hopeless
No matter how far"

—"The Impossible Dream", *Man of La Mancha*

WHEN THE BUBBLE EXPLODED IN 2000, US stock prices collapsed as speculative excess was drained from the market. The sudden growth in low-cost retail stock trading, a result of the widespread emergence of the internet in the mid-1990s and fueled by changes to securities regulation, was part of what led to the bubble and its subsequent collapse. These changes went on to have a lasting effect on the small company markets, which were essential for the survival of the venture capital industry.

The Bubble was merely the most visible sign, or result, of broader changes that had been leading to the ruination of the small company capital markets between 1975 and 2012. In most cases, the problems were caused by well-intentioned regulations or deregulations with unintended consequences. Starting in the late 1960s and continuing until the Bubble, four investment banks specializing in underwriting small, high-growth venture-backed companies gained a dominant hold on small company underwriting. They were Alex Brown in Baltimore, the oldest investment bank in the country, and the California-based banks, Hambrecht & Quist Group (H&Q), Robertson Stephens & Co., and Montgomery Securities.

Two of the "Four Horsemen," as the firms were sometimes called, shared an intertwined history. In 1969, Sandy Robertson, Robert Colman, and Ken Siebel started Robertson, Colman & Siebel. Thomas Weisel joined the firm in 1971, and his name was added to the masthead. In 1978, Tom became CEO, and he changed the firm's name to Montgomery Securities. Montgomery underwrote Yahoo! in 1996, and in a later reincarnation, Thomas Weisel Partners (or, TWP) financed Crocs Inc., Nuance Communications, Phase Forward Inc., and many other leading tech companies. (During its first year, TWP orchestrated Yahoo!'s $3.6 billion stock acquisition of GeoCities and played a role in the initial public offerings of Drugstore.com, Fogdog, Inc., FTD.com, InfoSpace.com, MapQuest.com, Netcentives, Red Hat Inc., Stamps.com, and TheStreet.com.)

The change at the top at Robertson, Colman, Siebel & Weisel led to the departure of Sandy Robertson and Bob Coleman, who then founded Robertson, Colman, Stephens & Woodman, which name was later shortened to Robertson Stephens & Co. in 1989. During the internet boom, from 1999 to 2000, Robertson Stephens underwrote seventy-four IPOs, totaling $5.5 billion, including MapQuest, E-Trade, Vericity, and Bebe.

Hambrecht & Quist was founded in 1968 by Bill Hambrecht and George Quist. Over the years, the partnership underwrote Apple Computer, Genentech, and Adobe Systems in the '80s. In the 1990s, they underwrote Netscape's IPO and Amazon's. Alex Brown, under the leadership of Don Hebb, was the leading underwriter of venture-backed companies on the East Coast.

By the early 2000s, all four firms were acquired. In 1997, Bank America bought Robertson Stephens, and Bankers Trust bought Alex Brown. Then, in 1999, H&Q was acquired by Chase Manhattan Bank, and NationsBank acquired Montgomery Securities. The reasons for the sales were multifold. All four firms were research-based. Regulatory reforms reduced the trading spreads and commissions they could charge, eliminating the vital profit center, selling public company stocks that the firms relied on to stay solvent during bear markets when the "IPO window" would close. At the same time, the federal government stopped enforcing Glass-Steagall, the legislation passed in 1933 in the wake of the stock market crash of 1929 and during the Great Depression to limit the risk-taking lending institutions. Suddenly commercial banks could own investment banks. Meanwhile, IPO investment banks were seeing their valuations surge, yet with their economic model threatened by regulatory change, and with sudden interest from large commercial banks, they took the opportunity to get out while the getting was good, selling their firms to commercial banks at historically high valuations.

After the Bubble, the number of IPOs dropped precipitously, and buying and selling stocks in small public companies was no longer profitable. With the loss of these small IPO investment banks, the institutional investors that formed the foundation of the small IPO market abandoned small companies in a quest to find liquidity. The best new internet companies would go public much later than previous-generation companies had, such as Intel, which raised $8 million at a $50 million pre-money valuation in 1971. The Bulge Bracket investment banks, such as J.P. Morgan and Goldman Sachs, entered the market to underwrite companies with $1 billion-plus market caps, also known as unicorns. They could only justify covering companies with $1 billion valuations because they had big bank overheads. There was no economic incentive to maintain coverage of smaller companies.

By 2010, the Age of the Unicorn was upon us. Both the venture capital industry and investment banks focused on $1 billion outcomes.

The age of the small offering was over. Venture-backed companies postponed offerings to avoid dilution. By 2017, $66 billion was invested, or in some cases trapped, in unicorn startups.

Regulatory pressures hurt the smaller banks a lot. Recognizing these trends, the Four Horsemen were sold, and IPOs for small venture back companies collapsed. In retrospect, the excesses of the bubble only masked the structural changes that led to the collapse of the small company equity markets. The Four Horsemen reemerged as asset managers. Robertson Stephens reopened in 2013. Bill Hambrecht started WR Hambrecht in 1998. Thomas Weisel Partners was founded in 1999, and Stifel acquired the firm in 2010. When Alex Brown was acquired, Brown Advisory (founded in 1993) and ABS Capital Partners (founded in 1990) were spun out as independent entities.

Collectively, the Four Horsemen underwrote thousands of high-tech and med-tech IPOs from the late 1960s until 2000. Their departure from the IPO market was only one of the factors in its collapse (as seen in the chart below).

A perfect storm of regulatory change largely destroyed the small IPO market. This market is what former president Jiang Zemin of China referred to when he called the Nasdaq "the crown jewel of all that is great about America." In 1975, the Securities and Exchange

Commission mandated the deregulation of the brokerage industry, abolishing high fixed commissions. The intent was good, to allow market competition to dictate commission levels, but the decision also ushered in discount brokerage and the collapse of the ecosystem of smaller institutional investors, investment banks, and stockbrokers required to support small IPOs.

In 1994, the SEC's antitrust suit pushed the Nasdaq to adopt new order handling rules, which cut the incentive for market makers to provide liquidity and support stocks. In 1996, anticipating this new world of low-cost trading and internet access, Charles Schwab introduced the concept of discount brokerage. Lower brokerage fees deprived retail salesmen of their livelihood, and they rapidly abandoned stockbroking to seek higher fees as asset managers. In 1996, 1997, and 1998, in rapid succession, the Manning Rule, the Order Handling Rules, and Regulation ATS (Alternative Trading Systems, otherwise known as electronic trading) combined to reduce trading spreads and brokerage economics dramatically. Small companies' liquidity provision, research support, and sales support disappeared.

Online brokerages reached 9.3 million accounts in 1999, executing 512,000 trades a day. Cheap trades encouraged day trading at the expense of long-term investing. That same year, the US Banking Act of 1939 was formally repealed, permitting commercial banks, insurance companies, and securities firms to operate under one roof. Financial conglomerates "too big to fail" formed overnight, decreasing competition, increasing systemic risk, and leading to the credit crisis of 2008.

Under the Glass-Steagall legislation, leverage was limited to a 3-to-1 ratio. After its repeal, leverage in financial institutions exploded to 100 to 1. Repayment of loans was no longer considered to be a requirement to make a loan. After the debt crisis in 2008, virtually no financial institution CEOs were criminally prosecuted because they were following incentives created by the US government to make housing available to everyone regardless of whether they could afford it. The US government, not the banks, caused the credit crisis.

In early 2000, Regulation Fair Disclosure (or Reg FD) was created to prevent the selective disclosure of important information by public companies to market professionals and certain shareholders. It mandated that when public companies disclose material nonpublic information, such as earnings and forecasts, to a limited group such as stockbrokers, the company must simultaneously make public the disclosure of that information. This effort to level the playing field and give people confidence in the market destroyed Wall Street's equity research industry while benefitting private equity funds, as distinct from venture capital funds, who were positioned to exploit the public markets with real-time reactions.

Substantial investing in alternative investment funds ensued. In 2001, the SEC phased in decimalization, pushing price competition to penny increments, and spreads disappeared, further damaging the incentives to provide research and liquidity. Quality research on small companies simply disappeared. From 1994 to 2001, the SEC drove the economics of trading spreads for small-cap stocks from one quarter per share to one cent, a 96 percent decline.

The Sarbanes-Oxley Act (or Sarbox) was passed in 2002. Its goal was to restore public confidence in the capital markets after the discovery of accounting fraud at Enron, WorldCom, and HealthSouth. Under Sarbox, the average cost of going public increased to $2.5 million, and the annual cost of staying public increased by $1.5 million annually. Ironically, Sarbanes-Oxley was implemented to address a problem created by large public companies, yet its impact was felt most by small companies that could least afford the cost.

In 2003, there was a global settlement between the Financial Industry Regulatory Authority (FINRA), the NYSE, NASDAQ, and the ten largest securities firms. It required those securities firms to separate research from investment banking. Analysts could no longer be compensated for investment banking business. Investment bankers were not allowed to have input into research compensation or coverage decisions, which led to a further decline in research for small-cap stocks.

The SEC caused a structural overhaul of the securities markets with Regulation National Market System (or Reg NMS) in 2005. This stripped away the remaining ability of NYSE specialists to support small-cap stocks on the Big Board and increase the attractiveness of quantitative trading. In 2007, the Exchange Rule Act's Rule 201 was amended, eliminating the uptick rule on short sales. This meant that short sales could occur at any price, unrelated to the previously traded price. This increased short selling and volatility, and it gave speculators the means to drive prices down with short raids. The effect of this perfect deregulatory storm of the first five years of the 2000s had dire consequences. Over the decade after the bubble, the capital markets were closed to 80 percent of the companies that needed them. Some speculate that this led to the loss of 22 million jobs since 90 percent of a company's growth occurs after its IPO.

The US equity markets have turned away from long-term fundamental investing to become the home of casino capitalism. The quality of brokerage research has declined markedly, while the quality of institutional research conducted by institutions has increased. Wall Street abandoned active sales coverage of long-term institutional investors; instead, it focused on high-frequency trading, derivatives, and a tiny number of high-commission-paying hedge funds. In 1990, the median IPO was $10 million in size, whereas, in the first half of 2009, it was $135 million. The number of IPOs fell from 520 per year (pre-bubble) to 120 IPOs per year (post-bubble). In 2000, the average holding period was five years, but in 2011, it was 2.3 months. The average holding period for high-frequency trading is 11–21 seconds. In 1990, 90 percent of trades were based on fundamental investing; however, by 2001, it was down to 30 percent. It has been reported by the Aite Group that over 70 percent of the volume of trading in US markets is done by high-frequency traders.

Different standards of transparency exist for brokerage and '40 Act institutional investors, like T. Rowe Price than for hedge funds. New products and venues increased opaqueness and increased risk. These include:

- **Black pools:** These are opaque, anonymous trade execution venues used by institutions away from traditional exchanges. Approximately forty black pools are said to be operating in the United States.

- **Hedge funds:** While an estimated 8,800 hedge funds are responsible for 30 percent of stock trading volume in the United States, they are not required to disclose anything, including trading activity or their use of leverage.

- **Naked shorts:** In June 2008, a report by J.P. Morgan indicated that 22 billion shares of stock had "failed to deliver." Most of these shares were likely the work of "naked short" sellers. The SEC has focused considerable attention on bringing dangerous short-selling activity under control since the credit crisis accelerated in the fall of 2008. Naked short-selling is the practice of short-selling affordable assets of any kind without first borrowing the security or ensuring the security can be borrowed and is conventionally done in short sales.

- **Predatory shorts:** These short-sellers target vulnerable, new-issue activity; they may short ahead of a marketed follow-on stock offering and legally cover in the open market after trading, or they may illegally trade on inside information and short ahead of PIPEs and registered direct offerings. They might take short positions in companies and then illegally disclose false negative publicity about them, aiming to cover their positions at a profit. These behaviors cost issuers hundreds of millions, if not billions, of dollars in lost proceeds every year. To date, the SEC has not vigorously pursued these short-sellers.

- **High-frequency trading firms:** These firms generate computer-driven order flow not supported by individuals making fundamental buy-and-sell decisions. They include proprietary trading firms (e.g., GETCO and Tradebot), statistical arbitrage hedge funds (e.g., Millennium and D.E. Shaw), and automated market makers (e.g., Citadel Securities, Goldman Sachs, and Knight Capital Group).

- **OTC derivatives and credit-default swaps:** These products may depend on offsetting transactions in traditional equity, debt, and options markets. Systemic risk elevates significantly due to the lack of a single regulator and central clearing party to oversee all related market transactions.

- **Credit surrogates:** When security complexity made it impossible for investors to conduct their own analysis, they relied on ratings from ratings agencies and insurers. The

ratings proved to be overly optimistic, especially those of
CDOs of ABSs and CDOs of CDOs (CDO-squared) whose
complexity exceeded the analytical and risk management
capabilities of the most sophisticated market participants.

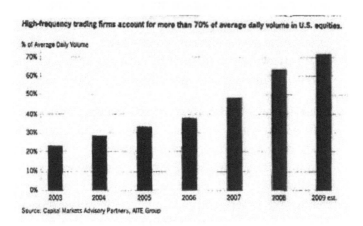

High-frequency trading firms account for more than 70% of average daily volume in U.S. equities.

Source: Capital Markets Advisory Partners, AITE Group

The structural changes in the market changed entrepreneurial
behavior. In 1982, NEA had a getaway for portfolio CEOs in the
Napa Valley. I asked them how many wanted to build a company for
the long term, and 80 percent replied positively. In 2008, at a similar
type of retreat, that number was reversed—only 20 percent wanted
to build for the long-term. The venture capital industry was also
affected by the structural problems in the market.

Time to Liquidity Continues to Increase
Median Time From Initial Equity Funding to IPO

The average time for a company to reach liquidity increased from 5.4 years in 2003 to 8.1 years in 2016. This lowered a fund's internal rate of return and made it harder for the asset class to raise money. It is a fact that venture firms that cannot raise money continue to exist for another ten years as they liquidate their old portfolios, so in 2007, 90 percent of the capital in the industry was controlled by 470 firms.

Another manifestation of the capital markets crisis was the delisting of companies. Before 1997, the US was performing in line for IPOs with other developed markets; after 1997, the number of listed companies declined by almost 33 percent. During this time, Hong Kong increased the number of listed companies by more than 91 percent. When weighted for changes in the real GDP, the US decline in listed companies was almost 53 percent between 1991 and 2008. Japan, Australia, Toronto, and London all outperformed the US in this area.

By the late '90s, I was aware of a tidal wave approaching our capital markets. It was like standing miles inland and watching as a ten-foot surge of water crossed the ocean on its way to the shoreline, though the wave wouldn't reach its destination until the crash of 2000. By then, it was a 250-foot wall that would decimate the innovation economy.

In the early 2000s, I formed Inside Venture with Mona DeFrawi. Our idea was simple: to develop an alliance between the top healthcare and technology venture capital firms. We would have a conference annually, inviting the new generation of small company banks, the institutional investors who invested in late-stage private companies, the top venture capital firms, and their best portfolio companies. The hope was that we would introduce our best portfolio companies to financial institutions three years before they went public. The institutions could do their research and get to know management over time. Big firms like T. Rowe Price, J.P. Morgan, Fidelity, and Wellington were invited, as were small firms like Wasatch, Maverick, Essex, and OrbiMed. A year before a portfolio company went public, we asked the institutions to participate in a private placement, hoping they would be the lead investors in a public offering.

Though we tried to interest the new generation of the Four Horsemen, Jeffries, Piper Jaffray, Cowen, JMP Securities, and Leerink Swann, we failed because those firms thought they could do it better on their own. If InsideVenture took off, they probably thought, would institutional buyers need bankers? After all, the institutions had their own research.

We financed InsideVenture for roughly a decade with the fees we charged at the conference and investments made by the venture firms. The internet made it easy to find small-growth companies to raise money without going to conferences. The venture capital firms lost confidence and refused to fund InsideVenture. We sold the nonprofit to Barry Silbert, an energetic entrepreneur who founded SecondMarket, a private firm that sold secondary interests in private companies over the internet. He dreamed of being able to offer primary shares over the internet, much like Bill Hambrecht was doing. At that time, SecondMarket was selling secondaries of all the best tech companies, including Google, LinkedIn, and Facebook.

As a result of this ten-year quixotic adventure with Inside Venture, I got to know David Weild, the former vice chairman of NASDAQ and CEO of Weild & Co. At the time, he was an advisor to the global accounting, tax, and advisory firm, Grant Thornton. It was here that his research into capital markets was first published.

The Grant Thornton work provided data and analysis of the IPO crisis for stakeholders who had an interest in the capital markets for small companies. Much of the information and data on the crisis that I have previously mentioned in this chapter has been lifted—nearly verbatim—from those Grant Thornton reports.

During his career, David participated in thousands of equity offerings, including those for NVIDIA, Celgene, Facebook, Netflix, and JetBlue. His studies have been cited in the *Wall Street Journal, The Economist,* and *Businessweek.* He provided testimony to the House of Representatives and the SEC on small and emerging companies; in addition, he has spoken at the Group of 20 and the Organization for Economic Cooperation and Development. Even the 2012 Jumpstart Our Business (or JOBS) Act relied on studies performed by David, with *Forbes* going so far as to call David "the father" of the JOBS Act. For ten years, we devoted much of our time to trying to fix our Humpty Dumpty capital markets. I played Sancho Panza to his Don Quixote.

In 2011, under Secretary of the Treasury Timothy Geithner, a special committee was formed called the IPO Task Force. Its mission was to examine and recommend changes to existing securities regulations and market practices. It was chaired by my good friend Kate Mitchell, a co-founder of Scale, a Silicon Valley-based venture firm that invests in early-stage tech. Another good friend, Mary Miller, was also very involved in the work. She left her position as director of the fixed income division at T. Rowe Price to be the assistant secretary of the treasury for financial markets, and later, the undersecretary for domestic finance under Geithner.

If David Weild was the father of the JOBS Act, then Kate Mitchell, a founder of Scale Venture Partners, was its mother. She assembled a committee consisting of venture capitalists, entrepreneurs, securities attorneys, academics, accountants, public investors, and investment bankers. She put together a contact list of various individuals who were asked to provide input to the task force, including me, Joe Grundfest of Stanford Law School, Bill Hambrecht of WR Hambrecht + Co., David Weild of Weild & Co., Dixon Doll of DCM, Mark Heesen of President of NVCA, Duncan Niederauer of NYSE, Scott Cutler of NYSE, Edward Knight of NASDAQ, Bob McCooey of NASDAQ, Barry Silbert of Second Market, Francis Currie of Davis Polk, Lise Buyer of Class V Group, and Greg Becker of Silicon Valley Bank.

The JOBS Act, also known as the Crowdfunding Act, was intended to encourage funding for small businesses. President Barack Obama signed it into law in 2012. It created ways for companies to use crowdfunding to issue securities over the internet in a somewhat similar fashion to Bill Hambrecht's Dutch auctions. It also reduced some of the regulatory disclosure requirements for companies with less than $1 billion in sales. David Weild was also heavily involved with two other provisions of the JOBS Act: one permitted the use of general solicitation in private placements, and the other was Regulation A+ (or Reg A+), which permitted "IPO Lite." Both proved critical for the formation of small company capital.

Kate's great accomplishment was to arrive at some provisions that would pass muster with the hundreds of differing competitive interest groups. My approach would have been to radically regulate and limit hedge funds and program trading, lower capital gains rates for long holding periods, and allow increased brokerage commissions and eliminate trading in spreads. Too many powerful oxen would have been gored with my approach. One does not use a sledgehammer to tune a piano.

During the process of crafting these incentives, David sent a note to Kate in 2011, saying he felt the JOBS Act was a good step forward but did not go far enough. He thought the daunting challenge to the IPO market was not the cost of going public but the fact that the public markets were structured such that they destroyed the commissions and trading spread essential to support IPO distribution, support, and fundamental research. He recommended the following:

1. Larger tick sizes and spreads on trading to incentivize reinvestment in stockbroking, equity research, and to provide liquidity (a tick is the minimum incremental amount at which you can trade a security).
2. The end of what he dubbed "one-size-fits-all markets" and new legislation to create a new type of stock exchange—which have since been created and are today called venture exchanges—that would be optimized to support small company capital formation, their investors, and their investment banks.
3. A JOBS Act 2.0
4. Limits on synthetics, derivatives, and index funds (putting controls on index funds is a big ox because index funds are replacing active management).
5. Limiting leverage to a 3:1 ratio.
6. Restoring the provisions of the Glass-Steagall Act.

The bottom line is that the JOBS Act has done a lot to restore the small company capital markets, as evidenced by the dramatic recovery of IPOs. The question remains, however: Will crowdfunding lead to a whole new form of speculative excess and abuse?

XV.

SCOTT SANDELL, FOREST BASKETT, AND EXPLORATORY DRILLING

*"If people are doubting how far you can go,
go so far that you can't hear them anymore."*

—Michele Ruiz

WHEN SCOTT SANDELL'S PARENTS TRIED to get him to play Little League baseball, he failed miserably and wanted to quit the team. His father was understanding and said, "It's fine if you want to quit the Little League, but do not make a habit of quitting. If you wish to be successful in life, you do not quit." Scott followed this advice and soon discovered that he liked winning.

Though Scott Sandell is now NEA's third managing partner, his road to the top wasn't a smooth one. He started his career at the Boston Consulting Group, then joined C-ATS Software as the company's first salesman, later founding and running its European subsidiary before attending business school at Stanford. During and after business school, Scott was a product manager at Microsoft, working on Windows 95. He also earned a bachelor's degree in engineering sciences from Dartmouth College.

Growing up, Scott loved the woods. This passion led him to the Boy Scouts, which drastically influenced his life. In eighth grade, he was head of the troop, three years younger than any other troop leader. By his junior year in high school, he was an Eagle Scout, teaching leadership.

Once at Dartmouth, Scott devoted himself to crew. When he started practicing with the team as a walk-on, it was clear that he was better than his crewmates. On the second day, Scott was asked to stroke the JV boat while the freshmen, who had not rowed in high school, learned how to row. That winter, all the freshmen were combined into one team. He was especially careful to be "one of the guys," although he was more advanced than his teammates and was elected team captain.

Scott figured out how to be less visible because, in a team sport, you have to be part of the team. You can't be above them. He dreamed of the Olympics, but those hopes were dashed by two herniated discs. Still, rowing in competition during college had a lasting impact on his career.

In 1996, Scott joined NEA, and over the years, he learned the secret to a successful venture capital career. He liked to compare it to oil drilling. There are two types: wildcat and exploratory drilling. You drill a wildcat well when you have analyzed the geological characteristics of an area and think you know where the oil field is likely to be; the odds of striking oil with wildcat drilling are about one in a hundred. With exploratory drilling, you determine which direction the oil field goes from an established well, and you start drilling to follow the field. Here, your odds of success are close to one in three. In venture capital terms, wildcat drilling is to discover the internet; Facebook and Amazon are exploratory drillings. To get to that point, though, Scott had to learn many lessons.

As a consultant, Scott introduced a company to NEA, and although NEA did not invest, the firm ended up hiring Scott after they turned down the company. He met Nora Zeitz, an associate, during his interviews in Baltimore, and recalled his first thoughts on NEA's value system during an oral history interview conducted in 2015:

"Nora was up in this little tiny office on the top floor of the Baltimore building, which is a fabulous building. She thinks that I am going to be offered a job and wants to make sure I know what I am getting myself into.

"She says, 'If all you want to do is make money, this might not be the right firm for you.'

"I say, 'Why is that?'

"She answered, 'Because if you sit around the partners' meetings long enough, you'll find out that a lot of decisions are made in ways that are suboptimal to purely making money over the short term. NEA tends to side with what's good for the company, even if it's sometimes not in the interest of NEA immediately because our partners are more interested in building companies than they are in making personal fortunes.'

"As it turned out, this is highly appealing to me, but I don't know if she is conveying this to scare me away or intrigue me. It is a critical signal, and I am very attracted to NEA because I do not see myself as a financial person. In fact, of all the disciplines of business, that's probably the one in which I have the least interest. I see myself as an entrepreneur or a business leader, but not as somebody who is only going to be an investor. I am much more interested in the process of creating great companies. That is really what gets me excited about venture capital."

Dick Kramlich, Mark Perry, and to a lesser extent, Peter Morris, were Scott's mentors at NEA. Scott floundered at first, prompting Dick and Mark to ask him to leave the firm, but he wanted to stay, so he asked for more time to prove himself. Scott used his second chance to canvas the partnership and get everyone's perspective on what he was doing wrong and what he could be doing better. Their comments were insightful. Wisely, he also used the chance to establish better relationships. Scott was enthusiastic about creating new enterprises and trying to help them succeed because it was the most challenging kind of investing. It was also definitely the riskiest. It took courage, discipline, perseverance, and creativity to help start new companies in new fields. But Scott thought that if you were interested in business and you wanted to hone your skills to the highest level, there was no better place to do that than venture capital.

Scott soon saw the bigger picture and drew lessons from each new company he was involved with. He has a talent for understanding new concepts quickly and figuring out what's important. He quickly dove into the core issues of any new business, unafraid of new technology, which was not true of all NEA partners. He also never invested in things he didn't understand or in a company that wasn't better than its competitors.

Scott was more of a businessman than a technologist. The most important ability he looked for in others was the soundness of their reasoning. For example, does an entrepreneur make ethical judgments based on facts before distilling them into a decision? When you're a founder responsible for the success of others, it's essential to be confident and ethical in your choices. Also, can the entrepreneur establish a connection, build rapport, and deal with each person while recognizing each one is different? For Scott, emotional intelligence is fundamental for leaders and founders. These small companies are made up of a small number of people who, in effect, are the business. If the leadership cannot figure out how to get these people to work together effectively, then they are not going to step off the starting line.

Scott's first investment for NEA was Mission Critical Software, a systems management software solution for Windows NT. He had worked for Microsoft, and he had an advantage over the people in Silicon Valley because he knew what opportunities were surrounding that specific product and that Microsoft was unlikely to pursue something similar on its own. In addition, Mission Critical's product would be far more valuable after NEA invested. The product had high margins. It was only a question of how much money NEA stood to gain. Scott felt he needed to make money without losing any along the way, and over his first four years at NEA, his perseverance paid off. Ten million dollars turned into $40 million.

The next two years were spent focusing on just that one software company's success—to the detriment of everything else—because he believed that if that company failed, he would lose his job. He was involved in Mission Critical to the point that he didn't help any of his NEA partners with their company's problems. Mission Critical would not have survived without Scott's passionate guidance.

In 1998, Scott learned about the company WebEx from his father-in-law at the time, Douglas Ayer, who was also a venture capitalist. They invested in the company together, and Ayer turned out to be Scott's most significant mentor during his first five years as a venture capitalist. WebEx had developed a piece of software that connected computers over the internet, allowing those computers to share what was on their screens. They could link two computers or a thousand.

WebEx created a virtual meeting space on the internet called Online Meetings Today. Creating such a "space" was a complicated, highly technical process because you had to maintain multiple, simultaneous real-time connections over an inherently unstable or unreliable network.

What Scott did not realize when he met WebEx's founders was that they had shopped the deal up and down Sand Hill Road. Kleiner Perkins had turned it down. Benchmark had turned it down. Everybody had turned it down, partly because the founders were not out of central casting. They were brilliant immigrants from different places, who did not have the standard resumes and did not speak English with a perfect American accent. But Scott and Douglas Ayer saw that they were utterly brilliant, competent, forward-thinking entrepreneurs.

Twenty minutes into WebEx's pitch meeting at the NEA partner's meeting, Scott was convinced that NEA should invest, and he assured NEA it was a worthwhile investment despite its high valuation. The company was already successful, boasting $3 to 4 million in recurring, subscription revenue. (Subscription revenue from software is far better than selling products.) Plus, WebEx's technology was differentiated; it would be hard to replicate. Scott also saw a need for it in the market. Their customer adoption program was fabulous, because the customers loved it, and it took on a viral status. Every time a WebEx customer set up a meeting on their platform, they introduced a new potential subscription customer to the service. The leverage in their business model was incredible: once they had multiple servers, the only other costs were customer acquisition and support. It was the first web business to have this SaaS (software as a service) recurring revenue model, which was later made famous by Salesforce.com.

Presenting to the NEA partners meeting, Scott met Joe Graziano, the former CFO of Apple. Joe had had a conflict with the WebEx founders and didn't want NEA to do the deal. One of NEA's difficult partners agreed with Joe and tried to kill the deal, but Scott won. Later, that same NEA partner tried to fire Scott, but Dick and I blocked it. Eventually, we had to fire the difficult partner because, among other things, he was always trying to fire our best investors, Scott and Peter Morris.

Fortunately, NEA made the WebEx investment, and in 2006, Cisco Systems bought WebEx for $3.2 billion. WebEx's founders, Min Zhu and Subrah Iyar, had a fascinating partnership. Subrah, the CEO, ran the business, while Min ran the technology and the operations as President and CTO. This business was unlike most others because they did not just invent technology to package and sell, they created a service.

Very seldom does a company create a technology, pioneer a new business model and a new sales model, at the same time as delivering their service to customers. One of the challenges of this new model was that it was impossible to hire an ordinary executive for such a job where the model of success was unproven. If you said, "I want someone with the experience to run sales and marketing," you'd be on the wrong path because no one had ever created a sales and marketing operation like WebEx's before. What's more, few vice presidents of engineering were also capable of running a service while a technology that was continually evolving. Min did both. WebEx invented this approach on the fly.

Another novel development was that Min and Subrah ran the company as a partnership. Because there were so many new things to invent all the time, it was best to have two people working closely together with complementary skill sets. Though Min and Subrah never made any key decisions without consulting each other, they often disagreed, heatedly. Scott would help them sort it out.

Being on the board was both challenging and rewarding. Scott had great respect for Min and Subrah. In return, to have their trust and respect was a big deal. Scott spent a lot of time listening to and trying to understand each of them. That was one of his vital contributions over the four years he worked closely with WebEx. He spent many nights and vacations on WebEx's problems because the founders worked all the time. As immigrant entrepreneurs, they seemingly never took vacations and holidays.

After a disagreement with Subrah, Scott was asked to leave the board. At the time, WebEx had $100 million a year in recurring revenues and was growing 40–50 percent per year. With new, powerful executives on the board, Scott felt he was no longer essential to the firm's success, and he agreed to leave.

Subrah's disagreement with Scott had begun when Scott said WebEx should raise more money, that their balance sheet was not strong enough. Scott had met resistance specifically when he said that he was willing to sponsor a PIPE (private investment in public equity) into the company. Perhaps Subrah assumed that Scott's motives were driven by self-interest because it could be advantageous to NEA to invest at a low price, but Scott's agenda was to help the company, whether or not NEA profited from it. WebEx's stock price had been beaten down, and both founders felt that it was unfairly valued.

Scott said to Subrah, "Let NEA invest at $8 a share. I'll put in $10 million or $20 million. The partnership has approved it." But Subrah and Min felt the price should be $10. The stock was trading at $7 or $8. Scott replied, "The market says $8, it should be $8." WebEx went to Alex Brown to market a private placement that was done at $10. They left out NEA.

After leaving the WebEx board, Scott continued to exhibit one of his greatest skills: retaining relationships in tough times. Min began to bring Scott startup ideas, some through his network in China. Initially, the ideas were not good, but Min had enthusiasm. He was such an incredibly brilliant guy that he could see things most people couldn't. It seemed he could see the future. While he was honing his instincts, it became Scott's job to help keep Min from making mistakes.

Scott was convinced NEA should invest in China when Min invited him to visit the country. On his first trip, Min introduced Scott to Datong Chen and Ping Wu, the founders of a company called Spreadtrum Communications, Inc. It was immediately apparent to Scott that NEA should invest in this company. It was the largest ever first-round investment that Scott had sponsored—$23 million bought NEA 20 percent of the company. The company's pre-money value was about $60 million, which seemed like a high price. One of the unique characteristics of the WebEx investment was that Scott was sure it would work. The business model was proven. He was already on board while other people were looking at what was missing. To Scott, however, it was evident that whatever was missing could be added, which would raise the value of the stock. He calibrated the risks differently than everyone else.

Spreadtrum Communications invented the first single-chip baseband chip for cell phones based in TD-CDMA, plus the software that ran on top of it. Scott's investment thesis was that these chips would be crucial to the dominant computing platform of the next two decades—the cellular phone. Spreadtrum did not, however, have the dominant product in the industry. There were other, much larger companies already making such chips. But Spreadtrum had the most integrated and advanced architecture.

Scott met Spreadtrum in 2003, and NEA invested in March of 2004. Spreadtrum had also created the first TD SCDMA smartphone processor (after NEA invested), which was a fully integrated, single-chip solution to China's first mobile standard. In Beijing, the government announced they were issuing the first licenses to the carriers for TD SCDMA deployments, giving Spreadtrum the full benefits of the largest and fastest-growing mobile market in the world—China. Spreadtrum designed the chips in Sunnyvale, California, and manufactured them in China. The company targeted the Chinese market, which was open to new entrepreneurial vendors.

At 58 years old, Min was about six feet tall with an athletic build, and he was very fit for a man his age. He was a distinctive-looking guy. If you ever met him, you would not forget that he was intense, incredibly passionate, and excitable—much more so than the typically reserved Chinese businessman.

As a young man, he had been recognized as one of the smartest high school students in China, which would have been a great distinction, were it not for the Cultural Revolution. Intellectuals were expelled to the countryside and forced into labor camps, and since he was singled out as one of the brightest, Min was treated the worst. He was sent to a labor camp for eight years. When he was speaking with his province's commissar, he promised, "I will make our province the most prosperous in China." He started a barrel manufacturing company, and soon his province was the fastest-growing in all of China. At the end of the eight years, a father and a husband by that time, he won a scholarship to university.

Min finished university at the age of 36, then won a scholarship to Stanford University for engineering management. He had to leave his family behind for the first year because the meager scholarship was not nearly enough to support a family in the US. Min spent his first year working odd jobs while living in someone's backyard in Menlo Park. During his second year, he became the manager of a local apartment complex. With opportunity, an apartment, and a salary to support them, he was able to bring his family to America. He engineered his own success to help his family.

✦✦✦

One of the most important things that Scott and Dick Kramlich did for NEA was hire Forest Baskett as a venture partner and then promote him to general partner. Forest was born in New Orleans, and as a child, had to overcome attention deficit hyperactivity disorder (ADHD). He went to Rice University in Houston to study physics, philosophy, and math, then earned his doctorate in computer science at the University of Texas. Forest's next move, in the '70s, was to Stanford University, where he was the first member of the Stanford faculty with a systems background to be granted tenure.

Forest started his Stanford career as a professor in the Department of Electrical Engineering and Computer Science. There, he hired Jim Clark, who went on to found Silicon Graphics and Netscape, and he shared an office with John Hennessy, the founder of MIPS Computer Systems, who would go on to become president of Stanford. During the 1970s, Forest helped in the formation of Sun, Silicon Graphics, and MIPS—three of the seminal companies in Silicon Valley.

Around 1986, Jim Clark persuaded Forest to become the CTO of Silicon Graphics, a fantastic company that attracted the best of the best. He was regarded as the most valuable CTO in Silicon Valley. The alumni of Silicon Graphics were the founders of successful companies and key innovators in technology. Because of his Silicon Graphics background, everyone in Silicon Valley knew him. Forest and Scott later went on to finance several companies founded by these alumni.

For thirteen years, Forest watched Silicon Graphics grow, eventually employing 15,000 people. The company initially developed 3-D graphics systems, then added large multiprocessors, or supercomputers. Silicon Graphics wound up in two non-complementary businesses: the high-margin business of supercomputers and the low-margin business of personal computer graphics. Later, when Silicon Graphics bought Cray, a supercomputer manufacturer, it was a disaster. Sales plummeted. Forest had experience in product development and acquisitions, which is a solid background for a venture capitalist, so he resigned from Silicon Graphics and joined NEA in 1999.

As a new NEA partner, Forest visited a conference that hosted a competition for early-stage companies, allowing them to demonstrate their products before an audience of venture capitalists, journalists, and others that might help them. Naturally, there was a rigorous selection process. Each chosen company got five minutes on stage, then the audience voted, and an award was given to the best company.

At this conference, Forest met the founders of Fusion-IO, a computer hardware company. The first year that Fusion-io won the award as the best company, Forest approached the founders, David Flynn and Rick White, and learned that they were already in late-stage discussions with Sequoia Capital. Sequoia was one of NEA's chief competitors. Forest came back to the office and said, "Scott, look, I met this interesting company. Would you be willing to meet with them?"

After a six-month process, NEA invested in the company. Early on, it looked as though it might be reasonably straightforward to determine who would lead the business in this new stage: David and Rick each proclaimed that he did not want to be CEO. Rick was the CEO at the time. David was the CTO. Both founders had decided that the new CEO they wanted to hire was Don Basile. Basile did help Fusion-io get out of a bad deal with Micron, a semiconductor manufacturer, but his approach was too abrasive. Passing Basile over led to a lawsuit, but Scott didn't settle. He had learned early in his career not to settle because if you do, you'll only invite more lawsuits.

Scott recommended David Bradford for CEO. David had been Fusion-io's vice president of business development and a kind of general counsel to the company. He looked thirty-five but was closer to sixty. Formerly the chief counsel for the software company Novell, he had an impressive legal background, and Fusion-io had many legal problems to address. More importantly, there was a real lack of confidence among the employees in the company. David was a stand-up adult who any reasonable person would instantly trust.

David Bradford soon cleaned up all the mess, which prompted David Flynn, the founder, to ask Scott for a meeting. He started by saying, "David Bradford is a great CEO for the company—just the right guy at the right time—but he's not the long-term guy. I think I should be the next CEO." David Flynn was the CTO, the technical founder of the company. Though he was forty and had no background running a company, he was a brilliant guy.

Scott did not immediately think Flynn would fit into the company in that position. He asked, "David, do you know what it means to be the

CEO? Do you know what that job's really all about? Do you know what it's going to be like five years from now when we're really successful?"

They talked about that for a couple of hours, but Scott was not convinced. He felt he should persuade him not to become CEO, or he should set up a process to figure out if he was the right guy. Scott said, "The first requirement of a leader is that people want to follow you. I would like your permission to interview all the people that work in the company to determine whether or not they would like you to be the CEO." He also told Flynn he was going to interview the board members as well.

Over the next month or two, Scott and Forest conducted a series of interviews with key employees. Steve Wozniak, the co-founder of Apple, in his first position after leaving Apple, had signed on as the chief scientist of Fusion-io. Wozniak said, "You know, he's really smart, he's really hardworking. There are some things he doesn't have, but he's earned the opportunity if he wants it, and he will make up for what he doesn't have with passion, drive, and ambition." Scott found that responses from other employees were similar, and Scott came to agree with them.

Fusion-io was one of Scott and Forest's best companies. The most important thing to Scott, after the management team, was the value proposition. At NEA, we have to ask, "What are they going to do to change the world, and how strong is their value proposition?" Fusion had an unbelievable value proposition. They were working with solid-state storage and flash memory, used in cell phones. Unfortunately, the cell phone, in general, was unreliable. Enterprises were not using cell phones when Fusion-io was founded, which meant they had to figure out how to build reliability into the cell phone.

Because David Flynn had a background in different related technologies, he could see what no one else had seen before. Today, Fusion is a market leader that delivers the world's fastest data (accelerating databases, virtualization, cloud computing, and big data). They created the market, they owned it, and today, they completely dominate it. After NEA invested, the company signed a distribution agreement with Hewlett-Packard, which was a tremendous validation. NEA then introduced the company to the CTO of IBM, who got excited about working with them. Overnight, they signed an agreement with IBM. They then signed another with Dell Computers, and it became clear all the server vendors wanted in on the Fusion-io action. Dell was the chief competition in the IBM deal. After losing the deal, Michael Dell offered $130 million for the company. Although David and Rick considered it, they decided the offer was too low. NEA invested at $27 million, and in 2011, Fusion-io went public on the New York Stock Exchange at a valuation of $1.4 billion.

Scott is very successful at building networks of VCs and entrepreneurs. He gives some credit for this ability to having both attention deficit disorder and dyslexia. In that oral history interview of 2010, he said, "I'm dyslexic, and I have ADD and all these other things that made it hard to get through school. But in our business, that turns out to be a great advantage because I can learn the way I want to learn. We all have different ways of learning. If I can talk to someone and ask the right questions, that's really helpful. I can direct the conversation. They are motivated to teach me. They're among the smartest people in the world, entrepreneurs. What a fantastic way to learn."

Scott considered himself a traditional VC. He said, "Nothing is more exciting than changing the world, and making new things happen that dramatically impact the way people live, work, and play, which was the original vision that Chuck Newhall, Frank Bonsal, and Dick Kramlich had when they created NEA. It doesn't work a lot of the time, and it's painful when it doesn't work, but when it works, it's spectacular. Facebook was completely re-architecting everything they did to use Fusion-io as their core technology; so was Apple." Scott took pride in this because he felt he has helped many entrepreneurs change the world, and that is what venture capital is all about.

Forest and Scott are masters of exploratory drilling, with Silicon Graphics alumni, with Forest's academic contacts, and with Scott's Chinese contacts. Forest described what they look for in a new company when he was interviewed in 2010: "We think about three primary aspects of a potential investment. One is the technology for the idea. What is it that this company wants to do? Two is the market. Is it a big market for this idea, or this product, or this technology? And three is: who are the people that are going to try to make this work? You can roughly characterize venture firms by the way they weigh those three aspects differently. For NEA, we put more emphasis on the people than either the market or the technology. Those three things are a tripod. You have to have all three legs be strong, but for us, we look really, really carefully at the people."

Forest also said selecting a CEO is not a one-decision action. "There's a truism that there are CEOs who can take a company from zero to $100 million in revenue, and there are CEOs who can take a company from $100 million to $1 billion. Those are frequently not the same people. We try to have that conversation with founders when we're talking about investing. If they're comfortable with that, then it's a signal that you've got someone who's flexible and wants the company to be successful, as opposed to someone who cares more about his or her own 'success' than the company's. It's important to have that conversation up front. We always try to do that. But even when we do, people don't always know what it is that's important to them. They think that it's the company, but when it comes time to make difficult decisions about leadership, either new leadership or shared leadership, it is hard for people. They have their baby, and don't want to give up their baby."

Forest said that to evaluate new investments, "we have a monthly meeting where we go over our portfolio, and we say, 'Is it category one? Is it category two? Or is it category three?' The category ones are the ones that we call needle-movers. These are the companies that we think will be so successful that they'll generate great returns for our limited partners.

"Category three are the ones that are not going to make a difference, or they've kind of run out of steam, or the market turned out not to be that great. It's time to move on, so find someone to buy them or shut them down. Finding someone to buy them is preferred. You have to shut them down when that doesn't happen. But the notion is, 'Let's not put a lot of our energy into these companies because they're not going to make a difference.' The category two companies are the hard ones. That's where most of our time goes. We're not sure, 'Are they going to break out and become successful, or are they going to turn into category three companies?' Those are the ones where we wring our hands a lot. We do what we can, and we get our partners to help us and try to figure it out. We frequently have companies in that category that get promoted up. Those are big successes for us personally. Those are the companies to which we add real value."

It was a privilege to work with Scott and Forest. They have been crucial contributors to NEA's success, particularly over the last decade.

XVI.

CREATIVITY

"Think left and think right and think low and think high. Oh, the thinks you can think up if only you try."

—Dr. Seuss

THOUGH I WAS AN ENGLISH major, not a scientist, my life has been spent in the company of scientists. I have been on the boards of nine pharma and service companies that focused on central nervous system disorders. These companies are Supernus, Sepracor, Vitae, Vela Pharmaceuticals, BrainCells Corporation, American Day Treatment, BehaveCare, and Lifemetrix. I have witnessed scientific explorations to the frontiers of the mind. As an investor, I have seen breakthroughs in neurobiology and psychiatry that helped me better understand the passionate and intense minds of creative entrepreneurs—those who dare disturb the universe.

The pioneering neurobiologists and psychiatrists who live on the edge of discoveries are my heroes. The study of the brain is still in its infancy, but thanks to these pioneers, our knowledge will grow. Being with these scientists has also provided me with insight that helped me understand what makes a successful entrepreneur.

One of the most critical developments in neurobiology has been the field's better understanding of the brain's chemical messengers: serotonin, norepinephrine, and dopamine. Each plays a significant role in mood disorders, such as hypomania, bipolar disorder, and attention deficit hyperactivity disorder. These messengers go from neuron to neuron across synapses, causing dopamine to be released, and, in turn, causing heightened emotional states and bursts of creativity. If the released dopamine takes the mesolimbic pathway, it triggers rewards.

Dopamine is the brain's pleasure chemical. But pleasure is only one of its facets. It also affects motivation, memory, behavior, cognition, sleep, mood, and learning. Its levels spike during periods of high stress, which encourages us to achieve great things or to avoid something dangerous. It boosts our spirits, urging us to take the high-risk path, with the higher reward, rather than the easy way out. Ambitious people with high levels of dopamine in the striatum and prefrontal cortex take risks and work hard. The brain can be trained to feed dopamine as needed. You attach a dopamine response to the task you want to achieve.

After watching warriors, entrepreneurs, artists, and scientists, I believe these heightened emotional states are the gateway to what we call creativity. Such people are not "normal" or "balanced." They are extraordinarily driven and possess superhuman energy. As an investor, one of my most important tasks is to assess how an entrepreneur will be able to channel this power toward positive ends while avoiding the dangers of its darker and more destructive side. Too often, I've seen the effects of gifted people's dark impulses within their companies—and within my own family.

The genetic basis of manic depression (bipolar disease), ADHD or ADD, and hypomania are well established. Over the past twenty years, we have mapped the human genome, and we are well on our way to identifying which genes or collections of genes influence individual diseases. For example, researchers have identified something very important to me, the single gene that is linked to post-traumatic stress disorder (PTSD), a condition called shell shock in World War I.

Sigmund Freud explained our actions in terms of sex and aggression; neurobiologists, in contrast, tend to regard mental disorders as nothing other than chemical imbalances, or chemical differences. The crusading neurobiologist thinks not in terms of treating patients, but of treating brains. The neurobiologist points to relatively new diagnostic techniques to support the concept. In modern medicine, positron emission tomography (PET) has made it possible to map the living human brain. It is possible to compare such a map of brain activity in an average, healthy patient to that of a patient undergoing a manic-depressive episode, and even to measure the effect of new drugs on such brain activity.

As with all "breakthroughs," caution is advised. The glittering PET images do not exactly show real brain action. They are, more precisely, simulated images of statistical analyses of many brain images correlated to morphological brain structures. A snapshot in time cannot reflect the state of an organ in continuous interaction with the whole organism, which is itself in continuous interaction with the environment.

I believe that over the next thirty years, psychotherapy and neurobiology will merge, providing us with more accurate insights into the human mind. The development of the brain will be seen as determined by genetics and the continuous interaction with the environment. The brain is continuously rewired by individual experience. Gene expression is, in fact, also modified by life experience.

I often think back to my last conversation with my grandmother when she was 99 years old. She told me my creativity made me very different from my parents. She also warned me that every gift comes with a burden. She said that I would overcome adversities that would overwhelm other men. She couldn't tell me what my burden would be: either she did not know or she felt it was best I discover it on my own. I now understand the responsibility I carry, and this process of discovery has been both exhilarating and painful. I have had to put in great effort and energy to live successfully with my ADHD, PTSD-caused depression, and hypomania.

The brain is continually transforming. Chemical imbalances are signposts, but they do not explain brain function. Illness of the mind must be viewed as the complex interaction of neurobiological, environmental, and social influences continuously interacting with each other. Pharmacological intervention is therefore never the simple, sole solution because the complex interactions that affect behavior are in perpetual flux. Perhaps, in time, therapeutic brain changes caused by psychotherapy will have their own brightly colored maps. Assessments of psychotherapists might someday actually guide the neurobiologist in discovering the biological basis of mood disorders.

✧✧✧

Let us examine the three states that I believe govern most entrepreneurial creativity. The first is hypomania, a mild form of mania, marked by elation and hyperactivity. Hypomanics are usually cheerful people who require little sleep but maintain high energy levels; they are often very sociable, talkative, highly confident, have flights of creative ideas, are prone to risk, and have high self-esteem. For them, pleasure is triggered by an exciting event, like making a discovery or making a lot of money. They are prone to be very impatient with failure and feel that life is, for the most part, a pleasurable experience.

I believe, from my decades-long quest to understand the brain science behind creativity, that roughly 80 percent of entrepreneurs are either hypomanic, have ADHD or ADD, or have bipolar disorder. In my opinion, 65–70 percent of the 80 percent experience hypomania. I've known hundreds of hypomanic CEOs, and many of my partners are hypomanic. The most notable example is Dick Kramlich. The rule of thumb is that a VC has a limited attention span and should only sit on eight boards. At one time, Dick sat on twenty-eight, attending three board meetings a day. I did a random sample of his CEOs and found that they felt Dick was their most active and important board member. At the same time he was president of the National Venture Capitalist Association, he was building multiple houses, and assembling a collection of video art that became one of the most important in the world.

For most people, having ADHD or ADD seems bad, as if the game of life did not deal you a good hand. But it can be quite the opposite. A person with ADHD has to channel their excess energy and disparate focus into a productive, rewarding life.

The symptoms sound scary. People with ADHD are disorganized and lose track of things. They are easily distracted, hyperactive, impulsive (acting first and thinking later), constantly interrupting, constantly moving, constantly answering questions before the person asking has finished the sentence. It is believed that 5 to 10 percent of all children have this disorder, and it is five times more prevalent in boys. Of the 80 percent of entrepreneurs affected by some sort of mental condition, I think 25–30 percent have channeled their ADHD to their benefit.

When I was in the fourth grade, I had an excellent American history teacher, Mr. Goodwin. His nickname for me was "Itch." Before he would start his lecture, he'd ask "Now, Itch, are you going to behave yourself?" In his classroom, we had wood and iron desks pushed together and bolted to the floor. He would climb up on one of the desks and walk around the classroom, from desk to desk, giving his lecture. He always looked as if he was teetering, ready to fall off the desk at any moment. He would straighten up and say things like, "How many of you have heard of the midnight ride of Paul Revere?" I would raise my hand because I was a Revolutionary War nut. I had probably spent the weekend playing with my toy soldiers and recreating the battle on Lexington Green. He would say, "Now, Itch, let someone else answer the question." While another student took their turn, I'd pretend I was Paul Revere, riding his horse by bouncing up and down on my chair.

Mr. Goodwin and I had an understanding, and I never forgot anything he said. I cannot say the same about math and science, where I found looking out the window and drawing on my writing pad to be much more interesting than listening to the teacher. Most teachers did not have Mr. Goodwin's tolerance for my shenanigans. I was forever getting punished and told I was a stupid failure— practically confined in a straitjacket. This treatment only encouraged my belligerence. Many ADHD children fail later in life because they lose their self-confidence from the barrage of criticism.

How did I survive past the age of 30? I developed highly structured routines. Nancy Dorman, NEA's administrative partner, introduced me to lists. Every day, I had a list, displaying my schedule. I then wrote notes, describing how I would accomplish the most trying tasks first thing in the day. I made special places for all the little things I perpetually lost: keys, wallet, bills, and paperwork. Whenever I traveled, I had a schedule that accounted for every minute of every day, and God help the person who tried to change my plans. I broke large tasks into a series of smaller ones and ran a victory lap whenever I completed a task. I became so hyper-focused on my goals that sometimes I forgot to eat or sleep; unfortunately, I often wore people out, including my wife and some of my partners.

I often think of my prehistoric ancestor. I imagine his tribe of hunters and gatherers sitting together in a cave, sewing hides or knapping flint. They would have been given strict orders by the tribe's leader to perform only their tasks and not be distracted by anything. But my ancestor with ADHD would be distracted by something going on outside: a twig snapping or something that didn't smell right. He would go to the mouth of the cave to investigate recklessly, ignoring the rest of the tribe and the flint he was supposed to knap, only to find a cave bear approaching the cave, intent on killing his tribe and reclaiming its lair. ADHD isn't great when you need people to knap flint, but it certainly expands your horizons so you can see things "normal" people miss. One person with ADHD, with hypersensitivity to "distractions," can save a tribe or create a company.

The entrepreneur and my ancestor share this expanded attention. Change can be frustrating, disruptive, and uncomfortable, but an executive with ADHD, who we will call Mr. ADHD, has lived with such constant change and shifting focus all his life, so he adapts instantly. The other thing is that Mr. ADHD has experienced defeat and rejection numerous times throughout life. He is therefore used to overcoming setbacks under any conditions. Mr. ADHD has developed functional impulsivity, making quick and often intuitively sound decisions when everything is uncertain. Mr. ADHD struggled to gain the approval of others as a child, and as an adult, he has developed a personality that has made peace with the uncomfortable feeling of not always pleasing others. Having been an underdog, he likes to help underdogs. His enthusiasm breeds contagious motivation. Having to accommodate the difficulties that came with ADHD has also made him abnormally persistent. His desire to please often makes him compassionate, a good conversationalist, someone who provides constant surprises, and has a good sense of humor to deal with stressful situations. He will shower his life partner with an unending flow of presents. ADHD means he always sees the world from a different perspective, which is called creativity.

Thomas Edison, Richard Branson, Ingvar Kamprad (IKEA), Paul Orfalea of Kinkos, Alan Meckler of Jupiter Media, Charles Schwab, Ellen Carey of Glassbreakers, and David Neeleman of Jet Blue have all shared anecdotes that indicate they have ADHD. Neeleman said his ADHD enabled him to take complications and turn them into simple solutions.

I recently had a very interesting conversation with Michael Classen, one of my son Ashton's associates, who helped me with this book. We were comparing notes on our shared experiences with ADHD and ADD and found our views to be very similar. We both agreed that with the disorder, you encounter adversity, which you learn to overcome with grit. We also agreed that facing adversity forces one to become self-reflective at an early age. You ask yourself, "Why am I different?" which can lead to unusually early self-awareness.

In my case, I think ADHD led me to seek out mentors, people who had what I lacked in certain areas. When you work with a mentor, you should rely on him or her to help you with decisions. I might add that mentorship is never a one-way street. You must try to always give as much or more to your mentor as you receive. But as I have commented many times earlier, the people with whom you choose to associate and work with dramatically affect your life.

To see the positive benefits of ADHD at work, I have to look no further than my own partners. I have described previously the way ADHD benefitted and helped shape the work of Frank Bonsal, Scott Sandell, and Forest Baskett.

If some people think it's improbable that ADHD contributes to entrepreneurial creativity and success, they will think it's outlandish for me to make the case that some entrepreneurs, maybe 2–5 percent of the 80 percent, are positively affected by bipolar disorder. I do not say this lightly. I say this as someone who has also seen how devastating that disease can be. My first wife Marsi, who had bipolar disorder, committed suicide. Yet, I can still see good things that come from people who suffer from the disease.

Let's consider the characteristics of bipolar individuals. They have mood swings that last seven days to one year, swinging between episodes of mania and depression. During mania, bipolar people experience euphoria and have a heightened level of accomplishment. They believe they are unstoppable in pursuit of their goals, and they are unnaturally happy in social situations. They are prone to substance abuse. They speak rapidly, in pressured speech, due to their racing thoughts. Many are irritated by things that wouldn't irritate most people. They experience periods of increased physical ability alternating with periods of lethargy.

During manic times, they have a decreased need for sleep yet do not feel tired. Sometimes, they miss work or appointments to pursue other activities they deem more important. At times, they become fatigued, going to bed early and getting up late. They often complain of chronic pain with no known cause. They ricochet between hopelessness, losing interest in activities they previously enjoyed, and manic periods, in which they rashly pursue their objectives and often experience hypersexuality, which can lead to infidelity. Finally, they can have suicidal thoughts which, combined with their compulsiveness, can lead to death by their own hands.

You might think surfing these vicissitudes of emotion would lead to lives of sad desperation. Bipolar disorder is challenging, but there are exceptions. There are bipolar geniuses who have channeled their challenges into world-stunning creativity. The following list is primarily based on the work of Dr. Kay Redfield Jamison, the author of *An Unquiet Mind: A Memoir of Moods and Madness,* who said: "We all build internal sea walls to keep at bay the sadness of life and the overwhelming forces within our minds. In whatever way we do this—through love, work, family, faith, friends, denial, alcohol, drugs, or medication, we build these walls, stone by stone, over a lifetime." She lists the creative, world-changing bipolar geniuses in her books. Here are a few examples:

Writers: Faulkner, Fitzgerald, Hemingway, Henry James, Twain, Conrad, Dickens, Melville, Tolstoy, Isak Dinesen, Walt Whitman.

Artists: Gauguin, Van Gogh, Munch, Michelangelo, O'Keefe, Rothko, Pollock, Turner, Picasso.

Musicians: Handel, Klemperer, Rossini, Tchaikovsky, Noel Coward, Beethoven, Elton John, Mozart.

Poets: Baudelaire, Blake, Coleridge, Dickenson, T.S. Eliot, Emerson, Boris Pasternak, Poe, Pushkin, Shelley, Dylan Thomas, Walt Whitman.

Military: Churchill, Lincoln, Sherman, Frederick the Great, Theodore Roosevelt, Grant, Patton, Meriwether Lewis.

Business: Disney, George Eastman, Ted Turner, Elon Musk, Steve Jobs, Estee Lauder, Henry J. Heinz.

Presidents: Coolidge, Madison, John Quincy Adams, Pierce, Lyndon B. Johnson.

Bipolar disorder is found in about 1 percent of the world population, but in 2.6 percent of the US population over the age of 18. While it is genetically based, no single gene is responsible; instead, there are biological differences between the typical brain and the bipolar brain. Life experiences like high stress, trauma, substance abuse (the incidence of this is between 30 and 50 percent among those suffering from bipolar disorder), and childhood abuse can heighten the risk. So do neurological disorders like traumatic brain injury, stroke, AIDS, multiple sclerosis, and epilepsy.

Lithium is the gold standard for treating bipolar disorder, and it has been for a long time. The chemical element was discovered in 1817 by Johan August Arfwedson and was used to treat gout. It wasn't introduced as a bipolar disorder treatment until 1871. In 1948, Dr. John Cade, an Australian psychiatrist, published about lithium's efficacy as a mood stabilizer, after which it became more widely used. The FDA approved it for the treatment of bipolar disorder in 1970. The long saga of lithium and the failure to develop more effective new drugs highlights the difficulty in developing central nervous system drugs.

My experience with bipolar disorder, as I have described, was personal: Marsi had it. After her March 13, 1982 suicide, I began an extended study of its effects.

I served on boards with three bipolar entrepreneurs and encountered several other people with bipolar disorder in my life. These people were not easy to live with, but they were hyper-creative. My interactions with Bob Jasse, founder of Chomerics, are described in Chapter IX, in which I discuss my long friendship with Dick Kramlich. Without Dick's help, Chromerics would not have been as successful as it was. It is to Bob's credit that he accepted Dick's counsel.

Another bipolar entrepreneur I encountered, I'll call him Mr. X, was one of the most successful businessmen in the last days of the twentieth century and the first years of the twenty-first. I knew a young venture capitalist on Mr. X's company's board, who said that he was going to ask his girlfriend to marry him on a Friday night, so he had selected the ring and asked their parents to join him that night for the celebration. On the morning of that Friday, Mr. X called the VC and told him he had to be in his office at 9:30 AM the next morning, Saturday. The young VC told him what he had planned that night, but the entrepreneur ignored him. Immediately, the VC panicked, canceled his engagement party, and left on a red-eye to California to meet Mr. X. On Saturday morning, the young venture capitalist walked into Mr. X's office, and the famous entrepreneur asked, "Why are you here?" Like Bob Jasse, this renowned entrepreneur used abusive behavior and generous rewards to control those around him. And yet, the company they worked on was a phenomenal success, and they had a productive ten-year relationship.

The last bipolar CEO I worked with was a noted doctor whom I asked to leave his company after he almost drove it into bankruptcy. He tried to control his board by threatening them with a lawsuit if they did not approve his decisions. After his departure, we hired a new, experienced CEO. The company went into a death spiral, however, because, as the company's new CEO discovered, its business model was a sham.

Overall, then, my batting average with bipolar CEOs has not been bad: two winners and one loser. In all cases, working with them took years off of my life but also added some great experiences I will never forget.

XVII.

DUCKS ON A POND

"If you really look closely, most overnight successes took a long time."

—Steve Jobs

WHEN MARSI DIED IN 1982, Dick took me aside and said, "You really should move to California. You'll live longer, be much more productive, and I will find you a beautiful, Californian wife who will understand venture capital and appreciate you. You see, I never invest in a company that is more than an hour's drive away from my home. I can attend three board meetings a day when you will have to travel three days to attend one board meeting in Parkersburg, West Virginia."

I returned with a smile, "Dick, I am going to change Baltimore." Between 1780 and 1830, Baltimore was the innovation center of the US, with the first railroad, the fastest schooner on the ocean, the Baltimore Clipper, indigo printing, the shortest route to the New American frontier across the Appalachian Mountains, and the first investment banks in the country. Other Maryland firsts in the late eighteenth and nineteenth centuries included the first mechanical dredging machine, the first metallic writing pens, the first umbrella factory, the first synthetic sweetening agent, saccharine, and linotype, the first machine to mechanically set type. Artists from Europe and other American cities came to Baltimore during this period to create some of the greatest classical beauty (fine arts, architecture, decorative arts) in the history of the US. This was the Baltimore I'd fallen in love with, but that city had long been lost. When we'd moved there, many of our friends were living off fortunes created two hundred years ago. "I am going to transform Baltimore into San Francisco," I insisted. It was the stupidest thing I ever said.

Of course I was jealous of California. When I'd moved to Baltimore in 1957, a nice home in Baltimore was as expensive as a similar home in Pacific Heights, San Francisco. At that time, the Baltimore house and the Pacific Heights house would have cost $150,000. Today that house in Baltimore might sell for $400,000. That same amount might have bought you a parking spot in Pacific Heights in 2010. The house attached to the parking space would have cost $25 million. California had the power to take whatever it had and make it better, faster, and more expensive.

I took Amy, my second wife, to see Baltimore's sweeping views of the newly created Inner Harbor. There, the lights illuminated sailboats, and the moon reflected on the water. The "Old City on the Bay," as H.L. Mencken called it, made Fisherman's Wharf look shabby. Amy and I were excited, and I said, "The ocean, the mountains, and the English countryside are all here—in a city that is being reborn." *Baltimore will give San Francisco a run for its money,* I thought. If Dick had been there, he would have smiled because I was forever the naive junior analyst.

In 1983, Amy and I went to dinner at the "Black Pearl," a glamorous, exclusive Newport restaurant that had just opened up an outpost in Baltimore. I ordered frog legs with fettuccine. When the plate arrived, the big bowl was filled with frogs' legs sticking out of pasta. As I looked at my dinner, I noticed that the frogs' legs were still covered with skin. Taking my fork, I discovered the distended corpses of whole, boiled frogs with grossly swollen bellies. Amy started to laugh. Dick would have said, "I think Baltimore has a little way to go." It was an omen.

Amy and I both knew it would be a big challenge, but there were national macro trends we thought would help the region. For instance, the federal government was breaking up the Bell monopoly that had ruled telephone communications from 1877 to 1982. When the marketplace opened to outside competition, small companies created Ethernet, local area networks, broadband communication, high-speed data communications, and so on. The communications gold rush was on, and Washington was a large market. Ultimately, companies like MCI, America Online, UUNet, Network Solutions, PSI Network, Telogy, Ciena, and Teligent would prosper in the mid-Atlantic, which I define as the region roughly a two-and-a-half-hour drive (without traffic) north and south of Baltimore. Along with communications companies, there was a need for software. A number of software companies were formed, including Mario Marino's company, Legent, in 1989.

At the same time, the biotech revolution was in full swing. Nobel Prize winners Dan Nathans and Hamilton Smith, from Johns Hopkins University, discovered restriction and enzymes that would allow scientists to manipulate the DNA chain. The biotech industry would eventually create many of Maryland's big ducks (i.e., successful entrepreneurial companies), such as MedImmune, led by Wayne Hockmeyer and David Mott; Human Genome Sciences, led by Bill Haseltine; and Life Technologies. The potential to cure disease with the new technologies coming out of these companies was mind-boggling. Three typhoons of innovation—in communications, software, and life science—that had been gathering since the 1970s and 1980s were about to make landfall on the shores of the mid-Atlantic.

In the 1970s, there was little entrepreneurship. Washington was a cow pasture for politicians chewing their cud. They were served by a group of relatively small businesses, aptly nicknamed "beltway bandits," that did various types of defense-related and data-management consulting projects for narrow profit margins. Baltimore was the land of pleasant living, with banks, insurance companies, real estate and accounting firms, and traditional manufacturing businesses. The most exciting event of the year was the Maryland Hunt Cup, where handsome heirs of the great Baltimore entrepreneurial fortunes rode in their pink jackets, chasing foxhounds through an idyllic countryside, while their rich wives from New York, Chicago, and Dallas dutifully refreshed the family fortunes that had run out. As far as entrepreneurial innovation was concerned, Baltimore was a backwater.

The Delaware Valley and Philadelphia were similar to Baltimore. In Delaware, around Wilmington, there was the great DuPont Company, which had created hundreds of millionaires living a bucolic existence in stately mansions. Philadelphia was dominated by big, traditional businesses, and of course, New Jersey was the home of Big Pharma.

It was common knowledge that no small entrepreneurial company could compete with Big Pharma any more than a small company could compete with IBM or AT&T. To the local managers of financial assets who handled the money of the foundations, endowments, brokerage firms, insurance companies, and so on, this was the gospel, the word of God. Everything in the region conspired against risk-taking. Insiders shunned anyone and everyone who subscribed to ideas out of step with their own. The Greater Baltimore Committee, which had been started to develop Maryland business, could not spell *entrepreneur.* It focused on taking expensive boondoggles to IBM's headquarters in New York to try to convince the company to move to Baltimore, a total waste of time and money.

I knew the region had assets that could create commercial innovation because it had capital, leading academics, government institutions, and the proper support structure. These assets included Johns Hopkins University, the National Institutes of Health, and the University of Pennsylvania, some of the most prestigious names in the healthcare field. On the technology side, the US Department of Defense and the Pentagon demanded ever more sophisticated telecommunications and computer systems. The John Hopkins Applied Physics Laboratory was a center of scientific innovation. If someone could capitalize on matching new technologies with their financial needs, something might happen.

To some extent, NEA, formed in 1977 and funded in 1978, was a catalyst for the region. A bicoastal firm that brought the California attitude to the mid-Atlantic, NEA attracted like-minded individuals and firms to join its entrepreneurial crusade, forever disrupting the region's comfortable but complacent status quo.

The region depicted on the map represents a geographic area similar to the size of the Greater San Francisco and the Greater Boston metropolitan areas. Mid-Atlantic Northern Virginia, Washington, D.C., Maryland, Delaware, Pennsylvania, and southern New Jersey. The Greater San Francisco area, of course, is in California, and the Greater Boston area is mostly in Massachusetts. The mid-Atlantic would be more challenging to galvanize than these other regions because you would have to get the venture capital, legal, accounting, and entrepreneurial communities across all the states to cooperate to some degree.

In the 1960s and early 1970s, there were only four venture firms in the region. Allied Capital in Washington, D.C., was founded by a group of local businessmen in 1958 as a small business investment company (SBIC), made possible by the Small Business Investment Act. It was led by David Gladstone and George Williams. Don Christensen founded Greater Washington Investors as an SBIC in 1959. It raised $5 million in an initial IPO in the 60s; Broventure, the venture arm of the Brown Family, formed in Baltimore in 1968, was led by Bill Gust and Phil English. Data Science Ventures, in Princeton, New Jersey, was founded by Mort Collins in 1968.

When Bill Gust was recruited to co-manage Broventure in 1978, as he remembered, "I was shocked. I didn't expect it to be like Silicon Valley, and Silicon Valley was nothing like it is now, but I didn't see any opportunities here for venture capital firms. It was a wasteland. NEA was raising its first fund, about $15 million, I think, but that was new to this region. When I showed up with Broventure money, it was family-owned, I pretty much made investments in California and New England. I only did a couple of deals in the region, in Baltimore and Hunt Valley. I think the reason for that is because it takes time to create a region like Silicon Valley. People forget that Silicon Valley did not begin with Steve Jobs, but goes back to the 1930s, when Hewlett and Packard left Stanford to form HP. They also had excellent engineering and business schools. Route 128 in Boston dates to the 1940s. These ingredients were not found anywhere else in the US.

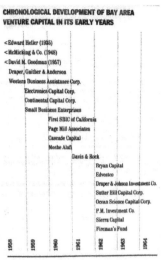

CHRONOLOGICAL DEVELOPMENT OF BAY AREA
VENTURE CAPITAL IN ITS EARLY YEARS

<Edward Heller (1935)
<McMicking & Co. (1948)
<David M. Goodman (1957)
Draper, Gaither & Anderson
Western Business Assistance Corp.
Electronics Capital Corp.
Continental Capital Corp.
Small Business Enterprises
First SBIC of California
Page Mill Associates
Cascade Capital
Moshe Alafi
Davis & Rock
Bryan Capital
Edvestco
Draper & Johson Investment Co.
Sutter Hill Capital Corp.
Ocean Science Capital Corp.
P.M. Investment Co.
Sierra Capital
Fireman's Fund

1958 1959 1960 1961 1962 1963 1964

The great flowering of venture capital in the San
Francisco Bay area reflected experienced management, aggressive research institutions, the presence
of high-tech headquarters and spawning ground companies. The city of San Francisco, while not a center
of entrepreneurship, contributed to the entrepreneurial climate with its extensive resources and services.

"In Baltimore, the economy ran on real estate and commercial banking. The Baltimore business community was clueless. I still remember some of them saying, 'Who would name a company Apple?' They did not understand the power of technology for creating small companies on little capital, companies that would create jobs. That kind of understanding didn't come until the '80s."

In early 1987, Frank Adams of Grotech Ventures and I founded the Mid-Atlantic Venture Capital Association (or, MAVA). I had spent a good deal of time attending the Western Association of Venture Capitalists conference in California, where venture-backed companies made presentations to raise equity, and venture capitalists networked with other venture capitalists, public investors, investment bankers, and the lawyers, accountants, and other service providers. When I was a T. Rowe Price analyst, these conferences had provided my best investment ideas, but I knew they did more for me than just that. The East Coast was rather gloomy as we made our way through the energy crisis. California was exhilarating, and its optimism was contagious. In the mid-Atlantic, too, we were looking for the next Intel, Apple, or Genentech, but first, we had to create an association that would bring those small growth companies with venture capital and the right support structure. I had also attended similar meetings in Boston, and I knew it wasn't simple to create a venture capital ecosystem overnight.

How could we do this? I pondered. NEA could not finance it on its own. I went to see Selig Solomon, at the Maryland Department of Economic Development, with Ray Bank, a young NEA associate who became very helpful in creating MAVA. Selig was a businessman who instantly understood the value of the idea we were proposing. He did not believe what the politicians thought, that the only way to get economic growth in the region was to attract IBM to move to Baltimore with a tax break.

As we were both duck hunters, we shared the ducks-on-the-pond theory, which goes something like this: if you are sitting in a blind on the Eastern Shore and have your decoys out, and three hundred yards away, a single duck sits and suns itself, then no self-respecting duck will try to land in your pond during the whole day. If you have five hundred ducks in your pond, you might get fifty ducks to try to land every eight hours. But if you have ten thousand ducks sitting on top of each other in your pond, then every duck in the world will try to land in your pond. Ducks are entrepreneurial companies. Boston and San Francisco were ponds with ten thousand ducks.

The reasons entrepreneurial companies cluster together were multifold. Certainly, proximity to other, similar companies had many positive business benefits. It also ensured that the region would develop the infrastructure that supports such companies. Still, in my mind, the real reason was personal. If you were in Parkersburg, West Virginia, and your high-tech company went bankrupt, you had to move to a new state to get a job. If you were in San Francisco, and your company folded, you only had to walk down the street to get a job the next day. You did not have to leave the state, and your children did not need to change schools. It was clear that we needed to attract ducks, and the VCs to back them, and that an association was the first step to building that ecosystem. I needed a partner, though.

I found one in Frank Adams, a founder of the Maryland-focused venture capital firm Grotech. In the early 1980s, Frank had been executive vice president of Peterson, Howel, and Heather (PH&H), a Hunt Valley firm whose primary business was automotive fleet leasing and corporate relocations. He'd headed PH&H's international business, buying troubled companies and turning around their businesses. Frank was characterized as a maverick entrepreneur inside a large company. He left PH&H, where he was very happy and had been asked by the firm's chairman, Jerry Geckle, to head strategic planning to take over a bankrupt computer manufacturer, TMS.

Frank preferred fighting on the front lines rather than a rear staff position where he could do little more than offer advice. Mr. Geckle said about Frank, "I've always admired people with the guts to wade into things that are tough and get them done."

TMS was a miserable situation. According to Frank, "The product was terrible, the management worse, the marketplace dying, and the company's reputation toxic." Frank turned the company around, leaving it to take over another troubled company, Telemanagement Systems. He then turned that around and sold it.

Frank made money but was not ready to retire. In 1985, Frank Bonsal, an NEA co-founder, introduced Frank Adams to Ed Segar, a former Donaldson, Lufkin, and Jenerette venture capitalist. They wanted to start a venture firm that focused on investments in the mid-Atlantic region. Together, they formed Grotech and approached Sewell Watts of then Baker Watts Investment Bank to help raise the capital. Sewell agreed to take on the assignment for a piece of the general partner Carry in lieu of a cash fee. The project was given to a young banker names Roger Novak. Baker Watts eventually raised $2M from high-net-worth individuals, Adams raised $10M from USF&G through his old boss, Jerry Geckle, CEO of PH&H, who introduced him to Jack Mosley, CEO of USF&G.

By this time, Ed Sager, living in Wayne, Pennsylvania, faded away, and Adams ran the firm with just a secretary. After successfully investing the first fund in local companies, he set about raising Grotech II in 1987. It was at this time that Roger Novak was hired to complete a team already staffed with two other partners with significant operating experience and an advisory group. Novak left the firm in 1993. Grotech continued investing primarily in regional companies over the next 30 years. Roger Novak would go on to fund another venture capital firm with Jack Biddle called Novak Biddle.

Frank commented on the conditions of venture capital in Maryland when Grotech was founded: "At that time, NEA was here, but was mainly investing outside the area because there was not a lot of entrepreneurial activity going on in the mid-Atlantic. Grotech Partners

I was a rather small fund, about $12M. I wanted Grotech because I saw it as a way to get venture capital into promising local companies. We helped Alton Labs, which produced a very big return. We created Grotech II in 1987 and then III in 1991."

Because Grotech was a mid-Atlantic-focused fund, Adams encountered a degree of prejudice. When pursuing investors, he all too often heard, "Why should we put money into the mid-Atlantic?"

Roger Novak described the opportunity in the mid-Atlantic: "I was interested in large-scale networking, which was prevalent in the government, and in the security of the networks. I thought these would make their way into the commercial world. But the initial players were government. Alton was dealing with an agency in Fort Meade, south of Baltimore. Verity became a big win and originally was working for an agency at Langley, Virginia. Secured Computing came out of work for an agency at Fort Meade. I realized we couldn't take the national security part out, but we did take a subset out, and these became the first telecommunications firewalls."

There was, Frank Adams admitted, a learning curve. "In those years, we were more conservative than the California crowd. We looked more to established companies, ones with a track record, before we would fund them. The California people influenced us to go for it faster, be riskier. We were more stuffed suits, and they convinced us to go more in the directions that blazed first. This was especially true of NEA because they had a California office with Dick Kramlich and that caused the Baltimore office and Grotech to be more aggressive at an earlier stage.

"Still there was the feeling that more could be done. What activity there was centered on Baltimore. Investors thought northern Virginia was horse country. Chuck Newhall and I put Mid-Atlantic Venture Association together because we felt if we didn't do it, no one would. We wanted to create a critical mass here. What we needed in this region was to attract entrepreneurs. We had to persuade competent people to leave good jobs with established companies. If we attracted them here, they would start fast-growing companies that would, in turn, attract more venture capital. We felt that what we were really doing was starting a process that might take thirty years."

For me, Frank Adams was the perfect partner. For NEA, MAVA was nice to have. For Frank, MAVA's success was a necessity. Best of all, we agreed on everything. When we started NEA, the mid-Atlantic was not a hospitable place for venture capital or entrepreneurship. There were exceptions, including T. Rowe Price and Alex Brown, but the rest of the business community was indifferent to startups or somewhat suspicious that there was a scam going on.

About six months after NEA opened its doors, we got a call from *The Baltimore Sun* asking us if we would give them an interview. We said yes, and a week later, a reporter arrived at our doorstep looking like he was about to suffer a heart attack. He was almost crying. He acted like this was a stupid assignment he had only grudgingly accepted, and that the launch of NEA was nothing compared to real news like Bethlehem Steel, the largest employer in Maryland, closing its doors and laying off employees.

Years later, the *Sun* would write that NEA raised all its money in Baltimore and invested it in California. The truth was, by the late 1980s, less than 1 percent of NEA's capital came from Maryland, and 10 percent of it was invested in the mid-Atlantic. But these stories are representative of how most local institutions were very skeptical of the venture capital business. Even today, NEA is vastly better known in California than it is in Baltimore.

Not all the media was hostile. Tim Baker, a contract writer for the *Baltimore Sun,* tried to set the record straight: "Since the duck-hunting season will open soon, it's time to blast away at that old canard about how Baltimore's mean-spirited venture capital firms bankroll startups in Boston and northern California but won't invest in Maryland's own high-tech companies.

"For example, earlier this year a local business school's survey piously reported that our venture firms have invested 90 percent of their capital out of state. Take New Enterprise Associates, Maryland's largest venture firm. It has made 175 investments, but only twelve of them in Maryland. Sounds terrible, doesn't it?

"We're told over and over that these venture firms deprive local entrepreneurs of the capital needed to build this region's high-technology future. But it won't wash. Indeed, there are so many good angles from which to fire away at this theory that it's hard to know where to start shooting.

"The theory rests on the assumption, usually tacit, that our venture-capital firms have exported to other states' capital which they raised here in Maryland. In fact, Baltimore venture capitalists have never succeeded in raising much money around here. Most of their money has come from out-of-state investors.

"For example, NEA's eight funds have raised $577M since 1978. But only $7M came from Maryland. On the other hand, those eight NEA funds have invested $32M in Maryland companies. NEA's out-of-state limited partners invested another $25M in NEA's Maryland investments. As a result of these leadership investments, these companies have now attracted more than $219M in additional public equity funding. That is 276 million dollars being invested in Maryland companies due to NEA.

"NEA's experience is typical. Grotech Partners in Timonium raised $50M from out-of-state institutional investors last year. So far it has invested $10M. From that pool $6M went into Maryland companies along with an additional $2M in co-investments from out-of-state which Grotech arranged. Last month those companies attracted another $15M in public equity.

"This year may represent a breakthrough year for venture-capital investment in this state. Since January, four venture-backed Maryland companies have completed initial public stock offerings: Genetic Therapy, Medimmune, Integrated Health Services, and Microprose. This is a major accomplishment. Add nine other new offerings in the rest of the mid-Atlantic area, and together they amount to a significant chunk of all the venture-backed initial offerings in the country this year—more than the fabled entrepreneurs in Silicon Valley and the San Francisco Bay area. Venture capital firms, the MAVA members will start companies that eventually will bring billions of dollars of investments to the mid-Atlantic."

There was one other notable exception to the otherwise pervasive hostility toward venture capital in the regional media. That was Edwin Warfield, who ran a local daily newspaper, *The Daily Record,* and a business magazine, *Warfield's.* If Frank and I were MAVA's fathers, then Edwin was its godfather. He spent three decades covering what was going on in the entrepreneurial world, and he closely followed the stories of MAVA and other venture capital firms in the region.

There were also a few people besides the VCs concerned about the lack of entrepreneurship in the region. Robert Embry, Jr., was one of them. As president of the Abell Foundation, which is dedicated to enhancing the quality of life in Maryland, Bob was acutely aware of macroeconomic trends. With insufficient local entrepreneurship, he knew that Maryland would continue to fall behind other states. In the late 1980s, Bob's assistant, Tim Baker (who'd written the favorable *Sun* article), approached NEA and Alex Brown to establish a regional seed venture firm. John Nehra, a general partner at Alex Brown, was brought in to run it, and we started Catalyst Ventures in 1989. Bob went on to fund other regional funds, including one led by Barbara Plantholt of Johns Hopkins University. Hopkins eventually established its own venture firm, Triad, with Barbara at the helm, in the early 1990s. Bob was also instrumental in getting Calvert Social Venture Partners, led by John May, started. Eventually, Bob was directly or indirectly responsible for thirty to forty investments being made in local startup companies. Catalyst Ventures was a 3.5x fund, and NEA decided to bring the regional investing in-house, hiring John Nehra as a general partner.

In the beginning of venture capital in the mid-Atlantic region, Baltimore became the center of activity. In the early 1980s, a number of firms started there, including Alex Brown, led by Bruns Grayson; Emerging Growth Partners; T. Rowe Price Ventures, led by Terral Jordan; Arete Ventures Limited; and Grotech, led by Frank Adams, to name a few. However, in Washington, D.C., and the Delaware Valley, the stage was being set for similar developments. In a sense, MAVA became a rallying point for those in the region outside of Maryland interested in venture capital. In truth, it was the combined efforts of entrepreneurs, venture capitalists, and service providers that created MAVA.

Washington, D.C, developed more slowly than Baltimore, but for years, there had been a lot of entrepreneurial activity there, funded by VCs from outside the region. In the late 1960s, US Time Sharing Inc., a company that sold computing time to the government, went public. It served as a training ground for the developers of subsequent Washington-based software companies. Bob Cook and Dan Dyer worked there. Mario Marino moonlit there while he was in the Navy. Dan Dyer went on to establish Scientific Time Sharing Corporation in 1969. Mario founded Legent Corporation in 1973; eight years later, Bob Cook founded VM Software. As time went on, most of these companies came to focus on remote computing and software. CA Technologies bought Legent for $1.8 billion in 1995, at that time the biggest acquisition in the software industry.

Headquartered in Washington, D.C., MCI Communications was founded in 1963 by Jack Goeken and led to great success later by Bill McGowan. MCI went head-to-head with AT&T in the early 1990s and became the second-largest long-distance service provider in the US MCI was instrumental in encouraging the Sherman Antitrust Act legislation that broke the Bell monopoly. In 1997, World Com bought MCI for $47 billion, the largest merger in history at that time.

Perhaps the biggest star in the Washington, D.C. firmament was America Online, originally called Quantum Computer Services, which started as a web portal and an online service provider in 1985. The idea for America Online was Bill von Meister's and the company was first led by Jim Kimsey and Steve Case. By 1999, the company had 12,000 employees and $5.5 billion in revenue. It was sold in 2015 to Verizon for $4.4 billion.

Another big win for the region was John Puente's Digital Communications Corporation, founded in 1971. By 1999, it was Hughes Network Systems, grossing over $1 billion.

The mid-Atlantic region created big ducks, including MCI and AOL, but they were sold and left the pond. The region did not have the kind of companies like Hewlett Packard and Intel that would continue to flourish, sprouting new companies for close to a century.

In the 1970s, however, government procurement changed, hastening a shift to relying on outsourcing. Gary Golding, of Edison Partners, described how the Washington, D.C., software community developed, "The first MAVA Fair, in '87, was a significant energizer. A lot of things were coming together then. You had Steve Case at Quantum, which would become AOL, Marshall Graham at The Source [Telecomputing Corporation], and Emmit McHenry at Networking Solutions. You had Scientific Time Sharing Corporation, where lots of people gained experience [becoming] software entrepreneurs. MCI and DARPA [Defense Advanced Research Projects Agency] were successful and spinning off talent that started up new companies. You had Ernst & Young, whose people were dominant in entrepreneurial services, helping startups. Law firms Shaw Pittman and Hogan & Hartson were putting together deals for entrepreneurs. Washington had its equivalent of *Warfields*. It was called *Techway*, and it covered all the entrepreneurial activity in the region."

Mario Morino recalled that the mid-1980s was a crucial time, "One problem was that, in this region, we were noted for service firms, and to venture capitalists, service firms just don't have the multiples that they like. They want to see the kinds of profits a software products firm can command. By '86–'89, this was beginning to happen. Service firms became more important and started earning the kind of money venture capitalists appreciated. They took more of an interest in being here and investing here."

In the 1980s and 1990s, the Washington technology sector was thriving. MCI and DARPA spun off a lot of talent that shaped new tech companies. Steve Case started America Online. NEA and Accel funded UUNet. Grotech funded PSI Net. Tom Scholl founded Telogy in 1984. A year earlier, Stephen Walker started Trusted Information Systems (TIS), a pioneering company in cybersecurity that focused on internet networks. In the 1990s, Kevin Burns founded Sage Software Consulting. After its sale, he would go on to run Lazard's venture arm in Washington.

While all this was going on, the healthcare field had an explosion of activity, too. Some of this was due to Dr. Bernadine Healy, the director of the NIH, who enabled NIH scientists to patent and commercialize their discoveries.

With Dr. Alen Walton, a former Harvard Medical School professor, at the helm, Oxford Bioscience Partners from Westport, Connecticut, began to invest in the region. Investments included Martek Biosciences, developers of microalgae healthcare products, Genetic Therapy, and Human Genome Sciences. Even more important were the activities of Health Care Ventures, led by Wally Steinberg and Dr. Jim Cavanaugh, which helped start Genetic Therapy, Human Genome Sciences, MedImmune, and a host of other companies.

Similar work to create an ecosystem for startups and venture funding was being done in the Philadelphia region. The Delaware Valley Venture Group was created in 1983 by the Philadelphia Chamber of Commerce and the Philadelphia First organization, with the help of leading local companies and universities to stimulate the growth of venture capital in the region.

The Delaware Valley area did not have the long, historic presence of such firms as Broventure and Allied. Data Science Partners was first established in Princeton, New Jersey. Data Science Partners invested nationally in early-stage high-technology companies and had made significant investments in the mid-Atlantic region. On the other side of the Delaware River, in Radnor, Pennsylvania, TDH Ventures was led by Jim Doherty; founded in 1973, TDH invested the majority of its capital in the region.

Like the Baltimore-Washington corridor, the Delaware Valley region gained most of its venture firms in the 1980s, as firms began to cluster in Philadelphia and Princeton, such as SR One, led by Brenda Gavin, which was the venture capital arm of GlaxoSmithKline, focusing on healthcare investments. Most of these firms had both a national and regional focus.

The bellwether venture event in Philadelphia was the founding of its first national venture firm, Philadelphia Ventures, in 1983. The firm was led by Charles Burton and Tom Morse. Charles, or Chief to his friends, was the driving force behind the Delaware Valley Venture Group in its early years, and he made sure it coordinated with MAVA. Chief had worked at INA with John Ridell, who helped to drive NEA's initial funding. The group's membership grew from two firms in 1983 to over fifty in 1999, seventeen of which managed over $1 billion in capital.

Hillman Ventures in Pittsburg, led by Philip Paul, was one of the largest investors in venture capital and private companies in US history. Henry Hillman believed in American entrepreneurship, and in the 1970s and 1980s, he put his money where his mouth was. The firm provided capital to such venture partnerships as Kleiner Perkins Caufield & Byers, Brentwood, InterWest Partners, Alpha Partners, NEA, and TA Associates. It helped to spawn companies like Hybritech, Tandem Computers, Genentech, and Teradata.

The leading Princeton venture firms were Accel Partners, Domain Associates, DSV Partners, and the Edison Venture Fund. Founded in 1983, Accel was the largest venture fund in the region and the recognized leader in the telecommunications, software, and healthcare arenas. Domain, founded in 1985 and led by Jim Blair, invested exclusively in healthcare companies, nationally and regionally. DSV Partners, one of the oldest early-stage venture firms in the country, invested in health and information sciences companies, while the Edison Venture Fund, founded in 1986, was the largest venture fund with a strategic focus on the mid-Atlantic region. By the late 1990s, the mid-Atlantic was humming.

Jamie Hamilton, a Washington, D.C., entrepreneur who was the first hire at FreeLoader, noted that in the Baltimore-Washington region, much had changed for high-tech employees by the 1990s. "In '85, they wouldn't have talked stock options because they did not know what stock options were. By the late 1990s, they are savvier, like the California people, and they come in saying they want X percent and the stock strike price that would suit them.

"There are new venture capitalists here, too," Hamilton continued. "The older venture capitalists are like they always were, but the new ones are more like the California ones. They are quicker, want to make the deal faster before it slips away. In California, there is competition for deals, and now that is happening here. Venture capitalists have to be faster on their feet. In California, they would meet you and invest right away. That was not done here until recently. Traditionally, in this region, it was bread and butter; crafting deals that made sense, doing due diligence, going for real businesses, not intangibles. But now it's great for entrepreneurs here to have venture capital firms fawning over you. You are now in the driver's seat, so long as you have a good idea."

The mid-Atlantic was becoming exceptionally active. Gary Golding, of Edison Partners, estimated that between early 1997 and the middle of 1999, local venture capitalists funded between sixty and one hundred companies. "The big firms such as Carlyle, Columbia led by Jim Fleming, and NEA have all raised $300 million in this time for small companies, and lots of the money has gone into this region. Suddenly, the Reston dream is realized. Their communities spread about . . . even the notable California law firms are moving in, notably Cooley Godward," "So we've reached a sort of critical mass," Golding said in that interview. "The bigger successes have developed the managerial and entrepreneurial talent that leaves and starts second-generation companies. The more experienced and better people are going to make better quality companies in which to invest. The climate is going to attract better people from outside, too. They will see that they can move their families here, and in case they have to leave one company, there are others which they can go and not have to uproot their wives and children. This kind of critical mass has been achieved in Silicon Valley and Boston, but not in places like Pittsburgh."

In his oral history interview, Roger Novak, of Novak Biddle Venture Partners, echoed this. He said, "There is now a great deal of momentum. There are skilled engineers, some with money, and an infrastructure that includes PNC, Silicon Valley Bank, and Imperial, led by April Young, all of which understand venture lending, and lawyers who understand the deals."

What is necessary to create an entrepreneurial ecosystem? In my opinion, there are six elements:

1. You need world-class, academic research in the region. The mid-Atlantic had that in spades, coming from institutions such as Johns Hopkins, the NIH, DARPA, the University of Maryland, and the University of Pennsylvania.

2. You need venture capital firms in the region. In 1970, there were four venture firms in the mid-Atlantic. When I stepped down as chairman of MAVA, there were well over 120.

3. You need many managers with significant entrepreneurial experience in a variety of industries. In 1970, the mid-Atlantic was an entrepreneurial desert, but today we have lots of small company managers with the right expertise.

4. You need to encourage large, innovative technology and medical companies to spin out employees for startups. This is the mid-Atlantic's weakness because the best companies in the region are often sold.

5. You need ducks on a pond—a host of entrepreneurial companies.

6. You need time. It takes twenty years to get a venture ecosystem started and forty years for things to come to fruition. Over this kind of time frame, MAVA helped change the mid-Atlantic from an entrepreneurial desert to a significant entrepreneurial region. At the high point, the mid-Atlantic had more venture-backed companies than Boston, and its share of capital raised by the overall US venture industry went from half a percent in 1970 to 20 percent in 1990.

The following table highlights MAVA's impact:

Total Number of Venture Capital Firms in the US

1970	200
1990	600

Mid-Atlantic Venture Capital Firms

1970	4
1990	120

Mid-Atlantic Share of Venture Capital IPOs

1970	1%
1990	28%

Mid-Atlantic Share of Venture-Backed Companies

1970	1%
1990	20%

Venture Capital Dollars Raised in Mid-Atlantic (as % of Total)

1970	.05%
1990	20%

Number of Venture Capital-Backed Companies in the Region in 1990

San Francisco: 879

Boston: 365

Mid-Atlantic: 475

The creation of the entrepreneurial ecosystem in the mid-Atlantic was the work of many. The venture community started with the first four firms already mentioned, and the community grew with the funding of NEA in 1978. In the early 1980s, Chesapeake Venture Management; New Venture Partners, led by Howard Wolfe; Boulder Ventures, led by Larry Macks; and Arete Ventures opened their doors. Several venture firms based outside the region also established a significant mid-Atlantic presence, including Oxford, Alan Patricof, Kleiner Perkins, Sevin Rosen Funds, InterWest Partners, Charles River Ventures, Venrock, and Greylock Partners.

In 1989, Columbia Capital, based in Alexandria, Virginia, was founded by Jim Fleming to invest in the telecom industry. Not long after, Triad started work out of Johns Hopkins, and Calvert Social Venture Partners got up and running, too. In the 1990s, several other mid-Atlantic firms joined the fray, including Novak Biddle Venture Partners; FBR Technology Venture Partners, led by Gene Riechers; Carlyle Venture Partners, an offshoot of the Carlyle Group launched to invest in emerging technology companies; and Woman's Growth Capital Fund, led by Patty Abramson. And this is only a partial list. It does not include the firms expanding the venture universe in Philadelphia, Delaware, or New Jersey.

Almost as important as establishing the venture firms was the growth of service providers, the law and accounting firms, that focused on entrepreneurial companies, such as Arthur Andersen, led in this era by Jim Brady; Ernst & Young; Hogan & Hartson; KPMG, led by Michael Joseph; Price Waterhouse Coopers (before it became PricewaterhouseCoopers, in 1998), led regionally by Larry Alleva; and Coopers & Lybrand, led regionally by Pat Deering; Piper Marbury; and Venable, Baetjer & Howard.

Charles Heller of the Dingman Center for Entrepreneurship at the Smith School of Business at the University of Maryland played an important role in the 1990s, too. Silicon Valley Bank even set up a regional office in Arlington, Virginia, to finance venture debt, which many local banks were hesitant to provide. Imperial Bank was a local exception that stepped up to finance ventures. Several regional banks did, too, such as Ferris, Baker Watts, and the Friedman, Billings, Ramsey Group. To create an entrepreneurial ecosystem is the work of many hands.

I stepped down as chairman of MAVA. I was followed by Frank Adams, my partner in founding MAVA. Frank was followed by Art Marks, soon to be a former NEA partner. Art was followed by the capable Patrick Kerins, then a Grotech partner, now an NEA partner. In 2002, Julia Spicer was hired as the executive director of the organization. The chairmanship changes every three years, but Julia has been the unwavering constant since she started. Unfortunately, the twenty-first century would not treat MAVA kindly.

As discussed, after the 1990s, the biotech world changed dramatically. Biotech required significant financing, and the outcomes were binary, pass/fail only. Fortunes were being made elsewhere, in funding consumer internet companies, the cloud, and statistical analysis system (SAS) software. Gradually, limited partner-type investors came to fund only technology venture firms and began avoiding biotech partnerships. The number of medical-only venture firms declined precipitously in this era. In the biotech heyday, however, half the IPOs in this region were healthcare.

After the bubble burst in 2000, the valuations for communications companies collapsed, and tech capital was only finding its way to internet products and services. If mid-Atlantic venture opportunity was a three-legged stool balanced on biotech, communications, and software, now only software remained intact, although I am sure biotech and communications will eventually recover. Ultimately, the effect was that the number of large venture funds in the region declined severely.

Simultaneously, the large funds left were finding conferences increasingly irrelevant, asking themselves, "Why go to a conference when you can surf the web instead?" Conferences were MAVA's primary funding source and raison d'être. While Julia and the MAVA leadership managed to refocus MAVA on startups and angel investors, these organizations don't usually have the resources to spend a lot of time and money supporting a trade organization like MAVA. In my time there, several hundred venture capitalists and service providers gave thousands of hours combined to support MAVA. Increasingly, Julia had to do everything herself.

The good news is that the entrepreneurial economy is now embedded in the mid-Atlantic. Industries and regions go in and out of fashion, but because the venture industry is extremely cyclical,

I remain convinced that the mid-Atlantic will come to play a more significant role in American innovation.

The consciously guided evolution of a venture ecosystem did not only occur in the mid-Atlantic, San Francisco, and Boston. In the past twenty-five years, similar ecosystems have also been created around Seattle, Minneapolis, Austin, New York City, and Los Angeles. Attempts to recreate such a system around the Research Triangle area in North Carolina have failed, despite the efforts of many people.

All regional ecosystems go through periods of boom, bubble, and bust, created by waves of innovation and reciprocity. Most regions surf the national trends to some extent, sometimes being more protected or sometimes more exposed depending on their regional DNA. We succeeded in bringing ducks to Baltimore's pond, building symbiotic relationships between companies, but California—and to a lesser extent, Boston—have proven capable of producing new waves of innovation over and over for eighty years, continually spawning new, vital technologies around which companies are created.

XVIII.

BETTER OUTCOMES, LOWER COSTS

"I have not failed. I've just found 10,000 ways that won't work."

—Thomas Edison

"BETTER OUTCOMES AT LOWER COSTS" was my mantra when I financed twenty different healthcare service companies. If one chose to follow the largest three of these, post-acquisition, throughout their lives as acquired divisions of bigger companies, you would see today that they have combined revenues above $400 billion.

I backed three CEOs in healthcare service provider businesses who built multibillion-dollar companies. All three were greedy. Two were accused of having misrepresented their financial results. It was easy to do so when their companies grew through acquisitions or via industry roll-ups. All three encountered significant challenges in their respective markets, though only two of them would survive acquisition and go on to become giants in their industries. The third, with the CEO who paid himself too much, went into bankruptcy and its parts were sold. The parts were significantly more valuable than the whole.

The lessons from my experiences with all three CEOs showed me the three issues to watch while building a healthcare service provider business. First, several of the CEOs succumbed to enhancing their results illegally, which is easier when half of your growth comes from acquisitions. The CEOs bought companies valued at 3x revenue multiples, but they were valued at 7x revenue multiples when they became part of the larger, public companies. To have value as a public company, roll-ups should always be accompanied by robust internal store-for-store growth, but you must check on how that store-for-store growth is calculated since there are many ways to fudge those numbers. Companies that enhance acquisitions numbers and store-for-store growth wreak havoc on investors.

The major second issue was government intervention. Many government officials believe that for-profit medicine has no place in the US healthcare system. No matter how much a for-profit company saves patients on total healthcare costs, if the company makes "too much money," then their reimbursement levels will be slashed. I believe that patients are hurt when reimbursement rules are changed rapidly and with little appreciation for the unintended consequences.

The third problem healthcare service providers experienced came from CEOs wanting to expand an unproven business model too rapidly, creating a cash-consuming monster. I once financed a provider who tried to build a chain of outpatient centers that treated morbid obesity, a costly disease with radiating comorbidities such as chronic obstructive pulmonary disease, heart disease, and cancer. The chairman was number two in the running to be CEO of one of America's largest medical device companies and then ran an unrelated leveraged buyout of a blood bag company that was a successful investment. He based his obesity model for his new startup on a profitable clinic run by one of Harvard's best doctors. He rapidly expanded to ten to twelve clinics with two venture financings.

Soon, all his clinics were drowning in losses. Investors told him they would not finance the company until he made some of the existing clinics profitable. In a fit of pique, he tossed the company keys to me and led his management team out of the door, saying, "If you don't like the job I am doing, you run the company." The board brought in a turnaround CEO, who spent a year trying to make the model work, but the facilities just could not break even. The core problem was that the insurance companies worried that if they paid for our expensive treatments, then other providers would demand a similar reimbursement for their inexpensive weight loss programs.

Ultimately, the company went bankrupt. I learned to beware of expanding unproven delivery systems, especially when you have arrogant big-company management teams in place.

In the early 1990s, I started to shift my focus from providers to managed-care companies, including Amerigroup and Bravo Health. Jeff McWaters, CEO of Amerigroup, and Jeff Folick, CEO of Bravo Health, were two of the finest and most dedicated leaders I have encountered in my career as a venture capitalist. Their companies encountered great difficulties, often caused by government interference. In the end, they both triumphed, producing better outcomes at much lower costs. Both CEOs, like George Washington at Valley Forge, overcame "fearful odds" to accomplish great things. Initially focused on the Medicaid population, Amerigroup lowered costs and improved patient outcomes with case management. A narcotics-addicted pregnant woman can cost the healthcare system $1 million in care of a drug-addicted baby, but if you incentivize proactive doctor's visits by paying the mother $20 per weekly appointment, it dramatically reduces the number of drug-addicted babies born. The program saved lives and preserved the health of thousands of babies.

Bravo Health patients were case-managed beneficiaries that had dual-eligibility in Medicare and Medicaid. For the most part, they were elderly, poor inner-city patients with several chronic illnesses and very few years to live. When they got sick or needed care, they were usually treated in emergency rooms, hospitals, and nursing homes—the most expensive provider platforms in the American healthcare system. For an elderly patient, the quality of life in the emergency room is equivalent to the quality of life in a torture chamber. Bravo's approach to the problem was simple: every week, transport the patients to a community clinic or a general practitioner's office, then practice preventative medicine rather than reactive medicine. They were treated with simple, low-cost interventions. One of the most pervasive problems with caring for the elderly is that they do not take their medications. Bravo understood this, so the company called its patients to see that they complied with and took their medicines. They called the patients' families as well to ensure they were involved daily in the patients' care.

Bravo Health started in 1993 in the Baltimore basement of 1119 St. Paul Street, NEA's office. Chip Linehan, a young NEA partner, and I had become intrigued with the idea of starting a company that provided daycare for elderly, inner-city patients. With other partners, Chip's father, Earl Linehan, had built the most extensive private nursing home company in the US, and David Carliner was one of Earl Linehan's key partners. When Meridian was sold, Chip hired David to develop a business plan for a company, called Elder Health.

After one year of doing research and drafting a business plan, Chip and David set out to hire a CEO. They first used a top executive recruiter who spent our money and accomplished nothing, so I called Jeff McWaters of Amerigroup, and he recommended Mike Steele, an accomplished managed-care executive. We hired Steele. We then raised a $12 million series A round from NEA, Larry Coleman of Coleman Swenson Booth, Scott Meadow of Frontenac, Carter Beese of Riggs Bank, and Meridian Partners, all of which were venture partnerships.

The first Elder Health facility opened in 1994. The trick in starting a healthcare services company is not to open a lot of facilities until you have proven your economic model at the facility level. Unfortunately, the initial Elder Health model was flawed. It took four years to gather enough patients to break even in that one facility. With a viable model, profitability should be achieved in closer to six months to a year.

In the late 1990s, Elder Health was out of money. We raised another big round from several existing and new investors, which included Mike Aspinwall of GE Capital and Nader Naini of Frazier Healthcare Partners. The financing was delayed because GE wanted a legal opinion that the company was in compliance. Several lawyers balked at giving this opinion, worried about the liability of guaranteeing our compliance, but David Carliner found a lawyer who was willing to risk the potential liability. We succeeded in financing the company one week before it would have had to declare bankruptcy. This would become standard operating procedure until we found a new CEO. Two steps forward, one step back, alternating between victory and defeat.

The company, after months of negotiations with Humana, signed a deal where Elder Health would provide patient care while Humana handled claims processing, but Humana pulled out because they were losing money. Next, Elder Health thought they had a deal with Blue Cross Blue Shield of Maryland to provide care for a large number of patients, only to read in the *Baltimore Sun* that BCBS was withdrawing from the Medicare market. The company spent a year trying to get a big contract, only to lose it the day before the contract was to start. This happened several times.

At the height of the Bubble, Chip was asked to move to the West Coast to focus on tech deals, although he continued to attend some of the Elder Health board meetings. I took over as the lead investor, meeting with Mike Steele for an hour or two twice a month. We concluded the adult day care model did not work and that we should change the company's focus to become an HMO.

In 2000, we became an HMO. It was the fastest HMO approval in the country, plus, we had acquired an HMO that had a relatively large book of business. The acquisition strained the company financially. Not only did we have to pay to purchase it, we had to set aside a large cash reserve to pay for patient care, in the event we failed to manage the business properly. Around 2002, we altered our HMO strategy to focus on case management of patients. The strategy was better outcomes at lower costs.

The problem was that we did not grow fast enough. We failed to meet budget, so in 2004, we restructured the company, hiring Jeff Folick as CEO. Jeff had met Chip when they both sat on the board of AgeWell. Jeff was the former COO of PacifiCare, a giant HMO, and had more than thirty years of managed care experience. He was impressive and had a Rolodex of contacts. When Mike left Elder Health, the company had $500 million in revenue and substantial losses. Jeff turned that around in twelve months. Jeff's value went far beyond having the contacts that made accelerated growth possible. Leadership was his greatest attribute.

David Carliner said of Jeff's leadership style, "While we had a great team of people who were incredibly committed to our mission, the team was demoralized. We had gone years missing targets and projections, and many people on the team felt like we just couldn't win. When Jeff took over the company, he got people to believe in themselves again and created a culture where people gave their all for themselves, for Jeff, and for the mission. He brought new people into the organization who were drawn to work with him who contributed significantly. He was truly an inspirational leader who built incredible loyalty."

Dick Kramlich always told me, "You are only one person away from having a great company." In this case, he was right. Jeff renamed the company Bravo Health—how fitting! An accolade for a brilliant performance. Bravo produced results that would have its investors clapping for years.

Jeff continued to face the same types of problems the company had always faced, but he solved them. For instance, when the Centers for Medicare and Medicaid Services (CMS), the major regulatory agency, found that Bravo was not in compliance with some of the Medicare regulations, it could have been the end of the company. Jeff showed the agency there were errors in their calculations and the company was in compliance. Although the government changed reimbursement levels seven times during Jeff's tenure, requiring the company to change its way of doing business, Bravo's sales still grew dramatically, and profit margins increased. The company expanded beyond the dual-eligible market into traditional Medicaid and Medicare markets. It also started to supply its patients with generic drugs.

Jeff had been commuting from Los Angeles to Baltimore for five years, and the brutal commute was taking a toll. He asked the board to find a local CEO. At the same time, Chip, Nader Naini, and Jeff all thought the Obama administration might destroy Medicare Part C reimbursement, so in August 2010, faced with that prospect and the fact that Jeff would move on, the board voted to sell the company to HealthSpring, Inc., a similar company based in Nashville, for $545 million.

In October 2011, Cigna acquired the combined company for $5 billion, an incredible step-up that would have valued Bravo closer to $2 billion. I always believed you went with the jockey, not the horse, and I knew the odds of finding another Jeff were low, so I had voted against the sale. I disagreed with it because the price was too low. The probability that our reimbursement would be changed was high, and NEA's healthcare team needed a big victory to keep our jobs. At that time, the dollar value of the Bravo gain was the seventh-largest in NEA's history.

If I had to describe my efforts related to Bravo, I would say I believe I played a substantial role in changing the company's strategy to HMO and case management. I also provided advice and counsel to both Jeff and Mike Steele during times of trouble. Most importantly, I kept the board focused on building a great company when most others would have happily closed its doors. David Carliner described my role as follows:

"As I was deciding to come to NEA to be 'incubated,' I was told by many people to be wary of venture capitalists. People said to me that venture capitalists were short-sighted with time horizons that couldn't exceed five years, solely focused on the bottom line with no place for values. I was concerned about these warnings but felt that NEA and Chuck were different. In hindsight, given all the trials and tribulations that we went through, I know that those concerns could be true for some venture capitalists but certainly were not true for you. I couldn't have been more impressed with your focus on the long-term. From the very beginning, you made it clear that you wanted to build significant companies that really improved upon the way healthcare was delivered and made patients' lives better. You understood the importance of culture, values, and mission to the company's success. You taught me that to be successful in your business, you need to first and foremost bet on people that you trust with big ideas and let them do their thing. I appreciated the fact that you trusted us with the specifics and focused your attention on how to help us build our shared vision for the business."

You might think this behavior should merit special attention. It should not. This is what venture capitalists do. It is their job description.

Jeff McWaters graduated with a degree in accounting from the University of Kentucky and married his high school sweetheart, Cindy. Jeff also joined Ernst & Young in 1979; then, in 1980, he went to work for Hospital Affiliates, which had begun to acquire and manage health maintenance organizations. Jeff was in the right place at the right time. As a young man, long before Amerigroup was founded, he learned the inner workings of the emerging Medicare and Medicaid populations, and he learned about how to run a business when he helped open Cigna's Managed Care division in Dallas, Texas. In 2002, he told Managed Healthcare Executive, "We didn't have a checkbook when we started. We had no policies or procedures, no infrastructure, no computer system, nothing! We did it all from scratch." That's the perfect way to train an entrepreneur.

In 1986, Jeff helped Dr. Ronald I. Dozoretz start Options Mental Health in Norfolk, Virginia. Jeff was the CEO, and the company developed and managed mental health and substance abuse programs for the Medicaid population. It was one of the first case-management programs in the country. The company grew to $500 million in sales and was profitable. As Jeff said, "It became clear to me that the Medicaid and uninsured populations were both very large and growing. They were still being managed by a 1960s era healthcare system. Patients could not be seen, and doctors were not getting paid enough." In the early 1990s, some states turned over their Medicaid populations to HMOs.

In October of 1994, Jeff started Americaid Community Care, drafting the business plan at his kitchen table. The new case-management company was focused on the Medicaid population, particularly children and expectant mothers. Americaid planned to concentrate on a limited number of disease "states" such as prenatal care, asthma, diabetes, and sickle cell anemia. The company's goal was to send patients to primary care physicians, which was less expensive than sending them to hospitals, nursing homes, or emergency rooms, where care delivery is costly for chronic illnesses.

Americaid would take over the role of the social worker. The company provided transportation to the doctor and helped patients with the problems of daily life. The young Medicaid population offered higher profit margins than older populations because younger people had more cooperative attitudes, responded more quickly to treatment, and recovered rapidly. There was little competition from the larger HMOs, who were focused on an older population. He chose Virginia Beach due to its central location, excellent quality of life, and workforce, not its market.

Jeff approached Sage Givens about backing Americaid. Sage was in the process of forming Acacia Venture Partners, backed by Paul Wythes, the founding partner of Sutter Hill. Jeff and Sage had been introduced by Joe Hutts, the CEO of PhyCor, which is now Evita Health Inc., one of the hottest healthcare service companies at the time. Sage and I had worked together for years, and she sent me the deal. We both saw the potential and NEA and Acacia committed to Americaid immediately, but Sutter Hill, who was also considering the deal, proved to be a bit more difficult.

Jeff presented his plan for Americaid on the Thursday before Thanksgiving, in California, but he had been told to only submit a three-page outline. When he got there, it turned out Sutter Hill wanted more. They gave him six days over the Thanksgiving holiday to write a complete business plan and return to California to make a full presentation. He wrote the plan on his dining room table, having to travel forty minutes to the airport each way because he had no office equipment to copy or fax. Sutter Hill loved the plan, which turned out later to be an accurate projection of the first company's three years. To put that in perspective, in the venture business, only 1 percent of startup plans are this accurate.

Americaid closed on an $8 million financing, funded in two $4 million tranches. Getting licenses and rapidly building revenue was nearly impossible, but Americaid managed to find a way. Since the company could not market directly to members, it invited Medicaid community leaders, consultants, outreach social workers, and clergy to focus groups where representatives detailed how the Americaid program worked. Information about Americaid programs was placed in churches, supermarkets, Head Start programs, and daycare centers. The company also relied on word of mouth to market its services. In 1996, Americaid had $23 million in revenues and lost $10.9 million, but the model was proven—only volume was needed.

In 1995, Americaid raised an additional $16 million from Sierra Ventures, where they worked with Jim Tananbaum (a partner before he founded Prospect); Accel Partners, with Gene Hill; and the Princeton University Investment Company's Randy Hack. Before Americaid closed the financing, it could hardly make payroll. Although the company had revenue, it was required to set aside vast regulatory reserves in case Americaid had not forecast its medical loss ratios correctly. Therefore, the profit and loss statement showed Americaid losing $1 million a month, but the actual results were far better. The company changed its name to Amerigroup.

In 1997, Amerigroup raised another round of financing from Ferrer Freeman & Co. in Greenwich, Connecticut, where they worked with co-founder Carlos Ferrer. By the end of the year, the company had 41,000 members, $64.4 million in revenue, and had lost $8.9 million. Profitability would soon follow. In 1995, the company was almost put out of business by Representative Henry Waxman of California. A long-time enemy of for-profit medicine, Waxman co-sponsored legislation that would have required an HMO to have 25 percent commercial business and 75 percent Medicare and Medicaid business. To add 25 percent commercial business would have been an impossible task for Amerigroup. Working with the states in which

Amerigroup operated, the company managed to help kill the law, which opened up enormous opportunities for the industry.

Amerigroup doubled in size in 1999. Premiums reached $392 million, and that growth led to new frontiers. It was clear the company had financing needs only the public market could provide, so between 2000 and 2001, the company attempted three public offerings, which failed. Overcoming every possible adversity, in the summer of 2001, the company finally filed with Bank of America and UBS Warburg. The company was about to go public on September 11, 2001, when the planes crashed into the twin towers. The offering was canceled when Jeff and his management team were presenting at a conference in San Francisco. They could not return to the East Coast for eight days. The company resubmitted its prospectus with ten amendments suggested by the underwriter to make the offering more attractive. On November 5, 2001, the offering was completed, raising nearly $75 million, and marking Amerigroup one of the first companies to go public after 9/11.

The much-needed funds went to general corporate and acquisitions. At the end of the year, the company's membership was up to 472,000, while premiums reached $889 million. A delay in the offering enabled the company to attain an even higher price for its stock because, after three years of waiting, it had become much larger.

By 2002, the company had grown to $1.15 billion in revenues, with more than 600,000 members. A few months later, when the company moved from the Nasdaq to the New York Stock Exchange, it added another 265,000 members and revenues approached $1.6 billion. In 2004, the company's membership exceeded two million, and the company was flush with cash. Amerigroup was recognized by *Fortune* as "one of America's most admired companies," and by *Forbes* as "one of America's best-managed companies."

Jeff retired in August of 2007 at the age of 51. He had built an extraordinary management team with a high minority population. The company had a $2 billion market cap and, in 2008, had revenues of $5 billion. He pursued a political career and was elected a Virginia state senator. Half a decade later, the revenues of the company he built had grown to $8.9 billion, and, in 2012, the company was acquired by Wellpoint (now Anthem) for $4.9 billion.

While Amerigroup continued its case-management innovations,

doctors were compensated for keeping patients healthy, not for the number of procedures performed. Preventative care was made a priority. Amerigroup provided physical fitness programs, bulk purchasing of drugs, and medical equipment for patients, including eyewear, hearing aids, vitamins, and so on.

When Jeff left the company in 2007, he said, "The issue we set out to address at the state level in 1994, access, quality, and cost containment, remain the central challenges facing our nation's overall healthcare systems. The time is now for those of us in healthcare to take some lessons we've learned in Medicaid and apply them in a broader, more comprehensive way, ensuring access for all Americans."

Commenting on his career as an entrepreneur in a newspaper interview, Jeff said, "You work like crazy, partly because you really believe in your product and your people, and partly because you are too scared to do anything else. You improvise, take calculated risks, and create a results-driven culture of integrity, excellence, and drive to improve every day . . . for true entrepreneurs and world-class operators, the dream never goes away. What happens when the dream is realized, when the challenge of taking a company public has been accomplished? You look for a bigger challenge!"

XIX.

A FAREWELL TO ARMS

"If you want to live your life in a creative way, as an artist, you have to not look back too much. You have to be willing to take whatever you've done and whoever you were and throw them away."

—Steve Jobs

ON DECEMBER 18, 2010, I planned to leave to go to our house in Utah for Christmas vacation. The mountains had good snow, and I was looking forward to skiing over the break. Three senior healthcare partners, who had been with NEA for years, asked me to meet with them at 2:00 PM. I valued them as much as I would value brothers. I had backed the oldest partner in three companies as CEO. I brought him into NEA as a general partner. I had pointed him and the two younger partners to many pharmaceutical and healthcare company deals that I or my contacts had originated. I was happy to do so because the oldest of these partners had much more technical and operating experience than I did. I had often recommended to my friends that they ask him to go on their boards instead of me. Whenever newspaper reporters called me, I referred them to him so that he could get the visibility. I had referred some of the best deals that crossed my desk to the two younger partners so they could generate the investment records one needed to become a general partner.

Before the meeting, I wondered what was on their minds. The meeting was in a small conference room. I entered, and the three of them were sitting across the table from me looking serious. The older partner started the conversation by being very direct, as usual. The gist of what he said was this.

"Chuck, you do not have the technical or operating experience to direct the med team in the future. You have recruited an incredible team of doctors, scientists, and CEOs to direct the firm's investments, but you have a strong personality. You need to get out of the way and let the new team run the show."

I was asked to resign from the management committee that ran the firm, not to make any new investments, and not to talk at med team meetings. The older partner now was doing all the talking. My younger partners sat with grim faces, folded hands, saying nothing. I had no idea whether they agreed with what the older partner was doing, but they did nothing to stop him or object to what he was saying. I, therefore, assumed they supported everything he was proposing and the manner it was being said.

It was as if a mortar round had exploded in my face. I was back in the valley of the shadow of death in Vietnam. My hands started to shake, I was sweating, and I had trouble hearing. I knew the nightmares would follow. My PTSD kicked in, and I had trouble concentrating for the rest of the meeting. I had no idea whether they discussed this with the management committee or other general partners. Peter Barris, NEA's managing partner, knew because later he said I was brave to confront them. He clearly knew I was being asked to leave the partnership since a few minutes after the meeting he was ready to discuss the terms of my departure. He knew about the meeting and may have caused it to occur, but I do not think he knew how it was being handled. I do not think Dick Kramlich, Scott Sandell, or Mark Perry, the other members of the management committee, were consulted. In retrospect, I wish Peter had told me himself. The three healthcare partners were close to me in our partnership. At this point in my career, nearly 75 percent of my time was spent working with them in some way. If the three of them didn't want me, it did not matter what my other partners thought.

Fortunately, Jim Swartz gave me a plan for an occasion such as this. He said to me after the Bubble: "You lead, you follow, or you get out of the way." I could no longer work with these three men who I had thought were my brothers. I felt that I had just been shot, gangland-style, in the back of the head. It was time to get out of the way.

Most importantly, I felt I could not disrupt the function of the med team which I had built. The team was just getting back on its feet after it was almost eliminated during the bubble. NEA could not afford a public squabble, whether it was justified or not. Realistically the three of them were more important to NEA's healthcare future than I was. In their opinion, I did not have the technical knowledge necessary for today's biotech investing . . . so be it.

I admit I was not technically strong, but technical knowledge had never been the contribution I provided. The two younger partners were not technically strong either, and we had hired the older partner precisely to bolster NEA's technical know-how. Now, with Dave Mott managing the healthcare team and the new hires, NEA had never been stronger. I had made a lot of successful investments and had passed a lot of successful deals along to my partners. I originated deals and showed them to my friends, Jim Blair at Domain Ventures and Tony Evnin at Venrock, who also showed me their deals. I relied on their technical expertise, and they relied on my ability to help companies, to make entrepreneurs believe in themselves and they trusted me to be fair and do the right thing. That's why deals kept coming across my desk. I also had a very extensive network of CEOs and chief scientific officers of biotech companies, big pharma companies, and numerous friends in academic medicine. I always did a lot of due diligence on my own. It was difficult because, many times, equally qualified advisors differed. I often had to call in scientific consultants and patent attorneys.

I was not offended by my health care partners asking me to leave because I respected their opinions. What I objected to was how they informed me of their decision. There was no honor in it. Upon leaving the meeting, I went to the office of NEA's managing partner, Peter Barris, and resigned from the management committee of the company. I asked to receive one year's severance, paid over two years. I only told Dick, Scott, and Mark Perry what happened and asked them to say nothing. They assured me they had known nothing of this. I believe that as far as the rest of the firm and the limited partners were concerned, it was business as usual. My version of this story could be wrong, but I only knew what I was told and what I observed.

I voluntarily gave up half of my carried interest in NEA XIII, as

I was asked to by my older healthcare partner, but the partnership kindly vested me fully in NEA partnerships I through XII, including half of XIII. The next two years were torture. In retrospect, I should have taken the severance and left, but I still felt I could contribute to the firm, and I thought a sharp break would be harmful to NEA.

In leaving NEA, I knew I would be leaving my dream, which had dominated my life. Without my sacrifices, without the support of my first wife (who committed suicide), there would be no NEA. I knew I would have to cut myself out of everything and that long-standing friendships would disappear. This was important since most of my best friends were my NEA partners and limited partners. I had little time for all but a few social friends. It would take me four years after that meeting to recover and stop the nightmares of artillery barrages. Dave Mott, the new manager of the med team, kept kindly asking me for my opinion at med team meetings, in my last two part-time years at the firm, but I avoided giving them.

What amazed and hurt me, though, was not being given any credit for the ways I had helped my partners' careers. Dick Kramlich once asked my older partner, the one who asked me to step aside, who had originated his best investments. He told Dick he was solely responsible for all of them. I was shocked and wanted to accuse him of lying, but I said nothing. At that time, I wanted to keep the rest of the firm from knowing what was going on, and after all, I was getting out of the way. Maybe my older partner believed what he said—self-delusion happens often—but the total betrayal and lack of gratitude hurt me deeply.

One problem that caused me more pain was entirely of my own doing. I had anticipated getting my NEA salary until I was seventy. I was financially unprepared. To fund our living expenses until NEA's distributions started to flow, I had to sell half my art collection, built over forty years with obsession and loving care. It rubbed salt in the open wound. I still dream of the objects I loved and lost. I left the NEA office the week before Christmas in 2012, and I never went back.

Now, ten years after my departure from NEA, and after two glasses of wine, I find myself wishing that all those responsible in whatever way for my ignominious dismissal from the firm that I founded and loved will find themselves in the inferno, in the ninth layer of Dante's hell. The reason I can never forgive or forget is because they forced me to sell my collections. Those hundreds of items that sold over two days were not abstractions to me but the center of my life. They possessed me as much as I possessed them.

When I left NEA, there was one piece of "unfinished business" that I left for Scott Sandell and his other partners to solve. When we had started NEA, we had run it like a corporation, not a partnership. The founders had given 70 percent of their carried interest to new partners at the time we formed NEA III. We hoped this would enable us to attract the talent to build a partnership that would last a hundred years. Most other founders of leading venture capital firms did not give up this percentage of carry until their tenth fund. The founders and most of the partners felt that the founders should have a residual interest in a limited number of funds after they retire. This would be a reward similar to what founders of companies get when they leave the firm and continue holding the stock.

When Frank left NEA, we gave him a diminishing interest in the next three funds. Peter Barris, Dick's successor, felt there was a better way to do it. He hired a lawyer, George Stamas from Kirkland Ellis, to develop a solution. We first explored selling their interests to an outsider.

We approached Susequehana, a company that developed trading software for hedge funds. After several months, it became evident that it would never work. Susquehanna had investment horizons that lasted five to ten seconds. NEA's time horizon was five to ten years. We were from Mars and Sesequehana was from Venus.

George and Peter came up with another solution. NEA would form a management company that would own a percentage of the carry and fees. Owners of the management company were long-term employees who contributed to the firm's success. The management company was valued each year. When a management company member left, the remaining members would buy their interest with debt that was paid off when the management company received distributions. My debt took ten plus years to pay off. When Peter Barris retired from his management, he received three-plus times what a founder received.

The buy-out-of-debt approach failed. The debt grew so large that none of the remaining partners wanted to assume the liability. Scott got an outside investor to buy out the debt. Now when management committee members leave, they are given the declining interest in future funds as I did for Frank.

Things often happen for the best if you have a plan B, which, of course, I did. My oldest son, Ashton, founded his own venture firm, Greenspring Associates, in 2000. It had become an unbelievable success. Its story will be told in the last chapter of this book. Ashton asked me to join the firm as chairman of the board. He felt Greenspring and its young partners would benefit from what I had learned at NEA, He knew my connections could help and that I could help the firm find and make investments in good new healthcare deals. My youngest son, Adair, had joined Greenspring after a five-year stint at Jim Blair's Domain Associates, and today, we all work together. I resigned as chairman of Greenspring when Adair joined the firm in 2019. There were too many Newhalls on the roster.

Today, I don't have to make any tough decisions at Greenspring, but when my counsel is sought, I get to share my opinion and dig into the topics I have loved my whole life. It is truly the best of all possible worlds, which I would have never known had I stayed at NEA. Leaving also gave me the time to pursue my writing. For me, from childhood, writing was a necessity. It does not matter whether I was a good writer or a mediocre writer. But being able to put my soul on paper in the hopes that it will help others learn and live better and happier is what I wanted. Writing is one of the greatest loves of my life. *Je ne regrette rien.*

Six years after my departure from NEA, like my father and grandfather before me, I was diagnosed with Parkinson's disease, caused by genetics, a stressful life, and Agent Orange in Vietnam. Thank God I had six years to travel and write before it really started to affect me.

I have feared Parkinson's all my life. My grandfather died of it; so did my father. My father was diagnosed six months after he retired. It took him fifteen to twenty years to die, and I say that because they were years of dying, not living. I watched him deteriorate from a robust and lively man to a vegetable. Doctors in Florida moved around a lot, and he seemed to have a new doctor every six months. He would get pneumonia, and against his living will and our objections, the new doctors would douse him with antibiotics. My mother tried to take care of him at home, but it was killing her. When his nurse failed to show up for the night shift, he would lose control of his bowels and my mother would have to take off his clothes, drag him to the shower, and clean him up. She became very frail and very depressed. My father had put a loaded revolver beside his bed. When I found out, I confiscated it. Afterward, I forced him to go to a full-time care facility, against his will. He cried when the nurses took him out of his house on a stretcher.

My first wife's father was diagnosed with Parkinson's two years after Marsi, his daughter, committed suicide. He was a doctor, but he was friends with the local doctors treating him. When he got pneumonia, the doctors did not douse him with antibiotics, and he died peacefully a few weeks later. He did not want to be and was not a burden on his family.

My father was not so lucky, and it is not what he wanted to happen. For the last three years of his life, he laid on a bed with his arms and legs pulled under him. He could not see. He never closed his eyes. He would stare at the ceiling. He lost his mind about a year after we put him in the assisted care facility. Before that, he would wake up screaming from his nightmares. Taking care of him was devastating for all of us.

Last night, I had a dream. I was back at the University of Pennsylvania, having conducted a forty-eight-hour ambush patrol at the ROTC Army base at Indiantown Gap. I was exhausted and went into my officer's quarters for a quick lie-down while my men prepared for inspection. Captain Rose, my ROTC instructor, whom I respected greatly, burst into my room, shutting the door behind him. In a quiet voice, so that my men could not overhear, he said, "This is a disgrace! It is not leadership. You lead from the front. You sleep after they are asleep. You eat after they eat. You get up before them. You lead by example! You take greater risks than they do!"

My dream fast-forwarded, and I was standing beside Captain Rose's deathbed. He was a bitter, disillusioned old man. He said, "The Army is bullshit. Everything I taught you was wrong. Take care of yourself first. Forget the others. Many of the officers I know feel the same way because we were tricked into fighting in Vietnam, a war that had no purpose and accomplished nothing. There are a few legacy officers that disagree, the ones related to General Pershing or George Washington or some other General. I call them the legacy officers. But the rest of us just don't care. Live for yourself and take care of yourself."

Captain Rose disappeared into the fog in the mist, and in the next scene of my dream, I found myself standing in a Scottish moor, cold and wet. I thought to myself: "Captain Rose is wrong. The Vietnam War had a purpose. I am a legacy officer. I do care, although no member of my family went to West Point, we have all fought and died for duty, honor, country for 400 years. I will do the same."

In Vietnam, I always walked third in line. When we spotted an enemy, the point man went left and the machine gunner went right, opening fire. I faced the enemy alone, directing the squads behind me to maneuver and attack the enemy from both sides. But everyone in my platoon is now dead. I must charge the enemy alone. I have taught my sons how to live with honor. Now I must teach them how to die with courage as a warrior, as my ancestors have died before me.

I do not mean to imply that by looking at the sunset you should end life in a passive manner--quite the contrary. When I was in Vietnam, my favorite battalion commander, Lt. Col. Raymond Smith, would start his address to the troops by saying, "When the going gets tough, the tough gets going." When you get tired and disheartened, you need to get reminded of this.

During Covid, the deterioration of my health started to accelerate. Gracie the pug, my little girl, and a much-loved member of our family, set an example for me of how to live when you approach death. Grace, very much a lady, in her old age was very tiny and frail, but very tough. She was a lady as tough as my grandmother who raised me, who shot a hat off of a burglar's head when he was breaking into her house, or my great-grandmother, who shot and killed a Lakota Sioux warrior who attacked her family during a raid on the fort where she lived with her husband, Capt. Abbott and her children.

In her old age, Grace was blind and deaf, her body was failing, and her leg dragged behind her. She never whined or in any way indicated that she was not happy to be alive. Each morning she eagerly jumped off out bed, four times her body height, to land on a hard floor. She followed us around everywhere we went, moving as quickly as she could, somehow finding us in remote rooms far away from where she was sleeping. When we were sad, she was with us, sitting in our laps, looking up to us with loving eyes that could no longer see. When we came home, somehow she knew and met us at the door. In the last two years of her life, during the Covid-19 pandemic, she was with me 24 hours a day. She slept beside me or on the pillow next to me at night. During the day, while I was writing, she lay next to me on a pillow. Every hour or two, she would come over to me and paw my leg. I would pick her up, kiss her head three times saying "I love you," scratch behind her ears three times, and rub her tummy three times. I would put her down and she would go back to her pillow and fall asleep until the next time she would scratch my leg. Four times a day, Amy had to scrape what looked like sludge from her eyes with a Kleenex and apply eye ointment. She dreaded it, but she never complained or barked, and always kissed Amy when the treatment was finished. She enjoyed her food and treats even on the day she died.

Whenever someone entered the house, Gracie guarded it. If she knew the people, she would go over and greet them. If she did not know them, she would bark once or twice and go over and smell them, circling them two times. When she ascertained that they presented no threat, she would go back to her bed, lie down and fall asleep. She guarded our house even on the last day of her life.

Yes, my little girl was tough, and I, in my declining years, must be tough as well. As Dylan Thomas said in a poem to his father, "Rage, rage against the dying of the light."

Now I have both prostate cancer and Parkinson's disease. I find myself in the same place as Gracie. My sight is going, my body is deteriorating, and my memory is fading. It is so tempting to give up and just fade away. But I must not, for like Gracie, I have many lessons to teach and things to do.

My father always had a pill box in his bathroom that contained his medicines. I hated that pillbox because he was shackled to it and would never be free for the rest of his life. Now I have a similar pill box and I am shackled to it.

Most of all, I must never show anger. I cannot be angry at myself for not being able to do the things I did before Parkinson's. I must not be angry with my caregivers for not moving fast enough to do something I have asked them to do. I am lucky to have caregivers who love me and it is more difficult to be a Parkinson's caregiver than it is to be a Parkinson's patient. I must also be content and accept that each day I will inch closer to death.

I must spend each day doing exercises which I have been taught by my Parkinson's physical therapist, Adrian Ataiza. It hurts to do it; I would rather sit down and drift off to sleep. You must relearn every physical activity: how to get out of a car, how to hold your fork, how to eat (elbow on the table, not off), and how to walk. You must practice until they enter your muscle memory, and you never do the "little things" like you did before you had Parkinson's. If you do these things properly, you can slow the onset of the disease. I must monitor my nutrition (that means eating) and control my drinking, which I never have done well. When sitting down on the floor, sometimes the only way I can get to a place I can stand up is to crawl. Falls are a constant danger. Lifting heavy things is impossible. One of the most disturbing things is the loss of independence. I can no longer drive myself, and others must do the things I used to handle on my own. I refuse as much assistance as possible. If you cannot take the dog out at night because you stumble in the dark, take her out in the day. Everyday my blood pressure is all over the place. On the high side is 176/97; on the low it is 98/69. It is supposed to be 120/80. So I monitor it daily and take medicine to control it.

I must continually work to improve my memory and decision-making. I hate math and could never do memory exercises like sudoku, but now I plan my own memory games: "history, art, and literature sudoku," "list your favorite British and American romantic novelists," "who were ten American impressionists and how did their painting styles differ," "Is what happened in Dubrovnik, in the Croatian war of the late '90s, happening today in the US? In Dubrovnik, people who had gotten along for 2000 years suddenly tried to kill each other. Argue both sides." I must constantly play this form of cultural game whenever I am awake. Every day I force myself to learn new things, but most of the time I cannot remember happened yesterday. I leave pads of paper everywhere so I can write down things I need to remember and use my iPhone as an aide-memoire.

I must be as tough as Gracie, I must fight, fight, fight each day to ensure I can see as many sunsets as I can before "Taps" is played and the lights are turned off.

Gracie died June 28th, 2021, at 6.30 in the afternoon. She lived two and a half years longer than when we were first told to put her down. Together we watched a lot of sunsets.

I am almost finished with this book. Only our boys are left to speak. You, reader, are probably asking yourself why this guy who is writing a business book is talking about his dog and about fighting

Parkinson's disease. The reason is this: they teach the most important lesson a venture capitalist must learn . . . "Never Say Die!"

As a venture capitalist, I invested in scores of companies. At any point in time, I might have had ten companies facing a life-or-death crisis. At some point in the crisis, I reached a place where I wanted to lie down, cover my face, and give up. This is when I would punch myself hard and say: "Nil desperandum" ("never say die" in Latin.) The technique worked, and I would always hop up and start fighting.

One of my three founding partners, Dick Kramlich, was nicknamed "Never Say Die!" He was over 80 when he retired from NEA. He should have gone on a long, beautiful cruise with his wife to a tropical island. But what does he do? He starts another venture-capital partnership with two young pups that might be able to keep up with him. A good venture partnership will return three times invested capital. Dick's new partnership has the potential to return fifteen times invested capital, yes, 15x. What can I say . . . "Never say Die!", another of venture capital's truths.

XX.

THE APPLE DOES NOT FALL
FAR FROM THE TREE

Ashton Newhall

FROM A VERY EARLY AGE, I have encountered adversity in nearly every facet of life. As a young child, I tragically lost my mother, and my father struggled with post-traumatic stress disorder (PTSD) resulting from combat in Vietnam and his wife's suicide. At 6 years old, I received a diagnosis of dyslexia and ADHD and PTSD. I spent my late childhood and teen years learning how to not just cope with these disabilities but harness their benefits. I learned that I could multitask better than most and my success would be predicated on my work ethic. Used properly, adversity helps you succeed.

In the late 1990s, working for T. Rowe Price, I attempted to launch an internal venture capital business similar to the firm I would later found, Greenspring Associates. Ultimately, this initiative was not seen as a priority by the firm. Due to my high degree of conviction in the concept, I left my job at age 25 to start with Rupert Montagu, the son of my father's former partner, Greenspring Associates, then called Montagu Newhall Associates, out of a one-bedroom apartment. It took a year and a half to raise our first fund and many more to prove our investment model. Today, we manage over $17 billion and employ over one hundred and forty people.

Starting at T. Rowe Price

In the summer of 1996, before my junior year in college, I began an internship at T. Rowe Price in their marketing department. The program enabled me to shadow and participate in informational interviews with people in the various divisions of the company, to see what might interest me. One of these interviews was with Chris Newman, who later became a friend of mine and worked in T. Rowe Price's institutional sales group. Chris informed me it was unlikely anyone my age would be recruited into the institutional sales group; their minimum investments were $50 million and historically, no one had ever been hired out of college. As is the case with so many who have faced adversity, challenges such as these intensified my determination. I therefore asked Chris if he knew the fellow who headed the team and asked for an introduction. I soon met him. He was tall and had long blond hair, and his name was Todd Ruppert. (A few years ago, Todd retired from T. Rowe Price and is currently a venture partner at Greenspring Associates.)

Todd probably thought I was a bit brash when we first met. I remember saying, "You don't know me yet, but I know you are going to hire me." I am sure he thought that was a little bold at the time, but in the end, I think he appreciated my confidence. After the internship, I was invited back to work more closely with the institutional sales group and many of Todd's subordinates. After completing the program, I finished my senior year at Elon, and before I graduated, Todd hired me for the salary of $27,500 per year.

During the summer of 1998, I moved into a small one-bedroom apartment in Federal Hill, Baltimore, and began work with T. Rowe Price as a full-time institutional sales associate. During those first few months, I remained in close contact with Todd as he took me under his wing and became a mentor. Back in 1985, Todd was hired by T. Rowe Price to help lead their institutional sales group, so he was managing money for banks and insurance companies, as well as launching new product lines.

Stepping Back to Our Origin

In the 1980s, there was a growing demand among T. Rowe Price's US retail and institutional clients for access to overseas markets. Most agreed, however, that servicing those markets was not a core competency at T. Rowe Price of Baltimore. Therefore, the firm formed a joint venture with a London-based investment firm, Robert Fleming & Co. Robert Fleming was a pure money manager, just as T. Rowe Price was in the US. This joint venture was called Rowe Price Fleming Asset Management, and each party owned 50 percent of the new firm. It was set up so that T. Rowe Price could not do business outside the US, and Robert Fleming was not allowed to do business in the States. The new venture would manage the foreign holdings of the firm's institutional clients. So, in 1980, when T. Rowe Price launched their first international tech fund, it was managed by Rowe Price Fleming.

Todd became the head of institutional investing in 1993, and at this time, he supervised all T. Rowe Price's US business. A few years later, in 1998, Todd hired me. This was near the point at which Todd began to sense that Rowe Price Fleming, like many joint ventures, might become unstable. For that reason, Todd began traveling around Europe, using his vacation time and his own funds, trying to build a network of investment professionals. Around 1996, he encountered a private equity placement agency, Helix, in the business of placing European capital in American private equity funds. To expand T. Rowe Price's connections to European-based institutions, Todd bought a 10 percent stake in Helix on behalf of the firm.

Soon after, it became apparent how spotty the fee income stream is in private equity placement. You might earn a substantial fee when you raised a new fund, but that was the end of it until you raised another, several years later. In 1997, Todd decided to start an advisory firm at Helix called Altius Associates, which would serve as a discretionary manager of private equity portfolios and would smooth out Helix's lumpy revenue stream. The next year, Helix hired Marcus Simpson, who had managed private investments for the Virginia Retirement System, to open a US office for Altius. In his role at the pension plan, Marcus made substantial investments in NEA and became a good friend of my father. At Altius, Marcus hired Rupert Montagu, my future co-founder at Greenspring.

Shortly after setting up the US office of Altius, Todd invited me up to New York to meet Rupert, who, at the time, was a director of marketing. As fate would have it, Rupert's family and mine were good friends, going back to the 1970s, when far fewer people worked in the industry. It seemed funny that I did not know Rupert personally, since he had recently begun working in private equity. Rupert's father, Anthony Montagu, was the co-founder of Abingworth, the prominent London-based venture firm, which had a joint venture with NEA for fifteen-plus years, which is how he knew my father. Though I knew Rupert's father and mother pretty well, and I had met his brother and sister, I had never met Rupert. At that point, Rupert had been working at Altius for a few years. Before that, he was selling alcoholic beverages in Europe for Brown Forman. We were both relatively inexperienced in the venture capital industry, each of us with only a couple of years of experience under our belts.

Altius was an early success, having won mandates to manage the private equity portfolios of the State of Maryland, the California State Teachers' Retirement System (or, CalSTRS), and a handful of others. Given the early traction, T. Rowe Price was benefitting from having an equity interest in the earnings of Altius, which led Todd to consider doing something similar to Altius, but directly under T. Rowe Price. However, the majority of Altius's business was dedicated to large private equity buyout funds. Given my connections in the venture industry, the idea of creating a venture-focused fund-of-funds at T. Rowe Price stemmed from discussions between myself and Todd on the heels of the Altius experience. This was when Todd and I started to think through how such an initiative might work.

Up until this point, I had always thought that I would not work in venture capital because that was what my family had done for the two prior generations. I felt a need to forge my own trail, and by working in the institutional sales group at T. Rowe Price, I had chosen that alternative path. Despite my initial resolution, Todd put me on the venture project, and over the succeeding months, as Todd sent me out on more venture-related missions, I realized that I enjoyed this work much more than the traditional job for which he had hired me. Working in venture capital was fun for me and like nothing I had ever done before. Instead of asking people for their capital, I was pitching to oversubscribed venture funds about why they should take our money, and I was able to help T. Rowe Price gain coveted access to oversubscribed venture funds like Jim Swartz's Accel Partners. As time went on, it became apparent that I could be quite useful in this role at T. Rowe Price. That's not to say, however, that all was going according to plan.

Over the coming months, Todd and I further refined the product strategy. We had everything we needed, and we were on the verge of launching, when, in August 2000, T. Rowe Price made the largest acquisition in the firm's history.

The End of T. Rowe Price's Venture Initiative

In early 2000, Robert Fleming was acquired by Chase Manhattan Bank for $7 billion. After some deliberation, it was decided T. Rowe Price would purchase the 50 percent stake they didn't already own in Rowe Price Fleming, the original joint venture set up between the two organizations to provide international products to either's clients. On August 8, 2000, T. Rowe Price acquired that stake for $750 million, and for the first time in twenty years, the firm was allowed to conduct business internationally. Todd, who had spent years building relations abroad, was best suited to take on the role. He was promoted to president and CEO of what became T. Rowe Price Global Investment Services. Such titanic developments within the firm drew attention and resources away from our venture initiative.

In considering whether to keep the project afloat, the firm found itself reflecting on whether such an initiative fit T. Rowe Price, philosophically. At the time, the firm specialized in fee-for-service mutual funds, so very few managers received carried interest as part of their compensation. This kind of incentive structure and the active involvement in management as a member of the board of directors, which venture firms must do, was perceived to be outside the firm's core competency. Their mutual funds were doing well, and the consensus was not to compromise the goose that was laying the golden egg. At the same time, there was pressure to raise hedge funds, which were generating fortunes for those who knew what they were doing in those heady markets. A multibillion-dollar hedge fund seemed like a much more attractive place to which to allocate resources than a two-hundred-fifty-million-dollar venture fund. Overall, given T. Rowe's historic acquisition, and the minimal support we were receiving from the board, we knew the project's days were probably numbered.

One day, Todd called me into his office and read an email from a senior executive to whom Todd regularly reported. The email said something like, "I hope you are not continuing your work on the venture initiative, Todd, because we do not have board support for the fund-of-funds. I think you need to shut it down." The project was shut down, just like that.

Here we were, we had in place almost all elements necessary to roll out the new product, and yet, just like when my father founded NEA, the project was unlikely to resurface within T. Rowe. We had written our private placement memorandum (i.e., our business plan). We had lined up our service providers, including our law and tax firms. Our leads were Dick Testa of Testa, Hurwitz & Thibeault and Tom Holly of PricewaterhouseCoopers, who had also worked with my father when he was a general partner at NEA. I can remember when I was younger hearing my father's long phone calls with Dick on the weekends. There was continuity, a kind of lineage here—it almost seemed too serendipitous to quit.

It is also worth noting that, at the time, law firms and other service providers interviewed the fund managers rather than the other way around. In some cases, they were interested in investing more than just their professional time. In others, they were doing the due diligence themselves because if fund managers couldn't raise sufficient capital, they wouldn't get paid. I was a 24-year-old kid, receiving the *Good Housekeeping* seal of approval from Testa, Hurwitz & Thibeault and PWC, which was helpful throughout the fundraising. Having lined up these ancillary services, I was in a much better position to start my own firm.

Beginning of a New Chapter: Skiing in Verbier, Switzerland

After the project came to a halt, and after a few weeks had passed, I was in Geneva, Switzerland at the same time Rupert was there. We were both attending a European Venture Capital Association (EVCA) meeting. At that time, I was still covering T. Rowe Price's private equity interests, so I was still going to the annual meetings and conferences of the venture firms in which T. Rowe had an interest. After the EVCA meeting ended, Rupert and I took advantage of a long weekend and went skiing at Verbier.

One day, Rupert and I were on a ski lift going up the mountain, and he said, "You know, I've always wanted to start my own firm."

"I haven't necessarily always wanted to start my own firm," I replied, "but I really feel like we could do what we were going to do by ourselves, on our own."

By the time we had gotten off the ski lift, Rupert and I said, "Screw it! We'll go do it ourselves."

When I returned to the States, I remember the feeling of walking into Todd's office to tell him I was leaving. I was scared as hell because he had bet on this young graduate from Elon University. I was the youngest in the institutional sales group by twenty years, so I felt indebted to him. Nevertheless, I told him I wanted to leave the firm and work in venture on my own. To my surprise, he was supportive. He became one of the first investors in our fund.

I would later find out that Todd had asked George Roche, T. Rowe Price's CEO to sponsor a $1 million investment in our firm. George was an old friend of my father's, had supported NEA from the start, and was chairman of NEA's board of advisors. It was brought to an internal investment committee, which was not in favor of investing in our fund. From my understanding, George Roche was determined and was able to convince them to invest. George forced the issue through, and they invested. It is funny that in the late 1970s, it was Don Bowman, T. Rowe Price's CEO at the time, along with Cub Harvey who had to push TRP's unwilling board to invest in NEA (it is interesting to note that after retiring from T. Rowe, Cub Harry joined NEA as a partner). Without TRP's support for both our firms, we both probably would have had a more difficult time raising money and getting started.

Getting Started on Our Own

The premise of Greenspring Associates, then Montagu Newhall Associates, was simple: to provide investors with access and allocation to premier venture capital funds and direct investments—what is known as a fund-of-funds. At the time, I was blessed with one distinct advantage in pursuing this idea: close relationships with great venture capital general partners who founded some of the leading firms in the industry. My father, Chuck Newhall, had co-founded New Enterprise Associates, the largest early-stage venture capital firm in the world. My grandfather, Charles Watson Newhall Jr., led investments into private companies like Reaction Motors (the company that built the engine that helped Chuck Yeager break the sound barrier) on behalf of Laurance Rockefeller's family office. But upon founding Greenspring, I faced a massive challenge. Investors were unwilling to take a chance on a 25-year-old without proof that our firm could gain access to historically outperforming funds. As a result, as I will describe in detail later, I became the first investor in our fund, putting at risk a sizeable amount of personal and family capital. Rupert and I committed to four funds and paid capital calls personally for several months. My father guaranteed $18.5 million of these commitments to funds but refused to take any equity in Greenspring for the guarantees. As we raised money from new LPs the guarantees were released. Sixty percent of the money in our first fund came from venture capitalists who had founded their own firms. After some time, we were able to partner with a large family office and hold a first closing. We were introduced to this investor by Howie Wolfe, who at the time was a special partner of NEA and a friend of my parents. Having proven we had access to the best funds, additional investors committed.

Unlikelihood of Success

Indeed, many in the industry looked at us askance for being so young and especially for being so inexperienced. There were other reasons that we seemed to be such a long shot. For one thing, the tech bubble had just burst in March 2000, and technology companies were thought to be passé or worse. In general, venture capital was deemed one of the worst asset classes. It was an environment similar to 1977, when NEA was formed. In this environment, it didn't seem to make much sense for us to be raising a tech-specific, venture-focused fund of funds that would also charge an extra layer of fees to its limited partners. Not to mention, Rupert and I had limited investment experience and little to none with direct investing. That said, Rupert seemed to have a great personal portfolio, with an internal rate of return of over 100 percent, but it was all illiquid. It nearly went to zero in the years following the bubble's collapse. His early, noteworthy deals include Siroyan, the semiconductor company, and EyeStorm. It was enough to get us started, and along with my connections to some top-tier funds, we believed we had a chance.

Our story of youthful gumption has many of the same elements as those of other entrepreneurs. After Rupert left his job, he would come down to Baltimore and sleep on a blow-up mattress. My apartment had a television bigger than my couch—some old TV from the nineties that my parents had discarded, but I was happy to have it. I had also won a computer while I was working at T. Rowe Price. I was browsing the internet at the office and saw a banner ad that said, "Click here and win a free Compaq computer!" I thought to myself, "There is no way this is real." I clicked the banner ad anyway, entered my address, and the next thing you know, they sent me a free Compaq computer. It was little more than a motherboard, a screen, and a keyboard, but on that computer, Rupert and I wrote and processed all the initial work for what became Montagu Newhall Associates.

The Struggles of Raising Our First Fund

In the beginning, Rupert and I thought we would probably have access to a handful of top-quartile funds. We also knew these funds would be attractive to many high-net-worth individuals. Naturally, we did what we could to arrange meetings and introductions with wealthy prospects. After meeting with several prospective investors over several months, we seemed to have run into a roadblock. The investors were willing to give us their capital, but only under the condition that they were placed in top funds. On the other hand, Rupert and I needed to have possession of the money to commit to these funds. It was a Catch-22. Once this had sunk in, we felt that we had neglected something fundamental in our business plan.

At this point, we had gone several months without jobs or salaries or any luck in our new enterprise. This was one of our low points, where we might have given up. However, it was clear the only real solution was to make the capital commitments to these funds first. Then, once we had secured allocation, we had to go raise money to replace our commitments with limited partners. As described earlier, that was when my father provided the guarantees, even though he was initially skeptical that Rupert and I could pull this off. My father and our family still invested several million dollars in the first Greenspring partnership.

Those initial commitments were to Atlas Ventures, Oak Investment Partners, New Enterprise Associates, North Bridge Venture Partners, and Domain Associates. If it wasn't for Chuck Newhall, my father, and his endorsement of our strategy, I believe we would have never gotten off the ground.

It was scary to take on such liability. If we did not raise enough money to get the fund off the ground, we not only would have to put our project to rest but be on the hook for a substantial amount of funds. Luckily, based on those $18.5 million commitments, we were able to prove we could gain access to top-tier funds, and soon thereafter, we brought a family office that made venture capital investments on board.

That family office was Hank McCamish's, who was also a limited partner in my godfather's, Howie Wolfe's, fund. (Howie had been a special partner at NEA until he started his firm, where he continued to invest along with NEA.) Hank described himself as an "old peddler in the insurance industry in Atlanta" who figured out some big loophole for big corporations like Coca-Cola and made a killing. He had started a family office and was an active investor in venture capital deals. Hank, along with his lead investment officer, Roy Jones, said that given our family's $18.5 million underwriting of the commitments to our first funds, they would put up $15 million on the condition that they received a third of the fund's carry.

We hesitated for a moment at Hank's proposition. We had targeted a $25 million fund size, so giving up a third of the carry would leave us with little margin. However, Hank said he intended to do co-investments with us and that he would be able to arrange introductions with other prospective investors throughout the Atlanta area. As a result, we felt we had little choice, and Rupert and I closed the deal with Hank while in my parents' basement. (Back in the 1970s, NEA had done the same thing with its lead investors, Landmark [Howie's firm at the time] and T. Rowe Price.)

Shortly after, we were able to raise an additional $16 million, and we held our first close in April 2001 for a total of $31 million. Over a long ten months afterward, we were able to grind out an additional $21 million, and in February 2002, we held a final close for a total fund size of $52 million. This was quite a coup. Our first fund had brought us to approximately $520,000 in annual fee revenue, and Montagu Newhall Associates was officially in business. My father introduced us to three healthcare investments—Myogen, Bravo, and Pharmion—which produced good returns in a short period. Today, we still work closely with several NEA partners and continue to make mutually profitable investments together.

It was also worth noting that we had a meaningful number of investors from venture capital firms who invested personally. This has been a staple tenet or fundamental doctrine for our organization ever since: incentivize venture capital managers in whose funds we invest to invest in our own funds. This way, we have quality limited partners who share our opinions and whose financial interests are aligned with our own.

Finding a Next Level Partner: Jim Lim Comes Aboard

Having achieved reasonable success in raising Fund I, we began thinking about Fund II. We agreed that we needed to find a dynamic new partner who could help propel us to the next level. We were working hard to develop relationships with folks we thought could be the next generation of leaders in the venture capital fund investing business, which at that point was 80 percent of our strategy. A potential early-round draft choice was Jim Lim, who was the director of venture capital at Commonfund. Kevin Campbell, Rupert, and I had known Jim from our time spent actively networking at events and annual meetings, and all four of us were solely focused on the venture capital industry. Kevin was one of Greenspring's first employees, and he deserves the credit for the introduction.

I first met Jim in 2001 at the Venrock annual meeting in New York City at the Rainbow Room. I vividly remember running into him in the bathroom. He was standing with his hand on his head at the giant marble urinal that was bigger than my six-foot-four-inch frame. Jim said, "Do you ever notice when you come to New York City, you see friends you wish you'd never see again because they keep you out way too late?" I laughed, thinking, *I don't know who this guy is, but I like him already!* That marked the beginning of what would soon become a beautiful, long-term friendship. Still, it took many years to recruit him.

As Jim said, he "wanted to wait until the startup risk was removed."

A few years later, in early 2004, I invited Jim to the Waldorf Hotel in New York City for an interview. He commuted into the city from Connecticut, where he lived at the time, and where he worked for Commonfund. We had just begun fundraising for our second fund, and I had an American Express card, on which all our expenses were charged, including printing paper. Finally, I had reached a crucial minimum threshold for an American Express black card. My father had a similar card when he started NEA because it came with seemingly endless perks and discounts at hotels, restaurants, and special events. It felt like I had won a lottery. I could now stay at hotels with this card, and get upgraded at discount prices.

I was in New York, checking into the Waldorf, and the concierge said, "Sir, we are upgrading you to the penthouse suite." I felt like I had died and gone to heaven. To get there, I was escorted around back to a separate elevator by a butler. Once I had entered the suite, which was practically the entire top floor, I saw a fireplace, multitudes of couches, and a dining room table that seemed to stretch for miles.

I invited Jim up to begin the interview process, which in hindsight was probably the worst decision I could have made. I looked like a self-important 25-year-old dilettante entrepreneur extravagantly spending his client's money. As excited as I was to have it, I would have been better off without my Amex Black card that day. Ironically, the first time I was able to use its benefits was also the worst time. I was the son of a well-known venture capitalist trying to recruit the son of a Korean dry cleaner who would not be impressed by a show-off. I cannot emphasize enough how tone-deaf and embarrassed I was, which makes it even more astounding that Jim made the bet that he did.

At that stage in our business, there were two things we had to be able to do: fundraise and access top venture funds. As a start to our interview, I first asked Jim if he could introduce us to Sequoia Capital or Kleiner Perkins Caufield & Byers, as well as the other Tier 1 firms. He said no. I began to go down the list of second-tier firms. He rejected each one.

Then, I wondered, "What about fundraising?"

"Nope." Jim had a non-compete and non-solicitation agreement, so he could not help fundraise until his non-compete expired. On top of that, just like me, he had no direct investment experience.

Despite all these shortcomings and potential barriers to our successful partnership, we thought that our relationship would come to fruition over the long term and that given our backgrounds, we could put together a strong portfolio. Above all else, we observed that we had the kind of tenacity and friendship necessary to spend hours together, travel together, raise money together, and invest together. We also had shared values and goals.

Although neither of us had much to offer, we somehow saw past each other's inexperience and other flaws and understood intuitively that our strengths as a team would outweigh our shortcomings as individuals. If anyone were ever to question the sincerity of our commitment to such ideals as loyalty, trust, and teamwork, they wouldn't have to look much further than this story. It's funny: despite his overall success, the first fund that Jim was able to get us into turned out to be the worst-performing fund investment we ever had.

Fast forward to late 2004. Although the ultimate success for Fund I was still far from assured, we had gotten it off the ground and had a strong pipeline of investors for Fund II. This made Jim feel reasonably confident in our ability to raise a second fund. In October 2004, after our first closing in Fund II, Jim joined as a managing general partner.

My father's friend Ben Schapiro, who managed Questmark, a venture partnership that invested in late-stage deals, provided us with introductions to several investors that became limited partners in Fund II.

Jim left a lot behind when he left Commonfund. Unlike most other funds, Commonfund compensated their managers with carried interest not only from the funds they were specifically managing but also from all products across their firm. Even though he was in venture capital, Jim would collect carry from the buyout funds. In doing this, Commonfund was trying to nurture a culture of collaboration and integration across its various products. Consequently, when Jim resigned from Commonfund, he was leaving behind not just the compensation he was earning as a manager, but also a large sum of firm-wide profits for many years to come. Without getting into details, his overall comp at the time he was leaving was nearly equivalent to our firm's total revenue. When I think back to the decision he made, it is staggering what he walked away from. He acted on the courage of his convictions and proved so through his actions. It was fortunate that

Jim joined Greenspring because a few years later, Rupert Montagu left the firm to pursue other interests. We parted ways but stayed on good terms with each other. Rupert has remained a friend of Greenspring and a loyal supporter to this day.

ExactTarget—Jim's Deal

Jim's contacts have helped Greenspring in our fundraising but also with investment performance. Here is Jim's account of the ExactTarget investment, which will be followed by my account of the Cologix investment. These two stories illustrate Greenspring's investment practices.

"Before joining Greenspring in 2004, I was the director of venture capital at Commonfund Capital, an asset management firm based in Wilton, Connecticut. While there, I had gotten to know Scott Maxwell quite well, who, at the time, was a managing director at Insight Venture Partners. So in 2005, when Scott decided to leave Insight to start OpenView Venture Partners, we were very enthusiastic about being one of his anchor investors. As with the majority of our fund investments at Greenspring, we wanted to not only partner with OpenView at the fund level but also to invest directly alongside their firm. As it turned out, we were helpful to Scott's fundraising process, and when it was all said and done, Greenspring put together a group of investors that represented over half of OpenView's first fund.

"Soon thereafter, owing to our stable, trusting relationship, I got a call from Scott, who said, 'I think I have the perfect opportunity for you: great management team, and solid business, low downside, and it could be a three-times multiple.' If you know Scott, you will know he is more right than wrong. Luckily, he got the upside wrong on this one.

"Scott had first invested in ExactTarget, an on-demand email marketing suite, back in 2003; and after a period of strong growth, the team returned to the market to raise another round. There was a lot to like about the business. First and foremost, Scott Maxwell, who had been a trusted partner of ours for over three years, was very bullish on the company and on the management team's ability to execute. The company had never really missed plan, had grown about 20 percent quarter-over-quarter, and was highly capital efficient. So in 2006, Greenspring participated in the company's Series D round.

I joined as a board observer.

"ExactTarget's management team, especially Scott Dorsey, Scott McCorkle, and Tracey Dolan, was impeccable in the execution of its business plan, a trend that continued throughout our investment period. So unlike most companies, they did not need much assistance. Instead, Greenspring was influential in financing its growth when it would have been easy for the company to sell during the financial crisis.

"In 2008, a little over a year after our initial investment, ExactTarget was considering an IPO. However, given all the signs of a present and future financial crisis, they elected to stay private and raise additional private capital. At this point, we made a pivotal, risky decision that propelled our firm forward.

"Since late 2006, when we first invested in the company, management was consistent and unfailing in their execution, their growth had accelerated to an eye-popping 30 percent quarter-over-quarter, and they had adhered to their plan. On the downside, the email marketing technology sector was very competitive, with well-funded companies such as Responsys, ConstantContact, Silverpop, and Cheetahmail. Despite these factors, we had to ask ourselves, 'If we are going to live and die by one company, which one would it be?' Ashton and I both agreed that the one company would be ExactTarget. As a result, we pulled from numerous funds and placed substantial capital into the company's subsequent round, bringing our total position in the company to $53 million.

"After we had crossed the chasm of the financial crisis, ExactTarget had weathered the storm, and in March of 2012, the company completed a successful IPO, listing on the Nasdaq at nineteen dollars per share. Two years later, the business was acquired by Salesforce.com for $2 billion. To this day, the company remains Greenspring's most successful investment. However, if we had not invested over our pro-rata allocation, especially at a time when there was substantial risk, the company would have never been as impactful to our platform. In a similar light, without our platform business, and as a result of our relationship with OpenView, we would have never had the opportunity to invest. When you find exceptional business and, in this case, a once-in-a-generation management team, it is critical to have courage in your convictions."

Cologix—Ashton's Deal

To appreciate the origin of Greenspring's investment in Cologix, which resulted in one of the firm's most impactful investments, you must first understand our relationship with Columbia Capital. In 2008, I and other members of our team began spending significant time raising capital in Australia, despite many asset managers having written off the geography from their target lists. I originally started making trips to Australia after T. Rowe Price Associates entered the market and Marcus Simpson from the Queensland Investment Corporation. who I knew from Altius, had begun his tenure at Australia's sovereign wealth fund. T. Rowe Price Associates had also set up an advisory board there, of which one of the members was Lachlan Douglas, who worked at Principle Advisory Services and was the son of the original crocodile hunter, Malcolm Douglas.

The connection to Marcus, Paul, and Lachlan led to numerous trips to New Zealand and Australia at a time when most managers neglected the fundraising opportunity in the region. Soon after, the sovereign wealth fund became our largest investor, quite the feat at a time when upper-quartile venture performances were a mere 8 percent over the prior ten years. This partnership propelled our firm into a new era of custom, separate accounts. These personalized mandates employed custom-tailored strategies that sought to build a highly concentrated portfolio of top-quartile managers. To receive such sizable allocations to well-performing funds is a challenge, requiring strong relationships and oftentimes the ability to identify managers who are overlooked or undervalued. One of those managers at the time was Columbia Capital, a growth equity firm based in Alexandria, Virginia, focused on spectrum-related assets, telecommunication, and infrastructure investments.

Founded in the late 1990s, Columbia Capital was an investment bank running spectrum auctions; in the early 2000s, it expanded to the venture business. We were considering it as a potential manager for the custom mandate. Columbia was reformulating its team and strategy at a time when the market thought its performance was developing. We thought there was a solid opportunity. We believed in a couple of its fundamental attributes: the team was made up of very trustworthy, loyal people and transitioning to a new generation that we thought had extreme potential. In addition, the types of deals they were putting together, which they called "Columbia Deals," fit our direct investment criteria. They were proprietary-sourcing opportunities that had risk-return characteristics that we would do directly, with people who were highly referenceable, and both geographically and culturally aligned. As a result, we made a substantial commitment in 2008 to Columbia Capital V for $120 million.

In the context of their direct opportunities, one of the earlier deals they brought to us was Cologix, which was led by Grant van Rooyen, the CEO. Previously, Grant was working at Level 3 Communications, where he focused on data center colocation and interconnection services. Consequently, he knew the sector better than anyone. Grant had seen the good, bad, and the ugly, and Columbia Capital had been trying to recruit him for years. In 2009, Columbia Capital approached him to manage a roll-up strategy of data center operators focused on secondary markets across the US, and when the firm brought a strong initial asset to acquire, Grant left to launch the business.

Soon thereafter, I met with Grant, and we immediately hit it off. Grant was born in South Africa and had a strict upbringing in Australia. I had grown up with a military father who had had a similar upbringing. Grant and I spent significant time in Africa and Australia, so we initially bonded over all those similarities. However, as a result of his no-nonsense upbringing, he cut to the point quickly. It was the first meeting I had ever had where the entrepreneur interviewed me, not the other way around.

Grant said, "I understand Columbia likes you, but I do not know you. Why do I want you as a partner?" He was aggressive, and I loved it. That immediately put the meeting on tilt, and we got down to business.

In the end, we were able to sell our way into the deal as a result of Columbia's strong recommendation, our cultural alignment, and that Greenspring had a history in telecom-related assets (e.g., Neutral Tandem, a telecom company I invested in and helped enter new markets). At its core, we represented a trusted relationship that could help Grant and his team by leveraging our network, so in December of 2010, we co-led Cologix's initial round of funding with $3 million. Despite this, it is worth noting that until Grant got to know us better, he still would not let us join his board! In the years after, we continued to invest in follow-on financings, bringing our firm-wide exposure to a total of $30 million.

Cologix's management team was one of the most experienced teams with which I have had the opportunity to work. Suffice to say that they did not need much help, especially with Columbia Capital as a partner; however, we remained an active investor through strategic guidance and helping them hire investment banks, such as DH Capital, to make acquisitions.

From an investor perspective, the company faced a unique set of challenges throughout its life cycle. Fortunately, management was investing substantial capital alongside the syndicate (over $20 million). Weirdly, they were incentivized to keep prices low for follow-on financings. Moreover, there were times when some members of the management team wanted to invest more, but others with less liquidity did not want to face dilution. This resulted in tricky negotiations at times primarily because of the velocity at which we were acquiring assets. The ability to identify quality targets for acquisitions was a continuous challenge. At a time when prices for data-center-related assets were rising, being able to recognize clear synergies and to assess value in an intellectually honest way was essential. Fortunately, our management team proved to be specialists in this area.

The team successfully faced obstacles over the following seven years, acquired and integrated over ten businesses, and generated an 85 percent EBITDA compound annual growth rate; that produced a successful exit in early 2017 (when Stonepeak Infrastructure Partners acquired a majority stake in the business). The outcome returned over $150 million to Greenspring's platform, and we rolled a portion of our equity into the new company.

Upon reflection, if it wasn't for the "salt mine work"—the effort of going to Australia and spending a significant amount of time where others wouldn't—we would have never had the means to foster a meaningful relationship with Columbia Capital and partner with them on Cologix. Columbia deserves tremendous credit for such an outcome. From inception, they were integral in pivoting the company's strategy to focus on data-center consolidation in Tier 2 markets and were vital in setting the strategic vision that later resulted in a successful outcome. Moreover, they are the epitome of what we look for in great partners: management-friendly, team-oriented, and low-ego.

The marriage of great partners and an incredibly adept management team made Cologix into the business it is today.

Innovative Approaches

Although Greenspring's roots can be traced back to venture fund commitments, we also introduced a new concept to the traditional fund-of-funds model: incorporating direct and secondary investments into one "co-mingled fund." This model was met with tremendous skepticism in the beginning. Doesn't each investment type require a distinct skillset? How can limited partners effectively invest directly into companies? These were questions we faced.

I am proud to say we fervently disagreed with the critics. To this day, we believe that our model, a single unified investment team working across funds, directs, and secondaries, affords us synergies that few other firms can claim. Rupert Montagu, who was adamant from the beginning that we include directs in our fund-of-funds, was essential to setting this strategic vision for the future.

Direct-Only Funds as a Limited Partner

In 2007, we raised our first direct-only fund called Greenspring Crossover Ventures, a fund dedicated to investing directly in public and private growth companies. Before opening this fund, we did invest directly in venture-backed companies, but these investments were embedded within our co-mingled fund strategy. In those instances, investors let us do this despite having limited experience because it was part of what they really wanted us to do, as opposed to what they were hiring us to do. By launching the Crossover Fund, we stood on our two feet, proclaiming that we're going to not only be fund investors but direct investors.

Big risks open up the possibility for big losses. We knew that many in the industry had been put in the "penalty box" for adding too many new products or otherwise stretching their resources too thin. Investors would then cut back or abandon their GPs, punishing them with smaller fund sizes. At our scale at the time, that could have meant life or death, so we were taking a big leap of faith. We had safely jumped over early hurdles, but that didn't mean we were not worried. Fortunately, we have been able to generate a compound annual return on our directs of 23 percent since 2000, so our investors are quite happy.

One of the many things that we learned in launching Crossover was that we were not good at investing in public companies. We also learned that there was sufficient excess capacity in the direct deals we were already doing within the routine of our core fund-of-funds. At this point, like the flexible startup we needed to be, we pivoted our strategy and raised Greenspring Opportunities II (GO II). It was the successor to Crossover but would solely invest in private companies alongside our co-mingled fund-of-funds. Today, this has become the second-largest portion of our business.

There is undoubtedly an element of experimentation in our development as innovators in the industry. We did not know where we were going to end up when we launched the Crossover Fund. As far as its size was concerned, it was not going to contribute materially to our fee base. It turned out that without that experiment, we would have never raised GO II, and our direct business would have been relatively trivial compared to what it is today.

Separate Accounts

Some of the conventional wisdom when we began to grow dictated that there was no benefit to adding products to our platform. From an investor perspective, the problem comes down to which "master" a GP serves. If you manage only one product, the LP is the master and the only client. If you add additional products, then those LPs are no longer the single "master." Despite this stigma, we once again put the entire franchise on the line—this time for Australia's sovereign wealth fund. In 2008, around the time of GGP IV, we raised our first separate account, a $500 million fund with a custom mandate to deploy large financial commitments into a concentrated group of top-tier managers. Over the years thereafter, we not only proved we could launch custom strategies and provide reliable performances, but we showed that our new products did not detract from our older ones. We proved that new strategies benefited our entire platform by generating synergies, that it was not a zero-sum game. For example, since the fund strategy required us to place large sums of money into a concentrated number of managers, we were able to work with one of our closest, most successful partners to create their very own growth-stage fund to complement their early-stage strategy.

The benefit was two-fold:

1. Ability to provide substantial exposure to otherwise oversubscribed, proprietary companies and, as a result, generate outsized returns.
2. Enormous level of loyalty and trust in a top manager, which later led to better allocations and more robust direct and secondary opportunities.

Australia's sovereign wealth fund, British Petroleum, and British Air co-invested with Greenspring. Greenspring would invest $15 million for itself in a venture fund but represent a total investment base of $365M from its limited partner co-investors. VCs would appreciate this commitment and would let Greenspring price the last private round where they put up 85 percent of the money and Greenspring 15 percent. This led to excellent investments with half the time to liquidity. This pivotal moment in our business has enabled us to grow substantially by creating custom mandates for large institutional clients, all the while strengthening our platform.

I was a passionate advocate for the separate accounts and direct-only strategies. If I had not had partners who supported me, these initiatives would have never come to fruition, and we would not be where we are today. When I look back on these pivotal moments objectively, there is no reason why my partners should have supported me, but they did. For that, I owe them a tremendous amount of credit and gratitude.

Data as a Weapon & Portfolio Impact

We believe capital is a commodity and that success as a venture capital firm is predicated upon differentiation in terms of both investment model and a manager's ability to add value to its portfolio companies. We seek to differentiate our capital through the trusted relationships that we form, through capitalizing on our data advantage, and through our Portfolio Impact Program. As one of the largest investors in the majority of our managers' funds, we have access to granular information on a subset of promising venture-backed companies. In recent years, we have spent considerable time and resources on determining how best to use this information to make great investments. Our solution is a predictive deal-sourcing tool we call Beacon. The algorithm combines our own proprietary data with public, third-party data. Beacon then can sift through thousands of opportunities and hone in on ones that meet our criteria for success.

I knew that the success of the best venture capitalist had less to do with the money and more to do with the value those investors brought to their companies in the form of strategic guidance, introductions, and human resources. As a result, we sought to differentiate ourselves by applying the "general partner mentality" as a fund investor. To this day, we are the only venture capital fund of funds with a dedicated team exclusively focused on adding value to venture managers and their portfolio companies. Last year alone, this team, called our Portfolio Impact Team, hosted six distinct events that helped foster connections between our managers' portfolio companies and major corporations. Through these events and other ad-hoc efforts, our team made over 610 customer introductions and over 130 strategic introductions. We believe these efforts allow us to be more valuable partners and gain additional access and allocation to promising venture firms. While we offer a number of strategies, including our diversified fund, dedicated direct investment fund, venture secondary fund, micro-VC-oriented fund-of-funds, and growth-equity-oriented fund-of-funds, each serves to fortify the others.

Overall, since co-founding Greenspring, I'd like to think we have brought a fresh perspective to how the innovation economy is financed. I have four key takeaways:

1. Innovation is pervasive, and there are many great businesses outside of Silicon Valley.
2. Capital is a commodity and in and of itself is not a differentiator.
3. Helping management teams does not require a board seat.
4. Ownership should not be the priority objective; rather, being in the best assets with superior management teams is paramount.

While this is what we have focused on, these are past lessons. Just as the industry has changed dramatically since my father started NEA, the industry will continue to evolve, and so will we. Going forward, we hope to further differentiate ourselves through three main areas:

1. Continuing to invest in the power of the platform by adding innovative products and services.
2. Further enhancing the effectiveness and scale of our Portfolio Impact service to help the funds and companies in which we invest.
3. Leveraging our data advantage through advanced artificial intelligence.

I consider myself incredibly lucky to have been helped by my father and his partners at NEA. One of the reasons I was excited to share this story of my business experience is that I hope that in some small way, it enables me to help my children and others in the same way others helped me.

Footnote

This is an email I sent to Ashton and Adair's Godfathers, my partners, Dick Kramlich and Frank Bonsal. I also sent an email to Ted Newlin (an entrepreneur and good family friend), Jim Blair (founder of Domain), and George Roche (former CEO of T. Rowe Price), who are godfathers in spirit.

July 7th, 2021

I wanted to pass on some good news to you. It has been announced publicly that Stepstone Group, a multi-product private equity firm, is acquiring Greenspring Associates for 800 million dollars. The acquisition will strengthen Stepstone's venture capital and growth equity business. Stepstone has $464 biilion assets under management. Greenspring has $17 billion assents under management. Greenspring has about 140 employees and has achieved a 21% compound return on its funds since 2000. The reason for my email is not to brag but to thank you for the positive impact you had on our son's lives. You were godfathers, but more importantly, the way you lived your lives, the record of your achievements, and your friendship inspired both boys. They talk about you often. Amy and I wish to thank you for your contribution to Ashton and Adair's success. You are the first to hear.

The following is an email Ashton sent to all his employees that day:

Thank you for joining all hands in this momentous day. Our journey is far from over and there is plenty of work to do. This partnership with Stepstone will help us achieve our firm's goals and many things we haven't dreamed of yet. When many of us reflect on a transaction of this nature, what makes us the happiest is not the dollars paid or the industry accolades, it is the fact that our team gets to do this together. In that regard, we may have some new faces that will be added to the team who will make us even stronger and we look forward to welcoming them together.

Overall, we are most excited about changing the scale at which the innovation economy is financed with all of you! On behalf of the people in the world who benefit from the advancement of technologies as a result of all our efforts; we thank you in advance for the privilege to help shape the world of tomorrow. I, along with the rest of the leadership team, are looking forward to embarking on our continued evolution with each of you. Thank you for your many contributions to date that led Greenspring to where we are today. Let's get after it!

Best,

Ashton

Adair Newhall

I want to make a positive impact on the world, to preserve Marsi's, my deceased first mother's memory, and to honor my parents—particularly Amy Newhall, my second mother, who put in the hard work to help me become who I am today. This is what motivates and drives me. The bar was set high from my beginning. My brother Ashton and I were constantly reminded by our father about our ancestors' achievements, not to brag about them but to emulate them. Some of the ancestors are related closely, some distantly. They include General George Washington, General Robert E. Lee, Emperor Napoleon Bonaparte, Col. John Cross, General Sam Smith, Col. Frank Newhall, Capt. Walter Newhall, Evangeline Abbott Newhall, Captain Asa T. Abbott, and a host of others important to the history of our country.

Some of our relatives made names for themselves on a global scale, some by just helping the lives of others, both reinforcing my belief that I couldn't rest on my laurels. I developed a personal mission, almost an obsession, that I must depart this world leaving it better than when I arrived in it. Both my mother's death and Amy's example remind me to be compassionate to people who experience adversity. Without this ability to read people and relate to their concerns intuitively, I would be unable to lead effectively.

These motivations have driven me to succeed and have pushed me closer to my dream of becoming a successful venture capitalist. Preserving my birth mother's memory has been more challenging to achieve. I never really knew her. She shot herself in March 1983.

At 4 years old, I remember wandering throughout our hallways looking for my mother. A red light coming from the glass front door caught my attention. My father, crying over a body on a stretcher, noticed his sons looking at him. He attempted to compose himself, walked over to my brother and me, and hugged us. He told us that our mother would not be returning but that everything would be okay. This vivid picture of my mother's dead body on a stretcher is the only memory I now have of her.

Although traumatic, I have used this memory to strengthen myself. Rather than wallow in self-pity, I have learned to sympathize with people who have experienced true hardship. Human loss is hard to cope with, but sometimes just being a good listener can assist with the healing process. Compassion is one of the keys to success. Without it, you will fail to connect with fellow humans and fail to inspire, fail to heal, and fail to lead.

The other gift my mother's death gave me was a keen intuition. Preserving her memory reminds me to be observant of other peoples' words, and more importantly, actions. I rarely enter conversations without watching a person's mannerisms. It is these types of gestures that offer clues as to the true nature of the person you are talking with. My mother's death allowed me to become more introspective. At a young age, I quickly discovered the way to control my feelings was to monitor my behavior and that of others. This trait has been exceptionally helpful in business: detecting a lie through the twitch of an eyebrow or a change in voice tone can make or break the success of a project. A reflective and intuitive nature has leveled the playing field for me. The so-called geniuses I have met rarely possess the ability to read people. This skill, not tested by most standardized tests, is vital because an attribute of leadership is the ability to read people. Without instincts, you will fail to understand team members and how to motivate them properly.

After Marsi's death, my father married Amy, my second mother. What Amy offered our broken family was stability, unconditional love, and balance in a chaotic world. My biological mother battled bipolar disease and had been raised by a highly critical abusive mother, which made her unfit to raise her own children toward the end of her life. Amy was selfless. She gave up her career to raise us, took me to tutors three times a week, and waited in wintery parking lots for hours just to take me home. She went to all my games. One year, she attended more than 500. She nursed me when I was sick and drove me everywhere when I was well. Most importantly, she taught my father how to be a father.

He had to be home at 6:00 PM so he could have dinner with us and discuss what we learned that day. She made him devote two hours a night to helping with our homework. After that, he could work on NEA from 9:00 PM until 3:00 AM if he wanted. She planned magnificent vacations where we learned things and created the inseparable ties that today bind our family together. I am a product of two mothers—the one who gave me life and continues to inspire my life, and the one who also inspires me and made me what I am today.

Overcoming adversity motivates me to make a significant positive impact. Stress may be bad for your health in some ways, but without stress (adversity) you will never grow as a person. The loss of my mother was followed by my gloomy diagnosis of post-traumatic stress disorder, severe learning disabilities, including dyslexia, attention deficit disorder, and hyperactivity disorder. At four, my future was in jeopardy. In high school, early academic struggles convinced some of my teachers to question my potential. Despite the negative criticism from some of my teachers, I fed off any and every athletic and academic success. I was lucky to have very engaged parents that mentored and helped guide me to make better decisions. By the time I received my University of Pennsylvania (Penn) acceptance letter, I had become captain of the soccer, basketball, and baseball teams, co-head of the Vestry, and president of St. Paul's School. I also managed to get into Penn with an 1110 SAT score because I had a high GPA, worked very hard, and had the ability to lead. My first semester, I had a 3.0 GPA, and it improved each quarter. I also played Division 1 baseball for Penn my first two years. So much for standardized test scores. This approach, to view adversity as a challenge rather than an insurmountable obstacle, helped to temper my strong work ethic into steel. It also reinforces my belief in Abraham Lincoln's statement, "Only the test of fire makes fine steel."

Adversity followed me at the start of my professional career. I sought an investment-banking job that would allow me to work with venture-backed portfolio companies, provide an exciting and fast-growing environment, strengthen my analytical foundation, and place me in a smaller environment where I could make a quick, positive impact. Thomas Weisel Partners (a leading San Francisco small investment handling firm) fit the criteria, but after two months on the job, the technology bubble burst. The tech-centric TWP fell on hard times. The investment banking department experienced the most layoffs, as my analyst class decreased from twenty-six analysts to twelve. Over the next two years, my semiconductor team would be terminated, and I would be transitioned to a newly created healthcare team. By the time I left TWP, only seven analysts remained from my original class. Despite these challenges, I outlasted the worst technology downturn in US economic history. Although I lacked a business degree like most analysts, TWP valued my work and kept me on. This ability to survive and to succeed in harsh conditions helped me. Overcoming and defeating hardship would become one of my character traits.

After TWP, I sought a startup environment where I could improve my entrepreneurial skills and learn how to create value. ESP Pharma, an NEA portfolio company, offered me that entrepreneurial environment, plus it had a leadership program that would allow me to experience different facets of the pharmaceutical business, an opportunity to learn from accomplished veterans, and the chance to make a quick, positive impact. John Spitznagel, ESP's famous CEO, bet one of my father's partners that I would wash out in six months. Beginning as a salesman with no experience and little training, I was given the second-worst territory in the US.

Within the year, I changed the Washington, D.C., territory from the fifty-seventh to the twelfth ranked territory in the US (there were sixty total sales representatives). After this, John Spitznagel adopted me and personally guided my career. John gave me broad exposure to all aspects of the company. I was transferred to the finance department, where I created a *pro forma* analysis that led to the acquisition of Retavase®, an IV thrombolytic drug neglected by its former owner. Shortly after completing the analysis, I was assigned to the marketing department to relaunch Retavase®.

The Retavase® product launch provided me with an opportunity to test my leadership qualities, challenge my intellectual curiosity, and make a positive impact. Under a tight deadline, I led my six-person team by outlining their assignments and by providing guidance when asked. We had to research the thrombolytic marketplace, identify Retavase®'s growth factors, develop a new marketing strategy, and outline the tactical implementation for the sales force in two months. We had weekly meetings with the marketing, medical affairs, regulatory, and sales departments, as well as hiring a new advertising agency. This let me monitor my team's development and measure their performance. I recognized, throughout this, that my intuitive abilities assisted me more than my analytical or sales skills. Many employees benefitted from more supervision and guidance, while others desired more freedom. I was able to manage effectively by understanding my teammates, watching facial expressions and body movements, and reacting accordingly.

The new launch of Retavase® was important for patients with blood clots that block major arteries and veins. Starting with the product launch, US patients would be treated by the most efficacious form of thrombolytic treatment available on the market. This development allowed certain patients to live longer and healthier lives. The successful product launch meant higher profits for my company and accolades for my product team. While the spotlight shined brightly, I tried earnestly to push my team members to the front because their ongoing support meant success on projects we would work on together in the future. Praising them for their work helped me to form a more cohesive unit.

Working in the corporate development group at Esprit Pharma, helped me develop another skill set. I believe each role I played in the company gave me a new skillset and prepared me to create value on a larger scale. Sales experience fine-tuned my instincts and people skills. It strengthened my integrity when I marketed our drug for its selected indication fairly and honestly, never overstating what it did. The finance experiences at TWP and ESP Pharma improved my analytical abilities and organizational skills when completing projects under tight timeframes. The marketing experience strengthened my leadership qualities by offering me a meaningful assignment and a team that needed guidance to complete a successful product launch. Corporate development has improved my negotiating skills and taught me how to lead larger groups.

My next chapter began at the Darden School of Business at the University of Virginia. This formal business education would be the first time I could study business issues in an academic setting without worrying about slowing a critical M&A sale, an IPO, or a private placement. I was taught by academic luminaries such as Susan Chaplinsky, my corporate finance and private equity professor;

Ed Freeman, who taught ethics; and my father's former Harvard accounting professor, Brandt Allen, who had moved from Harvard to teach at Darden. The case method resonated with my learning style: it allowed students to struggle with the case and ask questions. The professors then guided us to an answer. The school couldn't have been a better fit. Nearing the end of my first year, in 2008, I couldn't imagine how I could improve upon my first-year experience. I was pleasantly surprised.

My future wife, Kathryn McCann, after having completed both a B.A and M.A from the University of Virginia, was far too inquisitive to just stay in the development office at Darden, where she was working. At the start of my second year, I noticed Kathryn auditing my classes, answering the complex questions to the cases assigned to my class. *Who was this attractive Southerner with this active mind?* I wondered. Although not a Darden student (she was auditing courses), her curious nature drew her to our classrooms, and that's when I first noticed my Virginian future wife. After a few shared social experiences with friends, I asked Kathryn on a double date to Upstairs, a restaurant she had never experienced before. To be accurate, she had visited the bar, but not the restaurant. The rest is history. We have two beautiful children and have been married for over seven years.

My second year was filled with planning for the UVA Summit, UVA's first nationwide event showcasing its technologies and entrepreneurs. I worked diligently on my elective classes that focused heavily on entrepreneurship, venture capital, and innovation. I had never before received an education as wonderful as my Darden education. The professors were positive and informative, an outstanding group of teachers and academic researchers who encouraged students to learn and lead out in front. Luckily, I had achieved enough at this point to warrant attention from Jim Blair, a fabled partner at the venture firm Domain Associates. All I ever wanted was to be a prominent healthcare venture capitalist. With good fortune, amidst an economic recession, I received an offer to work at Domain Associates in San Diego, one of the strongest healthcare-only venture capital firms in the nation.

My time at Domain Associates was a very positive experience. As the only associate at Domain Associates, I supported all nine of its partners in Princeton and San Diego. Fortunately, I was able to work with Jim Blair, the founder, the most. He taught me to be a gentleman above the fray, especially when conditions on the ground are deteriorating. He had gravitas in the boardrooms. I sat in awe of his work and came to appreciate working for the other Domain partners: Brian Dovey, Eckard Weber, and Dennis Podlesak. In 2008, I was promoted to principal.

I got to work on Applied Proteomics, Astute Medical, Otonomy Pharma, CoLucid Pharma, Bionano Genomics, and Xagenic. Each company represented its own promise and came with its own set of challenges. Many of these companies had inspirational CEOs, dedicated missions, and strong personalities on staff. My experiences at Domain helped shape how I contribute now on the boards that I sit on. Too often, I've observed massive egos or too little teamwork around what should be a common, constructive vision. I noted how different venture capitalists worked daily with their management teams. Some board members elect to dictate commands and never really help the company along the way. I respected the board members who rolled up their sleeves and helped the management teams grow their businesses. Initially, I helped management teams build complex financial models, but toward the end of my time at Domain, I was offering broader guidance and assisting at the board level. For a majority of my portfolio companies, I became a helpful and constructive team member who helped solve problems but did not focus only on mistakes. This was the Domain way, and I look back fondly at the time spent with these top company creators and extraordinary human beings.

All good things come to an end. In 2014, healthcare IPOs were in full bloom after a thirteen-year hiatus, and some of my companies, like Otonomy Pharma, went public. CoLucid Pharma was acquired by Eli Lilly. At this point, Kathryn, after graduating first in her class at Stanford Law School, was a corporate lawyer at Cooley Godward, getting crushed by the workload. Law was not Kathryn's only life mission, and as we planned to grow and be very involved in our family, she and I wanted to return to the mid-Atlantic region to be closer to our families. The opportunity to live closer to my parents and to work with my father and brother was very attractive to me.

My brother Ashton and I had been having a dialogue about his need to build the senior team at Greenspring and improve their direct investment capabilities. Fortunately, the Greenspring senior team thought it additive, not competitive, that another member of the Newhall family would join the investment team. In mid-December 2014, Kathryn and I moved from San Diego and returned permanently to the mid-Atlantic on January 3, during one of Baltimore's biggest blizzards ever. Welcome home!

My time at Greenspring Associates has been very worthwhile. No longer do I work on company creation efforts. Instead, I help evaluate, pursue, and recommend investments in new venture capital funds, direct investments, and secondary investments in established venture partnerships. I've enjoyed witnessing how the venture capital market invests on a global scale and drilling down on the projects that our team deems most interesting. Greenspring partners invest in the best global company creators in the venture capital space, picking the best direct and secondary investment opportunities. We source via our trusted relationships and superior data advantage.

Starting in earnest in January 2015, fundraising became my first priority. There is truly a cadence about company creation investing that is different from the cadence of venture platform investing. The evolution of my career has been incredibly meaningful but also challenging as I learn how to invest in information technology funds and companies, and not just rely on my healthcare investing expertise. Additionally, getting acclimated to a new team and fitting in has a natural learning curve. So far, with my direct investments, I've had a loss in a company called GreenChef and what looks to be a winner in Bright Health. Several other companies I have sponsored look promising. Over the past three years, Ashton has charged me with building Greenspring's healthcare practice and making direct investments. I have to knock the ball out of the park and increase Greenspring's healthcare investments.

More opportunities await. I have the courage to want to change the universe as an investor, as my father taught me. I should also mention that I have a religious or spiritual motivation that drives my business career. I believe in God and Jesus. I have a spiritual faith that I hold higher than any earthly desire. My three specific goals outside my family are consistent with this: to have a significant positive impact, preserve my first mother's memory, and honor my parents (It goes without saying that I also want to be an excellent father and husband while doing all this). These goals are the foundation of my character and ambition. It was my drive to make a positive impact that prompted me to defy skeptics' belief that a child with a severe learning disability could not succeed at the University of Pennsylvania, to work diligently and outlast massive firings at Thomas Weisel Partners during the worst technology downturn in US economic history, to catapult the D.C. sales territory to success in less than a year, and to complete and direct the Retavase® acquisition and product launch, at ESP Pharma.

I look forward to the future. I recognize that if I continue to apply the same amount of effort and intuition that I have applied to date, I will make a positive impact in this world. I identify with Leonardo da Vinci's quotation, "I wish to work miracles." And I have stable family and business foundations in my life that might have not been there but for Amy and my father. With those foundations, perhaps these miracles will be possible.

Footnote

In the second half of 2021 and the year 2022, Adair may have seven of his health care companies go public. The market for IPO's could disappear, we could have a war, or Covid19 could shut down everything. These events could delay Adair's IPO's. But if things remain the same, Adair could have a great year. However, if the market collapses and his IPO's decline, he will have to wait until the company's fundamental progress raises its market value. Seven IPO's in a single year is a significant achievement in building an exceptional investment track record.

ADDENDUM

WHEN I WROTE *DARE DISTURB the Universe*, I relied on the oral interviews of five partners to tell their stories. Those partners' achievements only describe a few of the ways NEA partners affect the destiny of world-changing companies. There remains the majority of stories that I have not told. I asked a few of my other former partners who are hardly mentioned in this book to ask their entrepreneurs about the contributions they made to their companies. These are a few of the responses.

NEA partner: John Nehra

"My entrepreneurial and venture career was born and nurtured inside NEA under the mentorship and guidance of John Nehra. John and I hatched the idea and developed the structure of one of the first medical device incubators in the world, ExploraMed, which set out to create a series of companies using some initial NEA dollars to explore, iterate, and invent new technologies based on a methodology I had developed at Pfizer. To this date, I still marvel at John's nose for seeing this opportunity and believing in me when perhaps few others did. Over the course of the past twenty-four years, John, ExploraMed, and I produced a string of businesses creating some of the largest exits in the history of medical devices and some of the largest returns to NEA as well. Throughout those years and continuing to this day, John's advice and counsel, his calm and confident way of reacting to and managing through challenges, his strong sense of ethics and what is fair and right, and his ability to leverage the long-term investment view of NEA maintaining the firms support through challenges ultimately resulting in amazing success, shapes how I think and truly everything we do. He truly created the focus on Medtech investing at NEA, and today the firm is one of the leading and most successful investors in Medtech in the world. Having NEA as an investor in our space is a badge of honor, which carries with it a huge amount of respect and also responsibility. Patients across the world owe a debt of gratitude to the role John and NEA have played in shaping the present and future of medical technology."

> —Dr. Josh Makower, founder and acting CEO (until a full-time CEO could be recruited) Endomatrix, Transvascular, Acclarent, Moximed, Neotract, Willow, Nuelle, and Vibrynt. Now an NEA general partner.

NEA partner: Kitu Kolluri

"When we started Velocloud Networks, we knew we needed a VC who would bring business acumen, market insights, and operational experience. Kittu was able to do all that and more. In the formative phase of the company, Kittu helped us valuable guidance in finding the right product/market fit and overcoming important go-to-market challenges. He has greatly contributed to the success of Velocloud Networks thus far. He is always available and goes out of his way to help out -something that we have cherished and appreciated."

—Ajit Mayya, cofounder & CTO, Velocloud Networks

NEA partner: Mark Perry

"NEA partners were incredibly supportive of the company and the people they invested in. Their board members focused on helping the founding team hire the talent they needed, thinking strategically about when and where to seek additional financing, and ensuring proper governance without being heavy-handed.

"NEA's role in my startup was particularly valuable during some of our more difficult decisions. About a year after NEA's initial investment and following a long search for a CEO, we had finally identified an extremely strong candidate. Unfortunately, we were facing a difference of opinion among some of our board members, leadership team, and particularly strong pushback from our employees. I recall the phone call with Mark Perry in which he strongly urged me to move forward with the hire. Mark allowed me to reach my own decision that it was the right hire and then agreed to back me in revisiting the decision if we were unable to win over the team after six months. It turned out to be a significant decision for our company: the hire of the new CEO helped us close our Series B and subsequent rounds and we were able to win the entire company over on the decision within 3 months. Without Mark's willingness to back my decision, I am unsure I would have proceeded with that hire given the magnitude of the internal pushback.

"Another recollection I have from working with NEA in the late '90s was how far they would go to back the company and its management team. I recall a board meeting in 2000 where the company's management staff had decided that the best course of action was to sell the company. We were seeing concerns in the telecom side of the market about investing in a startup company and we felt that our ability to win the market would be much less difficult if we were able to partner with a larger company. During the board meeting, NEA made it clear that the choice was in our hands—they fully backed the management team if we decided to continue working towards an IPO but that if we felt an M&A was the right path, they would support that as well. Venture capitalists have a reputation for pushing for the maximal return, even if it means higher risk for the outcome, but I didn't experience any of that behavior with NEA."

—Ian Eslick, CEO, Silicon Spice

NEA partner: Sarah Nayeem

"When Imara was being formed, the sickle cell space was largely being ignored and had worrisome complexities for biotech investment. We needed an investor in NEA and a BOD member in Sara Nayeem to see the vision for the market and apply a detailed lens on creating a differentiated offering. Over the past few years and through additional financing rounds, Sara has remained an important visionary for Imara and has provided useful guidance as a physician-scientist, as a board member, and as a friend. From digging in on clinical trial designs to providing input on positioning and data presentation, to making important investor introductions, Sara is always engaged, thoughtful, and constructive. Having her and NEA as part of the team has been invaluable to the company and to me as the CEO."

—Rahul D. Ballal, Ph.D., Chief Executive Officer of Imara, Inc.

NEA partner: Dr. Josh Makower

"The UroLift System Technology is truly a game-changing technology to treat men suffering from an enlarged prostate. Through Josh Makower's visionary leadership as chairman of the NeoTract Board, I was able to build the organization the right way, with a focus on clinical data, reimbursement, surgeon education, and sales rep training. These key strategic investments resulted in NeoTract being acquired by Teleflex for $1.1b. To date, the UroLift System has treated more than 100,000 men, is now part of the American Urology Association Guidelines and is covered by most insurance companies. Throughout this journey, Josh provided me and the team with tremendous guidance and support around clinical study development, fundraising, and commercialization. He also participated in numerous company and customer events. Most notably, Urologists Summits, where Josh would speak to the group about the genesis of the UroLift System and our vision for the future. Josh's leadership was instrumental in NeoTract's success. I am honored to call Josh a friend and mentor."

—Dave Amerson, Chief Executive Officer of NeoTract

NEA partner: Dr. Justin Klein

"Vertiflex delved into a very complex, eight-year, $50M IDE trial in 2008. We sought a leader, an investor who would have the wherewithal to endure this effort. We chose NEA and Justin Klein who sourced the Vertiflex investment. Throughout our ten years together, Justin has been tireless in providing medical, scientific, and business expertise, and mentorship to me, personally. Our business is flourishing as a result. Justin embodies the values of both NEA and Vertiflex, providing true leadership with an innovation that is truly impacting patient care for thousands."

—Earl Fender, Chief Executive Officer of Vertiflex

NEA partner: Patrick Kerins

"At Millennial Media, we built a market-leading company from founding to a billion-plus valuation in seven years. Patrick Kerins, general partner at NEA, was instrumental in guiding the company in a range of areas as we grew. His keen ability to clearly state and verbalize the company's current situation, such that we could make key choices as a board, repeatedly added key value to the company. His expertise and thoughtful guidance were prescient as we grew organically, acquired companies, hired bankers, executed on an IPO, and a secondary public offering.

"Patrick served as a personal mentor for me, shaping my skills, and my evolving understanding of the role of the CEO as it was changing along the journey. NEA, as a firm, provided opportunities to learn from and interact with other CEOs and asked the hard questions. This not only made us thoughtful but helped us envision and ultimately deliver market leadership. Ultimately, we asked Patrick to be our chairman, which should be significant evidence of his outsized impact as a venture investor. Best yet, I consider Patrick a friend."

—Paul Palmieri, CEO, Millennial Media

Venture NEA partner: Bob Croce

"I have had the pleasure to work with Bob Croce for close to 15 years in the capacity of a board member/CEO relationship. I consider Bob not only a mentor but also a friend. In the last fifteen years, Bob has brought significant value to my two companies. His experience as an operator and his relationships in the industry are two phenomenal traits that Bob brings to the table. He is always available, has strong emotional intelligence, and is a great listener. While sitting on the Board of Acclarent, Bob was instrumental in the acquisition by JNJ.

The trust he had developed over a thirty-six-year period was evident and played a huge part in the process. At Earlens, his commitment to patient care was contagious and the continuity he represented while a venture partner at NEA was much needed for the success of the company. The medical device community is fortunate to have Bob as part of it. I consider myself privileged and blessed to have had the opportunity to work so closely with him."

—Bill Facteau, CEO, Earlens

NEA partner: David Mott

"From the inception of TESARO, David Mott's contributions as a strategic thought partner and an enthusiastic supporter of our mission have been invaluable to me and the TESARO leadership team. Together we established a vision to transform the lives of people living with cancer. Dave's unwavering support throughout our eight-year journey from company founding to the acquisition of TESARO by GlaxoSmithKline was instrumental in helping us successfully develop meaningful products and bring these to tens of thousands of cancer patients. Our seven hundred and fifty TESARO Associates and our partners operating in the US, Europe, and Asia are extremely grateful to Dave and the NEA team for providing financial resources and strategic assistance in fulfilling our vision."

—Lonnie Moulder, Chief Executive Officer, TESARO, Inc.

NEA partner: Dr. Ali Behbahani

"Ali was an indispensable board member at Nevro and provided immense value to me and the board as CEO. At Nevro, we developed HF10 therapy, a paresthesia-free treatment proven to provide superior pain relief to more patients with back and leg pain. Ali played a leadership role on the board during some of the most important milestones of the company as we grew the company to a $400M business with nearly one thousand people and transformed the spinal cord stimulation space. Ali's investment during our Series C positioned us for our US launch, which was a critical value driver for the company.

He played a leadership role during our IPO and subsequently as the director with the most public company experience. Ali was always prepared, strategic, and wise in his approach and made an invaluable contribution to the success of the company. The best part of the Nevro journey was being able to go on it together."

—Rami Elghandour, CEO, NEVRO

Venture and general NEA partners: Mike O'Dell/Harry Weller

"Working with Mike O'Dell and Harry Weller at NEA has been one of the great pleasures of my professional life. The enthusiasm, scrutiny, and camaraderie of our initial conversations about tech and what Fugue was building showed me that they were more than investors. These folks were deeply thoughtful and knowledgeable about technology and were people I wanted to work with as a team.

"Through all stages of our development, from Mike pointing me to important ideas in the history of computing while we were developing our architecture, to Harry introducing me to brilliant and excellent advisors and contacts, NEA has been a partner in all aspects of the business. Changing the world is both hard to do and hard to convince yourself to try. Having others on your team who take it on with enthusiasm, knowledge, and resources is a critical ingredient. NEA has been this for Fugue."

—Josh Stella, CEO, Fugue

NEA partner: Mohamad Makhzoumi

"I have been an entrepreneur most of my life, hustling to sell lemonade and cut lawns from an early age. Learning from these early endeavors, I progressed to run divisions of large companies, start businesses funded by private individuals and institutional capital, and run companies backed by both venture capital and private equity. There are a variety of recipes for success but I can give you one that works: a promising company backed by smart venture capital.

"In the summer of 2018 we divested my business, Paladin Health, out of a well-run company. To be successful, we needed the right partner with a mix of intelligence, expertise and support: the right partner was NEA and the right Managing Director was Mohamad Makhzoumi. Mo and his team immediately helped us raise additional growth equity from intelligent capital partners and build an expert team of operators and directors, all while connecting Paladina to significant growth opportunities.

"Mohamad's connectivity and instinct were evident from the beginning. Shortly after close, we simultaneously worked through the build of our Board of Directors and next round of financing. Our Board of Directors came together quickly, many with experience in working with Mo as his access to talent is unparalleled. We created a team of Directors that has been immensely impactful in growing our business, creating efficiencies and implementing compliance. Mohamad was also adroit in his understanding of the need for clinical expertise—together, we added three physicians to our Board. The next round of financing was also facilitated by Mo and his connectivity—an oversubscribed round of $165M materialized not long after the offering and initial discussions. Large firms with successful track records like Oak HC/FT, Alta Partners, Greenspring Associates and Australia's sovereign wealth fund emerged as the most attractive options for capital, all of which had worked alongside Mo and NEA before. At that point, Paladina was propelled for rapid growth.

"Paladina has spent the last eighteen months in aggressive growth mode. Another area of Mo's expertise is an ability to judge talent and fit, and that skill has helped Paladina build out our executive team. Paladina has added nine new executives after joining forces with Mo and NEA. Mo was instrumental in the creation of that executive team due to both his ability to identify top talent and his skill in selling that talent on opportunity. Mo has become an integral part of our recruiting team and I rely on him to help move executive teammates across the finish line. Paladina has been very successful with this strategy.

"Finally, I would be remiss in failing to mention Mohamad's unique instinct to help companies grow their top line. Mo has been a tremendous partner to me in thinking strategically about both channel opportunities and M&A. To exemplify this point, Mo and NEA provided the credibility that Paladina needed to acquire a large competitor in Activate Healthcare. It is also worth noting that Mo has developed a talented and productive team of his own to support these types of transactions, thus easing the burden on our operating team. Mo was instrumental in closing the Activate deal and he remains a key contributor in our ongoing efforts to grow through acquisition. He is talented in negotiations and has a firm grasp on opportunities to create incremental value.

"Mohamad Makhzoumi has been a productive partner and friend to me in my journey with NEA over the past few years. I am thrilled that we chose Mo and NEA to build Paladina together. This is the essence of great venture capital—a partnership that supports, challenges and ultimately creates extraordinary value for everyone and everything it touches."

—Chris Miller, CEO, Paladina Health

NEA partner: Ed Mathers

"Based on reputation, I was eager to have NEA lead the series A round at Ra Pharma in 2010. I knew that their presence would induce some of the smaller interested parties to commit, but I didn't know any of the partners or what they could bring to the board room. Ed Mathers proved to be the clear-thinking leader on the board and an invaluable partner as we built the company and eventually completed a very successful exit. He recognized the value and broad applicability of our platform and gave us the resources to execute. He pushed me hard to build the right team, because he said that he invests in teams with the experience to respond to the inevitable failures by coming up with the next great idea. Although not one of the PhDs or MDs on the board, he always had the most insightful questions, whether about the science, operations, or business, and usually the kind where I'd ask myself "why didn't I think of that?". I always knew where we stood in Ed's mind because he always said exactly what he thought, which is not something every board member is comfortable doing. For me, I wouldn't want it any other way."

—Doug Treco, Former Ceo, Ra Pharmaceuticals

ACKNOWLEDGMENTS

THE FOLLOWING PEOPLE HAVE PROVIDED me with much-appreciated help in editing *Dare Disturb the Universe.* I could not have completed the book without their help. Marguerite Gong Hancock, Dr. Arthur Daemmrich, Bobby Franklin, Jill Prevatt, Dick Kramlich, Frank Bonsal, Scott Sandell, Dr. Forest Baskett, Jeff McWaters, David Carliner, Dr. Carrolee Barlow, Edwin Warfield IV, Dr. James Blair, David Weild IV, Ashton Newhall, Adair Newhall, Michael Classen, Jim Swartz, Joel Gordon, George Stamas, Peter Barris, Dr. Kay Redfield Jamison, Carrie Nyman, Mark Graham, Louis Citron, C. Sage Givens, Jack Khattar, Dr. Tony Evnin, Dan Laidman, Rachel Weller, Dr. Tom Nicholas, Peter Morris, and Origelsa Ligu.

I want to thank Carole Kolker and Mauree Jane Perry for doing the interviews of leading venture capitalists, many of which I used in writing this book. Completing these interviews and making them available to the public has not been an easy task.

I want to give special recognition to Rachel Moore Weller, my editor and the wife of my former partner, Harry Weller. She is an editor with a commanding knowledge of the venture capital business. Without her help, for which she refuses to be paid, this book could have never been written.

I also thank Sharon Redmond for her excellent photography.

Most venture capital firms do not keep historical records beyond the financial ones. NEA was no exception. When the firm's administrative headquarters moved from downtown Baltimore to Baltimore County, all the historical documents were destroyed except those I saved. They are the source material for *Dare Disturb the Universe.*

The accounts in the book are my personal views. I am sure others will disagree with some of them. I have sent drafts of the chapters in this book to the main people I have featured who are living, and I have tried to ensure the contents are accurate. Getting the comments back and continued editing delayed the publication of the book six years. I apologize for any factual errors that Dare Disturb the Universe might contain despite these efforts. It is a story I think hasn't been told yet and should be before more resources are lost. Sources for the quotations in the book are from seventy interviews funded by Pete Bancroft, the National Venture Capital Association, Harvard, the Computer History Museum, and me.

Ingram Content Group UK Ltd.
Milton Keynes UK
UKHW012234170423
420333UK00002B/45